The Impact of Legislation

The Impact of Legislation

A Critical Analysis of *Ex Ante* Evaluation

Edited by

Jonathan Verschuuren

MARTINUS
NIJHOFF
PUBLISHERS

LEIDEN • BOSTON
2009

This book is printed on acid-free paper.

Library of Congress Cataloging-in-Publication Data

The impact of legislation : a critical analysis of *ex ante* evaluation / edited by Jonathan Verschuuren.
p. cm.
ISBN 978-90-04-17020-9 (hardback : alk. paper) 1. Legislation—Europe—Evaluation. 2. Bills, Legislative—Europe—Evaluation. I. Verschuuren, Jonathan.

KJC5349.I485 2009
349.4072—dc22

2008053628

ISBN 978 90 04 17020 9

PRINTED IN THE NETHERLANDS

Contents

PART II

EX ANTE EVALUATION IN PRACTICE

CONCLUSIONS

Preface and Acknowledgements

Since the past decade, legislative processes around the globe are being rationalised by introducing *ex ante* evaluation. Legislators, politicians, and the public at large increasingly demand new laws to have a particular effect and no unwanted side-effects. Various instruments are applied that all have in common that they must predict the effect of new legislation. These instruments range from small tests into one specific topic, for instance the effect of a new piece of legislation on the environment, or on the economic position of small and medium sized enterprises, to a full swing regulatory impact assessment that assesses all probable and possible effects of new legislation.

Although many publications on '*ex ante*' evaluation of legislation praise instruments such as regulatory impact assessment as being extremely useful, scepticism is in order as well. Is it not as difficult to predict the future effect of a new set of rules in our complex society as it is to predict where our society as a whole is going? This sceptical question was put forward by some of the researchers of the newly established Research Group for Methodology of Law and Legal Research at Tilburg University, The Netherlands. We decided to invite some of Europe's top specialists in the field of *ex ante* evaluation of legislation. We made sure that these specialists had a background in various disciplines such as law, social science, political science, and law and economics.

The group of authors that was thus formed, met on several occasions in Tilburg, to discuss draft chapters. The result is a comprehensive, critical, book on the pros and cons and on the opportunities, limitations and challenges of *ex ante* assessment of legislation. We think such a book is badly needed in the current debate on regulatory impact assessment. The editor wishes to thank all the authors for embarking on the project and for spending so much of their precious time writing on and discussing about *ex ante* evaluation. Thank you very much!

24 October 2008

Jonathan Verschuuren
Tilburg University
The Netherlands

Contributors

Koen Van Aeken completed his PhD (2002) in the social and political sciences at the University of Antwerp with a doctoral dissertation on the evaluation of legislation. Since 2006, he works at the Law Faculty of Tilburg University as an assistant professor, teaching sociology of law and conducting social-scientific, empirical research on matters of legislation.

Eberhard Bohne, M.A. (Univ. of Wisconsin), holds the Chair for Public Administration, Policy and Law for Environmental Protection and Energy at the German University of Administrative Sciences Speyer since 1996. He also serves as Head of Section III at the German Research Institute for Public Administration, Speyer. He is Co-Chairman of the Transatlantic Policy Consortium, a network of about 40 North-American and European Universities and research institutions in the field of public policy and public administration. His research activities focus on comparative empirical and legal analyses of environmental regulatory politics in the European Union, the liberalization of the electricity and gas markets, and on theoretical concepts of administrative decision making from an empirical and normative perspective.

Rob van Gestel is professor of theory and methods of legislation at Tilburg University. He finished his PhD thesis on Self-regulation in environmental law in 2000. Van Gestel was visiting scholar in the field of legisprudence at the KU-Brussels in 2004 and is one of the founding fathers of the Research Group for Methodology of Law and Legal Research, which was established in 2006. Van Gestel is now vice-chairman of the Dutch Association of Legislation, member of the International Association of Legislation, visiting professor for the European Academy of Legislation, and co-editor of the Dutch Journal of Legislative Studies, RegelMaat.

Hans Gribnau is senior lecturer at the University of Tilburg and professor of tax law at the University of Leiden. He teaches methodology of tax law and procedural tax law. His current research interests lie in the quality of tax regulation, the instrumental use of tax law, and governance and fiscal ethics. His latest publications include 'Soft Law and Taxation: EU and International Aspects' and

'Soft Law and Taxation: The Case of The Netherlands' (both in Legisprudence) and 'Constitutional limits to taxation in a democratic state: The Dutch experience' (in Michigan State Journal of International Law).

Robert Hoppe is full professor in Knowledge and Policy Studies, in the Department of Science, Technology, Health and Policy Studies (STeHPS), at the Faculty of Management and Governance, University of Twente. His manifold research interests involve policy and knowledge, governance of expertise, science-policy interaction; methods in policy analysis and design; and long-term policy dynamics. On *ex ante* (and *ex post*) policy evaluation he published a.o. 'Beleidsnota's die (door)werken' ('Policy Papers with Impact') (Coutinho, Bussum, 2004, 3rd edition). He served as an expert-member of the local Audit Chamber of the Enschede City Council (1998–2006). He is a frequently invited speaker for conferences in academia and professional and administrative communities. He is on the Board of the 'Policy Studies Journal' and 'Jaarboek Kennissamenleving' ('Yearbook Knowledge Society').

Linda Senden has LL.M degrees of International law, Dutch law and European studies from the University of Amsterdam. She obtained her doctoral degree at Tilburg University in 2003 on the thesis 'Soft Law in European Community Law. Its Relationship to Legislation' (Hart Publishing Oxford, 2004). In 2004 she was appointed professor of European law at Tilburg University. She has a wide interest in European regulatory and lawmaking issues. Her publications in this area include: 'Co-actorship in the Development of European Law-making' (with Hirsch Ballin, TMC Asser Press 2005), contributions to the book 'The Coherence of EU Law: the Search for Unity in Divergent Concepts' (OUP 2008) and various international and Dutch articles on alternative rulemaking in the EU and the open method of coordination. She also teaches a master course on Governance in the EU.

Pierre Larouche is Professor of Competition Law at Tilburg University and Co-Director of the Tilburg Law and Economics Center (TILEC). He is also a professor at the College of Europe (Bruges). A graduate of McGill University, he clerked at the Supreme Court of Canada, obtained his masters from Bonn University and his PhD from the University of Maastricht. He practised EU law at Stibbe in Brussels from 1993 to 1996. Thereafter he worked with Walter van Gerven on the Ius Commune Casebooks Project. His teaching and research interests include competition law, telecommunications law, media law, basic EU law and the common European law of torts, with the help of economic analysis and a comparative perspective.

Patricia Popelier is professor at the University of Antwerp, president of the Belgian Interuniversity Centre of Legislation (ICW) and vice-president of the International Association of Legislation (IAL). For her PhD thesis on 'legal certainty as a principle of proper law making' she received the F. Collin Award 1998. She teaches courses in public law and legislative studies and is author of several books and articles dealing with issues of public law, legislative studies and evaluation of legislation. She is member of the editing board of the review 'Tijdschrift voor Wetgeving' (Journal for Legislation).

Anne Meuwese holds a law degree and a PhD, awarded cum laude, from Leiden University. She has studied at Sciences-Po Paris and Oxford and worked as a research fellow at Exeter University for two years, before coming to Antwerp on a postdoctoral Marie Curie fellowship in 2008. Between March and July 2005, Anne was a trainee at the unit 'Better Regulation and Institutional Matters' of the European Commission's Secretariat-General. Anne has taught in several professional training courses on impact assessment and better regulation and she has published extensively on the subject, including a monograph entitled 'Impact Assessment in EU Lawmaking' which appeared with Kluwer Law International in 2008.

Sylvia Veit studied political science at the University of Potsdam and at the Free University of Berlin. In 2004, she was awarded with a PhD-scholarship from the Graduate School of Modern Governance at the University of Potsdam. Since 2006, she has been working as a research assistant at the Chair of Political Science, Administration and Organization at the University of Potsdam. Her major research interests are within the fields of public administration, central government organization and public sector reform, particularly better lawmaking and debureaucratization. She published several scientific articles and reports on better regulation topics. Within her PhD-project, she has undertaken intensive empirical research about the implementation of regulatory impact analysis in Germany and Sweden.

Victoria Verlinden started in 2003 as a junior lecturer/researcher at the University of Antwerp Law Faculty. She is working on a PhD on the institutional aspects of regulatory management and the organisation of the Belgian regulatory process, under the supervision of Patricia Popelier. In 2004, she joined the Regulatory Management Unit ('Kenniscel Wetsmatiging') for a couple of months, supporting, guiding and assessing the Flemish Government's regulatory management. In several articles she has stressed the need for evaluation (*ex ante* and *ex post*) to obtain a qualitative regulatory process.

Jonathan Verschuuren holds a PhD, awarded 'cum laude', at Tilburg University. Since 1999, he is a full professor of European and International Environmental Law at Tilburg University. He currently is the Vice Dean for Research at the Faculty of Law at that university, as well as the Director of the Tilburg Graduate Law School. His research mainly focuses on the role of international and EU environmental law in legal practice. Verschuuren has written more than 200 publications in the field of environmental law, including several books and many articles in outstanding refereed journals throughout the world. He is a visiting professor at the University of Connecticut (USA), North West/Potchefstroom (South Africa), Leuven (Belgium).

Henk Vording is a professor of tax law at Leiden University, the Netherlands. He currently is the coordinator of the research programme 'The boundaries of fiscal sovereignty' at Leiden university, as well as the over all research coordinator of the law faculty. He has chaired several advisory commissions on tax law matters. Vording has published many outstanding international publications in such journals as the British Tax Review and the Bulletin for International Taxation.

Jan Vranken, professor of civil law and civil procedure (1983–1997) and Advocate General at the Dutch Supreme Court (1992–1997), currently holds the chair on Methodology of Private Law. He also is co-director of the recently established Research Group for the Methodology of Law and Legal Research. His main fields of research and teaching are methodology and jurisprudence. He wrote more than three hundred and fifty publications, among them twelve books. He co-authored and (co-)edited 22 books. He is or was a member of various editorial boards of journals and book series. Because of his merits as a legal scholar he was awarded the Royal Honour in the Order of the Dutch Lion and a doctorate honoris causa at Leiden University. He is a member of the Royal Dutch Academy of Science.

Research Group for Methodology of Law and Legal Research

Compared to the methodology of judicial lawmaking and, to a lesser extent, that of legislation, the scholarly concern with the methodology of legal research is sparsely, all over the world. With the aim to strive for an internationally renowned cutting edge position in this new field of research, the Research Group for Methodology of Law and Legal Research was established in June 2007 at the Tilburg University Faculty of Law (The Netherlands).

The Research Group is working on three research areas. The methodology used by legal scholars is the primary focus of the first area. Legal scholars often analyze and discuss judgements and, consequently, adopt the methodology that is used by magistrates. This approach is no longer self-evident. Current trends to conduct European, international, contextual, comparative, inter- and multidisciplinary research, prompt new perspectives in the legal discipline. As these trends have confronted legal scholars with a wide range of methodological problems, the use of a clear and sound methodology has become an important prerequisite for achieving scientific progress.

The second research area focuses on theory and methods of legislation. Without trying to deny that drafting legislation is and should be a process of political deliberation, there is a growing need to objectify and underpin legislative activity by scientific research. It is of the utmost importance to pay more attention to fact finding, (*ex ante*) evaluation and so-called evidence based lawmaking by developing theories and methods that will enhance the quality of legislation in a time in which the influence of, both international and supranational law, and private rulemaking, is steadily increasing.

Theory and methods of judicial law-making is the third research area. Traditionally the legitimacy of courts' decisions in different societies has been studied as a function of the proper role of courts in society generally. From this point of view, regardless for and in which society a court fulfils its adjudicating task, whether or not its decisions are legitimate depends on the content of the argumentation used (legal quality) and the way this argumentation is made public (public quality). And the question to be answered is whether or not a court oversteps the limits of an abstract conception of the judicial function. However, a serious drawback of such a way of analysing is that it tends to look at just a limited set of aspects of the legitimacy of court decisions. Therefore, another more fulfilling methodology of judging the legitimacy of courts decisions should be used: i.e. a method which also pays due attention to the specific institutional context in which a court fulfils its task. From that point of view, whether or not a decision of a court is legitimate, depends not only on the content of the arguments publicly used, but also on the aforementioned institutional setting in which the court has to function.

More information on the work of the Research Group can be found at its website at <www.tilburguniversity.nl/faculties/law/research/methodology/>.

Abbreviations

ACCOP	Act for the Compensation in the Administrative Objection Procedure (Netherlands)
ACTAL	Advisory Board on Administrative Burdens (Netherlands)
BGBl	Bundesgesetzblatt (Germany)
BR	Better Regulation
BVerfG	Bundesverfassungsgericht (Germany)
CAF	Common Assessment Framework
CBA	Cost-benefit analysis
CEO	Chief Executive Officer
CEPS	Centre for European Policy Studies
CLWP	Commission's Legislative and Work Programme
COBA	Commission for Policy Analysis (Netherlands)
DG	Directorate General
EC	European Community
ECJ	European Court of Justice
ECOFIN	Economic and Financial Affairs (Council)
EEAC	European Environment and Sustainable Development Advisory Councils
EEL	*Ex ante* evaluation of legislation
EIA	Environmental Impact Assessment (Directive)
EP	European Parliament
EU	European Union
FDI	Foreign Direct Investment
GALA	General Administrative Law Act (Netherlands)
GDP	Gross Domestic Product
GFA	Gesetzesfolgenabschätzung (Germany)
GGO	Gemeinsame Geschäftsordnung der Bundesministerien (Germany)
IA	Impact assessment
IAB	Impact Assessment Board
IIA	Inter-Institutional Agreement (on better lawmaking)
IPPC	Integrated Pollution Prevention and Control (Directive)
ISC	Inter-Service Consultation
M&A	Mergers and acquisitions

MNE	Multinational enterprise
NBEPA	Netherlands Bureau for Economic Policy Analysis
NGO	Non-governmental organisation
NKR	Nationaler Normenkontrollrat (Germany)
NPM	New Public Management
OECD	Organisation for Economic Co-operation and Development
OIRA	Office of Regulatory Affairs
OMB	Office of Management and Budget
OMC	Open Method of Coordination (EU)
PDCA	Plan – Do – Check – Act cycle
PPBS	Planning Programming Budgeting System
R&D	Research and Development
REACH	Registration Evaluation Authorisation and Restriction of Chemical Substance (Regulation)
RIA	Regulatory impact assessment
SASV	Semi-autonomous social fields
SCM	Standard Cost Model
SME	Small and medium-sized enterprise
TEP	The Evaluation Partnership
TQM	Total Quality Management
UK	United Kingdom
US	United States
USA	United States of America
YCA	Youth Care Act (Netherlands)

Introduction

Chapter 1

Ex Ante Evaluation of Legislation: An Introduction

Jonathan Verschuuren and Rob van Gestel

I. *The Rise of* Ex Ante *Evaluation of Legislation*

'"Better Regulation" is afoot in Europe.'[1] At the EU level, as well as at the level of many of the Member States, the legislature is seeking to improve the quality of legislation and reduce administrative burdens. In this process, much attention is focussed on '*ex ante*' evaluation or impact assessments.[2] There is a wide variety of such assessments, some more or less limited to cost-benefit analysis,[3] while others have a much wider scope such as most (Regulatory) Impact Assessment (RIA or IA). Sometimes they simply encompass predictions on the basis of previous (ex post) evaluation research, more often impact assessments are carried out according to a specific methodology. In literature, four reasons for the rise of prior assessments have been distinguished.[4]

---

[1] This is the first sentence of Jonathan B. Wiener's article 'Better Regulation in Europe' (2006) 59 *Current Legal Problems Yearbook*, p. 447.

[2] See for an extensive overview of the developments concerning the introduction of impact assessments at the EU-level Anne C.M. Meuwese, *Impact Assessment in EU Lawmaking* (Kluwer Law International, The Hague 2008). For experiences in other countries C. Kirkpatrick and D. Parker (eds.), *Regulatory Impact Assessment: Towards Better Regulation?* (Edward Elgar, Cheltenham 2007) and, earlier, OECD, *Regulatory Impact Analysis. Best Practices in OECD Countries* (OECD publications, Paris 1997).

[3] Especially in the US there is a long tradition of cost-benefit analyses of legislation. *See* R.A.J. van Gestel and M.L.M. Hertogh, *What is regulatory pressure? An Exploratory Study of the International Literature* (Chapter 5) (Scientific Research and Documentation Centre of the Dutch Ministry of Justice, The Hague 2006), and also R.W. Hahn and R.E. Litan, 'Counting Regulatory Benefits and Costs: Lessons for the U.S. and Europe' (2005) 8:2 *Journal of International Economic Law*, pp. 473–508.

[4] R.A.J. van Gestel, 'Evidence-based Lawmaking and the Quality of Legislation. Regulatory Impact Assessments in the European Union and the Netherlands' in H. Schäffer and J. Iliopoulos-Strangas (eds.), *State Modernization in Europe* (Ant. N. Sakkoulas-Berliner Wissenschaftsverlag-Bruylant,

1. The growing complexity of legal systems in Europe where national parliaments and European institutions have become co-actors in a multi-level network of lawmaking feeds the quest for a reduction of uncertainties in the legislative process;
2. The emphasis on output parameters and monitoring of policy results in what is often called "new public management". If one considers legislation to be an important tool to stimulate economic growth, create jobs and safeguard sustainable development, it is obvious that the public will also confront legislators with an increasing interest in the effectiveness and efficiency of laws. This also explains a growing attention for principles of accountability and good governance;
3. The growing fear for regulatory accretion – the danger of rules breeding more rules – that could lead to an increasing evasion of legislation emphasizes the importance of creating thresholds in the law-making process to prevent the promulgation of superfluous laws and regulations;[5]
4. RIA's can provide standards for the process of policy formulation, by showing how consultations, costs and benefits, and trade-offs between policy choices have been taken into account by the legislature. This can make the legislative process more transparent.

Researching the possible or probable effect of a proposed piece of legislation, especially in a situation where uncertainty exists with regard to the problem, as well as the possible solutions, indeed may be more useful than traditional ex post evaluations. Such evaluations have at least three flaws. Firstly, most evaluations of laws in the past have failed to feed the lawmaking process because of bad timing. The policy cycle usually revolves quicker than the research cycle, with the result that 'real time' evaluations often have little influence on law and policymaking. Secondly, ex post evaluation is demand-driven, with few opportunities of cross-fertilization of evaluation results.[6] Thirdly, once a piece of legislation has been enacted, it will be difficult to change it substantially, let alone to totally revoke the draft-Bill, even when evaluation shows that the legislation has little or perhaps even an adverse impact.

However, the various kinds of *ex ante* evaluation methods are sometimes also met with criticism. The instrument appears to be misused by the authorities,

Berlin 2007), pp. 139–165. The author refers to various other relevant publications on the topic.

[5] J.B. Ruhl and J. Salzman, 'Mozart and the Red Queen: The Problem of Regulatory Accretion in the Administrative State' (2003) 91:4 *Georgetown Law Journal*, pp. 757–850.

[6] *See* R. Pawson, *Evidence-based Policy: A Realist Perspective* (Sage, London 2006), pp. 8–9. *Also* Van Gestel, *supra* note 4, pp. 139 et seq.

for instance by only considering the preferred option,[7] by not looking into the possible side-effects, and generally by a lack of imagination as it comes to alternative ways of regulation.[8] In addition, the used methodology is often unclear,[9] the instrument is frequently applied after the basic design of a new policy or new legislation has already been set, and it often primarily focuses on effects that can be easily quantified and monetized. Therefore, Wiener proposes to broaden the instrument to also include

> attention to multiple risks, moving beyond a narrow focus on cutting administrative costs or simplification for their own sake, toward criteria that address benefits as well as costs; centralizing expert oversight so that impact assessments actually influence decisions, both to say 'no' to bad ideas and 'yes' to good ideas; and undertaking ex post evaluation of policies for adaptive policy revision and for improvement of *ex ante* assessment methods.[10]

II. *Definitions of* 'Ex Ante' *Evaluation of Legislation*

In this book, the application of various methods of '*ex ante*' evaluation of legislation, such as regulatory impact assessments, simulations, experiments, in various fields of law at various levels (i.e., national, EU) are studied. We consider '*ex ante* evaluation' to be:[11]

> Future oriented research into the expected effects and side-effects of potential new legislation following a structured and formalised procedure, leading to a written report. Such research includes a study of the possible effects and side-effects of alternatives, including the alternative of not regulating at all.

This is a rather broad definition that includes various instruments applied both at a national level and within international organizations, such as the EU and the OECD, to assess the impact of drafted or yet to be drafted legislation, but

---

[7] In the UK, the National Audit Office concluded that in 2004, this was the case in 70% of the RIAs (example given by Van Gestel, *supra* note 4, pp. 139 et seq.).

[8] R. Baldwin, 'Is better regulation smarter regulation?' (2005) *Public Law*, pp. 485–511.

[9] *See* for instance Wolfgang Köck, 'Gesetzesfolgenabschätzung und Gesetzgebungsrechtslehre' (2002) 1 *Verwaltungs-Archiv*, pp. 1–21.

[10] Wiener, *supra* note 1, p. 508.

[11] This definition is based on the definition that was used by the Netherlands Court of Audit in a 2000 report on the organization of policy assessments: Parliamentary Docs. II, 1999–2000, 27 065, Nos. 1–2, p. 18 (available at its website <www.rekenkamer.nl/9282000/d/p115tk27065_2.pdf>). We added the criteria of the formalized procedure and the written output.

excluding informal consultation processes.[12] Both internal and external assessments are included in our definition. Sometimes the assessment is made within the competent authority, in other examples there is a more independent body that either carries out the assessment or controls the quality or validity of the assessment.[13] Another difference between various forms of *ex ante* evaluation is that some of these instruments assess the impact on a whole range of interests, while others only assess the impact on a specific interest, such as gender, the environment, low income groups, small and medium sized enterprises, or the economy. The instruments that cover a wide variety of aspects usually are called Regulatory Impact Assessment (RIA) or simply Impact Assessment (IA). The DIADEM database on the practice of IA in the EU Member States defines IA as follows:[14]

> A systematic, mandatory, and consistent assessment of aspects of social, economic, or environmental impacts such as benefits and/or costs, affecting interests external to the government, of proposed regulations and other kinds of legal and policy instruments, to i) inform policy decisions before regulation, legal instrument, or policy is adopted, or ii) assess external impacts of regulatory and administrative practices, or iii) assess the accuracy of an earlier assessment.

This definition shows that *ex ante* evaluation as defined in our book is a broader concept than RIA or IA. Since 2003, the European Commission applies an IA to all legislative proposals with the following key objectives:[15]

1. Improve the quality of Commissions proposals, in particular by facilitating a more systematic, coherent, analytical, open, and evidence-based approach to policy design, and by providing a thorough, balanced and comprehensive analysis of likely social, economic and environmental impacts.
2. Provide an effective aid to decision-making, in particular by providing policy makers with relevant and comprehensive information on the rationale behind proposed interventions, and their likely impacts, and by enabling policy makers to assess trade-offs and compare different scenarios when deciding on a specific course of action.
3. Serve as a valuable communication tool, in particular by fostering internal communication and ensuring early and effective co-ordination within the

[12] It is, however, needless to say that both formal and informal consultations can and often will play an important role in the process of conducting an impact assessment.

[13] The latter is the case at the level of the European Union where the European Commisson in 2006 established an Impact Assessment Board. *See* for the tasks and composition of the board: <ec.europa.eu/governance/impact/iab_en.htm>.

[14] Taken from the European Network for Better Regulation (ENBR) Handbook 'How to perform the DIADEM data collection', by Claudio Radelli, Bruno Dente, Scott Jacobs, Colin Kirkpatrick, Anne Meuwese, Andrea Renda, 31 July 2006, p. 5.

[15] Taken from the 2007 Evaluation of the Commission's Impact Assessment System by John P. Watson and others (Richmond, April 2007), p. 3.

Commissions, and by enhancing external communication by making the policy development process more open and transparent to external stakeholders.

III. *Goal and Methodology*

Literature on such topics as 'better regulation' or on '(regulatory) impact assessments' is quite abundant. Most of these publications, however, are journal articles focussing only on a specific element of regulatory assessments. More comprehensive books on the topic are scarce. They either only consist of practical guidelines to conduct assessments,[16] do not go beyond sketching the politics and philosophy behind the various 'better regulation' schemes,[17] or only focus on the EU IA system.[18] A comprehensive critical legal analysis of the various forms of '*ex ante* evaluation', focussing on legislation, rather than on policies, is still lacking. The aim of the book is to develop such a critical analysis, and, ultimately, to thus assess the prospects of *ex ante* evaluation of legislation. What are the benefits of *ex ante* evaluation and what not? Under which conditions should which form of *ex ante* evaluation be applied? What should be their role in the legislative process?

Under auspices of the Tilburg University Research Group on Methodology of Law and Legal Research, we have brought together specialists from the field of legislative studies within Europe to provide such a state of the art analysis through studying various forms of '*ex ante* evaluation' in various countries and on the EU level. The book has been written by an interdisciplinary group of academics. The authors mainly stem from various fields of law, but also from the fields of political and social sciences. All have a special expertise on legislation. To achieve the comprehensive result that lies in front of you, draft contributions were discussed within the group of authors on two occasions in Tilburg (August 2007 and February 2008). During intensive workshops abstracts and draft chapters were discussed. Subsequent discussions took place through email.

---

16 Andrea Renda, *Impact Assessment in the EU. The State of the Art and the Art of the State* (CEPS, Brussels 2006).

17 Neil Gunningham, P. Gabrosky, *Smart Regulation: Designing Environmental Policy* (Clarendon Press, Oxford 1998). Exceptions can be found in smaller articles, such as the critical article by Robert Baldwin, 'Is Better regulation Smarter Regulation?' (2005) *Public Law*, pp. 485–511.

18 Giandomenico Majone, *Regulating Europe* (Routledge, London 1996).

IV. *Research Questions and Approach*

In order to answer the question what the prospects of *ex ante* evaluation of legislation are, two paths are followed. First, we focus on the context of *ex ante* evaluation, then we will focus on some specific forms of *ex ante* evaluation: what doe they encompass and what are the experiences with these instruments?

The first part of the book (chapters 2–6) deals with the background of *ex ante* evaluation of legislation. What is the political, economic, or public policy background against which the instrument of *ex ante* evaluation has emerged? Why have they emerged, and what are the (common or different) goals of the various forms of *ex ante* evaluation? Also the political and methodological constraints of *ex ante* evaluation of legislation are researched.

In chapter 2, Popelier and Verlinden show how *ex ante* evaluation has developed from various perspectives, i.e., the perspective of legislative theory (the rational lawmaker, the governance approach), and economic theory (administrative simplification, deregulation, economic advantages of 'good regulation', regulatory impact assessment). The authors also show that *ex ante* evaluation can be relevant in legal practice, for instance in case decisions by courts.

As this chapter shows that economic arguments have been the main reason for the rise of various forms of *ex ante* assessment of the effect of proposed legislation, the entire next chapter is devoted to the economic approach. Larouche critically analyses the various economic rationales behind *ex ante* evaluation in order to be able to assess the quality of the assessments.

Chapters 4 and 5 focus on the political and institutional context of *ex ante* evaluation. In chapter 4, Bohne shows that there are political and institutional constraints that make an objective, true scientific, assessment difficult if not impossible. Instead, *ex ante* assessments are part of the political process. The author looks into such political and institutional constraints to research the productivity of *ex ante* assessments.

In chapter 5, Hoppe takes the policy process in which decision-making on new legislation takes place as a starting point, to assess the benefits and limitations of the various forms of *ex ante* evaluation of legislation. What is the instrument's current and potential role given the specific character of the politically oriented policy processes? The author thus sets the boundaries within which the instrument has to be used.

In the final chapter of part I, chapter 6, the methodological aspects of *ex ante* evaluation are reviewed. Van Aeken, a social scientist who wrote a dissertation on the evaluation of legislation, critically reviews the methodology that is used in various forms of *ex ante* evaluation and assesses the scientific quality of the assessments. He sets out to answer the question whether a prospective evaluation can be more than just 'guesstimating' the impact of legal interventions. Furthermore, Van Aeken criticizes the fact that in practice only a very limited number of methods and techniques are applied to the bulk of *ex ante* evaluations.

The second part of the book discusses past and current experiences with various forms of *ex ante* evaluation in different countries and at the EU level. What are the experiences with *ex ante* evaluation? What subjects have been dealt with? What methodology has been used? What was the outcome of the evaluation? Where in the legislative process, and by whom, has the evaluation been carried out, and how (if at all) have the results been used by the legislature? The chapters in part II (chapters 7–10) of the book thus not only describe current practice, but also critically analyse the practical effect of *ex ante* evaluations on the quality of legislation.

In chapter 7, Senden en Meuwese focus on the development of the European Commission's Impact Assessment system at the EU level and the various goals that such assessments have. One of these goals is deregulation and the promotion of alternative modes of regulation, such as the use of self-regulation, co-regulation, and soft law. Authors evaluate whether these alternatives have actually been used more often since the introduction of Impact Assessments.

The following chapters all focus on national forms of *ex ante* evaluation of legislation. In chapter 8, Veit looks into the experiences with the implementation of *ex ante* evaluation in Sweden and Germany. *Ex ante* evaluation sometimes already dates back to the 1970s and 1980s. The author has made a detailed study of all legal proposals that were submitted in both countries in 2006, as well as of all German draft bills from 1999 and 2003 to show how assessments look like and to find an answer to the question why national assessment requirements are not always met.

Chapter 9 assesses the accuracy of *ex ante* evaluations through studying later ex post evaluations ('feedback research'). Van Gestel and Vranken do so by conducting a case study concerning the *ex ante* evaluation performed by the Dutch Council of State because that is what comes closest to a comprehensive impact assessment. In the Netherlands, like in France, the Council of State advises the government and parliament on legislation. As this institution already exists for quite some time, it is interesting to see how they assess the expected effect of proposed legislation and whether their assessment in the end proved to be correct or not. Authors do so by selecting a number of bills and compare the *ex ante* evaluation by the Council of State to ex post evaluations of the same bills that have been carried out later.

The empirical part of the book ends with a chapter on an issue where legislation was introduced without any form of *ex ante* assessment, i.e., in the field of corporate tax law in the Netherlands. In chapter 10, Vording and Gribnau review the legislative process of the 2007 corporate income tax reform in the Netherlands by focusing on the various stakeholders involved. How have the interests of these stakeholders been used by the legislature, and would this have been different when some form of *ex ante* evaluation would have been applied? Would a full *ex ante* evaluation of aims, options, and effects of corporate income tax reform – in retrospect – have been a useful tool in the legislative process?

Chapter 11 is the concluding chapter of the book. This chapter focuses on the future. What are the prospects of *ex ante* evaluation of legislation? What are the benefits and what is the downside of *ex ante* evaluation? Under which circumstances should it be applied and when should it not be applied, given the instrument's limitations? These questions will be answered using the data offered by the nine preceding chapters of the book.

Part I

Context of *Ex Ante* Evaluation

Chapter 2

The Context of the Rise of *Ex Ante* Evaluation

Patricia Popelier and Victoria Verlinden

I. *Introduction*

The trend to evaluate laws corresponds with the spirit of contemporary times. Cartesian rationality has been replaced by the so-called *kosmos* principle,[1] the core of which can be expressed in terms such as complexity, contingency, uncertainty and relativism. This spirit manifests itself in philosophical theories on reason and rationality, in the emergence of social sciences, in legal views on law, society and the law maker and in economic theories on management and public management in particular.

In this chapter, we will not explore the various theories developed in the last decades. Instead some examples will illustrate the central thesis. This thesis proceeds from the establishment that although nowadays the idea of absolute rationality has been defeated, laws derive legitimacy (partly) from rationality. Various disciplines consequently have focused on evaluation as the key to a present-day concept of 'rationalism'. This chapter is about the rise of *ex ante* evaluation, not about pitfalls or weaknesses which might cause its fall. Our goal is to sketch some of the theories that explain why evaluation has become such a hot topic during the last decade. The next chapters will address the effect *ex ante* evaluation really has. The term '*ex ante* evaluation of legislation' is used as a general term for all sorts of evaluation during the preparation of legislation. When specific evaluation mechanisms are referred to, they will be shortly defined.

All kinds of theories support our thesis that rationality has been transformed into rationalism. In this chapter, we will combine descriptive and normative

---

[1] On the evolution from *taxis* to *kosmos*, *see* Friedrich A. Hayek, *Law, legislation and liberty*, Part 1, *Rules and order* (Routledge & Kegan Paul, London 1977), pp. 12 and 37. *See also* Neil Maccormick, 'Spontaneous order and rule of law: some problems' (1986) 35 *Jahrbuch des Offentlichen Rechts der Gegenwart*, p. 3.

elements to explain the rise of *ex ante* evaluation of legislation. In order to maintain this focus, we cannot analyse the political rationality that sometimes collides with the formal rationality of evaluation mechanisms. In chapters 4 and 5, this will be extensively shown by Bohne and Hoppe.

Above all, both prospective and retrospective evaluations are important elements of present-day concepts of rationality as a process of rationalisation (II). Thus evaluation is part of a rational decision making model which has been promoted in theories on legislation. At the same time, it fits in economic and management theories applied to administration and regulation, called 'New Public Management' (III). These are the theoretical foundations of a practice, the importance of which has been recognised from both an economic and a legal perspective. The first evaluation procedures are usually focused on the evaluation of financial effects. The importance of *ex ante* evaluation from an economic perspective has given rise to influential OECD studies and recommendations.[2] The fight against overregulation and administrative burdens discharged into a more integral model of rational decision making (IV). Whereas national states often initiated evaluation for budgetary reasons, a broader economic perspective makes room for a broader model such as a regulatory impact assessment.[3] In a more implicit way, the idea of evaluation as the key to rational decision making has manifested itself in a legal perspective, through jurisdiction of European and constitutional courts (V).

II. *A Present-day Concept of Rationality*

In many democracy theories, rationality is an important aspect of the legitimacy of government:[4] both for the use of government power in general and for the binding force of laws in particular.

Democratic institutions have sometimes been analysed as *irrational* by definition, especially in many Public Choice theories.[5] Nevertheless, modern concepts

[2] *See* for this influence Heinz Schäffer, 'Towards a more rational and responsible lawmaking process' in U. Karpen (ed.), *Evaluation of Legislation* (Nomos, Baden-Baden 2002), pp. 146–148.

[3] *See e.g.*, Italy, Alessandro Palanza, 'Evaluation of Legislation in Italy' in U. Karpen (ed.), *Evaluation of Legislation* (Nomos, Baden-Baden 2002), pp. 31–43.

[4] *See* Patricia Popelier, *Democratisch regelgeven* (Intersentia, Antwerp 2001), p. 326 and particularly pp. 54–65 and 88–100.

[5] According to Gerry Mackie, *Democracy defended* (Cambridge University, Cambridge 2004), pp. 9–43, Riker is the founding father of a trend which he describes (and criticises) under the name of "democratic irrationalism". This statement on democratic irrationalism is shared by legal authors outside the field of Public Choice, *see e.g.* Karel Rimanque, 'Forms of State in Science-Fiction' in B. Suykerbuyk (ed.), *Essays from Oceania and Eurasia* (UIA, Exa en Progressef, Antwerp 1984), pp. 19–25.

of men, state, liberty, democracy and rule of law have, in the glow of enlightenment theories, been founded on the idea of rationality.[6] The Enlightenment brought the secularisation of legitimacy principles, which referred to human instead of divine origins.[7] The democratic movement has grown from the belief in men as rational beings.[8] Rational beings are autonomous and sensible beings, capable of making their own plans and decisions on a rational basis and thus taking responsibility for their own decisions.[9] As rational beings, they should be guided by rational laws. Irrational laws disturb people's autonomy and therefore lack legitimacy.[10] Rational laws on the other hand are issued by rational and thus accountable law makers.[11]

However, the concept of rationality has evolved and so have theories on the rationality of laws. The emergence of the modern state was lead by the belief in absolute rationality. This concept, which dates from the eighteenth century, was based on unity, order, stability, coherence and certainty.[12] The codification movement illustrated the belief that reality could be projected in law books. Thus law and lawmaker were seen as rational in every aspect: perfect and complete. The qualities of these laws are described in several theories on the paradigm of the rational lawmaker. They include the presumption that the law is clear, effective and in accordance with reality and societal values.[13] They still influence legal

---

[6] *See more ample* Patricia Popelier, *Rechtszekerheid als beginsel voor behoorlijke regelgeving* (Intersentia, Antwerp 1997), pp. 100–102, regarding the "rule of law" (*Rechtsstaat*) as a rational principle and Popelier, *supra* note 4, pp. 84–88, regarding democracy as a rational principle.

[7] *See also* Philippe Gérard, *Droit et démocratie: réflexions sur la légitimité du droit dans la société démocratique* (FUSL, Brussels 1995), p. 108.

[8] *See also* Jack Lively, *Democracy* (St. Martin's Press, New York 1975), p. 6.

[9] *See among others* Walter Bogs, 'Das Problem der Freiheit' in E. Forsthoff (ed.), *Rechtsstaatlichkeit und Sozialstaatlichkeit* (Wissenschaftliche Buchgesellschaft, Darmstadt 1968), p. 512.

[10] 'Rational' laws however are not necessarily 'just' laws. Nevertheless, a concept which describes rationality as a process, including transparency, weighing of interests, consultation and evaluation, has a better chance to produce laws which are not contrary to concepts of justice.

[11] *See also* Patricia Popelier, 'Do instruments of direct democracy meet standards of democratic and proper law making?' in L. Mader and U. Karpen (eds.), *The Participation of Civil Society in the Legislative Process* (Nomos, Baden-Baden 2005), pp. 103–104 on the legitimacy crisis as a rationality crisis.

[12] François Ost and Michel van de Kerchove, 'Rationaliteit en soevereiniteit van de wetgever: "paradigma's" van de rechtsdogmatiek?' (1986) *Rechtsfilosofie en Rechtskritiek*, p. 133.

[13] *See among others* Norberto Bobbio, 'Le bon législateur' in B. Hubien (ed.), *Le raisonnement juridique* (Bruylant, Brussels 1971), pp. 243–249; Leszek Nowak, 'De la rationalité du législateur comme élément de l'interprétation juridique' (1969) *Logique et analyse*, pp. 65–86; François Ost, 'L'interprétation logique et systématique et le postulat de rationalité du législateur' in M. van de Kerchove (ed.), *L'interprétation en droit* (FUSL, Brussels 1978), pp. 97–184; Ost and van de Kerchove, *supra* note 12, pp. 125–140 and Zygmunt Ziembinski, 'La notion de rationalité du législateur' (1978) *Archives de Philosophie de Droit*, pp. 175–187.

thinking and practice, for example in interpretative methods. This paradigm of the absolute rational law maker corresponded with the paradigm of the sovereign law maker[14] and the inviolability of Acts of Parliament.

Modernism and postmodernism however have put subjective experiences in the forefront. One of their legacies is relativism: in present times the concept of rationality is a relative one. Models of law and rationality have thus evolved from *taxis* to *kosmos*. According to the former, society and legal orders are organisations with full control and complete knowledge of all relevant facts. Reality however has turned out to be far more complex and dynamic. In the latter model, relations emerge and dissolve in a spontaneous way, not all determinant factors or their mutual influences are known or recognisable. In this concept, rationality is no longer conceived in absolute terms. Instead it is a relative and subjective concept.

It has become apparent that people's behaviour is not always rational: it is not efficient or contrary to preferences or objectives. This is explained by the concept of 'bounded rationality': when making rational choices, people are limited by internal and external boundaries, such as uncertainties, information costs, limited memory capacities and cognitive biases.[15]

Thus Stephen J. Morse describes some commonsense observations on the present-day concept of rationality.[16] Rationality refers to a minimal form of coherence between desires, beliefs and actions. It includes the ability to be flexible and responsive to relevant changes in one's situation and environment, the ability to perceive and weigh facts and to act for good reasons. Also, what rationality demands "varies with context and will be defined according to normative social, cultural, historical, moral and political expectations."

Many of these insights can also be applied to the law and the lawmaker. Rationality is dependent on its context. Many laws which seem irrational to legal practitioners can be explained from a political context. The lawmaker is bound by external limits. Often he has to decide on the basis of incomplete information. He is bound by internal limits. He can't escape decisions based on cognitive biases or prejudices. So rational laws in the end are the product of a complex intellectual process which makes use of tools to seek and analyse information within certain boundaries (for example time pressure) and to draw decisions from this assessment.

---

[14] Ost, *supra* note 13, p. 133.

[15] *See among others* Francesco Parisi and Vernon L. Smith (eds.), *The Law and Economics of Irrational Behavior* (Stanford University Press, Stanford 2005), p. 613.

[16] Stephen J. Morse, 'The jurisprudence of craziness' in Parisi and Smith (eds.), *supra* note 15, pp. 229–230.

So the rational quality of laws depends on specific situations and needs, on tradition, cultural and social context. Rational law makers do not make perfect decisions. They do however adopt responsive and justifiable decisions. Popper defined rationalism as an attitude of willingness to listen to critical arguments and to learn from experiences.[17] Thus the idea of absolute rationality, leading to decisions based on truth, is replaced by the idea of *rationalism*: an ongoing process of rationalisation,[18] leading to decisions which are justifiable on the basis of present information and context and adaptable to changes in insights and environment.

III. *The Role of* ex ante *Evaluation in Theories on Legislation and Governance*

A. *Legal and Sociological Theories on Legislation*

In the last decades of the twentieth century the idea was explored that legislation and law making could become the object of science. Rationalisation of legislative methods and empirical sociological research to base decisions on, were part of endeavours to outline this 'science of legislation' or 'legisprudence'.[19] Schäffer described rationalisation of the law making process as the primary objective of a science of legislation.[20] Krems defined the *Gesetzgebungslehre* as part of this science, designed to improve the quality of the law and the law making procedure.[21] Elements are: the choice of aims and means and prognoses of possible effects.[22] It all comes down to *ex ante* evaluation: the careful preparation and consideration of legislative alternatives.

The paradigm of the lawmaker's rationality has been adjusted in the light of the evolving concept of rationality, described above. Wroblewski has thus sketched a model of an ideal law making process to further the production of

[17] Karl Popper, *The open society and its enemies* (Routledge & Kegan Paul, London 1969), part II, p. 225.

[18] Servatius W. Couwenberg, *Modern constitutioneel recht en emancipatie van de mens*, deel 2, *Liberale democratie als eerste emancipatiemodel* (Van Gorcum, Assen 1981), pp. 15 et seq.

[19] *See* Luzius Mader, 'La législation: objet d'une science en devenir?' in Z. Bankowski *et al.*, *La Science de la législation* (Travaux du centre de philosophie du droit, P.U.F., Paris 1988), p. 15.

[20] Heinz Schäffer, 'Rationalisierung der Rechtsetzung' in H. Schäffer (ed.), *Theorie der Rechtssetzung* (Maunz Verlag, Vienna 1988), pp. 199–240.

[21] Burkhardt Krems, *Grundfragen der Gesetzgebungslehre* (Duncker & Humblot, Berlin 1979), pp. 38–43.

[22] *Ibid.*, p. 16.

rational laws.[23] Qualities of rational laws, which were earlier on described as undisputable features of law, now serve as criteria for the drafting, preparation and evaluation of law. There is no longer the presupposition that the law maker has knowledge of the domain and the problems which need to be regulated.[24] Instead, the lawmaker needs to make use of social and positive scientific research to support decisions.

A rational decision making process produces laws which endeavour to reach specifically defined aims in the most efficient way. It uses a system of information gathering and evaluation. This system has to deal with internal and external boundaries. It has to try to avoid cognitive biases, attend to control points, and gather as much as possible relevant information in the least costly and time consuming manner. It has to take into account that decisions might need adjustment, because mistakes are always possible, the decision making process has to deal with bounded rationality and circumstances can change.

This insight is perceptible in many theories on legislation and the law making process. Noll stressed the need to subject legislation to controlling mechanisms to see if it meets certain quality criteria. He wanted to get rid of the idea that law is the accidental product of the conflict of political forces; instead the law making process needs guarantees to make law more objective.[25] To him, the question that matters regarding the quality of legislation is: how can laws influence social behaviour in a desirable way?[26]

Ex ante evaluation was part of the answer. Essential in this evaluation mechanism was the institutionalisation of a contradictory procedure, in order to obtain facts and data on which the formulation of legislative aims and solutions are based. This procedure involves, amongst others, the consultation of stakeholders and specialists.[27] *Ex ante* evaluation further consists of the development of alternatives, prognosis and assessments of possible effects and the weighing of priorities and costs.[28] Afterwards, the lawmaker must be open to *ex post* evaluation, to measure actual effects and side-effects.[29]

---

[23] Jerzy Wroblewski, 'A model of rational law-making' (1979) *Archiv für Rechts- und Sozialphilosophie*, pp. 187–201.

[24] *See also* Luzius Mader, *L'évaluation législative* (Payot Lausanne, Genève 1985), p. 100: in legal dogmatism the rational lawmaker is a presupposition, in legislative science it is an ideal.

[25] Peter NOLL, *Gesetzgebungslehre* (Rowohlt, Reinbek bei Hamburg 1973), p. 95.

[26] *Ibid.*, p. 63.

[27] *Ibid.*, p. 94.

[28] *Ibid.*, pp. 107–137.

[29] *Ibid.*, pp. 146–161.

Specialists, however, do not account for absolute truth or executable decisions: therefore the lawmaker must always be open to corrections.[30] Noll thus introduced the idea of an active instead of reactive, rational, planning legislator.[31] Since Noll, the idea that *ex ante* evaluation forms part of a rational law making process is based on a widespread consensus.[32] So, to name but a few, Schäffer enumerated the assessment of necessity, the assessment of practical and financial feasibility, acceptance and analysis of future effects as elements of the rationalisation process.[33] Mader has stressed that a rational decision making system has to be open to information, critical arguments, thinking in alternatives and self correction.[34] He describes evaluation as "an essential part of legislative methodology",[35] which leads to a dynamic and experimental concept of legislation.[36]

Meanwhile, legal theory has evolved from an instrumental view on legislation to a governance approach, based on Teubner's ideas on reflexive law.[37] In this model, regulation builds cooperative relationships with the private market. Consultation of stakeholders, which is part of a system of prospective evaluation, can be part of that model. Other techniques include forms of self-regulation and assign regulation power to nongovernmental entities. This way, the private sector is drawn into a governance model, sharing regulating responsibilities with governmental authorities.

Lobel enumerates participation, subsidiarity, flexibility, adaptability and dynamic learning among the features of a governance model.[38] As she puts it into words: "the business of government agencies becomes 'regulatory research and development' rather than regulatory decision making'.[39]

Traditional instrumental law relied on professional expertise to base decisions on. The governance model engages more actors and involves citizens in various stages of the legal process.[40] In this model *ex ante* evaluation does not only concern the evaluation of costs and benefits as assessed and calculated by specialists. Consultation of the public at large and stakeholders in particular is important to measure and gain acceptance and to come up with alternatives.

---

30 *Ibid.*, p. 96.

31 According to Mader, *supra* note 24, p. 24.

32 *Ibid.*, p. 43.

33 Schäffer, *supra* note 20, pp. 232–236.

34 Mader, *supra* note 24, pp. 100–101.

35 Luzius Mader, 'Evaluating the Effects: A Contribution to the Quality of Legislation' (2001) *Statute Law Review*, p. 121.

36 Mader, *supra* note 24, p. 7.

37 For an overview *see* Orly Lobel, 'The Renew Deal: The Fall of Regulation and the Rise of Governance in Contemporary Legal Thought' (2004) 89 *Minnesota Law Review*, pp. 361–367.

38 *Ibid.*, pp. 372–404.

39 *Ibid.*, p. 399.

40 *Ibid.*, p. 373.

So RACHLINSKI and FARINA give specific attention to thinking in alternatives and careful evaluation, to avoid cognitive failures which occur especially when specialist play a specific role in the decision making process. Self confidence and blinkers may blind specialists and make them rigidly rely on old recipes even when circumstances have evolved. Thus a careful lawmaker does not exclusively rely on specialists, but also looks for new approaches through the participation of stakeholders and the public at large.[41] NOLL already stressed the importance that not only lobby groups are being heard, but also interested parties which may be less organised.[42]

RACHLINSKI and FARINA also explain why the law maker may deliberately reject the most rational solution if this alternative encounters public opinion's resistance: "*the policy scientist's regulatory failure may be the political philosopher's success story*".[43]

B. *The Application of Management Theories in Governance Theories*

In the governance model described above, the private sector shares regulatory responsibilities with government authorities. Simultaneously, management theories designed for private entities are applied to government authorities. As LOBEL states: "A recurring theme of the new model is that state and government agencies should learn from the practices of private organisational models and market based management theories".[44]

In this part, we want to examine some interesting evolutions that show how the gap between private entities and government authorities is getting smaller. One of the finest examples is the rise of New Public Management (NPM) in the eighties (1). The NPM-paradigm plays a part in the rise of *ex ante* evaluation of legislation during the last decades.

Also, management theories and corporate governance theories provide reasons to integrate *ex ante* evaluation into the law making process. There is the significance of internal control in corporate governance theories (2) and DEMING's PDCA-cycle (3). These theories are an illustration of a climate in which evaluation is getting more and more important, both in the private and the public sector.

---

[41] Jeffrey J. Rachlinski and Cynthia R. Farina, 'Cognitive Psychology and Optimal Government Design' (2002) 87 *Cornell Law Review*, p. 589.

[42] Noll, *supra* note 25, p. 56.

[43] Rachlinski and Farina, *supra* note 41, p. 592.

[44] Lobel, *supra* note 37, pp. 365–366.

1. *New Public Management (NPM)*

Governance theories have been greatly influenced by the paradigm of New Public Management.[45] New Public Management seeks to enhance the efficiency of the public sector, by applying methods from the private sector.[46] It addresses beneficiaries of public services much like customers (a parallel with the private sector) and addresses citizens as shareholders. Therefore it is not exactly a political theory but more of an organisational theory. Since the 1980s this management philosophy has been used by governments (trying) to modernise the public sector.[47]

This focus on customer satisfaction and management tools in the public sector was connected to the evolution in theories on quality in the private sector. Sixty years ago, quality of products was mainly measured from a producer's point of view, focusing on statistics and features. Quality was thought of as "*the intrinsic features of the good or service itself, as seen by those producing it.*"[48] Throughout the years, a consumer oriented perspective prevailed, stressing the needs of the users of the product. These theories gradually evolved and merged into a new general theory, combining all aspects. This Total Quality Management (TQM) has got a much broader scope than previous perspectives on quality. TQM aims at embedding awareness of quality in *all* organisational processes, with a focus on customer satisfaction and lower costs.[49] Quality can only be provided when every single process has been carefully considered. Therefore, TQM is about communication, information, transparency, training and innovation.[50]

These principles have found their way into the public sector, in terms of NPM. Within NPM, specific quality models, such as the CAF-model, have been created

---

[45] "New Public Management" is a collective name for similar theories that was invented afterwards. *See* Tom Christensen and Per Lægreid, 'New Public Management: Puzzles of Democracy and the Influence of Citizens' (2002) 10(3) *Journal of Political Philosophy*, p. 268.

[46] *See e.g.* Jan-Erik Lane, *New Public Management* (Routledge, London 2000), p. 256; Christopher Hood, 'A Public Management for All Seasons' (1991) 69(1) *Public Administration*, pp. 3–9 and Patrick Dunleavy and Christopher Hood, 'From Old Public Administration to New Public Management' (1994) July-September *Public Money and Management*, pp. 9–16.

[47] *E.g.* Margaret Thatcher's approach in the UK during the 1980s. *See* Tony Cutler and Barbara Waine, 'Managerialism Reformed? New Labour and Public Sector Management' (2000) *Social Policy and Administration*, pp. 318–332.

[48] Christopher Pollitt and Geert Bouckaert, *Quality improvement in European Public Services* (Sage, London 1995), p. 16.

[49] *See* Nick Thijs, 'Het managen van kwaliteit in de publieke sector' (2004) 1 *Burger, bestuur en beleid*, p. 42 and more ample: John S. Oakland, *Total quality management: the route to improving performance* (Butterworth-Heinemann, Oxford 1994), p. 463.

[50] This evolution has never stopped. Recently, *Six Sigma* has been promoted as a new way of combining TQM insights with statistic approaches. *See* Thomas Pyzdek, *The six sigma handbook: a complete guide for green belts, black belts and managers at all levels* (McGraw-Hill, New York 2003), p. 830.

in order to translate TQM for a public environment.[51] It is interesting to see how self evaluation (or self assessment) has become one of the most important tools in these models. Quality and evaluation are inseparable in this model – as they are in *ex ante* evaluation theories.

Governance theories should not be considered to be a part of the NPM theories, but it is obvious that they share certain points of view. This is shown clearly by Radaelli and Meuwese, who discuss the 'Better Regulation' programs in Europe. Their analysis confirms that ideas from NPM are similar to those in Better Regulation policies, without stating that "Better Regulation is just yet another manifestation of NPM".[52] The differences should be acknowledged, but the analysis reveals that the two fields have communicated – via ideational transfer processes, or simply via catalysts such as communities of consultants and international organisations.[53]

New Public Management is not universally accepted as the best way to organise a public administration. Most heard is the criticism that the private and the public sector differ too much to translate management tools from one to another.[54] New theories have come up, slowly ousting NPM. Nevertheless, New Public Management theories acknowledge valuable insights and stress the importance of a broad quality managing system. Organisations should regularly assess all of their processes and citizens should be treated as customers. Transparency and communication are a must in order to keep them satisfied. This is where *ex ante* evaluation comes in: public impact assessment can provide the transparency about the decision making process that is needed to inform citizens and to create democratic legitimacy.[55]

---

51 The Common Assessment Framework (CAF) is a total quality management tool that has been specifically designed for the self-assessment of organisational performance in public-sector organisations. The European Institute of Public Administration provides trainings and seminars: *see* <www.eipa.eu>. Another useful model, originally designed for the private sector, is the EFQM-model, designed by the *European Foundation for Quality Management, see* <www.efqm.org>.

52 Just one example: the economic policy orientation and the governance ambition of Better Regulation are quite unique. *See* Claudio M. Radaelli and Anne C.M. Meuwese, 'Better Regulation in Europe: Administration, Public Management, and the Regulatory State', Paper for ECPR Rennes 11–16 April 2008, pp. 16–17.

53 *Ibid.*, p. 17.

54 *See* Stephen Page, 'What's New about the New Public Management? Administrative Change in the Human Services' (2005) *Public Administration Review*, p. 713 and Alan Doig and John Wilson, 'What Price New Public Management?' (1998) 69(3) *Political Quarterly*, p. 274. About the debate on NPM: Ali Farazmand (ed.), *Privatization of Public Enterprise Reform? International Case Studies with Implications for Public Management* (Greenwood Press, London 2001), p. 265 and B. Guy Peters, *The Future of Governing*, 2nd ed. (University Press of Kansas, Lawrence 2001), p. 260.

55 Transparency is also needed in an open, deliberative democracy. Decisions are only "democratic" when every citizen has had the opportunity to participate in the deliberative process. *See* John

2. *Corporate Governance*

NPM is particularly interesting for governments as it focuses on the organisation of public administrations. Nevertheless, it could be inspiring for the public sector to take a look at the private sector, and more particularly, at corporate governance theories.[56] These theories were initially successful in the United States during the 1980s. As a result of several corporate scandals, good governance of companies has also become a hot topic in Europe.[57] In 1999, the Organisation for Economic Co-operation and Development (OECD) formulated principles of corporate governance in five areas, e.g. 'The role of stakeholders' and 'Disclosure and transparency'.[58] There is no single model of good corporate governance, but the OECD has brought together some common elements.[59]

Corporate governance is a term that refers broadly to the set of processes, customs, policies, laws and institutions affecting the way in which a corporation is directed, administered and controlled.[60] It provides a structure allowing the company to set its objectives and to determine the means to attain those objectives and to monitor its performance.[61] Corporate governance also specifies the roles of different participants in the organisation and the relationships among the many players involved (the stakeholders).[62] Governments have similarities with corporations when it comes to satisfying different sorts of stakeholders:

S. Dryzek, *Deliberative democracy and beyond: liberals, critics, contestations* (University Press, New York 2000), pp. 1 and 85.

56 On the OECD website, public governance and corporate governance are both labelled as "governance", <www.oecd.org>.

57 In the UK, the fraudulent collapses of the Maxwell-emporium and the BBCI-bank have led to the Cadbury Report: Adrian Cadbury, "*The Code of Best Practice*", *Report of the Committee on the Financial Aspects of Corporate Governance* (Gee and Co Ltd, London 1992), <www.ecgi.org> (Just one of many comments: Vanessa Finch, 'Board Performance and Cadbury on Corporate Governance' (1992) *The Journal of Business Law*, pp. 581–595.) About the impact of the infamous Enron-scandal (US): John Armour and Joseph McCahery (eds.), *After Enron: Improving Corporate Law and Modernising Securities Regulation in Europe and the US* (Hart Publications, Oxford 2006), p. 718.

58 OECD, *OECD Principles of Corporate Governance*, SG/CG(99)5 (OECD, Paris 1999), p. 25.

59 The differences show in Eddy Wymeersch, 'The Corporate Governance Discussion in some European States' in D.D. Prentice and P.R.J. Holland (eds.), *Contemporary Issues in Corporate Governance* (Clarendon Press, Oxford 1993), pp. 3–23 and Klaus J. Hopt, 'Gemeinsame Grundsätze der Corporate Governance in Europa?' (2000) *Zeitschrift für Unternehmens- und Gesellschaftsrecht*, pp. 779–818.

60 *See* definitions in Eric Causin, 'Corporate Governance: le gouvernement d'entreprise' (2002) 61/62 *Le droit des affaires*, p. 74 and Hans Wilmots, *Een praktische kijk op administratieve organisatie en interne controle* (Standaard, Antwerp 2002), p. 15.

61 OECD, *OECD Principles of Corporate Governance*, SG/CG(99)5 (OECD, Paris 1999), p. 2.

62 Vrajlal K. Sapovadia, 'Good Corporate Governance: An Instrument for Wealth Maximisation', MBA Department of Saurashtra University Conference, India, 2003. Available at SSRN: ssrn.com/abstract=955289 (consulted in February 2008).

citizens, lobby groups, agencies, civil servants, political parties, etc. Thus corporate governance might provide useful insights for the law maker. In the context of this article, it is interesting to focus on the way quality is being monitored and evaluated. Internal control and external control are the keywords.

One of the corner stones in corporate governance theories is the need for a structured system of internal control within every (decision making) process. Internal control is broadly defined as a process, effected by an entity's personnel, designed to provide reasonable assurance regarding the achievement of prescribed objectives. Every process should be designed in a way that mistakes are filtered out by the administration itself.[63] The operational level should reach the standards that are formulated by the management.

There seems to be a similarity with the law making process: leading politicians formulate policy plans that are to be carried out by the civil servants. A first level of internal control should be carried out by the administration who prepares the draft bill: the facts and figures have to be correct. Afterwards, Parliament independently assesses these draft bills.[64] This is where *ex ante* evaluation comes in: it is a promising tool to make sure that the necessary assessments are carried out by the administration. It also makes the parliamentary control easier: Members of Parliament have immediate disposition of all relevant facts and figures.

Internal control is not sufficient to guarantee flawless products. In corporations, external stakeholders also exercise control over the organisation. E.g. an annual audit by an independent auditor provides an objective assurance on the way in which financial statements have been prepared by the management and presented. External and internal controls need each other. An external specialist cannot supervise every single process within the company. Internal control on the other hand does not work properly if there is no external control on a regular basis.

External control can also play a very important role during the law making process. Independent institutions should be able to take a look at draft bills. In Belgium e.g. there is an independent advice by the Council of State before draft bills can be submitted to Parliament. These advices often show (juridical) flaws in draft bills, a fact that stresses the necessity of external control. Furthermore external control can be useful once the bill has been passed. It is important to follow up the impact and side effects of legislation. In that way the need for external control can be an argument to plead for *ex post* evaluation as part of a

---

[63] *See* <www.coso.org>, the website of The Committee of Sponsoring Organizations of the Treadway Commission. This U.S. private-sector initiative's major objective is to identify the factors that cause fraudulent financial reporting and to make recommendations to reduce its incidence.

[64] In Belgium, this causes a problem, as ministerial cabinets take over large parts of the decision making process from the administration, thus avoiding existing structures and filters.

structured law making process. External control could then be carried out by an independent institution – such as the Anglo-Saxon Law Commission – or on a more modest scale through the remarks in the reports of the national Ombudsman.

A last focal point of corporate governance is the access to and disclosure of relevant information. The OECD outlines this demand: "*Where laws and practice of corporate governance systems provide for participation by stakeholders, it is important that stakeholders have access to information necessary to fulfil their responsibilities.*"[65] This demand can also be translated in terms of the lawmaking process. In a deliberative democracy citizens should participate in and be consulted about policy decisions. In order to assess the impact of these decisions, citizens need all the relevant information about the subject. *Ex ante* evaluation is a tool that can solve this problem: a good impact assessment contains the available information and presents it in a clear way. Several options are discussed and the possible (side) effects are listed. Hence *ex ante* evaluation can provide in the demand for transparency.

3. *The PDCA-Cycle*

A third organisational tool that provides new insights in the law making process is DEMING's PDCA-cycle: Plan – Do – Check – Act. DEMING was a mathematician and in the 1940s one of the first to elaborate an economic and statistic concept of quality. One of his baselines is that the management of a corporation needs to think of the future instead of the past. Processes can only be improved by using past data to act on future processes.[66] DEMING turned away from *ad hoc* quality initiatives and designed a permanent and well structured self-maintaining quality program. This was highly innovative and had a worldwide impact. Most famous is DEMING's PDCA-cycle:

Graphic 1 – PCDA-Cycle (DEMING)[67]

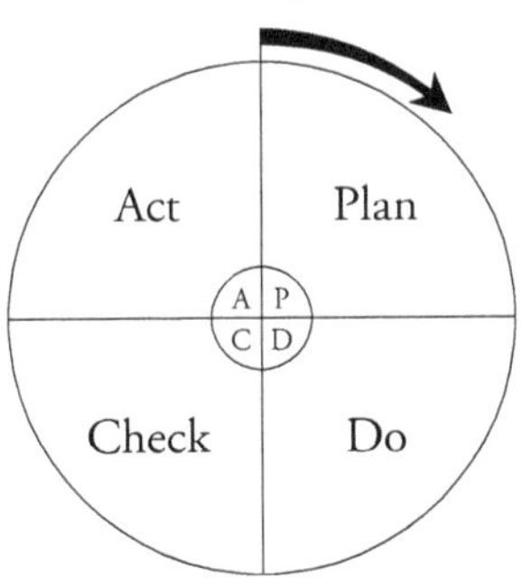

[65] OECD, *OECD Principles of Corporate Governance*, SG/CG(99)5 (OECD, Paris 1999), p. 18.

[66] William E. Deming, *Out of the crisis* (Massachusetts Institute of Technology, Center for Advanced Engineering Study, Cambridge, 1991 (12th edition)), p. 15.

[67] Image from <commons.wikimedia.org/wiki/Image:PDCA.gif>.

Deming's PDCA-cycle consists of four basic steps to design new processes and to take business decisions:

- *Plan*: Establish the objectives and processes necessary to deliver results in accordance with the requirements. Which transformations are needed? Do you have enough data to make a decision?
- *Do*: Implement the processes. If there is uncertainty about the effects, start on a smaller scale.
- *Check*: Monitor and *evaluate* the new processes against the objectives and report the outcome.
- *Act*: Review all steps (Plan, Do, Check, Act) and modify the process to improve it before its next implementation. Apply the actions that are needed.

Later on, 'Check' was replaced by 'Study'. Thus, the PDCA-cycle turned into the PDSA-cycle, but the content remained the same.

This cycle delivers useful insights for structuring the law making process. First there is a need for plans, for a policy.[68] A company, similar to a government, needs to know where to go. However there can be no policy without an access to correct data. Deming shows that policy is useless when it cannot be implemented. Nevertheless relevant data are not always available. Sometimes it is necessary to organise a pilot project in order to gather the necessary information.[69] The law maker should not be afraid to try out new methods in order to collect these data.

However the most important lesson is that according to Deming's cycle, prospective and retrospective evaluations are essential elements of every process. First the law maker needs a vision, a policy, a clear objective. Data have to show that the policy can be implemented. The policy and its effectiveness can be specified and examined during the *ex ante* evaluation. However the law making process never ends; it is a cycle. Evaluation *ex post* is necessary to assess and improve former decisions and to refine the methods used during the evaluation *ex ante*. Deming shows us that evaluation has two sides, i.e. *ex ante* and *ex post*, which cannot function apart from each other.

---

[68] This need can also be found in corporate governance theories: CG has to create a structure through which the *objectives* of the company are set. *See supra* para. 26 and note 60. *See also* OECD, *OECD Principles of Corporate Governance*, SG/CG(99)5 (OECD, Paris 1999), pp. 19–20: "Disclosure should include [...] *material information on* [...] *company objectives*." and p. 23: "*The board should fulfil certain key functions, including: reviewing and guiding corporate strategy,* [...] *risk policy, annual budgets and business plans; setting performance objectives,* [...]."

[69] In Flanders, these pilot projects ("proeftuinen") have become a well accepted way of working in the field of educational law.

4. *Conclusion: The Rise of Evaluation*

Governance theories acknowledge that state and government agencies should learn from the practices of private organisational models and market based management theories.[70] Looking at those private market models, it is remarkable how important evaluation has become. In NPM self assessment has become one of the key organisational methods. At the same time, transparency is put forward as a crucial demand. Corporate governance shows us that internal and external controls are basic conditions to manage a company. These controls can be translated into *ex ante* and *ex post* evaluation. Also stakeholders should be informed and consulted. *Ex ante* evaluation provides a tool for that as well. Finally the PDCA-cycle acknowledges the importance of *ex post* evaluation: *ex ante* evaluation is never complete without it. Thus the rise of *ex ante* evaluation can be situated in a larger context which includes both the public and the private sector.

IV. *An Economic Perspective*

The idea that legislation should be processed in a rational way, of which *ex ante* evaluation is a crucial element, has found its way to legislative practice. According to Schäffer, "facing the many new challenges of the modern state and considering the urgent requirements to use the scarce resources economically, there is a pressure for rationality in legislation".[71] *Ex ante* evaluation has no doubt been boosted by this economic incentive: better regulation decreases company costs and thus stimulates a country's economy.

Therefore evaluation techniques were introduced in governmental guidelines. Especially federal states such as Germany, Switzerland and Austria were pioneers.[72] At the same time states and international organisations have become more aware of the economic significance of laws.[73] Most illustrative is the evolution within the model of regulatory management that has been developed by the OECD.

The OECD was founded in 1961 and unites the governments of countries committed to democracy and the market economy. Its aim is to support sustainable economic growth, boost employment and contribute to growth in world trade.[74] The OECD reports on regulatory reform are determined by this economic perspective. Regulatory reform was approached in a narrow way, focussing on reducing state interference. At first suggestions were made to cut red tape and

---

[70] *See supra* para. 16.

[71] Heinz Schäffer, 'Evaluation and Assessment of Legal Effects Procedures: Towards a More Rational and Responsible Lawmaking Process' (2001) *Statute Law Review*, p. 136.

[72] *Ibid.*, pp. 142–143.

[73] *See* e.g., Radaelli and Meuwese, *supra* note 52, p. 15.

[74] <www.oecd.org>.

reduce administrative burdens. Complaints were voiced about 'regulatory inflation', rising compliance costs, and burdensome administrative formalities.[75] The OECD focused on the growing *quantity* and costs of regulation, rather than on the *quality* of regulation. This narrow economic point of view often leads to mixing up quantity and quality of regulation.[76]

In the 1990s however, the OECD realised that also the *quality* of regulations concerns the conditions for sustainable global economic growth. Policy makers recognised that makeshift approaches to reform were insufficient. Economic prosperity can be stimulated by all-round good regulation. In 1995 the OECD summarised its new point of view: "*Regulatory quality is crucial for economic performance and government effectiveness in improving the quality of life of citizens. The quality of regulations is becoming even more important as rules are internationalised, and national regulations affect the world trading system.*"[77] The OECD mainly started working on regulatory quality because economic growth and the efficient use of economic resources are promoted by high-quality regulations.[78] Nevertheless the OECD acknowledged the need for transparency of government regulation,[79] thus slowly widening its scope.

The 1995 Recommendation was a milestone: it was the first international standard on regulatory quality. It contained a guiding checklist of good decision-making principles, consisting of 10 questions. In 1997, these questions were transformed into eight principles of good regulation.[80] These principles are well known and have stood the test of time. In 2005 they have been updated, but only small changes have been made. According to the OECD, good regulation should:[81]

(i) serve clearly identified policy goals, and be effective in achieving those goals;
(ii) have a sound legal and empirical basis;

---

[75] OECD, *Recommendation of the Council of the OECD on improving the quality of government regulation*, 9 March 1995, OCDE/GD (95)95, 11, <www.olis.oecd.org/olis/1995doc.nsf/LinkTo/OCDE-GD(95)95>. (Cited as OECD Recommendation 1995).

[76] About quality and quantity of regulation, *see* Patricia Popelier, *De wet, juridisch bekeken* (die Keure, Bruges 2004), pp. 23–24.

[77] OECD Recommendation 1995, p. 3.

[78] OECD Recommendation 1995, p. 7.

[79] OECD Recommendation 1995, p. 7.

[80] OECD, *The OECD Report on Regulatory Reform. Synthesis* (OECD, Paris 1997), pp. 27–28. *See* <www.oecd.org/dataoecd/17/25/2391768.pdf>. (Cited as OECD Report 1997).

[81] OECD, *OECD Guiding principles for regulatory quality and performance* (OECD, Paris 2005), p. 3. *See* <www.oecd.org/dataoecd/24/6/34976533.pdf>. (Cited as OECD Guiding Principles 2005).

(iii) produce benefits that justify costs, considering the distribution of effects across society and taking economic, environmental and social effects into account;
(iv) minimise costs and market distortions;
(v) promote innovation through market incentives and goal-based approaches;
(vi) be clear, simple, and practical for users;
(vii) be consistent with other regulations and policies; and
(viii) be compatible as far as possible with competition, trade and investment-facilitating principles at domestic and international levels.

The economic scope of these principles is clear: regulation should not interfere with market mechanisms and should be clear and easy to use. The economic focus stays: in 2005 the OECD stated that "*the goal of regulatory reform is to improve national economies and enhance their ability to adapt to change.*"[82] Nevertheless the OECD is looking further. The concept of regulatory reform has changed over the last decade. In the 1990s efforts were made to reduce the scale of government, but these were often carried out in single initiatives. These isolated efforts were not as successful as expected. Slowly the idea grew that a regulatory environment favourable to the growth of economy needs a broader and more structured system, built upon a complete regulatory policy. Such policy needs a coherent, whole-of-government approach: removing unneeded regulations is still important, but needs to be integrated in a larger structure. Thus the OECD stresses its first recommendation: "*Adopt at the political level broad programmes of regulatory reform that establish clear objectives and frameworks for implementation.*"[83] The principles for good regulation should be part of this elaborated framework: they will not be successful just by existing. They must be put ahead as objectives and regulatory processes must be designed in a way that allows to monitor and attain these objectives.

How does *ex ante* evaluation fit into this whole-of-government approach? The OECD states that evaluation is an essential part of a regulatory policy: "*Assess impacts and review regulations systematically to ensure that they meet their intended objectives efficiently and effectively in a changing and complex economic and social environment.*" The OECD pleads for two types of evaluation: *ex ante* ("assess") and *ex post* ("review"). *Ex ante* evaluation should be effected as a so called Regulatory Impact Analysis (RIA): a formal and structured way of assessing (side) effects of new regulation. Governments should make sure that RIA plays a key role in improving the quality of regulation and that it is conducted in a timely, clear

[82] OECD Guiding Principles 2005, p. 1.
[83] OECD Report 1997, pp. 27–28 and OECD Guiding Principles 2005, p. 1.

and transparent manner.[84] RIA is also a great tool to monitor the principles of good regulation. While assessing the effects of draft regulation, it should become clear if the draft is necessary, simple, efficient, consistent, etc. RIA has all the assets to become the principal tool of a regulatory policy.

The OECD is an ideal platform to assess RIA systems throughout the world, via thematic studies and country reviews.[85] The collected good practices are excellent starting points to maximise the benefits of RIA. Looking at the efforts to promote RIA as part of regulatory reform, there is no doubt that the OECD finds *ex ante* evaluation to be an essential part of a regulatory system. This has certainly contributed to the rise of *ex ante* evaluation throughout the world.[86]

The OECD is not the only international organisation that has formulated guidelines for regulatory reform and impact assessments. The European Union (EU) is also very active in this field. This gives an extra boost to regulatory reform within European Member States. As for impact assessments, the EU shares the same economic drive with the OECD. The EU intends to realise the *Lisbon objectives*: the European Council has set the overall target to develop Europe as the world's most dynamic and competitive economy by 2010. *Ex ante* evaluation is said to make a contribution to these plans. The EU has published some important Impact Assessment Guidelines,[87] which will be discussed by Linda Senden and Anne Meuwese.

V. *A Legal Perspective*

The courts do not explicitly state that the lawmaker is legally obliged to evaluate laws. On the contrary, the Belgian Constitutional Court does not hold itself competent to criticize a law *because* it is not based on preparatory studies and analyses.[88] Of course, the more evaluation tools such as regulatory impact assessments become institutionalized, the sooner a legal obligation to perform an

84 OECD Guiding Principles 2005, p. 4.

85 *See* <www.oecd.org>.

86 E.g. the eight Flemish principles for good regulation have been based strongly upon the eight OECD principles. *See Gids Kenmerken van goede regelgeving*, Brussel, Ministerie van de Vlaamse Gemeenschap, 2003, <www.wetsmatiging.be/downloads/gids%20Kenmerken%20van%20goede%20regelgeving.pdf>.

87 *Impact Assessment Guidelines*, Brussels, European Commission, 15 June 2005. (europa.eu.int/comm/secretariat_general/impact/docs/SEC2005_791_IA%20guidelines_annexes.pdf.)

88 Constitutional Court no 51/2003, 30 April 2003, *Official Gazette* 12 June 2003 (*see* <www.courconstitutionnelle.be>).

ex ante evaluation might become judicially enforceable. At this moment this is not yet the case in the European Union and in its Member States.[89]

However case law of both national and European courts illustrates that evaluation is in fact a legal obligation. The Belgian Constitutional Court can annul laws if they are not proportional; the European Court of Human Rights can condemn countries for the same reason. The assessment of the proportionality of a law may depend on the performance of due care in the preparatory process, including the execution of consultations and studies. In the next chapters, some examples will be given related to both *ex ante* (*sub* 1) and *ex post* (*sub* 2) evaluations. The purpose of this analysis is to illustrate that legal reasoning supports the idea of evaluation as keystone for rational decision making. The analysis concerns the Belgian Constitutional Court and the European Court of Human Rights, but the case law of courts such as the European Court of Justice or the German Constitutional Courts could equally have served our purpose.

A. Ex Ante *Evaluation*

Constitutional Courts examine the proportionality of laws, either directly or through the equality test or fundamental rights. This way courts judge the rationality of laws. Laws are 'not clearly unreasonable' when they are justified by plausible arguments supporting a legitimate aim, balanced against other plausible arguments. Careful preparation, including research and consultation, influences the outcome of the question whether a law can reasonably be justified.

1. *The Belgian Constitutional Court*

The Belgian Constitutional Court can reject the government's arguments when it seems that the lawmaker did not prepare the law properly and was not informed by experts. The Court will do so when scientific studies do not support the lawmaker's proposition. For example, the Constitutional Court annulled a law which introduced a difference in treatment of two categories of fertilizers, because scientific studies submitted by the petitioner proofed the law to be based on false premises.[90]

In the case of legislative schemes regarding aircraft noise disturbing people living near the airport of Bierset, the Court judged that the right to family life and privacy was violated. None of the submitted reports supported the statement that neighbouring people could live in their houses without disproportional

---

[89] *See* Anne C.M. Meuwese, *Impact Assessment in EU Lawmaking* (Wöhrmann Print Service, Zutphen 2008), pp. 167–176 and 271–272 on review of impact assessment by the European Court of Justice with comparative notes on review on IA in the UK and the USA.

[90] Constitutional Court No. 1/1993, 7 January 1993, *Official Gazette* 19 January 1993 (<www.courconstitutionnelle.be>).

inconvenience – for example because the option to insulate their houses would force them to always stay inside with closed doors and windows.[91] Regarding the treatment of packing dependent on its reusable character the Court explicitly stated that the difference must be based on scientific data concerning the environmental implications.[92]

On the other hand the government can justify legislation referring to scientific studies or statistics on which its decision was based. For example, the claim that a law concerning sick-leave was discriminatory because it did not take into account the fact that the risk of falling ill increases with age, was rejected with reference to statistics the lawmaker had used in formulating the regulation.[93]

However the value of scientific analyses and reports must not be exaggerated. The lawmaker may base a judgment on global factors or reasonable suppositions or hypotheses. Also it is possible that scientific research is not of any help, for example because there is no scientific unanimity. So the Constitutional Court judged that because of the lack of scientific unanimity on the harmful environmental effects of polyvinyl chloride, the lawmaker when imposing environment taxes could on the basis of known facts reasonably assume that polyvinyl chloride packing creates greater environmental hazards than other kinds of packing.[94]

The Court thus takes into account elements of 'bounded rationality', such as information costs.[95] The Court reminds the lawmaker to estimate future consequences and make a fair balance on that basis. The lawmaker however must base legislation on research and analysis which are reasonably available. On the basis of that information he must estimate the effects, profits and losses associated with the effects in order to reach a fair and proportionate balance of interests.

2. *The European Court of Human Rights*

In the *Hatton* cases concerning night flights the European Court of Human Rights made very clear that it can set standards for the organisation of the

---

[91] Constitutional Court No. 51/2003, 30 April 2003, *Official Gazette* 12 June 2003 (<www.courconstitutionnelle.be>).

[92] Constitutional Court No. 195/2004, 1 December 2004, *Official Gazette* 10 December 2004 and Constitutional Court No. 9/2007, 11 January 2007, *Official Gazette* 30 January 2007 (<www.courconstitutionnelle.be>).

[93] Constitutional Court No. 134/98, 16 December 1998, *Official Gazette* 5 January 1999 (<www.courconstitutionnelle.be>).

[94] Constitutional Court No. 7/95, 2 February 1995, *Official Gazette* 1 March 1995 (<www.courconstitutionnelle.be>).

[95] *See* Patricia Popelier, 'De (ir)rationale wetgever vroeger, vandaag en in de toekomst' in B. Peeters and J. Velaers (eds.), *De grondwet in groothoekperspectief* (Intersentia, Antwerp 2007), pp. 86–88.

decision-making process. [96] The European Court refers to procedural aspects especially in cases relating to issues in which national authorities maintain large discretionary competence. The Court considered that in decisions affecting environmental issues, the Court may "scrutinize the decision-making process to ensure that due weight has been accorded to the interests of the individual". To that end it is "required to consider all the procedural aspects". The Court stresses that the lawmaker must act in due care, relying on appropriate investigation and study, guaranteeing a proportionate decision through permanent evaluation and monitoring, based on integral balance of interests through transparency and participatory procedures.

In other cases the Court has judged laws justified because they were based on careful preparation and evaluation too. In the *Evans* cases the Court upheld a law allowing the biological father to withdraw his legally required consent at any time before the frozen embryos were implanted in the applicant's uterus. As a justification the Court referred to the decision making process. According to the Court the law was "the culmination of an exceptionally detailed examination of the social, ethical and legal implications of developments in the field of human fertilisation and embryology". This examination involved a commission of experts, a Green Book for public consultation and representations from interested parties included in a White Paper.[97]

On the other hand the lack of careful evaluation is an element that can support the assessment that a law is not justified. In the *Lecarpentier* case the French lawmaker referred to motives of general economic interest to justify retroactive intervention to counter the effects of a judicial decision concerning a mortgage loan. The Court stated that there was no indication that the decision would have an impact on the financial sector and endanger economic activities. It condemned the lack of reliable evaluations of the virtual costs of pending and future judicial disputes in similar matters and disapproved of the fact that the Members of Parliament had not obtained precise information.[98]

B. Ex Post *Evaluation*

The Courts accept that rationalisation is an ongoing process. Therefore the rationality of a law has a dimension of time. New developments and unforeseen

---

[96] Hatton v. United Kingdom, 2 October 2001, European Court of Human Rights, no. 36022/97 and Grand Chamber, 8 July 2003, <www.echr.coe.int>. *See also* Fadeyeva v. Russia, 9 June 2005, European Court of Human Rights, no. 55723/00 which, however, concerned individual measures against a specific enterprise, not legislative action.

[97] Evans v. United Kingdom, 7 March 2006, European Court of Human Rights, no. 6339/05 and Grand Chamber, 10 April 2007, <www.echr.coe.int>.

[98] Lecarpentier v. France, 14 February 2006, European Court of Human Rights, no. 67847/01.

events may render a law ineffective or disproportionate. *Ex post* evaluations may either incite the lawmaker to adapt a law or prove the reasonableness of a law.

1. *The Belgian Constitutional Court*

The Belgian Constitutional Court induces the lawmaker to evaluate enacted legislation. The prospect of evaluations *ex post* may help to justify an enacted law. Once the law is in force the lawmaker must indeed evaluate to keep laws in pace with subsequent social or technological change. A law can be justified in the light of future evaluations, for example when periodic evaluations are announced to help the lawmaker to clarify and adapt legislation and to keep it within bounds of proportionality.[99]

For example, the Constitutional Court agreed that the different treatment of workmen and clerks initially corresponded with an actual difference in the kind of work performed by workmen on the one hand and clerks on the other, the former doing manual work, the latter intellectual. However, nowadays the reality of such a distinction has faded so that legislation which provides workmen with a less advantageous statutory regime is contrary to the equality and non-discrimination principle.

In another case the Court annulled a provision stating that the period for making a claim for child maintenance expires three years after the man had alleged intercourse with the mother leading to the birth, but was not married to the mother and did not recognize the child. According to the Court, the reduced term was justified in 1908, when after several years it was difficult to establish proof of sexual intercourse. Since 1987, however, the law admits proof by all legal means. Nowadays, scientific techniques make possible proof of sexual intercourse which is more reliable than the traditional witnesses and can be established long after the actual intercourse.[100]

In a recent case a legal provision dating from 1900 was challenged. This law provided for a simplified procedure for compensation claims regarding damage to vegetation and fruit caused by rabbits. According to the Constitutional Court this special procedure was justified in 1900 because the "unbridled multiplication" of rabbits constituted a plague to farmers. However, the factual circumstances have changed, since illnesses have reduced the amount of rabbits in a considerable

[99] Constitutional Court, No. 42/97, 14 July 1997, *Official Gazette* 3 September 1997 and Constitutional Court No. 136/2000, 21 December 2000, *Official Gazette* 23 January 2001 (<www.courconstitutionnelle.be>).

[100] Constitutional Court No. 79/2004, 12 May 2004, *Official Gazette* 10 August 2004 (<www.courconstitutionnelle.be>).

way so that they no longer constitute a plague. Therefore, the special procedure in favour of the victims of this kind of damage was no longer justified.[101]

2. *The European Court of Human Rights*

The European Court of human rights stresses the importance of new legal, social and technological developments to evaluate the proportionality of legislative intervention. In the *Wessels-Bergervoet* case it considered that the unequal treatment in social security provisions for men and women whose spouse worked abroad was no longer justified in the context of modern social attitudes. Although the basic regulation concerned had been subsequently amended, the Court condemned the regulatory regime on the finding that the original regulation still had discriminatory consequences, for example in the calculation of pensions.[102]

In earlier decisions, the Court stated that a Member State could deny the right to transsexuals to change their sex in registration files, but it warned that this would no longer be proportionate when significant scientific developments would make possible the biological transformation of a man into a woman or *vice versa.*[103] In more recent case law the Court found that in the context of scientific, social and legal developments the right of post-operative transsexuals to change the indication of their sex in birth certificates and their right to marry a person of the opposite sex from their post-operative one could no longer be denied.[104]

The lawmaker must not only keep pace with evolutions in a national context. He should also keep an eye on legal developments in surrounding states. For example, the European Court condemned the Turkish legislation according to which marriage has as a consequence that the wife loses her family name and obtains her husband's name, even if the couple wishes her to keep her name. To that end the Court referred to the fact that equality of men and women is a prominent value in the member states of the Council of Europe and the United Nations. More specifically, it referred to the consensus between member states in favour of a family name on terms of equality. The Court added that since November 2001 Turkish reforms were in line with the trend to give men and

---

101 Constitutional Court No. 44/2007, 21 March 2007, *Official Gazette* 25 May 2007 (<www.courconstitutionnelle.be>).

102 Wessels-Bergervoet v. Netherlands, 4 June 2002, European Court of Human Rights, no. 34462/97, <www.echr.coe.int>.

103 Rees v. United Kingdom, 17 October 1986, European Court of Human Rights, *Publ.E.C.H.R.* Series A No. 106 and Cossey v. United Kingdom, 27 September 1990, European Court of Human Rights, *Publ.E.C.H.R.* Series A No. 184.

104 I. v. United Kingdom, 11 July 2002, European Court of Human Rights, no. 25680/94 and Christine Goodwin v. United Kingdom, 11 July 2002, European Court of Human Rights, no. 28957/95, <www.echr.coe.int>.

women an equal position in family life, so that the law regarding the family name was no longer coherent.[105]

Ex post evaluations can also help to uphold a law which has become controversial after a specific incident. For example the European Court considered that the Italian law providing for a progressive social reintegration of detainees was reasonable, despite an incident in which a detainee after having obtained the favour of an alternative measure had killed a passenger. The Court's assessment was supported by the evaluation *ex post* of the law, executed by the government and establishing that the percentage of crimes committed by detainees having obtained the favour of similar measures was very low.[106]

VI. *Conclusion*

This chapter proceeded from the proposition that laws derive legitimacy partly from rationality. Rationality, however, is an evolving concept. Nowadays, rationality is considered to be a relative concept. We have defined it as an ongoing process of rationalisation, leading to decisions which are justifiable on the basis of present information and context and adaptable to changes in insights and environment.

In this context, evaluation is the key to rationalisation. As such it takes up a prominent position in several influential theories on legislation, governance and public management, both from a legal and an economic point of view. Evaluation in this context is not merely an option in the organisation of regulatory management. The proportionality test executed by constitutional and European courts turn it into a legal obligation. The execution and results of *ex ante* and *ex post* evaluations support the assessment of laws as being either proportionate or not.

This is the front office story, a formal and rational framework that has lead to the rise of *ex ante* evaluation of legislation. Of course, there is more to it, especially when the theoretical views are implemented in a highly political world. A modern concept of rationality, however, has to take into account its complex and relative nature. Rationality is context-bound. Therefore, the concept of rational law making has to take into account political rationality and strategies. Rational procedures, including participation, transparency and evaluation, at least force the law maker to make political motives explicit.

---

105 Unal Tekeli v. Turkey, 16 November 2004, European Court of Human Rights, no. 29865/96, <www.echr.coe.int>.

106 Mastromatteo v. Italy, 24 October 2002, European Court of Human Rights, no. 37703/97 <www.echr.coe.int>.

The value of evaluation should therefore always be assessed in the context of a relative concept of rationality. In this respect one should keep in mind SCHÄFFER's remark that public, politicians and parliaments may not have unrealistically high expectations: scientific consulting does not solve every problem. Instead it broadens the horizon and determines the limits of political action.[107] This means that evaluation does not lead to 'truth', to automatic, depoliticized decisions. Instead it might help the lawmaker to explain his actions and the public to accept the chosen solution – even if for some a certain law is not the most favourable one, or if subsequent unforeseeable events prevent the realisation of the legislative goal.

[107] Schäffer, *supra* note 2, p. 151.

Chapter 3

Ex Ante Evaluation of Legislation Torn among its Rationales

*Pierre Larouche**

I. *Introduction*

This chapter seeks to enrich the debate by bringing economic theories to bear on the discussion of *ex ante* evaluation of legislation. To the extent the rationale for *ex ante* evaluation of legislation is investigated in the literature, the analysis is usually based on political science or public administration. The economic literature on *ex ante* evaluation assumes one rationale without more.[1] This chapter takes the more open starting point of the former disciplines and combines it with insights from the latter.

Through his teaching and research, this author has been exposed to the literature and policy discussion concerning *ex ante* evaluation of legislation and has often come across evaluations regarding various legislative or regulatory initiatives. It has always struck him how *ex ante* evaluation seems to mean all things to all people. One of the main difficulties in dealing with *ex ante* evaluation of legislation is that while a broad consensus exists that *ex ante* evaluation is desirable, that consensus is based on a wide range of rationales, which may not always coincide with each other. Most everyone agrees on the main elements of *ex ante* evaluation of legislation, but views seem to differ on why *ex ante* evaluations are carried out. Few authors, with the notable exception of Meuwese,[2]

* The author wishes to thank Jacques Pelkmans in particular, as well as Filomena Chirico, Anne Meuwese and the participants in the working group on *ex ante* evaluation of legislation at Tilburg University for their help and their useful comments. The responsibility for the content remains the author's alone.

1 Namely quality improvement, *see infra*, heading III.B.

2 See her recent work: Anne Meuwese, *Impact Assessment in EU Lawmaking* (E.M. Meijers Instituut, Leiden 2008). This paper builds on the work of Meuwese (which was of invaluable help)

investigate the rationale(s) behind *ex ante* evaluation, as opposed to the practice of *ex ante* evaluation or their broader effects.

Of course, this matters little if the various rationales/functionalities do not imply any practical difference in how *ex ante* evaluations are conducted and used. Unfortunately, that is not necessarily the case.

Hence this chapter tries to structure the discussion of *ex ante* evaluation of legislation by starting with the fundamentals, that is to say the rationales for introducing *ex ante* evaluations in the first place. Why do we have them? What is their purpose? This chapter is concerned with *ex ante* evaluation of legislation as an institution or regime, and not with individual evaluations in specific instances. Furthermore, given the usual research topics of this author (competition law, economic regulation), EC law is usually referred to, but the discussion is framed as much as possible in general terms which should apply to any jurisdiction.

After briefly setting out a descriptive definition of *ex ante* evaluation of legislation (II), this chapter examines a series of potential rationales for *ex ante* evaluation, trying to ascertain how useful they are to explain *ex ante* evaluations and to work some of their main implications for the conduct of such evaluations. A number of mainstream rationales, typically alluded to in the literature and in policy documents, come first (III). They are followed by more complex rationales based on specific strands of economic theory (IV) and so-called deviant rationales, which have explanatory force but are not necessarily desirable (V). The conclusion pulls all of these rationales together and sees if they can co-exist or not (VI).

II. *A Working Definition of* Ex Ante *Evaluation of Legislation*

In Chapter 1, *ex ante* evaluation of legislation is defined as follows:

> Future oriented research into the expected effects and side-effects of potential new legislation following a structured and formalised procedure, leading to a written report. Such research includes a study of the possible effects and side-effects of alternatives, including the alternative of not regulating at all.

The current chapter relies upon that definition.

In order to make the definition somewhat more concrete, however, and given the EU law background of the author, the description set out in the Commission's

---

and seeks, with the help of economic analysis, to broaden the range of rationales beyond what Meuwese took into account on the basis of law, political science and public administration.

Impact Assessment Guidelines will be used as a working description of an *ex ante* evaluation of legislation.[3] If the EU-level Impact Assessment is used as a model, an *ex ante* evaluation

(i) takes place ahead of the legislative action
(ii) comprises the following analytical steps:
   1. Identify the problem.
   2. Define the objectives.
   3. Develop main policy options.
   4. Analyse their impacts.
   5. Compare the options.
   6. Outline policy monitoring and evaluation; and
(iii) includes stakeholder consultation and collection of expertise.

For the purposes of this chapter, the above definition and working description are sufficient; it is assumed that the working description covers most if not all instances of *ex ante* evaluation. The various rationales surveyed in the rest of this paper all fit this working description. They often also imply certain additional characteristics or elements, which will be presented together with the rationale in question.

III. *Mainstream Rationales*

On the basis of the policy documents on *ex ante* evaluation of legislation and of the literature, a number of recurrent rationales can already be distinguished. For instance, in one short paragraph in its Impact Assessment Guidelines, titled "Why is Impact Assessment important?", the Commission managed to collapse no less than four distinct rationales together:[4]

> All policy-decisions should be based on sound analysis supported by the best data available. The Commission's impact assessment system helps the EU institutions to design better policies and laws. It facilitates better-informed decision making throughout the legislative process. It ensures early coordination within the Commission and it takes into account input from a wide range of external stakeholders, in line with the Commission's policy of transparency and openness. It helps to

[3] European Commission, *Impact Assessment Guidelines*, SEC(2005) 791 (15 June 2005). For the purposes of this paper, the newer *Draft Impact Assessment Guidelines*, <ec.europa.eu/governance/impact/consultation/docs/ia_guidelines_draft_text_final_en.pdf> (27 May 2008) will be used (*see* pp. 21 et seq.). They do not differ from the 2005 Guidelines as far as the scope of this paper is concerned.

[4] Draft Impact Assessment Guidelines, *ibid.*, p. 3.

> ensure coherence of Commission policies and consistency with Treaty objectives and high level objectives such as the Lisbon and Sustainable Development Strategies. It improves the quality of policy proposals by keeping EU intervention as simple as possible. Finally, it helps to ensure that the principles of subsidiarity and proportionality are respected, and to explain why the action which is being proposed is necessary and appropriate.

That paragraph sets out four distinct rationales for *ex ante* assessments:

- *Improvement in quality* of decision-making: this is the main rationale coming through this paragraph, with references to "better-informed decision-making", "coherence and consistency", "improv[ing] the quality of policy proposals by keeping EU intervention as simple as possible";
- *Democracy* via participation in decision-making, through the "input from a wide range of external stakeholders";
- *Transparency*, which is mentioned as such together with openness of Commission policies;
- *Justification*, as put forward in the last sentence of the excerpt.

A survey of the literature such as conducted by Meuwese[5] allows for other mainstream rationales to be added to the list, namely:

- *Accountability*, in that the *ex ante* evaluation of legislation "highlights the trade-offs" to be made by the decision-maker and enables it to be held accountable for its choices;
- Another variant of *democracy*, where the *ex ante* evaluation of legislation complements representative democratic mechanisms by offering a forum for deliberation.

In addition, a basic rationale is often simply assumed, namely the *collection of evidence* concerning the matter to be decided. It is dealt with first (A), followed by the main rationale featured in the economic literature, namely quality improvement (B) and then the rationales which appear to rest on legal principles, namely justification, transparency, accountability and democracy (C).

A. *Collection of Evidence*

Under this rationale, the *ex ante* evaluation serves as a device to gather and order all relevant evidence on which decision-making is based. This is a more 'notarial' function, where the *ex ante* evaluation is a convenient and structured repository for all the input that went into a decision.

---

[5] A. Meuwese, *supra* note 2 at pp. 44–53. The two rationales set out in the main text correspond to the "highlighting trade-offs" and "structuring the discourse" models set out by Meuwese.

This rationale is not very useful, since it is neither powerful nor distinctive. Indeed, it does not explain many of the specific features of *ex ante* evaluations outlined above, Furthermore, it equally applies to other documents such as preparatory works, explanatory memoranda, interpretive notes, etc., which are commonly tabled alongside draft legislation or regulation.

It is worth mentioning, however, because it highlights one of the key issues relating to *ex ante* evaluations, namely whether they can be used later as evidence in judicial or other proceedings. *Ex ante* evaluations could be used in order to shed light on certain provisions, although their interpretive value as evidence of intent is probably limited since they are not prepared by the decision-maker itself.[6] *Ex ante* evaluations have a greater role to play in proceedings where the validity of an enactment (judicial or constitutional review) or the liability of the State is at stake. There an *ex ante* assessment provides useful evidence of the background to the enactment, which can be used to attack its necessity, its proportionality, its impact on fundamental rights, to name but the main ones.

If the function of the *ex ante* evaluation is to collect evidence, it would seem logical that the evaluation would be available in subsequent proceedings where the enactment for which the evaluation was prepared is debated. So far at European level, the ECJ has not yet used an *ex ante* evaluation as evidence in assessing EC law. In the only notable case where the ECJ mentioned *ex ante* evaluation,[7] the court noted that the impugned EC regulation[8] was not preceded by an *ex ante* evaluation, which did not lead to any immediate legal consequence.[9] At the same time, the lack of an *ex ante* evaluation clearly hampered the efforts of the Community institutions to prove that they had correctly exercised their legislative powers, and the regulation in question was partly annulled because it was disproportionate in the light of the available evidence.

---

[6] Especially if they are deemed to be a mere "aid to political decision-making, not a substitute for it": draft Impact Assessment Guidelines, *supra* note 3 at 2. On that account, the decision-maker forms its own opinion and the *ex ante* evaluation does not necessarily reflect what went on in the mind of the decision-maker. As discussed *infra*, notes 17–20 and the accompanying text, that quote might however give too little significance to *ex ante* evaluations.

[7] Case C–310/04, *Spain* v. *Commission*, 7 September 2006, ECJ, [2006] ECR I–7285, paras. 95 ff. This case is discussed in Meuwese, *supra* note 2, pp. 172–175.

[8] Regulation 864/2004 of 29 April 2004 amending Regulation 1782/2003 establishing common rules for direct support schemes under the CAP [2004] OJ L 161/48.

[9] *Supra* note 7, para. 103. As the Advocate General points out in her Opinion in this case, the Community institutions were not obliged to carry out an *ex ante* evaluation: Opinion of 16 March 2006, para. 82.

B. *Quality Improvement*

This is the mainstream rationale put forward for *ex ante* evaluations in the economic literature: the purpose of the evaluation is to improve the quality of decision-making and by the same token of the resulting measures.[10]

This is a very rich rationale, which ties together a number of strands. First of all, it builds upon the first rationale (collection of evidence) by giving it a more distinctive meaning: the function of the evaluation is to provide a framework to ensure that all available evidence is gathered and then analyzed in such a way as to improve its usefulness for decision-making. Secondly, it also has an institutional strand, as indicated in the above quote from the Commission Guidelines: the *ex ante* evaluation enables the various institutions involved in the decision-making to coordinate their actions by providing a common point of reference for their analysis. Thirdly, it can have a substantive flavour, where the Commission, in the same quote, links *ex ante* evaluations with subsidiarity and proportionality, two key principles applying to decision-making in the EC (and also elsewhere, at least as regards proportionality): the evaluation makes it easier to comply with these two principles, since it provides a sound analytical basis on which to apply them. Fourthly, in the longer run, *ex ante* evaluations can also become ingrained in the administrative culture – what Renda calls an 'evaluation-oriented culture'[11] – so that the quality of the work of the administration in general is increased.

Through all of the above strands, the quality improvement rationale unmistakably follows an expert, technocratic logic. The *ex ante* evaluations is then the province of the expert – whether he or she comes from the public authorities, from a consultancy, from politics or from one or the other interested parties. The experts gather to conduct the evaluation according to the established framework as set out in the working description above. They deliver a detached, objective and scientific assessment of the matter at hand.

The quality improvement rationale connects closely with a number of well-established elements of economic science. These are reflected directly in the *ex ante* evaluation framework. For one, the idea that as a first step the problem

---

[10] For instance, one of the leading independent studies on *ex ante* evaluations in Europe, Andrea Renda, *Impact Assessment in the EU – The State of the Art and the Art of the State* (Centre for European Policy Studies (CEPS), Brussels 2006), does not discuss at much length the reason why *ex ante* evaluation of legislation has been introduced in Europe, other than to mention briefly that it was meant to improve the quality of EC legislation (pp. 43–44), as if it were obvious. Indeed his whole book relies on the assumption that *ex ante* evaluations are there to improve legislative quality. *See also* Jacques Pelkmans *et al.*, 'Better EU Regulatory Quality: Assessing Current Initiatives and New Proposals' in J. Pelkmans and G. Galli (eds.), *Regulatory Reform and Competitiveness in Europe, Vol. I* (Edward Elgar, Cheltenham 2000), p. 461.

[11] Renda, *ibid.*, p. 22, when drawing lessons from the US experience.

must be clearly identified comes from the traditional public interest theory of regulation, whereby public authorities intervene to remedy market failures, i.e. instances where markets do not work as expected.[12] Once the market failure has been identified, one or more options are open to correct it, and this is what the evaluation is meant to study. At the same time, the evaluation also incorporates elements from the rival public choice theory of regulation, whereby the actors involved in deciding upon public intervention (i.e., the decision-makers) are also subject to the same behavioural assumptions as the market actors, i.e. wealth-maximisation and cognitive limitations. They are therefore also on the lookout for their private interest. Accordingly, next to market failures, government failures can also occur, i.e. situations where public intervention is driven by private interests rather than the public good and where the intervention ends up being more harmful than the market failure which it sought to address.[13] It is implicit in public choice theory that not every market failure can be solved, and hence that some market failures might be better left alone for lack of a solution which would enhance welfare overall. This explains why an *ex ante* evaluation should always consider a base scenario of no intervention.[14] More generally, in the presence of both market and government failures, decision-making is very likely to involve some trade-offs between the two: the identified problem should be solved to the greatest extent possible without thereby creating a larger problem somewhere else. This leads naturally into the cost-benefit analytical model which lies at the core of the evaluation.

The evaluation can even be presented as an antidote to those flaws in the legislative and regulatory processes which are exposed by the theory of public choice. By providing a "rational" basis to the decision-makers, the *ex ante* evaluation can force them to decide in view of the public interest and not of their private interest only. Meuwese presents this as "speaking truth to power",[15] and in her analysis highlights one key issue arising when economics provide the rationale for *ex ante* evaluations, namely the link between the assessment and the final decision-making.[16]

---

[12] *See* for instance William Baumol, *Welfare economics and the theory of the state* (Longmans, Green, London 1952). *See infra* notes 21–22 and accompanying text for a discussion of how these expectations should be defined.

[13] See for instance the fundamental contribution of George Stigler, 'The Theory of Economic Regulation' (1971) 3 *Bell Journal of Economics and Management Science*, p. 3.

[14] If intervention has already taken place and further intervention is contemplated, then the baseline scenario would be "staying with the current level of intervention", although "no intervention whatsoever" could also be envisaged: *see* draft Impact Assessment Guidelines, *supra* note 3, p. 26.

[15] Meuwese, *supra* note 2, pp. 45–47.

[16] Which Meuwese also identified as a key problem in the discussion of *ex ante* evaluations, *ibid.*, pp. 8–9.

Indeed, as far as the substance of the decision to be taken is concerned, economics-based rationales for *ex ante* evaluations are more exacting than other, law-based rationales examined below.[17] Even if there might not be a single truth to be pursued in decision-making, i.e. a single best decision which the decision-maker should be bound to take, nevertheless not all possible decisions are equal. If the aim of the assessment is to improve the quality of decision-making, in line with the above, then the evaluation is bound to narrow down the range of possible decisions. Moreover, the *ex ante* evaluation enables trade-offs to be identified, and the possible decisions can then be hierarchized according to the objectives which the decision-maker would like to pursue. If the maximisation of short-term welfare has priority, then decision *x* would be preferable, if the avoidance of longer-term risk[18] is the main objective, then decision *y* should be taken instead. The *ex ante* evaluation cannot be dissociated from the substance of the decision which it is meant to support, and the value of the evaluation can be directly measured by looking at the result achieved. The mere fact that an evaluation took place, on the other hand, does not suffice: even if the procedure was properly followed, the evaluation could still have failed to improve the quality of the decision-making if it, for instance, left some issues unexplored, failed to consider certain options or did not properly identify trade-offs. The 'improving quality' rationale would therefore be more result-oriented and not merely process-oriented.

At the same time, the Commission is its Guidelines – much like other authorities who carry out *ex ante* evaluations – is very adamant that "impact assessment is an aid to political decision-making, not a substitute for it".[19] In other words, decision-making remains in the hands of the political actors. Yet this statement can be interpreted in many ways, which we simplify to two for the sake of argument:

(i) The experts who prepare the evaluation cannot themselves take the decision, because only political actors can assume the political responsibility which goes with decision-making. With the evaluation, these experts essentially distill the matter down to a relatively manageable decision before political actors intervene to complete the work;
(ii) Irrespective of the *ex ante* evaluation, political actors remain free to take the decision which seems best to them. Of course, political actors will peruse and perhaps even use the evaluation, but their freedom remains intact.

[17] *Infra*, heading III.C.
[18] Properly discounted and in the light of the significance of potential consequences.
[19] Draft Impact Assessment Guidelines, *supra* note 3, p. 2.

Under the first interpretation, the *ex ante* evaluation and the decision are closely linked in substance: political actors are constrained by the evaluation. As a result of the evaluation, not every outcome is possible. Political actors take the necessary political decisions concerning the trade-offs outlined in the *ex ante* evaluations. Once these trade-offs have been politically arbitrated, political actors proceed to follow the assessment as far as the outcome is concerned. Only the first interpretation is truly compatible with the quality improvement rationale. Under the second interpretation, if political actors do not work with and within the constraints arising from the evaluation, then the evaluation cannot fulfill its purpose.[20]

It must be noted, however, that the extent to which political actors are constrained by *ex ante* evaluation of legislation is not determined only by their own statements, including that of the Commission quoted above. It crucially depends on courts, and hence on the value of evaluations in subsequent judicial or constitutional review proceedings, already mentioned above. If *ex ante* evaluations can be introduced as evidence in such proceedings – and even more strongly if a legal principle would emerge whereby decision-makers must take evaluations into account and address them in their decision-making – then the practice will conform to the first interpretation set out in the previous paragraph.

At the same time, the role and scope of economic analysis must be properly understood, especially if as just discussed the *ex ante* evaluation is meant to impose a constraint on the decision-maker. If the economic analysis includes a normative dimension, then the constraint on the decision-maker would be too strict. Such would be the case if the *ex ante* evaluation assumed, for instance, that maximization of total welfare is the sole valid policy objective, leaving no room for other economic or non-economic objectives. By the same token, this would reflect on the early stages of the assessment, since no problems would arise unless the market did not work so as to maximize total welfare. In such a case, the balance between the expert rationality of the evaluation and the democratic rationality of the decision-making would be upset, unless the decision-maker

[20] That problem is further compounded at the EU level, where a number of institutions hold a real power to influence the outcome of legislative procedures (and to a lesser extent, regulatory procedures as well). Contrary to most Member States, where government proposals escape relatively unscathed from the legislative procedure (as long as the government holds a stable majority in Parliament), in the EU Commission proposals can be modified significantly by the Council and the EP (at least when the co-decision procedure is applicable). The *ex ante* evvaluation is carried out by the Commission ahead of its proposal, but the other institutions have been under pressure to carry out their own assessments when they introduce modifications to the Commission proposals which go beyond what was investigated in the original *ex ante* evaluation. *See* Meuwese, *supra* note 2, pp. 99 et seq. for a study of the practice of the EP and Council.

is free to ignore the *ex ante* evaluation.[21] If the evaluation is to constrain the decision-maker, then the use of economic analysis should not venture into the normative; rather, the polity should provide the evaluation with the policy objectives against which it is conducted. At the early stage of problem identification, "market failure" would then be construed more broadly as a failure of the market – established on the basis of economic analysis – to attain the policy objectives set by the polity.[22] Similarly, at the later stage of analysis, the policy options would also be analysed and compared – using tools from economic analysis – as against those policy objectives.

As the previous paragraphs demonstrate, the quality improvement rationale is very rich and powerful. It provides a strong justification for a number of characteristics sought in an *ex ante* evaluation:

- The *ex ante* evaluation should begin without any *a priori* bias in favour of or against legislative or regulatory intervention. An *ex ante* evaluation could just as well end up finding that no serious problem exists or recommending that no action be taken.
- The *ex ante* evaluation should be conducted with an open mind. In particular, the choice of the options to be investigated – besides the baseline scenario(s)[23] – should include all options which at first sight appear worthy of investigating.
- The *ex ante* evaluation should be carried out early on, before any proposal has been formulated, so that it can improve the quality of the proposal while it is still in the hands of "expert" drafters and before it starts to be politically debated.

C. *Law-infused Rationales*

Alongside the more economics-infused rationale set out above, a number of rationales emanate rather from well-established legal principles. Economic analysis remains nevertheless relevant in understanding them.

---

[21] On the balance between the polity and the economy in economic regulation, *see* Pierre Larouche, *The role of the market in economic regulation*, Inaugural Lecture (Tilburg 2003).

[22] And thus of the well-known causes of market failure, including market power, information asymmetries, externalities or public goods.

[23] If the evaluation bears on an issue where the public authorities have not intervened before, the baseline scenario is "no intervention". If the evaluation takes place as part of a legislative or regulatory review, presumably two scenarios should be investigated in any event, namely "no change in current legislation or regulation" (the actual baseline in a review context) and "removal of legislation or regulation".

1. *Justification*
First of all, the purpose of the *ex ante* evaluation of legislation could be to provide a coherent *justification* for legislative or regulatory action.[24] This is a stronger version of the first rationale – collection of evidence – since it implies that the evaluation also presents a case to support the measure in question. At the same time, the justification rationale is weaker than the quality improvement rationale and should not be confused with it. The evaluation as justification does not have strong implications for the substance of the decision; the evaluation will have fulfilled its purpose as long as it provides a justification, irrespective of what that justification is. The justification rationale does not have much explanatory force nor is it very distinctive.[25]

2. *Transparency*
Secondly, *transparency* can also provide a rationale: the *ex ante* evaluation of legislation sheds lights on the decision-making process by presenting the evidence, setting out the problem and the policy options and then analyzing and comparing these options. By following the evaluation process or reading the evaluation report, stakeholders, other interested parties and more generally citizens can observe legislative and regulatory decision-making. While interesting and relevant, the transparency rationale remains fairly weak, and it is subsumed under the accountability and democracy rationales which follow.

3. *Accountability*
Building on transparency, the *ex ante* evaluation can aim to increase *accountability*. As a starting point, we can rely on principal/agent theory:[26] there is a principal and an agent, and the agent should act in the interests of the principal. Yet the agent might shirk, i.e. put its own self-interest above that of its principal, without being detected, because the agent tends to possess more or better information than the principal (information asymmetry problem). Mechanisms must be put in place to ensure that the agent does not shirk, i.e., that it has incentives to act in the interests of the principal. Accountability mechanisms, among others, force the agent to answer for its actions.

The evaluation, if well conducted (complete and transparent), contributes to accountability by enabling the principal to check upon the work of the agent. Actually, the assessment intervenes in two distinct principal/agent relationships.

---

[24] In line with the general obligation incumbent on public authorities to provide reasons for their action: see for instance Article 253 EC.

[25] And indeed Meuwese, *supra* note 2, p. 49 dismisses it as "too simplistic a goal for the impact assessment procedure".

[26] For an overview of principal/agent theory, *see* David E.M. Sappington, 'Incentives in Principal-Agent Relationships' (1991) 5:2 *Journal of Economic Perspectives*, pp. 45–66.

First of all, the legislative power taken as a whole is an agent of the polity (people). Secondly, within the legislative power, the administration is an agent of the actual decision-maker (be it the Legislature or the executive on the basis of delegated powers), since it usually carries out all the groundwork for the enactment of legislation or regulation, including carrying out the evaluation. The latter relationship corresponds most closely to the principal/agent theoretical model: the administration must work in the interest of the decision-maker, and the evaluation forces the administration to spell out its knowledge and its assessment of the various options, so that the decision-maker is not only well informed, but can also control the work of the administration and hold it accountable.[27] Within the former relationship, the purpose of the evaluation is more subtle: it can give the polity the necessary information to judge whether the legislative power is acting in the interest of the polity, i.e., in the general interest.

When the two principal/agent relationships are put together, it becomes apparent that through the *ex ante* evaluation, the administration is actually supplying the polity with a means to check on the Legislature and the executive. Here as well, the link between the evaluation and the decision-maker is crucial. Earlier, we saw that the quality improvement rationale could only work if somehow the decision-maker was constrained by the evaluation. From the reverse perspective, the accountability rationale provides a strong justification for that link: if the evaluation is presented as an expert, objective inquiry into policy options, then the decision-maker should answer for any departure from the evaluation. So the administration, when carrying out the *ex ante* evaluation, fosters both its own accountability towards the Legislature and the executive as well the accountability of the Legislature and the executive towards the people (the polity).

4. *Democracy in its Many Versions: Representative, Participatory, Counter-majoritarian*

A *democratic* rationale could also underpin *ex ante* evaluations. Interestingly, a number of potentially competing democratic models are served by *ex ante* evaluations. First of all, the evaluation can be seen from a more classical *deliberative* democratic perspective, as a forum where the actors officially involved in *representative* decision-making come to discuss and deliberate about policy in a structured fashion, with the help of the analytical framework of the evaluation.[28] The evaluation would then enhance the quality of democratic debate (in line with the quality improvement rationale set out above, but from a different angle). Of course, the evaluation could also produce a shift in the political balance between

---

[27] The Council and EP seem to use *ex ante* evaluations against the Commission for that purpose: *see* Meuwese, *supra* note 2, pp. 116–118, 121–125 (EP) and 136–139, 142–143 (Council).

[28] *See also* Meuwese, *ibid.*, pp. 51–52.

these actors.[29] The evaluation can also have a *participatory* purpose, i.e., to foster participation by stakeholders and other interested parties in the decision-making. The assessment would allow these parties to have a formal input into the decision-making process.[30] A different take on the participatory purpose of *ex ante* evaluations, based on game theory, is presented further below.[31] Finally, the *ex ante* evaluation could even have a *counter-majoritarian* purpose, in that it would enable the whole plurality of views and opinions held in society to be brought to the table, as opposed to the majority perspective which might prevail in the absence of an evaluation exercise.

While noble, these democratic rationales are lacking in explanatory force. In general, they tend to be too process-oriented: the purpose of the evaluation would reside in its process, and not in the result it achieves. That would be selling the evaluation short. The first one, relying on a classical representative model, does not add much; after all, the actors are supposed to deliberate when reaching decisions, so the assessment would be redundant (if representative democracy worked as it should). The last two ones are based on "alternative" theories, and they could position the *ex ante* evaluation as a democratic complement to legislative and regulatory procedures. Leaving aside the issue of how participatory or counter-majoritarian elements can be meaningfully introduced in a decision-making procedure based on representative democracy,[32] it is not clear why an evaluation (with the whole analytical framework as defined at the outset of this paper) is actually needed for that purpose. A simple consultation procedure might already suffice. Finally, democratic rationales are difficult if not impossible to reconcile with the more expert technocratic rationales such as quality improvement or even accountability: either the evaluation is meant to analyze policy options as objectively as possible, or it is a forum for more subjective debates between decision-makers, stakeholders and other interested parties. This might explain why, in the model of the draft Guidelines, consultation of

[29] *See* among others Chapter 5 by Robert Hoppe.

[30] As opposed to less open methods of exerting influence, such as lobbying.

[31] *Infra*, heading IV.B.

[32] This brings us back to the all-important link between the *ex ante* evaluation and the decision-maker. If the evaluation is to add a representative or counter-majoritarian element to legislative procedures, the decision-maker should somehow be bound or at least constrained by the result of the evaluation. Yet this would potentially clash with the representative democratic model underlying lawmaking. In her work, Meuwese discusses in great depth the constitutional implications of *ex ante* evaluations, finding that the status of the evaluation is currently in a state of flux at the EU level (*supra* note 1 especially the conclusions at pp. 265–270, 272–274, 280–281). The main representative institutions (Council, EP) seek to give some value to the *ex ante* evaluation, but they are careful to preserve their decision-making prerogatives. The Commission papers over the clash in its Guidelines, by stating that the decision-maker has the final say; as was seen above, this statement is open to discussion.

interested parties takes place at an early stage in the process, so that the expert, technocratic logic can re-assert itself afterwards. As seen further below,[33] under certain circumstances, consultation might be better explained via information asymmetries and game theory than democracy.

One interesting implication of the democratic rationales could be that the *ex ante* evaluation of legislation should be carried out by the public authority itself, if not by the decision-maker directly. It is difficult to see how the democratic purpose of an evaluation could be fulfilled if it is outsourced to a private party, such as a consultant, unless that private party is bound to respect certain rules in holding consultations and other forms of contacts with stakeholders and other interested parties. In the latter case, it might be preferable to leave the matter in the hands of a public authority, which enjoys greater legitimacy and greater expertise in political matters.

IV. *Complex and Specialised Rationales*

In the previous section, the mainstream rationales put forward for *ex ante* evaluations have been introduced and briefly analyzed. We now turn to another set of rationales which are typically not found in the mainstream literature: they rely on more sophisticated theory and might not be generally applicable to all *ex ante* evaluations. In certain cases, *ex ante* evaluations could serve to remedy information deficiencies (A) or secure commitment (B).

A. *Information Deficiencies*

A number of rationales considered previously focus on information, namely collection of evidence, quality improvement, justification, transparency or accountability. So far, in line with the mainstream discussion, it has been assumed that the required information was available, even if perhaps only to the agent (in the accountability rationale). This assumption is however inaccurate in the many cases where some information is missing.

If the missing information is *not available but can be generated*, the *ex ante* evaluation could be seen as a learning process, whereby the requisite information is first identified and then produced. Among others, the evaluation could then serve to correct cognitive biases.[34] Such biases can occur when probabilistic judgments are made on the basis of limited data which is subject to a bias from the observer: a well-known instance is the base-rate bias, where probabilities are

[33] *Infra*, heading IV.B.

[34] The seminal work on cognitive biases remains Daniel Kahneman *et al.* (eds.), *Judgment Under Uncertainty: Heuristics and Biases* (Cambridge University Press, Cambridge 1982).

assessed according to the representativeness of available data against prior stereotypes, without regard to the basic probabilities of these stereotypes.[35] One of the early steps in the evaluation would then be to try to identify cognitive biases which could affect rational decision-making and seek the requisite information to correct or at least counter-balance them.

Going one step further, the missing information could also be *unavailable and impossible to generate*. This is likely to occur where some long-term risks come into play, for instance as regards innovation policy, health and safety regulation, etc. Typically, a strong element of uncertainty surrounds matters such as the behaviour of investors, the future preferences of customers, the strength of demand, research achievements or harmful effects of new products. In such cases, the purpose of the assessment could be not so much to remedy the information deficiency, but rather to manage the uncertainty to the greatest extent possible.

The two information deficiencies rationales provide the strongest explanation for a feature of *ex ante* evaluation of legislation which is implicit in a number of the previous rationales (quality improvement, accountability, democracy), namely circularity. The evaluation becomes a discovery process. If, in the process of analyzing policy options (step 4 in the working description), a new policy option turns up which was not previously envisaged, then the evaluation must go back to Step 3 and feed that option into the analysis. Better still, it could be that the analysis of policy options leads to a refinement in the problem definition, in which case the evaluation is back at Step 1. Moreover, it is conceivable that additional consultations would be held if the evaluation loops back. This is all perfectly normal if the purpose of the evaluation is to generate missing information and deal with the consequences of uncertainty. The circularity of evaluation is a feature of the evaluation process, which unfortunately is not always apparent in the evaluation report which results from that process. The reports tend to picture *ex ante* evaluations in a more linear fashion.[36]

What is more, even if by definition a search for the purpose of *ex ante* evaluations implies that they are instrumental, the two rationales based on information deficiencies give perhaps the most intrinsic value to the evaluation.

---

[35] Amos Tversky and Daniel Kahneman, in the introductory chapter to their work, *ibid.*, pp. 3–20 at pp. 4–5, describe this bias by reference to an experiment where subjects are asked to assess the probability that someone is a lawyer or engineer by reference to a description of the person. The subjects were also told of the distribution of lawyers and engineers in the sample (the base rate). In contradiction with rational statistical analysis, the subjects in the experiments returned the same assessments irrespective of the base rate.

[36] It is also possible that the *ex ante* evaluation is conducted in a purely linear fashion, in which case it is of doubtful usefulness: see the discussion of legislative entrepreneurship, *infra*, heading V.B.

Especially where the information deficiency cannot be remedied, the evaluation can be seen as part of a larger work-in-progress, where risk management under conditions of uncertainty is the main task. The legislative or regulatory intervention will then typically involve layered decision-making (with a regulatory authority at the lower end of the decision-making chain, in order to enable flexibility and responsiveness) and built-in review mechanisms, where the current *ex ante* evaluation feeds into *ex post* review and the next generation of *ex ante* evaluation arising from such reviews. Decision-making then becomes a complex game involving public authorities and private actors,[37] which leads to game theory and the next rationale for *ex ante* evaluations.

B. *Commitment*

Game theory offers some useful insights which can enrich our understanding of *ex ante* evaluations in situations of uncertainty. In broad terms, an *ex ante* evaluation can be conceived as one step in a multi-period game involving the decision-maker and private actors.[38] In every period, the actors decide on their move depending on the prevailing conditions (including of course the legal framework). If the actors expect conditions to change in the next period, that expectation will affect their move in the current period. For instance, as regards investment in infrastructure, if actors expect that regulatory change might affect them adversely in the next period, they will refrain from investing as much as they could in the current period.

Against that background, the evaluation could contribute to provide a measure of certainty or predictability to private actors by laying out fully the background to a certain decision and thereby somehow committing the decision-maker to that decision. Indeed if the evaluation contains a solid analysis of the consequences of the various options available to the decision-maker, it can be assumed that the decision-maker is aware of these consequences, takes them into account and therefore will stay the course with its decision. The evaluation highlights and sharpens the choices open to the decision-maker, so that it is easier for the private actors to understand what the decision-maker wants to achieve. Accordingly, an element of uncertainty (uncertainty regarding regulatory change from one period to the other) is removed from the game or at least significantly reduced, so that the moves of private actors are not hampered by that element of uncertainty.

---

[37] The "regulatory space" paradigm set out by Leigh Hancher and Michael Moran, 'Organizing Regulatory Space' in Leigh Hancher and Michael Moran (eds.), *Capitalism, Culture and Economic Regulation* (OUP, Oxford 1989) is based on the same idea.

[38] *I.e.* the individuals and firms which are concerned by the decision to be taken (the "civil society" in governance literature).

By the same token, the evaluation would also foster acceptance of the resulting decision in the public at large. In legal terms, the evaluation would contribute to legal certainty and predictability.

In chapter 10, Vording and Gribnau point out that the reverse might also apply: the *ex ante* evaluation could also be used by the public authorities to elicit the information privately held by the actors. This can be seen as a further development of the participatory and information deficiency rationales outlined above. Participation of stakeholders and other interested parties is then desirable not just for its own sake as a form of democratic exercise, but also because it forces these private actors to disclose useful information to the public authorities. That information includes of course background data which feeds into the evaluation, but also – and perhaps more crucially – private preferences. If all possible options are on the table in the course of an evaluation, private actors cannot afford to limit themselves to posturing, as they might in an unstructured lobbying scenario where they can inform selectively in order to nudge authorities towards their preferred outcome. Rather, private actors must explain how their preferred outcome fits in the analytical framework of the evaluation (i.e., against the various public policy objectives and the general interest). They must also reveal what other outcomes might also be acceptable if the decision-maker did not follow their preferred outcome. In game theoretical terms, the private actors commit themselves more clearly and thereby decrease the uncertainty on the side of the decision-maker as to their expected behaviour (in response to legislative or regulatory action). This allows the decision-maker in turn to commit itself more decisively that it might otherwise have, which strengthens the rationale described in the previous paragraph (commitment from the decision-maker towards the private actors).

V. *Deviant Rationales*

All of the rationales covered so far cast *ex ante* evaluations of legislation in a positive or at least benign light: the evaluation serves a useful purpose. This contribution would not be complete if "deviant" rationales were not also surveyed, i.e. rationales under which the evaluation would play a more controversial, if not outright counter-productive role. They concern raising decision-making costs (A) and legislative entrepreneurship (B).

A. *Raising Decision-making Costs*

Using neo-classical economics, the evaluation could be intended to raise decision-making costs. In simple terms, if the cost of decision-making is c_0, the *ex ante* evaluation (EEL) adds to this cost and brings it to c_{EEL}. Note that the cost increase originates not merely from the actual cost of carrying out the *ex ante* evaluation, but also from the delay caused by the evaluation or from the increased political visibility brought about by the evaluation, which makes certain decisions more expensive politically. Assuming a linear and downward-sloping demand for legislative or regulatory intervention, the effect is as follows.

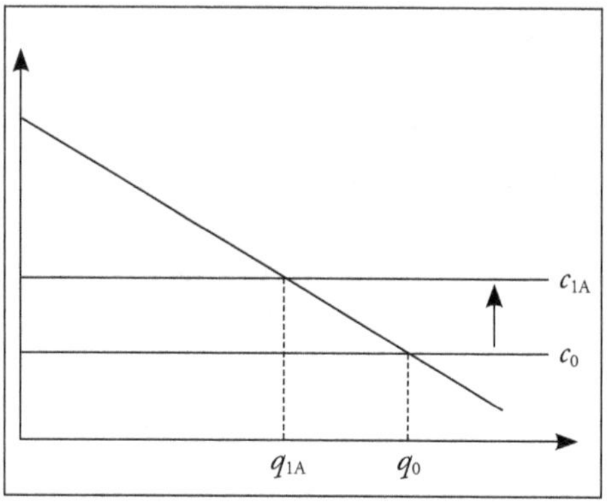

Through the increase in cost from c_0 to c_{EEL}, the quantity supplied is reduced from q_0 to q_{EEL}. In other words, if decision-making is more expensive, then the supply of decisions will dwindle.

Under this rationale, the evaluation is no longer a neutral process. It acquires a specific political bent, as part of a deregulation drive. The evaluation puts a brake on an overly enthusiastic legislative or regulatory power.

Historically, in the US, the UK and even at European level, *ex ante* evaluations were introduced as part of a larger movement towards "better regulation", which also had a strong deregulatory flavour.[39] In the specific case of the EU, *ex ante* evaluations are part of a broader Better Regulation programme,[40] which includes measures to simplify and reduce EC legislation,[41] and more recently a programme for reducing administrative burdens.[42] For the latter, a quantitative target of 25% reduction in burdens has even been set. That target is more real-

---

[39] *See* the historical reviews made by Renda, *supra* note 10, pp. 8–25 (US), 26–42 (UK) and 43–56 (EU).

[40] European Commission, *Better Regulation for Growth and Jobs in the European Union* COM(2005) 97 final (16 March 2005).

[41] European Commission, *Implementing the Community Lisbon programme: A strategy for the simplification of the regulatory environment* COM(2005) 535 final (25 October 2005).

[42] European Commission, *Action Programme for Reducing Administrative Burdens in the European Union* COM(2007) 23 final (24 January 2007).

istic than the typical political statements that "red tape will be cut by *x*%", and it has some methodological support.[43] Nevertheless, it proceeds from the same top-down vision: regulation is a burden which must be cut back, irrespective of the merits of individual instances of regulation.

In all honesty, while the Commission claims significant success for its Better Regulation programme,[44] that programme has yet to catch the attention of the general public.[45] In the meantime, the EU continues to produce legislation. The situation is perhaps not markedly different in other jurisdictions which have introduced *ex ante* evaluations. So there might be some merit to the proposition that the deregulatory rhetoric is necessary merely in order to ensure that evaluattion works neutrally, i.e. to provide a counter-balance to the natural propensity of the public authorities to expand their activities.

Nevertheless, if the evaluation is openly given a deregulatory rationale, some dangers are lurking. Firstly, an assessment which would begin with an *a priori* bias in favour of one or the other option (here in favour of not intervening or removing existing law or regulation) is not compatible with any of the rationales set out previously. The *ex ante* evaluation cannot be conducted openly and calmly under these circumstances. Secondly, a deregulatory rationale for *ex ante* evaluation opens the door to capture by conservative special interests. In the end, the evaluation could become a platform for political ends.

In any event, using an abstract level of regulatory output as a measure of the effectiveness of an *ex ante* evaluation regime might miss the point. It is true that, in theory, a number of assessments should lead to a finding that no legislative or regulatory intervention is needed. Still, few of these instances can be found. At the same time, *ex ante* evaluations are expensive and time-consuming, so that in practice the evaluation requirement could produce its effects upstream. One would then observe an improvement in the quality of legislative or regulatory initiatives, so that they pass the evaluation muster.[46] As Renda points out, the introduction of an *ex ante* evaluation requirement did lead to a change in culture in the US administration. It might still be too early to observe the same in the

---

[43] European Commission, *Measuring administrative costs and reducing administrative burdens in the European Union* COM(2006) 691 final (14 November 2006).

[44] *See* the latest report: European Commission, *Second strategic review of Better Regulation in the European Union* COM(2008) 32 final (30 January 2008).

[45] In political debates, it still sells to paint the EU as a regulatory Leviathan, as the recent Irish referendum on the Treaty of Lisbon showed.

[46] Whether the number of initiatives is actually reduced depends also on exogenous factors, i.e. whether socio-economic circumstances have evolved so as that legislative or regulatory intervention would be needed.

EU.[47] In a further step, if the quality of legislation and regulation improves as a consequence of *ex ante* evaluation, then the demand curve (the demand for intervention) might also shift, cancelling out the effect of the increase in costs.

B. *Legislative Entrepreneurship*

The second "deviant" rationale is in many ways the mirror side of the first. The *ex ante* evaluation could also be conceived as the business plan of the legislative or regulatory entrepreneur. Using a basic public choice model, the public authorities supply legislation and regulation, while the general public demands it. On the demand side, it is well established by now that there is a measure of competition among different interest groups in demanding legislation and regulation; the best organized interest groups – even if they might not be representative of the general interest – have an advantage. Similarly, on the supply side, public authorities cannot be seen simply as a monolithic entity. Within the public authorities, there are entrepreneurs who drive the supply of legislation and regulation. These entrepreneurs can act either out of a sense of vision in meeting pent-up demand[48] or more prosaically because they stand to make personal gains by satisfying demand. These gains can consist in either election (if the entrepreneur is a politician) or career advancement (if the entrepreneur is a civil servant).

The entrepreneur must work within the confines of the rules governing the production of law or regulation, however, so typically he or she will have to convince others within the public authorities of the need to adopt a certain measure. The *ex ante* evaluation could then be the business plan of the entrepreneur. Like any business plan, the purpose of the evaluation would then be to convince potential partners (i.e., the other actors needed to enact legislation or regulation) to work with and support the entrepreneur.

This rationale, more even than the previous one, does not reflect well on *ex ante* evaluations. If legislative entrepreneurship were the only reason why *ex ante* evaluations are conducted, the desirability of these evaluations should be questioned. Nonetheless, it is interesting to work out the implications of this rationale further. As a starting point, the evaluation would have the opposite effect when compared to the previous rationale: instead of hampering initiatives, the evaluation would support them. Consequently, the cost of the evaluation should be

---

[47] Renda, *supra* note 10, pp. 22–23.

[48] *I.e.*, the entrepreneur is ahead of the rest in seeing the need for legislative or regulatory intervention.

kept to a minimum; in order to do so, some corners might be cut short in the process. As a business plan, in any event, the evaluation should aim to convince more so than analyse objectively. This would imply for instance that:

- There is an *a priori* bias in favour of intervention, and more specifically in favour of a specific option;
- The set of policy options under study is pre-determined, so that the favoured option would already appear to have the best chances of success. In particular, for complex problems raising many issues, options are bundled across issues, so that the *ex ante* evaluation compares packages of options across issues instead of comparing the available options for each issue separately;
- The *ex ante* evaluation proceeds essentially in a linear fashion, without any need to step back to redefine the problem or add new options;
- The *ex ante* evaluation does not need to analyse all possible implications, as long as it appears reasonably complete;
- The *ex ante* evaluation can be conducted in parallel to the drafting of proposals.

On all these points, the *ex ante* evaluation as business plan is at variance with some of the key implications flowing from the rationales studied before. Accordingly, this rationale does not fit with the others and should be excluded.

Unfortunately, it is not possible to conduct an empirical study within the scope of this contribution to detect how often *ex ante* evaluations appear to be mere business plans for the legislative entrepreneur. Nevertheless, this author has come across a number of such evaluations, in areas such as competition law or electronic communications regulation. The same could probably be said in other areas of the law and in other jurisdictions. The business plan rationale for the evaluation appears alive and well.

VI. *Conclusion*

The previous sections can be summarized with the following table. The numbers in brackets refer to the heading number where each rationale is discussed.

Rationale	Strengths and weaknesses	Specific implications
Collection of evidence (III.A.)	Weak explanatory power Not distinctive	*Ex ante* evaluation available in subsequent proceedings
Quality improvement (III.B.)	Based on mainstream public interest and public choice theory Rich rationale Strong explanatory power for a number of *ex ante* evaluation of legislation features	Expert, technocratic rationality Evaluation follows the working description Evaluation constrains decision-maker Policy objectives to be specified by polity No *a priori* bias Openness towards all options Evaluation carried out before elaboration of proposal
Justification (III.C.1.)	Weak explanatory power Not distinctive	
Transparency (III.C.2.)	Weak explanatory power Subsumed under accountability and democracy	
Accountability (III.C.3.)	Rests on principal/agent theory (two relationships at stake) Strong explanatory power for link between evaluation and decision-maker	Evaluation available in subsequent proceedings Decision-maker must answer for departures from *ex ante* evaluation
Democracy – Representative, participatory or counter-majoritarian (III.C.4.)	Contradiction amongst democratic rationales Too process-oriented Limited added value of evaluation Limited compatibility with quality improvement rationale	Political rationality Outsourcing of *ex ante* evaluation to private party hard to justify

Table (*cont.*)

Rationale	**Strengths and weaknesses**	**Specific implications**
Information deficiencies – Generation of information or management of uncertainty (IV.A.)	Rests on behavioural economics (cognitive biases) and game theory Not applicable to all *ex ante* evaluations Rich rationale Least instrumental rationale	*Ex ante* evaluation must be circular (step back if necessary) Evaluation part of larger discovery process
Commitment (IV.B.)	Rests on game theory Not applicable to all *ex ante* evaluations Strong explanatory power for consultation procedures	Consultations in order to elicit information
Raising decision-making costs (V.A.)	Rests on public choice theory "Deviant" rationale Backed by historical context Evaluation openly politicized for deregulation	*A priori* bias against intervention
Legislative entrepreneurship (V.B.)	Rests on public choice theory "Deviant" rationale *Ex ante* evaluation totally instrumentalized Matches some observations	*A priori* bias in favour of intervention Choice of policy options rigged Linear evaluation Evaluation in parallel with proposals

In the light of the above, the following rationales can be ignored because of their weakness: collection of evidence, justification and transparency.

At least from an economics perspective, the richest and most powerful rationale remains quality improvement. It explains a large number of features of the *ex ante* evaluation. A number of other rationales are complementary to quality improvement and compatible with it. Accountability, for instance, provides a powerful justification for constraining the decision-maker on the basis of the *ex ante* evaluation. Rationales based on information deficiencies provide an elegant added explanation for the more complex *ex ante* evaluations, presenting them as discovery processes and emphasizing the circularity of the evaluation. The commitment rationale, based on game theory, explains the consultation requirement convincingly.

The democratic rationale, with its three variants, is somewhat more difficult to bring into the picture, since it does clash with the expert, technocratic logic which runs through the rationales listed in the previous paragraphs. Nevertheless, that is not an impossible feat. Furthermore, given that the political science and public administration literature emphasizes this rationale, it cannot be ignored.

The review of the various rationales has highlighted a number of open issues in the current understanding of *ex ante* evaluation of legislation which should be investigated in greater depth:

- The link between the evaluation and the decision-maker should be specified further. The position taken by the Commission ("aid to, but not substitute for decision") seems to downplay that link more than a number of rationales would require.
- The availability of evaluation as evidence in subsequent judicial proceedings should be explicitly acknowledged.
- The relationship between the expert, technocratic and political rationalities should be precised. On the one hand, the policy objectives which are central to the evaluation should be determined by the polity and not by a normative economic perspective. On the other hand, the actual analysis of market failures and of the impact of policy options should be carried out objectively, without biases or prejudices.

In closing, this leaves the two "deviant" rationales, where *ex ante* evaluation of legislation is politicized either against intervention (raising costs) or in favour of it (legislative entrepreneurship). They have been included in this paper not because they are desirable; in fact, they arguably pervert *ex ante* evaluation and create politically-motivated resistance against *ex ante* evaluation as an institution. Furthermore, they contradict the other rationales squarely. Some individual evaluations, however, do fit these "deviant" models. It is useful to keep these rationales in mind when studying individual evaluations, if only to be able to identify sub-par evaluations.

One can doubt whether the *ex ante* evaluation can be conceptualized with only one of these rationales. Leaving aside the "deviant" ones, it seems more appropriate to picture the *ex ante* evaluation as a multi-purpose instrument, following a number of strong and mutually reinforcing rationales. Once this rather dry but fundamental issue is dealt with, the life and practice of *ex ante* evaluations, in all its colour and diversity, can be more fruitfully and profitably investigated.

Chapter 4

The Politics of the *Ex Ante* Evaluation of Legislation

Eberhard Bohne

I. *Conflicts between Formal and Political Rationality in* Ex Ante *Evaluation*

A. *Formal Rationality*

As we have seen in chapter 2, *ex ante* evaluation of legislation is an offspring of the rational model of decision-making. This model consists, in simplified form, of the following steps:[1]

- Identify the decision problem,
- determine consistent objectives and preferences,
- identify all measures and alternatives for the achievement of objectives,
- analyze and assess the possible impacts of each alternative,
- evaluate alternatives against objectives,
- choose the optimal alternative,
- implement decision,
- evaluate decision outcomes.

The means-ends logic of this decision model is also called rationalist paradigm or economic rationality, since 'economic man' (*homo oeconomicus*) is supposed to make decisions according to this model. Here, the term 'formal rationality' is preferred to indicate that the model is not confined to economic decisions but can be applied to any type of decision and policy area.

---

[1] *See* David H. Rosenbloom, Robert S. Kravchuk and Richard M. Clerkin, *Public Administration. Understanding Management, Politics, and Law in the Public Sector*, 7th ed. (McGraw-Hill, New York 2009), pp. 314 et seq.; Nicholas Henry, *Public Administration and Public Affairs*, 10th ed. (Pearson-Prentice Hall, Saddle River NJ 2007), pp. 290 et seq.

Ex ante evaluation of legislation and its subcategories of evaluation like regulatory impact assessment (RIA) reflect the concept of formal rationality. According to the Commission's impact assessment guidelines,[2] an impact assessment consists of the following analytical steps:

- Identify the problem,
- define the objectives,
- develop the main policy options,
- analyze their impacts,
- compare the options,
- outline policy monitoring and evaluation.

It is evident that impact assessment is based on the concept of formal rationality.

Many similar analytical assessment instruments have been around for the last 50 years. Most prominent among them is benefit-cost-analysis which follows the same formal logic,[3] and has been used, for instance, for the deregulation of social and environmental policies in the US under the Reagan administration.[4]

Before the advent of *ex ante* evaluation of legislation, RIA and – in Germany – *Gesetzesfolgenabschätzung* (GFA) in the 1990s[5] the analytical activities which are subsumed under these concepts used to be part of programme evaluation. The scope of programme evaluation is much wider than the evaluation of legislation and covers any public or private policy.[6] Moreover, programme evaluation tends to focus on programme performance.[7] It is, therefore, an ex post evaluation of programme effects. If the programme evaluation includes an analysis of the

---

[2] *See* European Commission, *Impact Assessment Guidelines* of 15 June 2005 with 15 March 2006 update, SEC (2005) 791, p. 4.

[3] *See* Dennis P. Wittmer and Robert P. McGowan, 'Five Conceptual Tools for Decision-Making' in Jack Rabin, W. Bartley Hildreth and Gerald J. Miller (eds.), *Handbook of Public Administration,* 3rd ed. (Taylor and Francis, Boca Raton FL 2007), pp. 315–342, 333 et seq.

[4] *See* Susan J. Tolchin, 'The Political Use of Evaluation Research: Cost-Benefit Analysis and the Cotton Dust Standard' in Dennis J. Palumbo (ed.), *The Politics of Program Evaluation* (Sage Publications, Newbury Park CA 1987), pp. 249–269, 249 ff.

[5] *See* Carl Böhret, Gesetzesfolgenabschätzung (GFA): Heutiger Stand der Methodik und Erfahrungen mit der Integration in die Gesetzesvorbereitung in Deutschland, in Heinz Schäffer (ed.), *Evaluierung der Gesetze/Gesetzesfolgenabschätzung in Österreich und im benachbarten Ausland* (Manzsche Verlags- und Universitätsbuchhandlung, Wien 2005), pp. 31–45, 34 et seq.

[6] *See* Emil J. Posavac and Raymond G. Carey, *Program Evaluation. Methods and case studies,* 4th ed. (Prentice Hall, Englewood Cliffs NJ 1992), pp. 1–3, 15.

[7] *See* Kathryn E. Newcomer, Harry P. Hatry and Joseph S. Wholey, Meeting the Need for Practical Evaluation Approaches: An Introduction in Joseph S. Wholey, Harry P. Hatry and Kathryn E. Newcomer (eds.), *Handbook of Practical Program Evaluation*, 2nd ed. (Jossey-Bass, San Francisco CA 2004), pp. XXXIII–XLIV, XXXIII.

implementation process and structure, it is also called implementation research.[8] The past experience with programme evaluation and its instruments has to be taken into account in the further development of *ex ante* evaluation.

B. *Political Rationality*

Programme evaluation and its cousin *ex ante* evaluation of legislation are "inherently and unavoidably political".[9] Even if the *ex ante* evaluation is conducted in a non-partisan manner, its results may be used to support or prevent certain legislative actions. Consequently, already the conduct of the evaluation study can be drawn into the political process by relevant actors who provide no, false, misleading or incomplete information. Furthermore, the public authority which commissions an *ex ante* evaluation study has certain ideas and expectations about the need for specific legislative actions and their practicability, and will convey them to the evaluator. If he ignores them, the study is likely to be discarded as irrelevant. If he accepts them, he has become part of the political process. Finally, evaluation studies are often used as a political instrument to justify preconceived legislative actions.[10] This complaint has frequently been made of RIAs on the European level.[11] These political characteristics of *ex ante* evaluation of legislation must not be dismissed as accidental shortcomings of poor evaluation research. They are "inherent and unavoidable" and reflect conflicts between formal and political rationality.

Political rationality also follows a means-ends logic which, however, combines policy objectives with the objectives of gaining and/or maintaining power in government.[12] Exercising political power is a necessary condition for any legislative action.

---

[8] *See* Arnold Love, 'Implementation Evaluation' in Joseph S. Wholey, Harry P. Hatry and Kathryn Newcomer (eds.), *Handbook of Practical Program Evaluation*, 2nd ed. (Jossey-Bass, San Francisco CA 2004), pp. 63–97. For the most influential implementation study in Germany concerning air pollution control and water management regulations, *see* Renate Mayntz, Eberhard Bohne, Hans-Ulrich Derlien, Beate Hesse, Jochen Hucke and Axel Müller, *Vollzugsprobleme der Umweltpolitik* (Kohlhammer, Stuttgart 1978); for a recent comparative analysis and evaluation of industrial permitting regulations in eight EU member states *see* Eberhard Bohne, *The Quest for Environmental Regulatory Integration in the European Union* (Kluwer Law International, Alphen aan den Rijn 2006).

[9] *See* Dennis J. Palumbo, 'Politics and Evaluation' in Dennis J. Palumbo (ed.), *The Politics of Program Evaluation* (Sage Publications, Newbury Park CA 1987), pp. 12–45, 12.

[10] *See* Palumbo, *supra* note 9, pp. 13 et seq.

[11] *See* The Evaluation Partnership, *Evaluation of the Commission's Impact Assessment System* (Richmond-Surrey, April 2007), pp. 5 et seq. <www.ec.europa.eu/governance/impact/key_eu.htm>.

[12] *See* Carl Böhret, *Entscheidungshilfen für die Regierung* (Westdeutscher Verlag, Opladen, 1970), p. 44; Helmut Schneider, *Wirtschaftspolitik zwischen ökonomischer und politischer Rationalität* (Deutscher Universitäts-Verlag, Wiesbaden 1997), p. 29.

Experience shows that analytical evaluation instruments do not survive the political process if they ignore the demands of political rationality. The most prominent example is the former 'Planning, Programming, Budgeting System' (PPBS) which dominated government reforms and academic policy research in the 1960s and 1970s like the concepts of new public management today. PPBS passed away, inter alia, because analytically powerful instruments like benefit-cost-analysis ignored the political rationality of the budgetary process.[13] *Ex ante* evaluation will suffer the same fate if it fails to account for the political rationality of the legislative process.

C. *The Quest for Better Regulation*

Since the Commission's White Paper of 2001 'better regulation' has become a new mantra in Europe, and *ex ante* evaluation is seen as the philosopher's stone that will improve the quality of EU and national regulations.[14]

Ex ante impact assessments are required for new proposals of EC directives and regulations, and have to meet the requirements of the Commission's impact assessment guidelines of 2005/2006.

In 2000, the German Federal Government included a provision in the internal 'Joint Rules of Procedure of the Federal Ministries' (*Gemeinsame Geschäftsordnung der Bundeministerien* – GGO) which requires all federal ministries to prepare a prospective GFA (i.e., an *ex ante* impact assessment) for all proposals of legislative acts and statutory orders. There are no binding guidelines for GFAs. However, the Federal Ministry of Interior authorized the publication of a GFA-handbook[15] which contains GFA examples and provides guidance on the conduct of GFAs. Meanwhile, most OECD countries have adopted formalized RIA arrangements.[16]

However, neither the RIA documents of the Commission nor the GFA documents of the German Federal Government mention the conflict between formal and political rationality and its implications for the conduct and use of

---

[13] *See* Aaron Wildavsky and Naomi Caiden, *The New Politics of the Budgetary Process*, 5th ed. (Pearson-Longman, New York 2004), p. 190; Rosenbloom *et al., supra* note 1, p. 292.

[14] *See* Andrea Renda, Impact Assessment in the EU, *The State of the Art and the Art of the State* (Centre for European Policy Studies, Brussels 2006), pp. 43, 48.

[15] *See* Carl Böhret and Götz Konzendorf, *Handbuch der Gesetzesfolgenabschätzung (GFA)* (Nomos, Baden-Baden 2001).

[16] *See* Colin Kirkpatrick and David Parker, Regulatory Impact Assessment: An Overview, in Colin Kirkpatrick and David Parker (eds.), *Regulatory Impact Assessment. Towards Better Regulation?* (Edward Elgar, Cheltenham 2007), pp. 1–16, 10.

evaluation studies. The same thing can be said about the RIA literature. It is largely ahistorical, apolitical and technical.[17]

This chapter will, therefore, explore the functions and requirements of *ex ante* evaluations as part of the political process. On the basis of the analytical distinction between information deficits and information asymmetries using concepts of principal agent theory, the potential benefits and limitations of *ex ante* evaluations in the political process will be examined. The chapter concludes with some reflections on ex post evaluation.

II. *Types of Information Deficiencies*

The ultimate aim of an *ex ante* evaluation is to provide the lawmaker[18] with sufficient and clear information on the expected economic, social and environmental effects and side-effects of potential new legislation including legislative alternatives that can be used as a basis of comparison of those legislative options against each other and against the "no change option".[19] Thus, *ex ante* evaluation is an instrument to remedy the information deficiencies of lawmakers.

Legislative effects can consist of changes in human behaviour which is triggered by the legislation concerned. Effects on the economic and social system (such as effects on the unemployment rate) are aggregate effects of individual behaviour. Information on behavioural effects will be termed 'behavioural information'.

Legislative effects can also represent changes of physical, chemical or biological properties of man, environment and man-made objects (such as industrial installations) which result from the human behaviour affected by the legislation concerned. Information on these effects will be termed 'technical information'. For the analysis of the political functions of *ex ante* evaluation in the legislative process it is useful to divide information deficiencies into regulatory information asymmetries and information deficits. The criterion of distinction is whether or not the needed information is in the possession of the regulatees, implementing public authorities or third parties who have a special interest in the regulations.

---

[17] *See*, as an example, the contributions in Kirkpatrick and Parker, *ibid.*

[18] The term lawmaker is used here to denote any actor within the executive and legislative branches of government who is responsible for the drafting and/or adoption of regulations.

[19] *See* the *ex ante* evaluation of legislation definition in chapter 1 and European Commission, *supra* note 2, p. 26.

A. *Regulatory Information Asymmetries*

The term 'regulatory information asymmetry' is used here to denote the situation where the lawmaker lacks the necessary behavioural and technical information on the potential effects of new regulations while this information is in the possession of the regulatees, implementing public authorities and/or third parties who have a special interest in the regulations (e.g. interest groups representing regulatees). This situation poses problems for the lawmaker. Problems of information asymmetries are the subject of the principal-agent theory. Its concepts are useful for the analysis and development of *ex ante* evaluations.

According to principal-agent theory, any relationship between two or more actors where one actor depends on the action of another actor constitutes a principal-agent relationship.[20] The dependent actor is called principal, the other actor is the agent.

In the context of regulations, the lawmaker is the principal while the regulatees and implementing authorities are the agents. The compliance of regulatees with the regulations and the effectiveness of implementation by the authorities determine whether and to what extent the regulatory objectives set by the lawmaker (principal) are achieved. The relationship between the lawmaker and actors who are not regulatees but have a positive or negative interest in the adoption and/or implementation of the regulations can also be viewed as a principal-agent relationship. Actors who represent the regulatees (for instance business associations, professional associations) or public interests protected by the regulations (such as environmental groups) are agents of the lawmaker, because their activities support or impede the adoption and/or implementation of regulations prepared by the lawmaker (principal).

The relationships between the lawmaker and regulatees, implementing authorities or non-regulatees with a special interest in the regulations constitute regulatory principal-agent relationships. They are to be distinguished from other principal-agent relationships of the lawmaker, e.g. his relationship with evaluators or with other non-regulatees who have no special interests in the regulations. Since these relationships do not involve regulatory information asymmetries, they pose no specific problems for *ex ante* evaluation of legislation.

Principal-agent relationships are characterized by information asymmetries to the disadvantage of the principal. This means that the agents have more and better

[20] *See* John W. Pratt and Richard J. Zeckhauser, 'Principals and Agents: An Overview' in John W. Pratt and Richard J. Zeckhauser (eds.), *Principals and Agents: The Structure of Business* (Harvard Business School Press, Boston MA 1985), pp. 1–35, 2; Nicole J. Saam, *Prinzipale, Agenten und Macht.* (J.C.B. Mohr Paul Siebeck, Tübingen 2002), pp. 6 ff.; Eirik G. Furubotn and Rudolf Richter, *Institutions and Economic Theory. The Contribution of the New Institutional Economics*, 2nd ed. (University of Michigan Press, Ann Arbor Mich. 2005), pp. 162 et seq.

information than the principal. It is assumed that the agents use their information advantages to pursue their own objectives and interests. Consequently, the principal is faced with the problem to moderate or overcome this situation by influencing the agent or by other means. Principal-agent theory distinguishes four types of information asymmetries where relevant information is 'hidden' from the principal:[21]

- 'Hidden characteristics' denote properties of the agent (e.g. technical expertise, financial means) which are relevant for the activities of the agent but not known by the principal.
- 'Hidden action' delineates behaviour of the agent which cannot be discovered under normal circumstances by the principal (e.g. certain actions to deviate from technical or professional standards).
- 'Hidden knowledge' (or information) refers to special information of the agent which is necessary to understand and evaluate his actions (e.g. insider knowledge of technical or economic developments).
- 'Hidden intentions' are plans of the agent which are not disclosed to the principal so that he is misled or deceived about the agent's behaviour. Some authors subsume this information asymmetry under hidden characteristics.[22]

A main concern of principal-agent theory is to design and analyze the instruments which help the principal to cope with information asymmetries. The debate focuses on incentives, controls and sanctions which are intended to make the agent provide the necessary information and/or to prevent him from using his information advantage to the detriment of the principal.[23]

B. *Information Deficits*

There is another type of information deficiency which is not asymmetric and not related to a principal-agent relationship but relevant for lawmakers. This information deficiency is called here 'information deficit' and denotes a situation where the lawmaker lacks the necessary information on the potential effects of new legislation because this information does not (yet) exist (e.g. information on the still unknown causes of ubiquitous forest damages). The term 'information deficit' is also used to depict information deficiencies of the lawmaker which

---

[21] *See* Kenneth J. Arrow, 'The Economics of Agency' in John W. Pratt and Richard J. Zeckhauser (eds.), *Principals and Agents: The Structure of Business* (Harvard Business School Press, Boston MA 1985), pp. 37–51, 38 ff.; Elisabeth Göbel, *Neue Institutionenökonomik* (Lucius und Lucius, Stuttgart 2002), pp. 100 ff.; Saam, *supra* note 20, pp. 29 et seq.

[22] *See* Göbel, *supra* note 21, p. 103.

[23] *See* Göbel, *supra* note 21, pp. 110 ff.; Saam, *supra* note 20, pp. 31 et seq.

are not characterized by regulatory information asymmetries. Two cases can be distinguished.

In the first case the relevant information on potential legislative effects lies with non-regulatees who have no special interest in the regulations (for instance scientific data on dose-effect relationships of pollutants in the hands of an independent research institute). If the same information is also in the possession of regulatees and/or interested third parties, problems of regulatory information asymmetries do not arise. This is because the regulatees and interested third parties (agents) cannot exclude the lawmaker from the information which is also available elsewhere. Thus, there is simply an information deficit on the part of the lawmaker as long as he has not obtained relevant information from independent non-regulatees.

The second case is concerned with behavioural information on regulatees which is not 'hidden' from the lawmaker because it exists in standardized form. Examples are statistics of the Federal Statistics Office (for instance on waste disposal) and cost estimates on the basis of the Standard Cost Model which is used to identify the administrative burden of regulatees complying with regulatory information requirements (for instance filling in an application form). The costs are estimated with the help of standardized information concerning the wage and overhead costs of regulatees, the time to complete the required activity, the number of regulatees affected and the frequency that the required activity must be completed each year.[24]

C. *Relevance of the Distinction for* Ex Ante *Evaluation of Legislation*

As mentioned above, the purpose of an *ex ante* evaluation is to provide the lawmaker with sufficient and clear information on the effects of potential new legislation. This task is impaired by the problems of regulatory information asymmetries and information deficits.

If the *ex ante* evaluation is conducted by the lawmaker or regulatees, it is part of the regulatory principal-agent relationship with the problems of regulatory information asymmetries and information deficits. The same thing holds true if the *ex ante* evaluation is commissioned by the lawmaker or regulatees because in this case the evaluator acts on behalf of the lawmaker or regulatees respectively.

If the *ex ante* evaluation is initiated by an independent third party, the evaluator is not part of the regulatory principal-agent relationships. However, these relationships are the subject of the evaluator's analysis. Since the evaluation results

[24] *See* SCM Network, *International Standard Cost Model Manual* (October 2005), pp. 8 ff. <www.oecd.org/dataoecd/32/54/34227698.pdf>.

will be known and eventually used by the lawmaker, it is unlikely that regulatees and non-regulatees will disclose information to the evaluator which is harmful to their interests. Consequently, the constraints of the regulatory principal-agent relationships are likely to spill-over into the third party evaluation. This spill-over effect does not exclude the possibility that the third party evaluator enjoys more trust with regulatees and non-regulatees than the lawmaker and/or his evaluator, and can, therefore, obtain certain information which the lawmaker and/or his evaluator have no access to. In any event, the distinction between regulatory information asymmetries and information deficits is also crucial for third party evaluations.

On the basis of the distinction between regulatory information asymmetries and information deficits it can be shown that, in the context of regulatory information asymmetries, *ex ante* evaluation of legislation is merely a political instrument. Consequently, the *ex ante* evaluation can meet its proclaimed purpose only with respect to reducing information deficits.

The distinction between regulatory information asymmetries and information deficits is an analytical one. This means that in reality *ex ante* evaluations will be concerned with both types of information deficiencies. In this case the characterization of an *ex ante* evaluation as a political or analytical instrument depends on whether the main focus of the *ex ante* evaluation lies with regulatory information asymmetries or information deficits.

III. *Potential Benefits and Limitations of* Ex Ante *Evaluation in the Political Process*

A. *Functions of* Ex Ante *Evaluation for Better Regulation*

The key problem of EC and national legislation is not quality, but quantity.[25] The accelerating production of multitudinous detailed and complex EC directives and regulations is accompanied by an ever widening gap between legislative promises and their actual fulfilment. The over 20 years old promise of holistic assessment of environmental effects, first pronounced by the EIA directive, and 10 years later by the IPPC directive, is a prominent example for the credibility gap of EC legislation.[26] This gap results in a gradual erosion of the supranational

---

[25] In its White Paper on European Governance of 25 July 2001, COM (2001) 428 final, p. 18, the European Commission criticizes the large number of too detailed regulations and the accompanying regulatory complexity as the main problems of EC legislation.

[26] *See* Eberhard Bohne, 'The Implementation of the IPPC Directive from a Comparative Perspective and Lessons for its Recast' (2008) 5 *Journal for European Environmental and Planning Law*, pp. 1–33 (part 1) and forthcoming (part 2).

normative force of EC law. The preservation of effective supranational EC law rather than neo-liberal postulates of deregulation make restrictions on the EC norm production a top priority of better regulation. Similar complaints of overregulation can be heard in most EU member states.

Ex ante evaluation of legislation can contribute to a slow-down of the norm production by delivering information that certain regulations are not needed. However, experience[27] shows that information deficiencies concerning the need for certain regulations contribute to overregulation only to a small extent. The main causes are political and institutional factors.

Overregulation results, to a large extent, from continuous political pressure of interest groups on the European and national level. Industries, labour unions, farmers, handicraftsmen, service providers and self-employed professionals like doctors, pharmacists, attorneys etc. seek to protect their economic and other interests through regulations. Their quest for legal certainty is often the main cause for detailed regulations.[28]

Furthermore, the legislative process on the European and national level, from an institutional perspective, tends to be in the hands of semi-autonomous systems of government experts whose interests and joint efforts result in the production of voluminous and complex regulations. A case in point is the Water Framework Directive which has been called a "regulatory monster" in the German debate.[29]

---

[27] The author had been involved in lawmaking for some 20 years in the German Federal Ministries of Interior, and of Environment, Nature Conservation and Nuclear Safety.

[28] A bizarre example of unnecessary legislation is the German Horse Shoeing Act (Gesetz über die Reform hufbeschlagsrechtlicher Regelungen und zur Änderung tierschutzrechtlicher Vorschriften vom 19.04.2006, BGBl. I, S. 900). Today iron horse shoes are not the preferred method for the protection of horse hooves, since horses are no longer used for pulling heavy loads but for sports and hobby purposes. Under a 1940 regulation shoeing horses with iron shoes was the monopoly of blacksmiths who had to pass an exam and were certified by the government. Over the years, so-called horse therapists had emerged who treated horse hooves with other means than iron horse shoes. Their activities did not require a certification by the government. The lobbyists for the blacksmiths pressured the Federal Government to subject horse therapists to the blacksmith certification requirement in the 2006 regulations. Since no cases of maltreatment of horses by horse therapists or any other reasons of animal protection were known, the only effect of the regulation was to relieve blacksmiths from the competition of horse therapists. The certification requirement for horse therapists was quashed by the Federal Constitutional Court on constitutional grounds in 2007 (BVerfG, 1 BvR 2186/06 vom 03.07.2007 <www.bverfg.de/entscheidungen/rs20070703_1bvr218606.html>). The activities of blacksmiths and horse therapists should be left to the market and to the self-coordination of the profession. The Horse Shoeing Act illustrates how even relatively small interest groups can trigger regulations to protect their particular interests. Professional regulations of this sort are abundant in Germany.

[29] *See* Konrad Berendes, Die Wasserrahmenrichtlinie im Spannungsfeld politischer, fachlicher und rechtlicher Interessen, in Eberhard Bohne (ed.), *Ansätze zur Kodifikation des Umweltrechts*

Commission and national government experts form relatively homogenous groups in their respective fields. In environmental protection they tend to have an engineering or natural science background. Their professional socialisation often displays similar characteristics. Many of them have known each other for years. They gain social recognition and career rewards for producing regulations rather than for preventing them. They often develop a sort of common 'tunnel vision' on what constitutes the technically best solutions. The results tend to be detailed and technically complex regulations like the Water Framework Directive or the REACH regulation. These expert systems are, in practice, semi-autonomous and have partly got out of political control.

The political and institutional factors causing overregulation are not affected by an *ex ante* evaluation of legislation. Therefore, the potential benefits of *ex ante* evaluation for better regulation are rather limited.

B. *Consequences of Regulatory Information Asymmetries for* Ex Ante *Evaluation of Legislation*

1. *Influence of Regulatory Information Asymmetries on Data Collection*

A main part of *ex ante* evaluation is the collection of data on the economic, social and environmental effects of potential new legislation.[30] This requires causal models in order to identify potential regulatory effects.[31] Where models are not available, everyday experience with causal relationships must suffice. The data encompass behavioural and technical information and partly reflect regulatory information asymmetries to the disadvantage of the lawmaker.

The first step of data collection is to identify the likely effects of new regulations on the behaviour of regulatees, implementing authorities and third parties who are interested in the regulations. Information on these effects is behavioural data, and largely concerned with the regulatory compliance of regulatees. Compliance information is at the centre of potential conflicts between lawmaker (principal), regulatees, and implementing authorities (agents). The evaluation must, therefore, cope with the aforementioned (II. A) categories of regulatory information asymmetries.

The second step of data collection is to identify the potential economic, social and environmental effects which are likely to result from the regulatory behaviour of regulatees. These are technical and behavioural information.

---

in der Europäischen Union: Die Wasserrahmenrichtlinie und ihre Umsetzung in nationales Recht (Duncker & Humblot, Berlin 2005), pp. 9–22, 18.

[30] The Commission's Impact Assessment Guidelines (*supra* note 2, pp. 26 et seq.) contain detailed advice on data collection.

[31] *See ibid.*, p. 27.

The main problem of an *ex ante* evaluation with obtaining compliance information is the fact that it can only be obtained from potential regulatees and implementing authorities. These actors will provide information which serves their interests, or, at least, does not impair them. If the regulatees and implementing authorities support the new legislation, they are likely to play down compliance problems. If they reject the proposed legislation, there will be a tendency to exaggerate or invent compliance problems. A German example for the invention of compliance problems is the information provided in the 1990s by implementing authorities for the draft regulations on free access to environmental information. Then, a flood of information requests entailing enormous amounts of administrative work and costs were predicted which would lead to the break-down of German environmental administrations. Nothing of this sort ever happened. In retrospect, one can say, that the true motivation behind this false information was the administrators' distrust of the public which was, at that time, deeply engrained in German public authorities.

If the required compliance information lies with third parties who have an interest in the regulations, the information also tends to reflect the interests of third parties, e.g. observations on regulatee behaviour by environmental groups.

In sum, all agents involved in the collection of compliance data will act in a strategic manner preserving their interests. This result of the theoretical *ex ante* evaluation from the principal-agent perspective can be illustrated with a practical example of an *ex ante* evaluation.

2. *Examples*

In the early 1990s, the German Federal Ministry of Environment, Nature Conservation and Nuclear Safety planned to introduce binding administrative guidelines, inter alia, for the implementation of the general scoping provision in the Federal EIA Act (section 5). In order to assess the likely effects of the planned guidelines, a working draft of the guidelines prepared by the competent unit in the Environment Ministry, was tested by simulating permitting procedures under the Federal Immission Control Act and the Federal Water Management Act.[32] Representatives of permitting authorities, operators and environmental groups participated three days in the simulated permitting procedures for a power plant, a chemical installation and a land fill. EIA and the scoping procedure were then

[32] The regulatory test is described by Carl Böhret and Michael Hofmann, *Umweltverträglichkeit. Test von Umweltrecht im Planspiel* (Peter Lang, Frankfurt 1992). The test was conducted under the direction of Carl Böhret (German University of Administrative Sciences Speyer) and the author who was then responsible for the EIA regulations in the German Federal Ministry of Environment, Nature Conservation and Nuclear Safety.

new in German environmental law and politically very controversial. Generally speaking, EIA and scoping were considered obstacles to speedy permitting procedures by industries, a potentially powerful instrument of environmental protection by environmental groups, and a regulatory nuisance by permitting authorities. The test was, therefore, requested by the German Federal Parliament.

In the simulated permitting procedure for a chemical installation[33] the operator submitted an incomplete permit application arguing that the draft guidelines were confusing, and that scoping made the submission of a permit application within a reasonable time and cost range impossible. Thus, the actual ability of the operator to prepare a permit application under the EIA guidelines was 'hidden' from the lawmaker (hidden characteristics).

The environmental group refused to participate in the scoping hearing arguing that preparation time was too short and needed to be regulated in the guidelines. Thus, the actual ability and environmental expertise of the environmental group was 'hidden' from the lawmaker (hidden characteristics, hidden knowledge).

The permitting authority demonstrated regulatory toughness and formally dismissed the incomplete permit application on procedural grounds. With this decision the informal bargaining practices of permitting authorities which usually precede permit applications and permit decisions for a multi-million investment were 'hidden' from the lawmaker (hidden actions).

In sum, all test participants acted strategically, and tried to use the test for the promotion of their own interests.

An evaluation study based on a survey and interviews would have yielded similar results. The regulatory test only made the strategic behaviour of the regulatory agents more apparent than a study would have done. Given this situation, the Environment Ministry gained no better information from the regulatory test but used the test results to legitimize its EIA guidelines.

Current examples of regulations which would invite an *ex ante* evaluation in Germany are the planned introduction of a single environmental permit for industrial installations[34] and the revenue-cap regulation for the operation and maintenance of electrical power lines and gas pipelines which is to be implemented in 2009, and already hailed as the 'silver bullet' for generating competition in the German electricity and gas markets.[35] With respect to the single

---

[33] *Ibid.*, pp. 74 et seq.

[34] *See* The Draft Environmental Code, 1st book, sections 47 ff. of 19 November 2007 <www.bmu.de/files/pdfs/allgemein/application/pdf/ugb1_allgem_vorschriften.pdf>. For an overview of different models of an integrated permit, *see* Eberhard Bohne, 'Das Umweltgesetzbuch vor dem Hintergrund der Föderalismusreform' (2006) 4 *Zeitschrift für Europäisches Umwelt- und Planungsrecht*, pp. 276–293, 289 ff.

[35] *See* the Verordnung über die Anreizregulierung der Energieversorgungsnetze (Anreizregulierungsverordnung-ARegV) of 29 October 2007, BGBl I S. 2529.

environmental permit the constellation of political interests is similar as in the test case of EIA regulations. In the case of the revenue-cap regulations, many complex technical information which are in the sole possession of utilities and pertain to the operation of the electricity grid and the gas distribution system would enter the *ex ante* evaluation of legislation in addition to the compliance aspects. Regulatory information asymmetries seem to be even more pronounced with these regulations than with EIA and permitting regulations. This is because electricity and gas networks constitute natural monopolies which are not subject to competition and remain under the sole control of the network owner. Consequently, strategic behaviour of utilities is a common characteristic of the energy sector.[36] This means that any *ex ante* evaluation of the aforementioned regulations would have to cope with the strategic behaviour of the regulatees (regulatory agents).

However, the instruments proposed in the literature for the principal to prevent the agents from exploiting the information asymmetries are not available to the lawmaker and evaluator in *ex ante* evaluations. Lawmaker and evaluator cannot offer tangible rewards (i.e., money) to make the regulatory agents disclose true information. They are also unable to control or sanction strategic behaviour of the agents. Only with respect to implementing authorities situations are conceivable where the lawmaker (for instance a ministry) exercises control over certain authorities. However, with respect to *ex ante* evaluations on federal regulations these situations hardly occur, since the Federal Government has no controls over the authorities of the Länder which implement the largest part of federal regulations.

3. Ex Ante *Evaluation of Legislation as a Political Instrument*

All things considered, *ex ante* evaluation of legislation cannot overcome regulatory information asymmetries, and fulfil the purpose of regulatory analysis for which it is designed. In the context of regulatory principal-agent relationships *ex ante* evaluation is merely the continuation of politics with analytical means. It may be used by the lawmaker to legitimize planned regulations, or, in certain cases, to identify patterns of political conflicts likely to be caused by planned regulations. In short, *ex ante* evaluation of legislation is a political instrument in these cases.

However, one might argue that not all regulatees, implementing authorities and interested third parties exploit regulatory information asymmetries. Theoretically,

---

[36] *See* Heather E. Campbell, 'The Politics of Requesting: Strategic Behavior and Public Utility Regulation' (1996) 15 *Journal of Policy Analysis and Management*, pp. 395–423; Martijn Kuit, *Strategic Behavior and Regulatory Styles in the Netherlands Energy Industry* (Eburon, Delft 2002), pp. 123 et seq.

this situation may occur when certain regulations are politically uncontroversial. In this case, an *ex ante* evaluation is either superfluous because the potential effects of the regulations are known, or it is concerned with politically unimportant regulations (for instance procedural rules for archives). In either case, the *ex ante* evaluation is not worth the effort.

C. *Consequences of Information Deficits for* Ex Ante *Evaluation of Legislation*

When an *ex ante* evaluation is used to reduce the information deficits of the lawmaker, gaming strategies of regulatory agents cannot affect the collection of data. This is because the *ex ante* evaluation is concerned with information which is in the possession of non-regulatees who have no special interest in regulations. When the information does not yet exist (for instance information on specific dose-effect relationships), new research is necessary to obtain it. The *ex ante* evaluation, however, will not include this research under normal circumstances but may trigger it.

Ex ante evaluation for the reduction of information deficits are largely concerned with technical information (such as environmental effects of speed limits on freeways). With one exception, behavioural information is only involved if it refers to the behaviour of actors who are not regulatory agents (such as the impact of labelling requirements on consumer behaviour). However, behaviour of regulatees and other regulatory agents may be the subject of *ex ante* evaluations for the reduction of information deficits if it is available in standardized form. For example, the costs of regulatory information requirements are standardized on the basis of the Standard Cost Model and are now routinely part of the explanatory memoranda to new legislation in Germany. The problems of conducting *ex ante* evaluations for the reduction of information deficits are the same as for any other natural, technical or social science research.

IV. *Conclusions*

Since *ex ante* evaluations which are concerned with regulatory information asymmetries are political instruments, their conduct should not be mandatory. This obligation should be confined to *ex ante* evaluations for the reduction of information deficits.

Consequently, provisions on mandatory *ex ante* evaluations of legislation are to be modified. For instance, section 43 (1) No. 5 of the Joint Rules of Procedure of the Federal Ministries concerning mandatory GFAs should be amended, and restrict GFAs to the assessment of impacts which primarily involve information deficits but not regulatory information asymmetries. Section 43 (1) No. 5 could read:

> (1) The explanatory memorandum must explain:
> ...
> 5. the regulatory impacts (§ 44) insofar as the effects can be assessed on the basis of official statistics, the Standard Cost Model, or information provided by private and public persons and bodies whose interests are not affected by the regulations.[37]

Such a provision would restrict *ex ante* evaluations of legislation to the analytical functions which they can fulfil, and enhance their credibility. Otherwise, *ex ante* evaluations of legislation are running the risk of becoming discredited as merely political instruments. An evaluation of the Commission's impact assessment system has warned against this existing tendency.[38]

The proposed provision would not preclude studies conducted or commissioned by the lawmaker which are part of regulatory principal-agent relationships. These studies, however, could no longer take credit of the prestige associated with official *ex ante* evaluations. They would merely represent politically motivated studies which may nevertheless have an informative value in a given case. Last but not least, the provision would reduce bureaucratic assessment rituals and costs for the government.

Finally, given the political constraints of *ex ante* evaluation of legislation the focus of official impact assessment should be on the ex post evaluation of regulatory effects. While it is true that ex post evaluation also suffers from the political constraints of regulatory principal-agent relationships, these constraints are alleviated by the focus on existing regulatory facts rather than predicted impacts.

The influence of regulatory principal-agent relationships on ex post evaluations could be further reduced by setting up an independent Evaluation Commission made up of government officials, NGOs and experts from academia and relevant professions. In Germany, such a Commission was set up in 2006 for the evaluation of cost estimates on the basis of the Standard Cost Model.[39] Its mandate could be extended to conducting full GFAs.

The ex post evaluation of regulations should not be mandatory but subject to the discretion of the Evaluation Commission. The Commission has to determine whether the regulations are still necessary, and meet their prescribed objectives.

---

[37] The provision would read in German:

> (1) In der Begründung sind darzustellen:
> ...
> 5. die Gesetzesfolgen (§ 44), soweit sie auf der Grundlage amtlicher Statistiken, des Standardkosten-Modells oder von Informationen abgeschätzt werden können, die von staatlichen oder privaten Stellen zur Verfügung gestellt werden, deren Interessen von den Vorschriften nicht berührt werden.

[38] *See* The Evaluation Partnership, *supra* note 11.

[39] *See* Gesetz zur Einsetzung eines Nationalen Normenkontrollrates of 14 August 2006, BGBl I S. 1866.

Furthermore, a modified sunset clause should be introduced which provides for the expiry of legislation one year after the submission of an ex post evaluation, provided that the Commission has concluded that the regulations are no longer necessary, or need to be adapted to new developments. The expiry of the regulations can be avoided if the lawmaker decides otherwise within the one year respite.

Chapter 5

Ex Ante Evaluation of Legislation: between Puzzling and Powering

Robert Hoppe

I. *Introduction*

Those interested in the theory and practice of *ex ante* evaluation of policy proposals are living in paradoxical times. On the one hand, the heydays of *ex ante* policy evaluation lie at least three decades behind us.[1] In the 1960s and 1970s its enthusiastic embrace by scholars sparked off policy analysis as a new academic discipline in the US; and led to scores of new courses in Planning, Programming, Budgeting Systems (PPBS) and Cost-Benefit Analysis (CBA) in political science and public administration in Western Europe. At first, practitioners uncritically followed academic interest. Emulating US government practice, in the Netherlands, e.g., the Commission for Policy Analysis (COBA) was established. Its explicit purposes were (a) to add policy-analytic methods and techniques to the bureaucrats' toolkit of knowledge and skills; and (b) to establish high-level policy analysis staff units in every department.[2] Similar developments were seen in countries like the United Kingdom, Germany, and Sweden.

However, in the subsequent decades the interest in *ex ante* policy evaluation, PPBS and CBA waned for a number of reasons. First, in political and administrative practice attention shifted to implementation deficits of policy programs and

---

[1] *See* Wayne Parsons, *Public Policy. An Introduction to the Theory and Practice of Policy Analysis* (Edward Elgar, Aldershot and Brookfield 1996); Robert Hoppe, 'H.L. Klaassen, Besluitvorming en afhankelijkheid. Over de rol van de procesarchitect bij overheidsprojecten' (1996) 10:4 *Beleidswetenschap*, pp. 393–395; Beryl Radin, *Beyond Machiavelli: Policy Analysis Comes of Age* (Georgetown University Press, Washington DC 2000).

[2] *See* Hendrik L. Klaassen, *Besluitvorming en afhankelijkheid. Over de rol van de procesarchitect bij overheidsprojecten* (Eburon, Delft 1995).

projects adopted previously on the basis of very favorable *ex ante* evaluations.[3] Second, trial-and-error learning through *ex post* summative or formative evaluation of a policy's or policy program's outputs or even outcomes became the new trade mark of good policy analysis.[4] Third, empirical research into the actual uptake of scientific knowledge through *ex ante* policy analysis and other types of policy research showed very disappointing results for scientists.[5] On top of that, fourth, cognitive psychologists and social judgment researchers, in numerous experiments, showed that expert judgment was bias-ridden, and not necessarily better that judgment by lay people or experienced non-experts.[6] All in all, *ex ante* evaluation was disenchanted; *ex post* evaluation was lifted to the position of more cumbersome, but most sensible route for improving policy practice.

In view of these trends in the past, interest in *ex ante* policy evaluation experiences a strong revival. This goes both for the EU[7] and OECD[8] at the international level, and for national levels of government. In the Netherlands, e.g., experiences with CBA for large infrastructural works outsourced by public agencies to commercial consultants led to new national standards for the proper conduct of CBA.[9] The Department of Finance even managed to revivify old PPBS ideals and write these into novel comptrolling legislation for all levels of government under the new label "From Program Budgeting to Policy Accountability".[10] In the UK, the trend is manifest in the movement for Evidence-Based Policy.[11] Emulating ideas popularized through 'evidence-based medicine', the hope is that policy learning,

---

[3] *See* Michael Hill and Peter Hupe, *Implementing Public Policy. Governance in Theory and Practice* (SAGE, London 2002).

[4] *See* Evert Vedung, *Public Policy and Program Evaluation* (Transaction Publishers, New Brunswick and London 1997).

[5] *See* Robert Hoppe, 'Rethinking the science-policy nexus: from knowledge utilization and science technology studies to types of boundary arrangements' (2005) 3:3 *Poièsis and Praxis: International Journal of Technology Assessment and Ethics of Science*, pp. 199–215.

[6] *See* Kenneth R. Hammond, *Human Judgment and Social Policy* (Oxford University Press, Oxford 1996); Philip E. Tetlock, *Expert Political Judgment. How Good Is It? How Can We Know?* (Princeton University Press, Princeton and Oxford 2005).

[7] *See* European Commission, Communication from the Commission on Impact Assessment, COM 2002 276; European Commission, Impact Assessment Guidelines, SEC 2005 791.

[8] *See* OECD, Regulatory Impact Analysis (RIA) Inventory (Paris 2004).

[9] *See* Carel J.J. Eijgenraam, Carl C. Koopmans, Paul J.G. Tang, and A.C.P. Verster, Deel I. Hoofdrapport Evaluatie van Grote Infrastructuurprojecten. Leidraad voor Kosten-Batenanalyse, Onderzoeksprogramma Economische Efficientie Infrastructuur (Ministerie van Verkeer & Waterstaat, Ministerie van Economische Zaken, Nederlands Economisch Instituut, The Hague 2000).

[10] *See* Ministerie van Financiën, White Paper on Van Begroting tot Beleidsverandering (Sdu, The Hague 1999).

[11] *See* Cabinet Office, Better Policy Making: A Guide to Regulatory Impact Assessment (London 2003); Cabinet Office, Impact Assessment Guidance (London 2007).

eased by transparency and easier access to academic research findings and the results of evaluative research into the outputs and outcomes of previous policy programs made possible through the internet, may now well improve *ex ante* evaluation of new policy proposals beyond its previous limited levels.

As always, trends in policy analysis co-evolve with public opinion and policy agenda dynamics.[12] The growing political interest in sustainability issues is propelling a policy-analytic trend towards *Integrated* or *Sustainability Impact Assessment.* The idea is that traditional (macro)economic CBA and socio-economic policy advice for Profits and growth of Gross Domestic Product (GDP), ought to become integrated with modeling of sustainability aspects and *ex ante* evaluation of policy proposals along a much more complex set of evaluation criteria representing all aspects of sustainability, especially People and Planet in addition to mere Profit.[13]

In this chapter, another trend will take center stage. Since roughly the 1970s, people have become critical of the welfare state as over-sensitive and too responsive to citizens' political demands. In diagnosing this problem, structural deep causes like demand overload, and problem symptoms like fiscal crisis have gradually receded in the background of analyses. More and more, the quality and quantity of government regulation of the world of business, of civil society organizations and associations, and of the life of private citizens, came to be seen as the major evil-doers. This trend of the retreat of the legislator in public and political opinion has spurred the policy-analytic trend to *regulatory review or appraisal, regulatory impact assessment* – or, as it is has been defined in chapter 1 of this volume, *ex ante evaluation of legislation.* The idea is that by means of a comprehensive or selective use of *ex ante* evaluation political authorities may be better informed about the future consequences of legislative and other regulatory proposals. This would enable them to select the better proposals and eliminate the worse ones, thereby gradually improving the quality of government regulation for the economy, society and private citizens.

It is important to point out that *ex ante* evaluation is treated here as one, rather specific, subcategory of policy evaluation practices. Not only is there a distinction between *ex post* evaluation of outputs and outcomes causally connected to policies, policy projects and policy programs in the past; and *ex ante* policy evaluation based on forecasting or 'guesstimating' (as it is called by Van Aeken in the next chapter) possible future consequences of policy proposals. Equally important is the distinction between *policy, policy program* and *policy project.* A

---

[12] *See* Peter DeLeon, *Advice and Consent. The Development of Policy Sciences* (Russell Sage Foundation, New York 1989).

[13] *See* Marjolein Van Asselt, *Perspectives on Uncertainty and Risk* (Kluwer Academic Press, Dordrecht 2000).

government may have one or several policies, i.e. (implicit or explicit) major strategic guidelines for governmental actions for dealing with a particular policy problem or issue in the long run. A policy may or may not resolve itself into a routinised and continuous set of policy measures (a policy program), or into one-off, non-iterative policy projects. As the label *ex ante* evaluation implies, it is about *ex ante* evaluation; but it is neither about policy, programs or projects. *Ex ante* evaluation is unique in focusing on one particular type of policy instrument, rule-making or legislation. Although *ex ante* evaluation ought to be seen against the larger backdrop of policy evaluation practices, its specificity is to be found in its limitation to rules or laws.

Other chapters in this book describe, analyse, and evaluate some of these efforts at *ex ante* evaluation in different countries, levels of government, and policy domains. This chapter aims at a preliminary overall evaluation from a policy studies perspective. What may be said of the quality of present efforts at *ex ante* evaluation? Do they really live up to the high expectations suggested by the promises of its protagonists? Can they really contribute to more reflexive governance? Or will the present cohort of *ex ante* evaluations suffer the same mismanagement of expectations and subsequent decline as the previous upsurge of *ex ante* policy analysis and evaluation? Where illuminating and possible, I have gone beyond the experiences with *ex ante* evaluation of legislation reported in this book, which are limited to applications in continental Europe. After all, regulatory review originated in the USA. Like the UK, this country has a common law tradition. This may imply a more instrumental, utilitarian or pragmatist problem-solving perspective on rule-making and legislation.[14] It is beyond the remit of this article to speculate on whether or not this different attitude is a potential explanatory factor in the early rise of regulatory reviews in the USA and the UK compared to the rest of Europe.

My strategy in arriving at conclusions and evaluations is to look at *ex ante* evaluation of legislation from two contrasting perspectives. I will distinguish between a sacred and a profane story of the nature of public policymaking. In the sacred story, policymaking is collective problem solving; and policy analysis is merely cognitive decision support for political authorities – it is a form of *puzzling*. In the profane version, policymaking is a (civilized) political battle between protagonists and antagonists of competing policy proposals; consequently, policy analysis is a method of fighting – it is a form of *powering*. The second section is devoted to setting out these two contrasting perspectives. Sections III and IV look at *ex ante* evaluation of legislation through the lenses of the sacred and the profane

---

[14] *See* Richard A. Posner, *The Economics of Justice* (Harvard University Press, Cambridge 1981); Richard A. Posner, *Law, Pragmatism, and Democracy* (Harvard University Press, Cambridge 2003).

versions, respectively. From the sacred story perspective, *ex ante* evaluation can be shown to have numerous methodological flaws and shortcomings. From the contrasting perspective, the relative success of *ex ante* evaluation of legislation will be shown to depend on political contingencies. The fifth and final section discusses two possible strategies for using *ex ante* evaluation to achieve more reflexive governance: (1) approximation of the sacred ideal of policy analysis as puzzling by creating independent, more neutrally competent institutions for *ex ante* evaluation of legislation; or, alternatively, (2) to make the most of existing *ex ante* evaluation practices by building upon and strengthening suitable parts of the profane version of policymaking as powering.

II. *The Sacred and the Profane in Public Policymaking*

On the face of it, *ex ante* evaluation of legislation could simply be discussed as one element in the dominant paradigm of policy and conventional map of the policymaking process. This is, of course, the stages model of *instrumentally rational problem solving* (see chapters 2 and 4 of this volume). It tends to see policy analysis primarily as decision-support by policy analysts and evaluators for political authorities. The problem solving process usually begins with problem identification; as a next step, objectives are selected; subsequently, the process runs through stages of exploration and analysis of alternative options and their probable consequences; and issues in a weighing up of alternatives in light of several decision criteria, which leads up to a 'best' or at least 'optimal' or 'balanced' choice of policy measures. In other words, policymaking embodies rationality as a transparent, logical sequence of thinking movements issuing in the discovery of the best possible arguments in favor of one policy option.

On closer examination of the state of the art in policy studies, the dominant paradigm and model is contested.[15] A first rival paradigm sees *policy as structured interaction*, or play of power constrained by formal and informal rules on political strategies and tactics of partisan mutual adjustment among stakeholders and proximate policymakers. A second competing paradigm views *policy as social construction of meaning*, conferred in the battle between protagonists and antagonists of policies on concepts used in (competing) political and administrative discourses on social problems, policy programs and projects, but also political leadership and political obstacles or opposition. It is important here to clarify my response to this situation. *Whether or not one sees the existence of multiple*

[15] *See* Hal Colebatch, *Policy*, 2nd edition (Open University Press, McGraw-Hill, Maidenhead 2004).

accounts as problematic or not; and if not, how one sees the relationships between them, ultimately determines how one conceptualizes policy and policymaking.

Colebatch calls the accounts of 'policy as authoritative choice' and 'policy analysis as advice or decision support' the official or *sacred* account. It is used by politicians, proximate policymakers and experts as 'front-office talk' because it offers excellent rhetorical means to rationalize and 'sell' the outputs of policymaking to voters and citizens. After all, citizens expect government to respond to their problems; so the apparently rational movement from 'problem' through 'analysis', '*ex ante* evaluation', and 'decision' to 'solution' is common sense. It easily justifies the outsourcing of responsibilities for political judgment by ordinary citizens as 'lay' persons; and *vice versa*, legitimizes the prerogatives and specialized tasks of proximate policymakers, expert advisers or policy analysts, and political authorities.

However, the sacred account is used, both in theory and practice, not because of its empirical accuracy. Actually, the puzzle is rather why, in the face of mounting evidence for alternatives,[16] it is still the dominant account. Leading policy scholars accept that policymaking is not a rational, linear and sequential process; rather, they see it as discontinuous, contested, and dynamic, with only loose couplings between problems and solutions.[17] Equally important, the assumption of a unitary decision maker or single coordinator is palpably wrong. Policy decisions are the result of complex interest constellations and structured, but difficult to predict political interaction patterns between multiple actors, connected trough numerous mutual resource and path dependencies in complicated network structures.[18] And knowledge in policymaking is hardly an 'object' moving unidirectionally from experts to policymakers and authorities. Rather, knowledge is a joint construction produced during boundary work between policymakers and experts and public opinion and the media. Each party to the process uses information strategically in order to influence and bias the eventual authoritative definition of the problem and its underlying realities.[19] The doubts about the dominant paradigm of policymaking are not limited to academics quarreling over the interpretation of research data and theories. Perhaps more importantly, in policy practice too there is "...a disconnect between the analysts' perception of

[16] *See* Paul A. Sabatier (ed.), *Theories of the Policy Process*, 2nd edition (Westview Press, Boulder 2007).

[17] *See* John W. Kingdon, *Agendas, Alternatives, and Public Policies* (Harper Collins, New York 1995).

[18] *See* Charles E. Lindblom, *The Intelligence of Democracy* (Free Press, New York 1965); Walter Kickert, Erik-Hans Klijn, and Joost Koppenjan, *Managing Complex Networks. Strategies for the Public Sector* (SAGE, London 1997).

[19] *See* Charles E. Lindblom, *Inquiry and Change: the Troubled Attempt to Understand and Shape Society* (Yale University Press, New Haven 1990); *see* Hoppe, *supra* note 5.

self-worth (often drawn from the rational-actor model) and the real contribution that the individual makes in the nooks and crannies of the policy process".[20]

In essence, the dominant model serves as a social myth; it is a Platonic 'noble lie', without which practice is alleged to fall apart. It validates the outcome of policymaking processes as a rational account of how politicians make a difference. In itself, this shows that the problem solving account has strategic power-implications for the practice of policy work. For example, by saying, "We are talking just ideas now, not decisions", policymakers implicitly distinguish between policy analysis or *ex ante* policy evaluation, and policy adoption or decision-making. Drawing such a boundary implicitly reinforces status and power differences between proximate policymakers or analysts, and authorities and elected politicians who, in the regulated play of power, defend their monopoly on authoritative decisions against other policy players. Similarly, stressing "This is mere implementation!" implicitly commands street-level bureaucrats and non-state organizations in a policy network around some issue not to challenge the politically dominant problem definition or adjust policy objectives inherent in adopted policy designs. Yet, such challenges and adjustments might well merit the label 'rational' if they are reflexive responses to changing circumstances 'on the ground'. These examples alone suffice to show how puzzling and powering, intellectual cogitation and struggle for power, intertwine in real policymaking processes.

The challenger, called the *profane* or experiential account, is policy as structured interaction and rule-constrained power play. In such an account the 'advice' or 'decision support' by policy analysts is transfigured into a completely different story. Policy analysts become ordinary policy workers as 'political auxiliaries', as 'networkers' or policy 'diplomats', or as 'policy entrepreneurs'. Not analytical competencies, but negotiation, 'soft' coordination, maintenance of good contacts with other key players, and instigation of supportive or at least non-veto stances become key social skills for trained policy workers. In these types of 'back-office' account of policy, the rational solution, based on unshakable evidence and the persuasive power of the better arguments, is deconstructed as the lucky, victorious alternative which just happened to get more political support from stakeholders in processes of mutual adjustment based on calculated interests and 'deals'. Policy is not a rational solution to some problem; to the extent it is a cognitive or cultural phenomenon, it is *partisan analysis*[21] inspired by fixed commitments of important resources by vested interests and known stakeholders in routinized issue-machines. And here too, policy is part of shaping the

[20] *See* Radin, *supra* note 1, p. 183.

[21] *See* Charles E. Lindblom, *The Policy-Making Process* (Prentice-Hall Inc., Englewood Cliffs, New Jersey 1968), pp. 32–34.

political action itself. Saying "We need a gun control, anti-abortion, or climate change policy" and "Alternative A trumps alternative B in major dimensions of the problem" is a political claim for attention on other policymakers; it is a politically inspired attempt at problem framing or even for exclusive control over problem definition; it seeks commitment of (some of) *their* resources for achieving *your* policy objectives.

I want to stress that the sacred and profane, official and experiential, front- and back-office accounts of policy and policymaking are being actively used both in academic theory and political-administrative practice. These are plausible facts in the social construction account of policy. If policy is viewed as being part of political sense-making, as claims to control and fix the meaning of concepts used in political debates and struggles, it is only logical to apply this insight to the policymaking process itself. It means we may *subsume the sacred and profane accounts of policy under the social construction account.* The implication is that policymaking may be constructed or viewed as, indeed, encompassing puzzling (sacred, rational problem solving account), and powering (profane, structured interaction and power play account) because policy players are all engaged in exercises of sense-making and meaning-giving.

III. *Puzzling*: Ex Ante *Evaluation of Legislation as Policy Analysis*

Ex ante evaluation of legislation started its career as 'regulatory review' during the late 1960s and the 1970s in the USA.[22] It was President Nixon who first demanded the circulation within the executive branch of newly proposed environmental legislation. Under Presidents Carter and Ford centralized regulatory review was extended to all major policy initiatives with an economic impact estimated over $100 million per year. The system was perfected in Executive Order 12291, issued in February 1981 by President Reagan. He required CBA and centralized review for *all*, not just 'major' policy regulations. The required CBA was to be performed by the rule proposing agency itself. Thus, CBA as core analytical element in regulatory review is an *ex ante* evaluation activity performed and/or initiated by the relevant policymaking unit in the administrative part of the executive branch of government. The second element is centralized review, or a meta-analysis of such departmental *ex ante* assessments, by a body that is part of the Executive Office of the President; in this case, the Office of

[22] *See* among many others William F. West, 'The Institutionalization of Regulatory Review: Organizational Stability and Responsive Competence at OIRA' (2005) 31:1 *Presidential Studies Quarterly*, pp. 76–93.

Information and Regulatory Affairs (OIRA), as part of the Office of Management and Budget (OMB).

Although originating in a presidential political regime like the USA, the idea of regulatory review was supplanted to the Westminster democratic regime of the UK (Daffern & Wyatt, 2001), to the other types of democratic regimes of Continental Europe (like Germany and Sweden), and even to the European Union (EU)[23] (also see chapters 7 and 8 of this volume). In all cases, CBA as method of 'puzzling' has been combined with some stronger or weaker form of centralized overview, as mode of 'powering'. In the Netherlands, e.g., *ex ante* evaluations are formally conducted by the Council of State (as described in chapter 9 of this volume). But the development of a specific method of CBA for *ex ante* evaluation of legislation for compliance costs to business deriving from government regulations was entrusted, in 1998, to an *ad-hoc* but independent advisory commission, the Advisory Board on Administrative Burdens (ACTAL). Since then ACTAL's competency has evolved beyond the 'think tank' function of a policy and organizational infrastructure systematically aiming at the reduction of administrative burdens. Nowadays, there is one strong coordinating minister (of Finance), supported by one special-purpose interdepartmental project unit. ACTAL reviews all departmental *ex ante* evaluations for administrative burden reduction, assists departmental units in its analytic tasks, and prior to formal decision making or policy adoption, advises the Cabinet and Parliament about the quality and effectiveness of departmental regulatory proposals.[24]

Now, from a puzzling perspective, policy analysis is the art and craft of constructing and solving 'doable' problems for collective action; or, in other words, creating problems that can be solved.[25] *Ex ante* evaluation may be said to emerge from a long gestation process of problematisation of the role of laws and rules as major policy instruments. This was triggered by the neo-liberal political developments of the 1970s and 1980s. In the mood of citizens, the good intentions and achievements of the welfare state paled in comparison to its failures and perverse side effects. From well-intended and largely successful efforts to remedy market failures, the welfare state came to be seen as a major government or

---

[23] *See* Julia Hertin, John Turnpenny, Andrew Jordan, Mans Nilsson, Duncan Russel, and Björn Nykvist, 'Rationalising the Policy Mess? *Ex ante* policy assessment and the utilization of knowledge in the policy process' (Freie Universität Berlin, Forschungsstelle für Umweltpolitik, FFU-report 03–2007), 22 pp. (ISSN 1612–3026).

[24] *See* Actal (Dutch Advisory Board on Administrative Burden), Annual Report 2006 (The Hague 2006).

[25] *See* David Dery, *Problem Definition in Policy Analysis* (University of Kansas Press, Lawrence 1984); Robert Hoppe, *Het beleidsprobleem geproblematiseerd. Over beleid ontwerpen en probleemvorming* (– inaugural address; Coutinho, Muiderberg 1989).

regulatory failure.[26] Politicians like Carter and Reagan in the US, and Thatcher and Major in the UK, managed to win electoral victories through blaming centralized government and 'bureaucrat bashing'. In the concomitant newer philosophies of governance like the New Public Management (NPM), government reforms were clearly based on individualist, rational choice, and economic thinking. Its core assumption was to view "organizations as a chain of low-trust principal/agent relationships (rather than fiduciary or trustee-beneficiary ones), a network of contracts linking incentives to performance" (Dunleavy and Hood, 1994).[27] In NPM-thinking laws and regulations are no longer the unquestioned major instruments of governing they used to be. They are part of a larger set of policy instruments; and not necessarily the preferred tools (Hood, 1983).[28] As a matter of fact, in contemporary government practice legal expertise in the public sector is regaining part of its historical prominence because politicians and public agencies desire to be fully informed about the legal risks of engaging in all kinds of contractualized relations with firms or civil society organizations.[29] The once dominant paradigmatic view of legislation and regulation was gradually challenged by a neo-liberal reframing as compartmentalized legal designs leading to rule over-complexity and overload. From 'pet' policy instrument for legal professionals in ordering society, the impact of laws and rules on society and the economy was reframed as a risk and major contributor to uncertainty, economic underachievement and social disorder.

To become 'doable' policy-analytic problems, such political and ideological frame shifts have to be translated into or aligned with, to the extent possible, standardized and well-known disciplinary or professional concepts, criteria, models and theories. The neo-liberal ideological drift generally has boosted an economistic, public choice academic-professional framework in policy analy-

---

[26] West, *supra* note 22, interviewed officials working for OMB's OIRA, and found that "(a) common denominator among its personnel is the belief that government intervention has the potential to produce more harm than good, and (b) that the probable effects of agency rules should therefore be subjected to comprehensive analysis."

[27] *See* Patrick Dunleavy and Christopher Hood, 'From Old Public Administration to New Public Management' (1994) July-September *Public Money and Management*, pp. 9–17.

[28] *See* Christopher Hood, *The Tools of Government* (Macmillan, London 1983).

[29] In a recent employers' survey for the Public Administration curriculum at the University of Twente, this was vividly expressed: Legal quality care is no longer application of best practice in writing legal government texts, or of general principles of ethical and proper public administration. Rather, it has evolved into pro-active management of legal risks in three domains: multiple types of contracts in public-private partnerships, subsidising and tendering, especially in a EU-context, and regulatory transparency before policy implementation.

sis (Larouche, in chapter 3 of this volume).[30] In this framework the central, ethical benchmark and rationale for public policies begins with the concept of efficiency, supposedly attainable in a perfectly competitive economy. Market failures, other limitations of the competitive framework – prominent among which are some nasty properties of public and private goods like information asymmetries (see the previous chapter of this volume) –, and distributional issues, and government failures constitute clear rationales (and limitations) of policy interventions. For policy analysts looking for methods to structure and define the ideologically informed but analytically imprecise problem framings, public choice thinking offered plenty rationales for improving the quality and enforceability of rules first; and the reduction of the number of rules and even abolition of entire systems of legislation and regulation later. One could easily classify rule oversupply as a problem of government or bureaucratic failure. On top of that, for politicians using the rhetoric of blaming bureaucracy and reasserting the primacy of politics, this problem definition perfectly aligned with their ideological self-justification.[31]

To cut a long story short, considerations such as these have resulted in the choice of CBA as most suitable method of *ex ante* evaluation of legislation; a choice reflected in all handbooks or other types of central guidelines for conducting such evaluations.[32] This is a methodological choice that fits quite nicely with the sacred conception of policymaking as rational policy analysis for problem solving by political authorities. ACTAL, for instance, justifies this approach by three major arguments: "(1) *Measure* all existing and new compliance costs and internalized administrative burdens to...determine an *objective* measuring

---

[30] *See* the most popular introduction to public policy analysis in the US, David L.Weimer, and Aidan. R. Vining, *Policy Analysis.Concepts and Practice* (Prentice-Hall, Englewood Cliffs 1999).

[31] This is not to say that public choice was the only way of structuring the problem of rule pressure. In the Netherlands, e.g., NPM-like administrative and organizational thinking at the Department of Administrative Reform and Internal Affairs informs the idea of "Alternative Government" (*Andere Overheid*). One of its themes is to test all existing and new state regulation for unnecessary and superfluous administrative burdens on *citizens*. The Department of Justice attempts to tackle entire systems of legislation from a new philosophy of law perspective. In its project "A Usable Legal Order" (*Bruikbare Rechtsorde*) the ambition is to rethink the legal relationships between government, private citizens and firms in the general direction of a *self-guiding society*, where citizens and firms are enabled to solve their own problems through mediation and negotiation in out-of-court settlements. Yet, it would be fair to say that so far administrative-organizational and legal-theoretical problem structuring have been less productive in creating doable policy problems than the public choice frame.

[32] *See* respectively Carl Böhret, Gesetzesfolgenabschätzing (GFA) in Heinz Schäffer (ed.), *Evaluierung der Gezetze/Gesetzesfolgenabschätzung in Österreich und benachbarten Ausland* (Manzsche Verlags- und Universitätsbuchhandlung, Wien 2005), pp. 31–45; European Commission, *supra* note 7; OECD, *supra* note 8; Cabinet Office, *supra* note 11; <www.actal.nl>.

instrument, (and) a reduction objective… (2) (to) introduce one *objective* test that dovetails with the main point of Cabinet policy… (and) (5) express all regulatory pressure objectives in *one currency*: the euro."[33] (ACTAL, 2006:6)

The italicized (by RH) words clearly position CBA in the rationalistic, analycentric and neo-positivist epistemological ambitions of the linear model of policy analysis as knowledge transfer by experts to political authorities.[34] Needless to say, this model allows politicians to appeal to scientific expertise as a basis for their decisions. Only the EC guidelines, on paper, somewhat attenuate the positivistic aspirations. At least, they contain some post-positivist ideas that fit a more profane conception of policymaking: *ex ante* evaluation of legislation does not substitute for political decision making, but remains just an aid; in their final reports, analysts should not ignore but flag up uncertainties and pivotal assumptions in the analysis; and, finally, the analytic process is not entirely expert-driven but includes consultation procedures with stakeholders.[35]

In the reports on actual use of CBA and handbooks or guidelines for *ex ante* evaluation of legislation a lot of '*normal shortcomings*' show up. It turns out that, like in the case of handbooks on uncertainty analysis and risk management in environmental policy,[36] handbooks or guidelines on *ex ante* evaluation of legislation rarely inform actual practice (Veit, in this volume). No doubt, the most important complaint is that, so far, there are no clear signs that *ex ante* evaluation lives up to its promise of more 'enlightened' political debate and reflexive use of information in political decision making.[37] In that sense, *ex ante* evaluation of legislation does not differ from most other forms of *ex ante* policy analysis in the past and present.[38] There appear to be numerous causes. Frequently, *ex ante* evaluation of legislation is squeezed in at the very end; it occurs too late or too downstream in the policymaking process to make a difference (for a particularly

---

[33] *See* ACTAL, *supra* note 24, p. 6.

[34] *See* Robert Hoppe, 'Policy analysis, science and politics: from "speaking truth to power" to "making sense together"' (1999) 26:3 *Science and Public Policy*, pp. 201–210; Hertin *et al.*, *supra* note 23, pp. 9–10.

[35] *See* European Commission, *supra* note 7 (2005), p. 39.

[36] See Mark R. Powell, *Science at EPA. Information in the Regulatory Process* (Resources for the Future, Washington DC 1999); Annick de Vries, *Towards Do-ability: Dealing with Uncertainty in the Science-Policy Interface* (dissertation, University of Twente 2008).

[37] More generally, it is very hard to empirically demonstrate a causal link between policy evaluation and improved policy performance (*see* George A. Boyne, Julian S. Gould-Williams, Jennifer Law, and Richard M. Walker, 'Toward the Self-Evaluating Organization? An Empirical Test of the Wildavsky Model' (2004) 64:4 *Public Administration Review*, pp. 463–473.) Perhaps the interest in evaluation is just one manifestation of the power of the myth of benefits of so-called rational behavior.

[38] For the past, *see* Carol H. Weiss, 'The interface between evaluation and public policy' (1999) 5 *Evaluation*, pp. 468–486; for the present, *see* Hertin *et al., supra* note 23.

clear example, Van Gestel and Vranken in chapter 9 of this volume). In these cases, narrow instrumental or political use of marginal knowledge production by experts during an *ex ante* evaluation is the best that can be hoped for. As far as political use is concerned, interestingly, in the UK, "many desk officers hold the view that the function of (regulatory, RH) policy assessment is to justify the burden on business and citizens created by regulation".[39] If there is a lack of (additional) analytic resources (while being burdened to capacity by other, more important normal tasks) and insufficient policy-analytic skills or methodological myopia (Van Aeken, in the next chapter of this volume) non-use is very likely (see chapter 10 of this volume) – and even justified, I would add. Leaving *ex ante* evaluation of legislation to policy analysts that belong to the regular staff of lead agencies and departments, like in Germany (Veit, chapter 8 of this volume) and the EU, leads to a rather formalistic, 'ticking off' mentality. Says one German analyst: "The regulatory impact assessment is just a little hoop we have to jump through.... We try to assess the cost because we are required to do it."[40] Consequently, exploration of more than one policy option is often disregarded. Countries that entrust *ex ante* evaluation of legislation (also) to external bodies, like the USA, the Netherlands and Sweden (Veit, chapter 8 of this volume) appear to do a little better in this respect.

There are complaints about *comprehensiveness* in *ex ante* evaluations which also merit attention. Frequently, *ex ante* evaluations like CBAs are claimed to be lacking in promised comprehensiveness (Veit, chapter 8 of this volume).[41] In principle, CBA's attractiveness to policy analysts is that it allows them to decide whether investing in, e.g., wind energy production is better than administrative burden reduction, or the other way around. However, such conclusions are only warranted if all costs and all benefits of both options can be reliably measured and, properly discounted for future effects, expressed in monetary terms; and then related to utility functions expressing global economic efficiency or aggregate social welfare to determine their policy merit. The 'silo mentality' permeating bureaucratic politics normally prevents serious attention to aggregate social welfare. Rather, analysts in lead agencies and ministries focus on their own missions and objectives; a tendency hard, perhaps impossible to break.

This is even more so since measurement and expression of measurements in monetary terms is not possible for all problem dimensions. As is well known from other experiences, the urge to quantify has its opportunity costs. Even in the already limited case of *ex ante* evaluation for administrative burden reduction, some administrative burdens are easier to quantify than others. Visible,

---

[39] *See* Hertin *et al., supra* note 23, p. 12.
[40] *See* Hertin *et al., supra* note 23, p. 13.
[41] *See also* Hertin *et al., supra* note 23.

quantifiable reductions in administrative burdens are easier to achieve for business than for ordinary citizens. Information provision costs for enterprises implied by regulation are easier to capture in a Standard Cost Model, and consensual cost estimation is more likely for information costs than for other types of compliance costs. In the Netherlands, e.g., only in the year 2008 ACTAL is pushing to broaden the scope of its methods to include all compliance costs for enterprises. Similarly, the method was only recently pilot tested on administrative burdens falling on individual citizens. ACTAL follows a step-by-step target group approach, prioritizing citizens that particularly suffer from high administrative burdens like the chronically ill, the physically challenged, elderly social benefit recipients, and volunteer workers.[42]

In sum, only particular types of burdens for some social groups are measured, not all of them. Most conspicuously missing from *ex ante* evaluation's claim to comprehensiveness is that burden reduction is just assumed to be beneficial, on average, for the short and the long term. Especially non-economic costs and benefits are blended out of the consideration in the present practices for conducting *ex ante* evaluations. There is no Standard *Benefit* Model to logically complement the Standard *Cost* Model.

On top of that, *ex ante* evaluations suffer from serious intellectual impediments in the *forecasting* of policy effects necessary for proper CBA. Intellectual challenges to modeling and forecasting in the case of normal economically focused CBA are difficult enough. It is only fair to observe that the state of the art in forecasting outputs and outcomes in *ex ante* evaluations of legislation was and still is underdeveloped. Forecasting provides information about future states of society, particularly expected policy outcomes – both in the case of unchanged continuation of current policies, and in the case of policy adaptation or radical changes. Forecasts come in three shapes. *Projections* are based on the extrapolation of historical trends and data on the current situation into the future; if possible they use classical time-series analysis on an accurate data set reaching back far into the past. An example would be an extrapolation of the total number of rules contained in past and present laws or ministerial decrees. In the case of *ex ante* evaluation of legislation, extrapolative forecasting is still very much in its infancy. *Predictions* are derived from theoretical assumptions between causes and effects, combined with data about the past and the present. Econometric modeling of key economic indicators reflecting the (future) state of an economy is a well-known example. In contrast to some ecological and sustainability issues, theoretical forecasting in *ex ante* evaluations is way beyond reach. The third type of forecast is a *conjecture* founded in informed judgment, e.g. through conventional policy Delphi methods. But this is a questionable

[42] *See* ACTAL, *supra* note 24, p. 24.

method in the case of *ex ante* evaluation of legislation due to the alleged impact of information asymmetries between the legislator-cum-*ex ante* evaluation-analyst and those stakeholders who possess relevant information, but have a strategic interest in hiding it (Bohne, chapter 4 of this volume).

The response of academics and professionals to information asymmetries is circumvention-through-standardization. In the case of *ex ante* evaluation of legislation, this response is the rapid introduction and spreading of the Standard Cost Model (SCM) (also Veit, chapter 8 of this volume). In order to be able to start working toward improved forecasts, the Dutch government established the above mentioned temporary Advisory Board on Administrative Burdens (ACTAL). Similar advisory bodies with similar tasks were instituted in the UK, the *Better Regulation Commission*, in Germany, the *Normenkontrollrat*, and in Sweden, the intended *Regelråd*. ACTAL's first task was to design a method for zero-measurements for the year 2002 of administrative burdens on enterprises derived from departmental laws and regulations. The method devised is to let experts and representatives from business jointly produce agreed upon but standardized judgmental forecasts for particular types of administrative burdens. Standardization is necessary for comparable quantitative data about all types of administrative burdens caused by laws and rules across departmental domains. Standardization is achieved mainly by imposing one identical system of cost element structuring, the Standard Cost Model. Costs are expressed as amount of Euros. An interesting feature of the method is that the cost estimation procedure allows for consultative interaction between experts and business representatives by way of panels, interviews and surveys in the production of consensus judgments. The effects of information asymmetries are circumvented by application of statistical methods detecting gross overestimation by self-interested stakeholders, and by comparisons between several commercial branches and between different countries. Also, once a benchmark year has been agreed between experts and stakeholders, governments and experts use historical data analysis over a few years to justify further reduction targets for stakeholders in later years. This is similar to the way Statistics Holland assembles and calibrates its data for the production of economic indicators. It reflects the neo-corporatist culture and structure of government policymaking in the Netherlands. It is a very instructive example of how official 'facts', 'data' and indicator systems are, literally, socially and politically co-constructed by government experts and stakeholder representatives.[43] It is also a good example of how intelligent policy analysis (or puzzling) may inform more productive political interaction (or powering).

[43] *See* Theodore M. Porter, *Trust in Numbers: The Pursuit of Objectivity in Science and Public Life* (Princeton University Press, Princeton 1995); James C. Scott, *Thinking Like a State: How*

IV. *Powering*: Ex Ante *Evaluation of Legislation as Political Arena*

In section II I discussed an alternative depiction of policymaking as political struggle, in which policy analysis is not a substitute for politics, but is itself a method of fighting. In politics the questions, *Who evaluates what, for whom, how, when, and why?* define the nature and function of evaluation. And even though practices of (*ex ante* and *ex post*) policy analysis and evaluation can partly be measured by scientific standards, they are also political by nature.[44] In section II it was observed how politics as sense-making and meaning-giving implied that political talk about evaluation itself is part of the political process. By speaking of fact-finding and evaluation as decision-oriented and learning-enhancing activities, policy analysts and evaluators claim a most important role in policymaking; they compete with other players in the political arena for attention, status, and power. On top of that, analysis and evaluation of policy is not restricted to data collection or fact finding. Even though positivistically inclined policy analysts and evaluators deny it, other policy actors will not believe them and quickly point out the errors of their thinking.

In the case of *ex ante* evaluation of legislation, the essential political purpose has been to rein in bureaucratic freelancing; and the use of CBA has provided the political protagonists with an initial screening device. From a profane, political view of policy and politics, CBA was a power mechanism and, simultaneously, a 'scientific' mode of legitimizing their political purpose. Moreover, centralized regulatory review, whether by an Executive Office of the President (like in the USA), or by the Prime Minister's Cabinet Office (like in the UK), or by the Minister of Finance supported by an external advisory board (like in the Netherlands), also serves the political purpose of early warning system against policies that duplicate each other, or conflict with overall government policy guidelines, or the implementation of policy programs of other agencies.[45] The Dutch ACTAL makes no secret of this political role. In its mission statement it stresses that reducing regulatory pressure means (1) "to call in one strong coordinating minister with interdepartmental project management", (2) to device an objective test which "*dovetails with the main points of Cabinet policy*" (italics, RH), and also (3) to "commit implementation organizations, fellow authorities

---

Certain Schemes to Improve the Human Condition Have Failed (Yale University Press, New Haven 1998).

[44] *See* Carol H. Weiss, 'Policy research: data, ideas, or arguments?' in Peter Wagner and Björn Wittrock (eds.), *Social Sciences and Modern States: National Experiments and Theoretical Crossroads* (Cambridge University Press, Cambridge 1991), pp. 307–332.

[45] *See* West, *supra* note 22.

and fellow government bodies and supervisors to the objectives of reducing regulatory pressures".[46]

Clearance of departmental rule-making through centralized overview is a potentially significant addition to the normal power mechanisms through which executive political authorities (presidents, prime ministers, cabinets) may promote their political purposes through administrative processes.[47] Traditional means all have an *input* character: budgets, spending powers, appointments, cabinet agreements, persuasion and/or political deals with department ministers – and all this on condition of parliamentary approval. Centralized regulatory review, in principle if not in actuality, enables central government authorities and bodies to screen rulemaking as major administrative *output* of individual departments or agencies. Of course, central governmental authorities already reviewed departmental proposals and may subject them to central government approval, in a cabinet meeting or a prime minister's or presidential office, before being sent to parliament. But certainly centralized regulatory review enhances central government's capacity to influence the exercise of normally distributed jurisdictions of departmental and bureaucratic policymaking. This may not go so far as to oblige departments to have 'regulatory calendars' to centrally monitor their legislative efforts in detail (like under Reagan in the USA); or to send them 'prompt letters' to signal the urgency of some politically desired legislative initiative.[48] But the political 'groundwork' exists once *ex ante* evaluation of legislation and central regulatory review have been institutionalized. It will take quite some political alertness by individual ministers and agency heads to not let the possibilities for generalized political responsiveness inherent in this architecture overpower its original, single purpose of tackling regulatory rule pressure.

Thus, what is primarily an instrument for one particular policy purpose, serves equally as a potential means of centralizing power for key players in the government. Bohne (in the previous chapter) therefore correctly observes that *ex ante* evaluation, combined with central regulatory review, can be politically rational in marrying a policy logic of means-ends analysis to a political logic in gaining and/or maintaining power. In Germany, Sweden and the EU the centralized review element may still be more implicit and hidden. The limited powers of the federal government in Germany, and Sweden's allegedly 'rational' administrative culture may stand in the way of openly recognizing the political functions of *ex ante* evaluation-cum-central regulatory review. But the EC, after all the watchdog of the EU's political purposes and the only EU body

[46] *See* ACTAL, *supra* note 24, p. 6.
[47] *See* West, *supra* note 22, p. 79, p. 83.
[48] *See* West, *supra* note 22, p. 80, respectively p. 83.

competent to initiate new policy proposals, cannot but be aware of this informal and potential function.

Returning to the most important political question in *ex ante* analysis and evaluation, Who evaluates for whom?, some important differences meet the eye. In some cases, *ex ante* evaluation is conducted by lead agencies and departments through their own career civil servants. Centralized regulatory review is weak or absent. This appears to be the case in Germany, and the EU's departments in Brussels. Obviously, politicians believe that the quality of *ex ante* evaluation and its political impact are best served by respecting the stability of existing administrative organizations, the continuity of their personnel, and upgrading career civil servants' policy-analytic skills through central handbooks, guidelines, and special training. In other cases, centralized external bodies staffed by 'political appointees/missionaries' or 'gatekeepers' play a central role; although actual rule-making and design of legislative proposals remains a primary task of lead agencies and departments. This is clearly the case in the USA's OMB/OIRA as part of the Executive Office of the President under six administrations of both Republican (Nixon, Reagan, Bush sr., Bush jr.) and Democrat stripes (Carter, Clinton), and in the UK's strong Cabinet Office, with, consecutively, a Deregulation Unit under Conservative administrations (Thatcher, Major), and a Better Regulation Unit and Regulatory Impact Unit under Labour administrations (Blair, Brown). In the Anglo-Saxon world, bureaucracy and bureaucrats obviously are distrusted by politicians as inert at best, and acting in their own bureau political interests (maximizing budgets and policy scope, exploiting knowledge asymmetries) at worst. Hence, presidents and prime ministers have redefined the administration-politics dichotomy. They have severed the supposedly innovative political forces of *ex ante* and *ex post* policy analysis/evaluation from the inherently conservative mass of officialdom and vested political interests. Instead of defining CBA as part and parcel of a bureaucracy's neutral competence, they have used it as an instrument, wielded by external experts, for enhancing the bureaucracy's and career civil servants' political responsiveness.[49] Shapiro, a one-time political appointee heading OIRA, has observed that when politics and analysis openly conflict, politics always trumps analysis.[50]

Apart from these two opposite types, there are also mixed cases. In the Netherlands, centralized regulatory review is one of the formal tasks of the Council of State. The Council is an independent organization, external to the administra-

[49] *See* Aaron Wildavsky, 'The Self-Evaluating Organization' in Aaron Wildavsky, *The Art and Craft of Policy Analysis* (The MacMillan Press, London and Basingstoke 1979), pp. 220–224; *see also* William F. West, 'Neutral Competence and Political Responsiveness: An Uneasy Relationship' (2005) 33:2 *Policy Studies Journal*, pp. 147–160.

[50] *See* Stuart Shapiro, 'Unequal Partners: Cost-Benefit Analysis and Executive Review of Regulations', 2004 (<ssm.com/abstract=590241>) (referenced in West, *supra* note 49).

tive governmental apparatus. It tests the quality of legislation by administrative organizations; only after its approval, these may be sent to parliament for final adoption. In chapter 9, Van Gestel and Vranken will show that, from a policy-analytic and political point of view, the Council of State's centralized regulatory review is very weak. Due to its being understaffed and (from a policy-analytic point of view) underskilled, centralized regulatory review is too little; and due to its timing in the sequential process of policy advice, it is too late. However, the centralized regulatory review organized in the triad between the Minister of Finance, a central administrative body for interdepartmental project management made up of representatives of major departments, and ACTAL as well-staffed and expert advisory body, appears to be fully up to its task. One of its interesting features is that ACTAL somehow combines two distinct roles. On the one hand it acts as collaborative consultant and training center to single departments and agencies (also at lower levels of government); on the other, in its clearance of regulatory proposals and advice to the Minister of Finance, it acts in the heart of government as a 'watchdog' or 'gatekeeper' for the special purpose of tackling regulatory pressure. Whether or not these inconsistent roles can be played in the long run is an interesting topic for further research.

In Sweden, too, there is a huge difference between the weak form of centralized regulatory review organized through its Government Office and central agencies, and the more concrete and impact-rich *ex ante* evaluations conducted by Commissions of Inquiry (Veit, chapter 8 of this volume). The Swedish commissions are in fact special purpose task forces to study particular subject areas of policy implementation in depth. A number of characteristics are important for mentioning. First, frequently, the commissions mix expertise and political rationality in their composition: experts, public administration representatives, stakeholder representatives, and MP's. Second, commissions are supported by experienced commission-secretariats, which do most of the 'text-work' implied in policy reporting. Such secretariats, like their counterparts in the Netherlands,[51] become experienced boundary workers between commission members (as 'agents') and departments (as 'principals'); an experience which is an invaluable resource for creative and productive relations and the 'selling' of the commission report. Third, commission reports, and sometimes interim-reports, are published and therefore accessible to the general public. Fourth, reports are subjected to a protracted consultation procedure.

---

[51] *See* Roland Bal, Wiebe Bijker, and Ruud Hendriks, *Paradox van Wetenschapppelijk Gezag: Over de Maatschappelijke Invloed van Adviezen van de Gezondheidsraad* (Gezondheidsraad, The Hague 2002); Willem Halffman and Robert Hoppe, 'Science/policy boundaries: a changing division of labour in Dutch expert policy advice' in Sabine Maasen and Peter Weingart (eds.), *Democratization of Expertise?* (Springer, Dordrecht 2005), pp. 135–151.

What is most remarkable about them is that, although analysis is constrained by strict governmental instructions, time and budget limits, the puzzling, in the spirit of Lindblom and Wildavsky,[52] may be productive for the powering, compromising and consensus-seeking,: "The Swedish experiences therefore suggest that the political uses cannot be clearly separated from conceptual uses: a fair amount of 'enlightenment' sometimes occurs among the members of the committees *as they are confronted with and forced to assimilate various stakeholder positions, knowledge and perspectives*" (italics by RH).[53] What may be concluded from the examples is that the practice of *ex ante* evaluation of legislation is much more contingent upon political contexts than it is dependent on methodological precepts. What is actually needed is thorough comparative study of practices of *ex ante* evaluation for presidential, Westminster and more consensus-type democratic systems. Special attention should be given to conditions, like in Sweden's commissions of inquiry or the Netherlands' ACTAL advisory commission, where puzzling apparently strengthens powering in the sense of producing 'serviceable truths'.[54]

V. Ex Ante *Evaluation for More Reflexive Governance?*

Ex ante evaluation-practices inevitably lead to a major question: may the executive parts of governments and government organizations ever be or become self-evaluative? Does it make sense to mobilize *ex ante* or *ex post* evaluators as change agents against the alleged inertia and conservatism of normal bureaucracy and career civil servants? Or is it more plausible, as West argues, that "...it may just be unrealistic to expect that bureaucratic agents charged with accomplishing the policy objectives of...political executives can do so by remaining nonpartisan and objective."[55] In other words, does *ex ante* evaluation-practice suffer from the normal tendency that political responsiveness drives out neutral competence; or are there possibilities in *ex ante* evaluation of legislation for more reflexive governance? After all, by studying the potential impact of legislation and rule-application on the economy and society, public debate and political decision-making ought to become more informed and therefore enabled to arrive at more rational decisions. Reflexiveness about legislation and rule making as core governance instruments ought to lead to a wiser, more prudent use of those

---

52 *See* Aaron Wildavsky, *The Art and Craft of Policy Analysis* (The MacMillan Press, London and Basingstoke 1979); and *see* Lindblom, *supra* note 21.

53 *See* Hertin, *supra* note 23, p. 17.

54 *See* Sheila Jasanoff, *The Fifth Branch. Science Advisers as Policy Makers* (Harvard University Press, Cambridge 1990).

55 *See* West, *supra* note 49, p. 148.

same instruments. In my view, there are two, not mutually exclusive, routes for *ex ante* evaluation of legislation to achieve somewhat more reflexive governance. The first route is to set about approximating the sacred ideal of policymaking through combining powering and puzzling in the creation of neutrally competent, independent *ex ante* evaluation-institutions (Bohne, chapter 4 of this volume).[56] The alternative route is following Lindblom's advice to make the most of *ex ante* evaluation-practice by building on certain favorable ingredients of the profane story of policy-making.

More objective and balanced *ex ante* evaluation of legislation may be achieved by creating institutions that embody a reputation for neutral competence, independence as an antidote to (too much) political responsiveness, professional norms as a basis for interaction, and transparency as a resource for balancing views and shaming severe bias or abuse of analysis. Instead of having *ex ante* evaluation by centralized or departmental parts of the executive, the cases of commissions of inquiry in Sweden and ACTAL in the Netherlands, suggest that governments can also arrange for *ex ante* evaluation to be done at arm's length. Temporary advisory bodies or quasi-governmental think tanks outside of, but linked to executive agencies, may produce evaluations that are more credible and respected as neutrally competent in public debate. Their institutional design ought to reflect sufficient independence, but without becoming completely politically unresponsive. In order to be successful they would need a non-partisan leadership with tenure contracts independent from changing governments or elections; guaranteed funding that would not make them dependent on annual appropriations, but without giving them 'eternal' existence; and a regular analytical task which ties them into standard political routines, like budget policymaking or some annual or bi-annual state-of-the-nation reviews for parliament.[57]

Involving professions to make sure that professional and not merely political norms prevail in the practice of *ex ante* evaluation of legislation would also be desirable. Professional *ex ante* evaluation of legislation requires a balanced mix of three professions. Although the economic and the legal professions both provide norms relevant to *ex ante* evaluation across substantive policy areas, neither of these professions alone suffices. On top of that, as argued by Bohne (in chapter 4 of this volume) and above, *ex ante* evaluation badly needs *ex post* evaluation as a resource and quality check. This means that social science methodological

[56] *See* David L. Weimer, 'Institutionalizing Neutrally Competent Policy Analysis: Resources for Promoting Objectivity and Balance in Consolidating Democracies' (2005) 33:2 *Policy Studies Journal*, pp. 131–148.

[57] In the Dutch system for expert advice, all major three government-sponsored think tanks – the Center for Economic Policy Analysis (CPB), the Environmental and Nature Assessment Agency (MNP), and the Social and Cultural Planning Agency (SCP) – reflect these three design elements for independence.

expertise would also have to be part of the interdisciplinary set-up of professional *ex ante* evaluation (as will be elaborated by Van Aeken in the next chapter of this volume). One should be aware, though, that combining these three professional norms in one institute is not at all easy. Efficiency, justice, and scientific truth are not always mutually compatible professional values. Handling interdisciplinary professional conflict and prudence in balancing different professional angles will definitely be required of the leadership of a professional body for *ex ante* evaluation of legislation. Once such professional bodies exist, it may inspire faculties of law, economics and social science to train students with a special view to these job opportunities. Also, with the existence of specialized university training and bodies of independent, professional *ex ante* evaluation, (international) peer review may become an important factor in upholding professional norms and professional standardization in *ex ante* evaluation of legislation.

More than possible for *ex ante* evaluation in executive agencies, *ex ante* evaluation in advisory bodies or quasi-governmental think tanks ought to be transparent for a wide audience. *Ex ante* evaluations ought to be readily accessible to the public, for which internet portals provide excellent opportunities. Generally, *ex ante* evaluation-bodies should follow the practice of publishing proposed rules, invite comments from immediate and hopefully also some not-so-immediate stakeholders, and responding to comments in its final proposals. Especially the Swedish commissions of inquiry show that transparency has its rewards in learning among stakeholders and improved debates in parliament. The expectation of outsiders' scrutiny is a very important incentive for analysts and decision-makers to do a balanced and competent job, and argue their proposals in a comprehensive, fair, and clear way.[58]

Yet, the strategy of improving reflexive governance through creating neutrally competent, independent bodies for *ex ante* evaluation of legislation means creating a separate institutional niche at arm's length of normal practice. Numerous studies have shown that these arrangements suffer from problems of up-take of their analytical outputs in the everyday arenas of politics and policymaking. Therefore, a second strategy may also be considered. It follows from Lindblom's insight that, in politics, analysis is one way of conducting the political battle, but that one may still make the most of it.[59] In other words, instead of aspiring to approximate the sacred ideal of policy analysis in special institutes, one may also stick to the profane world of policy as political struggle over alternative policy

[58] *See* Philip E. Tetlock, 'An alternative metaphor in the study of judgment and choice: people as politicians' in William M. Goldstein and Robin M. Hogarth (eds.), *Research on judgment and decision making. Currents, connections, and controversies* (Cambridge University Press, Cambridge 1997), pp. 657–680.

[59] *See* Lindblom, *supra* note 21, pp. 21–27.

proposals and yet use a number of opportunities to improve *ex ante* evaluation 'from the ground up'.[60]

First, and contrary to the guideline and handbook approach which stresses rules for analytic method (like number of options, ways of quantification, *et cetera*), practitioners of *ex ante* evaluation could pay *more attention to process*. This involves mutually dependent issues like the scope and framing of the *ex ante* evaluation of legislation and which participants to select for what kind of involvement at what stage of the process. Asking such questions automatically generates ideas about who may learn what from whom; and how to integrate such different perspectives. Although high levels of conceptual learning may stay out of reach due to participants' unwillingness (information asymmetries) or sheer inability to transcend their own narrow self-interests, at least the odds for true policy-oriented learning are better than in purely administrative, expert and method-driven *ex ante* evaluation inside executive agencies or departments. Second, also in contrast to the technical emphasis in guidelines and handbooks on the importance of ideals of completeness and quantitative measurement issues, *ex ante* evaluation-analysts should be less wary of incomplete data and dare *rely on grounded, qualitative datasets*.[61] Meaningful policy research is not restricted to positivistic cost-benefit or cost-effectiveness analysis on which most *ex ante* evaluation is modeled. Third, and this is equally applicable to the alternative strategy discussed above, *ex ante* evaluation-analysts should not think of themselves as having a monopoly on 'expertise'. This hardly helps them to safely navigate the deep waters of the relationship between science, policy, and politics. It is much more productive to *think of themselves as 'boundary workers'*: people who know how to bridge the sometimes yawning gaps between science and political practice by both demarcating and coordinating these different institutional spheres in a creative division of labour.[62] Paying more attention to process, framing *ex ante* evaluation of legislation less positivistically, and defining it as boundary work, practitioners of *ex ante* evaluation could start doing a more reflexive job in the nooks and crannies of the normal world of bureaucratic politics.

However, perhaps the most important contribution to more reflexive governance can be made by sustained serious reflection on the relationship between the domain of law and the domain of public policy. Both in political and administrative practice and the academic discourses on public administration and political science, legal rationality is distinguished from professional/scientific, economic

[60] *See* Hertin, *supra* note 23, pp. 20–21.

[61] *See* Ray C. Rist, 'Influencing the Policy Process With Qualitative Research' in Norman K. Denzin, and Yvonna S. Lincoln (eds.), *Handbook of Qualitative Research* (SAGE, Thousand Oaks 1994), pp. 545–557.

[62] *See* Willem Halffman, *Boundaries of Regulatory Science* (Albatros, Boechout 2003).

and political rationality.[63] Legal rationality comprises all the requirements for confidence in the law: equality before the law, legal security, and protection (of citizens) against arbitrary (government) action. Economic rationality calculates the attainment of a maximum positive difference between benefits and costs, derived from the efficiency principle in perfect markets. Professional/scientific rationality aims at valid (theoretically related) statements of cause-effect knowledge of specific subject areas, which plays an informative and/or critical role in the policy practices in specific sectors of society. Political rationality, finally, sees to power maintenance for one's favorite collectivity; or, more broadly, it is the preservation of a sufficient amount of effective and/or symbolic problem processing capacity, and willingness to cooperate to this end, in a political system. The four rationalities in politics and policy may be considered as autonomous domains of discourse and practice in permanent boundary struggles. Each domain attempts to capture parts of the other domains by claiming the role of super-rationality overriding the other types. What is striking in the literature and practice of *ex ante* evaluation of legislation is the legal profession's naïveté about social scientific methodology; and its willingness to unreflexively sacrifice its substantively rational function of normative constraint for the sake of the other types of rationality in the politico-administrative system. This aligns well with a macro-political trend of the retreat of the legislator and the professional trend in public administration and policy analysis to consider rules, decrees and laws as just one possible, convenient instrument in the governmental toolkit.[64] However, in this toolkit-view of rules the legal acceptability of government actions is left undiscussed. (Public) law is supposed to serve a double function: both enabling legitimate government, and protect citizens from arbitrary action. To the extent prudent coping with ambivalences and ambiguities is political wisdom, keeping alive this continuous balancing between the functions of 'sword' and 'shield' of (public) law is the legal profession's most crucial contribution to reflexive governance. Applied to *ex ante* evaluation of legislation, it means it is high time for development of a Standard Benefit Model of legislation and rule-making for the present knowledge society.

---

[63] *See* Ignace Th.M. Snellen, 'Conciliation of Rationalities' (2002) 24:2 *Administrative Theory & Praxis*, pp. 323–346.

[64] *See* Christopher Hood, *supra* note 28.

Chapter 6

Pushing Evaluation Forward. Institutionalization as a Means to Foster Methodological Growth of Legislative *Ex Ante* Evaluation

Koen Van Aeken

I. *Problem Framing*

The aspiration of *ex ante* legislative evaluation is deceivingly simple: it aims at predicting snippets of the future. While this ambition is shared and understood by all people, from the farmer setting a date to harvest depending on weather estimates to the parents speculating about their daughter getting married to the right man, pursuing the means to realize this aspiration in a more systematic fashion tends to be of a very different nature. In early history, leaders relied on irrational and commonly religiously inspired rituals to unveil the future, maybe best represented through the consulting of the legendary prophetic figures of the Delphi Oracle, such as the priestess Pythia, Apollo's daughter.[1] Following the process of rationalization,[2] present day leaders and governmental administrations – as well as auditors, CEOs, experts, high ranking officials and many more –, are now scrutinizing the future in a much more rational way. In order to reduce arbitrariness and uncertainty related to the process of identifying the future consequences of current or proposed actions,[3] numerous methods and

---

[1] Menelaos Stephanides, *The Gods of Olympus*, translated by Bruce Walter, with drawings by Yannis Stephanides (Sigma, Athens 1997).

[2] Max Weber, *Die protestantische Ethik und der 'Geist' des Kapitalismus* (Scribner, Berlin 1934).

[3] *See* the definition of impact assessment by Henk A. Becker, 'Social Impact Assessment' (2001) 128 *European Journal of Operational Research*, p. 311. Becker defines IA as "the process of identifying the future consequences of current or proposed action".

techniques have seen the light, with consultation undisputedly ranking number one in terms of its popularity. Consultation is indeed so common that it is often overlooked as a form of *ex ante* evaluation.[4] It is without any doubt the oldest of the *ex ante* evaluation methods, since one of its simplest forms requires not much more than a conversation between some people. Indeed, the consulting of the priestess at Delphi could be regarded as a primitive form of *ex ante* evaluation. Rationalization, however, restyled the consultation process dramatically, thereby affecting, not in the least, the choice of persons whose advice was sought. Logical reasoning and exchange of knowledge gradually became regarded as essential features of the consultation process, leaving rites and rituals behind.

With the gradual advancement of positive-scientific reasoning and an increasing interest in planning complex industrial activities and affairs of the state, domains such as policy sciences and decision sciences emerged, bringing along techniques such as scenario analysis.[5] The advent of computer sciences caused a new revolution, making ever more intricate numerical methods accessible.

---

[4] Since the focus of this book is clearly defined as *ex ante* evaluation, discussions regarding methodology do not embrace methods and techniques restricted to *ex post* evaluations. Two remarks are at place here. First, I am a strong defender of the opinion (shared by others in this book), that good evaluation policy includes both *ex ante* and ex post evaluation. Integral evaluation, as I like to call it, forces the lawmaker to act prudently and carefully, requiring him to look back on the steps taken, so that the legislative equation takes into account both the external powers that can be foreseen and the factors that cannot be. Indeed, since *ex ante* evaluation is an attempt to guess what the future holds, it is by definition an imperfect attempt. Because of its true empirical nature (the effects of the law in question have been witnessed), *ex post* evaluation then helps to fill in the blanks and corrects the mistakes made earlier. This output can feed new *ex ante* research, thus bridging parts of the cycle of the elaboration of legislation. *See infra* and the contribution of Popelier and Verlinden to this volume, who emphasize the importance of the application of both *ex ante* and *ex post* evaluation. Yet all in all, the demarcation of the scope of interest of this book to prospective evaluation is a gentle sacrifice compared to the gain in topical purity and scientific exactness.

[5] *See* Liam Fahey and Robert M. Randall (eds.), *Learning from the Future: Competitive Foresight Scenarios* (Wiley, New York 1998). It is recommended as a well-organized anthology focusing on the practical application of scenario planning including war stories and clever insights. Each chapter is written by expert scenario practitioners. *See also* Robert E. Linneman and John D. Kennell, 'Shirt-sleeve approach to long-range plans' (2007) 55:2 *Harvard Business Review*, p. 141.

Micro simulation[6] or advanced time series analysis[7] became manageable tools due to cheap computing power. The build up of techniques over the years had some important effect: an ever growing variety of research contexts, data formats and research questions could now be tackled by the evaluator. This evolution has left its marks on the current state of affairs with regard to evaluation. Not only are evaluators confronted with ever more complex and challenging research contexts, but also, the expectations of the policy makers have risen sharply over the years. In nations with a well developed evaluation culture, policy makers, governmental departments and legislators now publish tenders describing in detail what kind of impact assessment they require, not afraid to set the standards to a very high level.[8]

In fact, with so much talk going on about the merits of *ex ante* evaluation and impact assessment, these 'great expectations' shouldn't come as a surprise. The direct impact thereof on evaluators is not to be underestimated: the evaluator should possess the skills to apply impact assessment in difficult contexts and should be familiar with the best method to tackle difficult evaluation questions. This holds for policy evaluation as well as legislative evaluation. It is the latter

[6] I enjoyed a first hand experience with micro simulation, reported in Koen Van Aeken, *Proeven van wetsevaluatie. Een empirisch geïllustreerde studie naar het hoe, wat en waarom van wetsevaluatie. Doctoral dissertation*, Chapter 5, 'Een evaluatie van de TIL' (University of Antwerp, Antwerp 2002), pp. 249–348. A good internet source is <www.microsimulation.org>. There is even a journal exclusively devoted to microsimulation: *The International Journal of Microsimulation*, of which the first volume was published in autumn 2007. A typical microsimulation exercise is included in the very first edition, namely Gijs J.M. Dekkers, 'The Financial Implications of Working Longer: An Application of a Micro-Economic Model of Retirement in Belgium' (2007) 1:1 *International Journal of Microsimulation*, pp. 10–25.

[7] Responsible for the popularization of time series analysis were George Box and Gwilym Jenkins, two engineers working on signal processing. Their models, of which ARIMA is best known, have inspired countless statistical analyses of larger number of data recorded at fixed time intervals – daily, weekly, monthly, yearly – allowing to make controlled estimates of future evolutions of the time series. Although this technique requires much technical skills and mathematical insight, it enjoys a fair share of popularity within the evaluation community, since it offers outstanding analysis potential of the typical (monthly) time series that are recorded by various administrations. In particular, it is a valuable tool to assess the impact of laws on variables (indicators) of which the values are systematically recorded and collected by governmental institutions. *See* for instance Sidsel Sverdrup, 'Towards an Evaluation of the Effects of Laws Utilizing Time-series Data of Complaints' (2003) 9:3 *Evaluation*, pp. 325–339.

[8] U.S. Congress even implemented federal legislation stating that evaluation research in the domain of education should live up to the highest standards in research design and statistical analysis, incorporating only models that allow for causal inference. A. Ginsburg and N. Rhett, 'Building a better body of evidence: new opportunities to strengthen evaluation utilization' (2003) 24:4 *American Journal of Evaluation*, p. 489.

topic that is investigated in this contribution, be it that there is a massive overlap between the two, due to the instrumental nature of legislation in the welfare state. Indeed, policy initiatives are commonly translated into legal rules and programmes, implying that the body of policy evaluation techniques is equally useful for legislative evaluation.[9]

Yet daily practice in the governmental departments of the Low Countries shows a somewhat different picture. Systematic empirical findings in the Dutch departments – gathered on the occasion of an empirical investigation into the nature of consultation processes supporting the elaboration of concept proposals for legislation – and proof from Belgian and Flemish governmental administrations indicate that just a limited number of techniques is applied in the bulk of evaluations and regulatory impact assessments. Moreover, the most common type of *ex ante* evaluation, consultation, is methodologically flawed in its implementation.

Methodologically less challenging approaches, like simple, written consultations, are much more in vogue than such techniques requiring knowledge of somewhat more advanced methods. This also holds for their intentions: the greater part of the Dutch respondents from the sample used in the research project mentioned above was reluctant to try new techniques. Their motivation to stick with familiar consultation processes was simple yet effective: they declared to be happy with the current state of affairs and felt no need for improvement, convinced that they did a good job.

The decision to apply a certain method or technique should be positively inspired by the features of the context of the evaluation and should not be negatively oriented by the restrictions to the set of techniques known to the evaluator. The method should fit the data, not (just) the evaluator. From a more general point of view, I firmly believe that legislation should benefit from the advancement in the field of evaluation sciences, not so because of the mere existence of various techniques, but because the intrinsic nature of legislation in the welfare state calls for much carefulness and prudence in designing legal rules. Likewise, the ability to employ the best suited technique in a sound way is a *conditio sine*

[9] Attributing an instrumentalist character to legislation in the modern state calls for resistance by quite a few legal scholars. However, when dealing with impact and effectivity, the formal appearance of the 'current or proposed actions' (as described *infra* in the definition of impact assessment) is of little concern for the methodologist. Evaluation of legal rules expands the scope of research questions with a legal one, inquiring into the juridical characteristics of the law-to-be, but the methodological fundamentals stay the same, whether the evaluation concerns programmes, laws or policies. Consequently, I do not distinguish between different formal aspects of different types of legal dispositions; the term 'law' is used in a very generic sense, and is synonymous to legal rules, regulation, legal interventions and so on.

qua non in order to develop *ex ante* evaluation towards its full potential, thus contributing to the overall quality of the legislation concerned. The relationship between the nature of legislation in the welfare state and evaluation is studied in section II of this contribution. In the following section (III), I suggest a tentative classification of methods and techniques, built upon a divide into two families, namely consultation and computation. Grounded on empirical findings in governmental departments in the Netherlands and Belgium, some important conclusions are drawn with regard to the characteristics of the application of these two families, such as asymmetrical use and resistance to innovation. Subsequently, I argue why this situation is undesirable. Section IV seeks to explain this situation, paving the road for a remedy which will be presented in section V. In that penultimate section, I promote the institutionalization of evaluation as a way to enhance the sound use of both consultation and computation in legislative *ex ante* evaluation. The embedding of evaluation in an organizational framework and other actions related to the process of institutionalization will not only tackle many of the methodological challenges, but offer additional advantages as well. Section VI concludes this contribution with a concise summary.

II. *Tackling the Challenges of Instrumental Legislation by Means of Evaluation*

A first question that pops up is: "Why should an evaluator be armed with advanced knowledge of research design, research methods and statistical techniques?" Answering this question begins with the search for the fundamental meaning of legislative evaluation. Evaluation studies can start from a number of basic central research questions, like assessing the efficiency, the effects, the impact, the social adequacy, the validity of the underlying policy theory, or the juridical correctness. However, researching the impact is the most fundamental and most common aim.[10] The quintessential rationale of impact studies is well expressed by that classic *motto* of the sociology of law:[11] 'law in action, law in the books'. Prospective evaluations allow us to gain some insight in the possible effects of rules-in-the-making, departing from the condition that the well-directed

[10] Note the following difference between effects and impact: the effects relate to the goals set forward by the legislator, whereas impact concerns all the effects generated by the law. As such, impact studies have the broadest scope. *See, e.g.*, Luzius Mader, *L'évaluation législative. Pour une analyse empirique des effets de la legislation* (Payot, Lausanne 1985) as well as Koen Van Aeken, *Proeven van wetsevaluatie. Een empirisch geïllustreerde studie naar het hoe, wat en waarom van wetsevaluatie. Doctoral dissertation* (University of Antwerp, Antwerp 2002), pp. 105–111.

[11] The phrase is attributed to Roscoe Pound.

intentions of the law-maker are often led astray by psychological, societal, cultural, economic and other non-juridical factors. With a good research design, the evaluator might be able to determine occurrence and amplitude of such events, which in turn will enable her of him to estimate the impact of these events on the projected regulating activities. As simple as it sounds, as difficult it is to carry out. It is, to start with, extremely difficult to determine which events will take place in the future. Next, calculating the effect of these events on the legislative project requires much effort and skill. This is furthermore complicated by the rise of multiple interaction effects between all of the events involved. Apart from the construction of a research design, a fair share of knowledge of socio-legal theory is necessary to comprehend the future evolutions.

Forecasting the future is undoubtedly one of the most intriguing challenges in science and far beyond. In ancient times, one visited the mythological oracle of Delphi in the hope of hearing Apollo's predictions through the Pythia, a priestess; in our days, in which scientific reasoning has forced irrationality to step aside, the priestess has been replaced by a panel of independent experts from whom one wishes to obtain forecasts in systematic interaction. The means may be different, but the end remains the same.

Predicting the effects of laws has always been an important topic in the socio-legal sciences. A main research goal has long been the quest for the identification of variables which could support or hinder the functioning of the law. If these variables could be detected and isolated, their future values could be filled in and the outcome would tell something about the effect of the law at stake. Many theories have been developed in this respect. Best known is probably the empirical study by the Norwegian scholar Vilhelm Aubert[12] (around 1950) on the working conditions of house personnel in his country. He presented a number of variables that could explain the terrible compliance hence low effectivity. An important factor was the lack of familiarity with the law in question. After Aubert, the explanatory scope of such attempts to explain the effectivity of laws in a systematic way was enlarged, *e.g.* by Rottleuthner[13] following Opp, who describes the effect of a law as a function of a number of variables, including the perceived authority of the rule giver, the perceived gains or losses in case of respectively compliance or breaching and so on. These schemes and likewise undertakings were however discredited by some as being too instrumental.

[12] Vilhelm Aubert, 'Enkele sociale functies van wetgeving' in Peper, B. and Schuyt, K. (eds.), *Proeven van rechtssociologie uit het werk van Vilhelm Aubert* (Standaard Wetenschappelijke Uitgeverij, Antwerpen 1971 orig. 1950), pp. 46–74.

[13] Hubert Rottleuthner, *Einführung in die Rechtssoziologie* (Wissenschaftliche Buchgesellschaft, Darmstadt 1987).

In 1975, John Griffiths[14] wrote a pioneering article in which he proposed to look at the *social working* of the law. He started from the observation that effectivity research almost invariably led to the conclusion that the law did not have the intended effects. In explaining the gap between intentions and outcomes, a number of factors can be distinguished. First, the lawmaker is not a normative monistic and homogenic instance, but rather one instance among many other rule generating entities, which is moreover plagued by ideological heterogeneity. Not only are the intentions of the law itself thus often ambiguous, but the law has to compete with many other sources of norms. In a seminal article, legal anthropologist Sally Moore defines 'semi-autonomous social fields' (SASV) as social groups with norm constructing abilities and sanctioning capacities.[15] Disregarding their level of organization, these fields can hinder (or support) the law to reach its goals. The different groups of employees in a hospital offer fine examples of a SASV; the nurses, e.g., create 'informal' rules that may deviate from the legally prescribed norms, *i.e.* state law but equally the rules of the hospital itself. Seen from the other side, the government may be unsuccessful in implementing new rules regarding, let's say, a cutback in the duration of coffee breaks, if the nurses themselves do not comply. The nurses have effective social means of enforcing their informal rules; if a colleague tries to break free from the informal regulations and wishes to adhere to the government's law, she might be severely punished. The SASV has not the power to put a nurse behind bars, but they can impose equally cruel social sanctions, such as isolating her from normal human interaction.

Griffiths points to more elements on the 'social working floor' which can render a law successful or unsuccessful, and may thus be helpful in understanding why evaluation is essential.[16] The second important cluster of factors deals with the norm addressees. The instrumental approach presumes that people are atomistic, rational individuals who interpret the law as intended by the lawmaker. In reality, people cling together, like atoms do in molecules, and their behaviour is far from rational at times. Moreover, they interpret the law often in their advantage. Peoples' behaviour as 'social animals' offers thus another partial explanation for the difference between the law in the books and the law in action.

Still another approach involves the psychology of man. In short, values matter. People are more likely to obey the law if they perceive the law as more legitimate. Furthermore, compliance is more easily obtained when the rules accord

---

[14] John Griffiths, 'Is law important?' (1975) 54 *New York University Law Review*, pp. 339–375.

[15] Sally F. Moore, 'Law and Social Change: The Semi-Autonomous Social Field as an Appropriate Subject of Study' (1973) 7:4 *Law & Society Review*, pp. 719–746.

[16] John Griffiths, 'De Sociale Werking van Recht' in Griffiths, J. (ed.), *Een kennismaking met de rechtssociologie en de rechtsantropologie* (Ars Aequi Libri, Nijmegen 1996), p. 469.

with their personal views on what is right or wrong.[17] While this may sound self-evident, it is a factor that is often ignored by law-makers since they regularly lack the knowledge about the values and beliefs system of the norm addressees. This situation typically occurs when the law at stake targets minority groups that hold on to values and convictions that deviate from the legislator's beliefs system. The same reasoning is applicable to legislation targeted to the majority as well, since the political elite presupposes that their values are shared by all. So, values, beliefs and attitudes construe another set of elements with explanatory power regarding the success or failure of legislative action.

Summarizing these studies, numerous societal, psychological, social-psychological and other factors break the simple causality chain that emanated in the minds and behind the desks of the lawmakers. Estimating the role and amplitude of the potential unfavourable or beneficial effects of all these intermediate factors on the functioning of the law thus becomes a concern of the evaluator. Fortunately, evaluators are not alone in this; they can rely on machines and humans to help them with their difficult tasks. All in all, estimating the future – to which *ex ante* evaluation essentially boils down – is a task of a gargantuan complexity. With so many intervening variables and possible outcomes, often radically different from the intended goals, much prudence is required when developing regulation. Fortunately, scholars, civil servants, policy makers *e.a.* can rely on an ever expanding body of knowledge regarding the effects of laws in real life, drawing from a wide range of resources. From an analytical stance, these sources could be labeled as practical, theoretical or methodological.

The first area of knowledge consists as such of insider insights – practical experiences lived and recorded by those involved in the ongoing planning, producing and implementing of legislation, which come in handy when elaborating new legislation. This is the most common source of knowledge within the administration. Next, theoretical insights are derived from disciplines such as sociology, psychology, political sciences, legal sciences, history, medical studies – or just about any field in which legal action can be planned. The public health system could hardly be developed without profound theoretical medical knowledge, just as reworking the fishery laws would be insane without general theoretical knowledge about the relationship between the fish stock and human intrusion. Theories, of course, are less convenient for the civil servant engaged in evaluation than the practical lessons learnt from colleagues, stakeholders and legislators. They often require careful study and pose considerable challenges when they are to be applied to a concrete situation, but are invaluable in pres-

[17] Tom R. Tyler, *Psychology and the design of legal institutions* (Wolf Legal Publishers, Nijmegen 2007), p. 6.

ent day programming of policy and legislation.[18] In fact, the evaluation of the underlying theory of policy, programs or regulation is as essential an evaluation research objective as impact, effectivity or efficiency are, as becomes manifest when browsing through educational basic texts on evaluation.[19] Thirdly, there exist various ways to treat existing findings and experiences (from the first and second sources) in a systematic way, and to handle purpose-collected data related to the laws-in-concept in an orderly fashion, allowing for in-depth statistical applications. This tandem of systematic data collection and analysis is the third resource exploitable by evaluators and is throughout this text referred to as methodology.

In practice, the use of theory often coincidences with the use of methods and techniques; to study the probable impact of liberating fishery regulation, e.g., data regarding the evolution of fish-stock are fitted into theoretical models describing these evolution in relationship to a range of variables. Seen from a reverse perspective, this means also that theory is lifeless without data; lawmakers are indifferent to a general theory, until the theory has been applied and can be understood in terms of real life effects, preferably expressed in numbers or simple interpretations thereof. As such, knowledge facilitating the elaboration of legislation through assessment of possible or probable impacts can be broken down into just two categories: the practical information transfer or exchange[20] between the lawmaker and the stakeholders on the one hand, and the theoretical-methodological knowledge useful for technical analysis on the other hand. I call the first category consultation, whereas the second category receives the name computation. These concepts are dubbed sometimes as stakeholder engagement and technical analysis. Both sets of terms serve their differentiating purpose well. Intuitively, it is clear that stakeholders' involvement and technicality stand worlds apart, a gap that is likewise expressed by the dichotomy consultation – computation. The following section explores this divide in a more systematic fashion.

18 P.H. Rossi, H.E. Freeman, M.W. Lipsey, *Evaluation. A systematic approach*, 7th edition (Sage Thousand Oaks 2004). Interestingly, the chapter on theory has become more voluminous and detailed compared to the previous edition of this well-known handbook. *See* also section V of this contribution.

19 *Ibid.*, p. 155.

20 Transfer is unidirectional by nature, implying that stakeholders are not involved; exchange, the two-way communication, is therefore to be preferred.

III. *Consultative versus Computational Methods*

A. *A Rough Taxonomy*

The phrasing above in terms of a dichotomy is not aimed *per se* at developing a strict classification of available methods and techniques. Rather, I suggest this particular distinction with a clear purpose: it facilitates an evaluation of the methodology of legislative evaluation. Expressed in somewhat more operational terms, this means that the (super simple) taxonomy presented here is useful to detect flaws, shortcomings or absence of evaluative methods in governmental departments. Remember that the very nature of legislation in the welfare state is the true motive for initiating evaluative action; legislation is thus intrinsically linked with evaluation; the common complexity of the context in which the future law will operate demands much sophistication from the legislator and his evaluators, a sophistication that must be played on the methodological front especially.

A first category of evaluation tools builds on collaboration of people involved in or affected by the law-to-be, including stakeholders and experts in the field. A formal definition is presented by Popelier *e.a.*: "Consultation refers to procedures in which the administration asks stakeholders and experts external to that very administration, for input regarding the further development of policy or proposed legislation, by means of consultation or advice."[21]

Useful techniques include:

- group interviews
- internet consultations
- citizen panels
- expert panels
- focus groups
- concept mapping
- Delphi-method
- workshop-method

No matter which technique is selected, the basic definition stays valid. The process always revolves around the opinions of people that are connected to the concept proposal of legislation. This implies that the resulting input into the legislative process is more or less subjectively coloured. The very selection of the parties

[21] Patricia Popelier, Rob van Gestel, Koen Van Aeken, Vicky Verlinden and Peter Van Humbeeck, *Consulteren over ontwerp-regelgeving: alibi voor vrijblijvendheid of prikkel tot actie? Een zoektocht naar internationale best practices en een toepassing op de Nederlandse consultatiepraktijk als referentiekader voor Belgische beleidsmakers en Vlaamse RIA-ambtenaren* (Politeia, Brussel in print).

which will be consulted is thus an important element of the procedure, since it sets the level of bias of the information that will be acquired.

A second set consists of methods and techniques that can be employed from behind a desk or a computer, relying on independent data collection and data analysis: the inside views and opinions of stakeholders (and other actors involved) are not taken into account. The terms computation and calculation do not imply a restriction to numerical methods, since both quantitative and qualitative techniques can be used according to the research context,[22] but they refer to the practice by which the evaluator actively processes raw, 'neutral' data. He does not merely obtain information, but uses this information, whereas in consultation the obtained information is subject to the views and convictions of the consulted people or organizations. Working with the data means independently and actively calculating or computing the desired outcomes, giving the advantage of greater objectivity (the 'middle-persons' are left out), accuracy (better alignment between research question and answer) and the possibility to attribute a level of confidence and exactness to the computed results (by using such measures as estimation errors).

In short, the concepts of calculation and computation describe a collection of evaluation methods and techniques that, in contrast with consultation, require active thinking about data collection and analysis, and allow significant autonomy and impartiality towards the stakeholders or administration. The term is most meaningful when positioned directly opposite consultation.[23] By way of illustration, some types are:

- goal attainment scaling
- prospective evaluation synthesis
- cluster analysis
- multi-criteria analysis
- patented techniques, like Metaplan©
- scenario building and -analysis
- simulation
- game theory
- risk assessment
- micro simulation
- modeling

[22] *See infra* for a discussion.

[23] Further research into this field might explore the distinction between stochastic models on the one hand, and models with determined parameters on the other. For a comparison of both types of evaluation models in the actuary business, *see* for instance <www.casact.org/pubs/dpp/dpp95/95dpp151.pdf>.

- time series analysis
- expert systems
- multivariate statistical techniques
- using existing reports, such as annual reports, budget estimates or audits
- extrapolating results from *ex post* evaluations of similar regulation in the past (spatial)
- using *ex ante* evaluations of similar regulation in other regions or countries (cross-sectional)
- experiments and quasi-experiments

Some remarks are definitely at place here. Consulted persons or institutions might base their advice on calculated data, while calculations might be partly based on estimated values, provided by experts in the field. Also, collecting data for *ex ante* evaluations often requires the collaboration of the administration, which might reduce the level of neutrality and impartiality of the evaluation. A third observation is of a more fundamental nature and concerns research paradigms, a topic untouched so far. While it is tempting to connect the dichotomy computation/consultation to the fundamental discussion on research paradigms, thereby linking consultation to the qualitative, post-positivist method and computation to the quantitative, positivist method, it is of no use. Apart from the fact that this discussion does not fit the ambition of this contribution, the seemingly obvious connection is faulty since some of the techniques labeled as computational can be applied as well in the positivist framework as in a post-positivist one. A good example is the discussion within the domain of risk assessment: the risks involved can be quantified by experts or qualified by stakeholders – hence the term 'perception' – resulting in quite different analyses.[24] Nevertheless, the technique is labeled computational. I presented this remark here because my call to include calculative methods in evaluation could wrongfully be understood as yet another indication that the positivist paradigm prevails in evaluation.[25] Indeed, a recurring critique in the specialized literature is that the quantitative methods take the lead with their detached, neutral, disengaged viewpoint, leaving less room for qualitative approaches that attempt to bring the human back into evaluation studies. As I hope it will be clear by now, I do not succumb to the 'domination of numbers'.[26] Instead, I would like to plead for openness, or the ability to choose from quantitative or qualitative methods, and likewise, from

[24] Paul Slovic, 'Perception of Risk' (1987) 236 *Science*, pp. 280–285.

[25] Abdul Khakee, 'The Emerging Gap between Evaluation Research and Practice' (2003) 9:3 *Evaluation*, p. 340.

[26] EEAC Working Group on Governance, *Impact Assessment of European Commission Policies: Achievements And Prospects*, <www.eeac-net.org/download/ EEAC%20WG%20Gov_IA%20statement_final_18-5-06.pdf>, 15 August 2008.

consultation or computation. Just as mixed models[27] are possible (combining quantitative and qualitative elements), evaluation studies containing consultation as well as computation might be very promising.

B. *The Case of the Flemish, Belgian and Dutch Government*

On the occasion of different studies relating to processes of *ex ante* evaluation, it became apparent that the civil servants engaged in legislative evaluation rarely applied methods and techniques outside the sphere of consultation. The analysis of a sample of Flemish RIAs conducted in 2007[28] and a survey among Dutch legislative lawyers[29] held in 2007 all grounded the conclusion that legislative *ex ante* evaluations are based upon weak methodological grounds. Striking facts are the following.

The standard RIA process contains six main steps: objectives, options, effects, implementation characteristics, consultation, information required for IF (Finance Inspectorate), with one of the steps being 'consultation'.[30] In other words, consultation is considered at the same level as the objectives or the options. Consequently, second-order importance is attributed to the method by which the options are calculated and compared. In the empirical study of the sample of RIAs studied, reporting thereof was overall extremely scarce or non-existent, reflecting the lack of a sound methodological basis for the evaluation. This is a first indicator of the one-sidedness of the methodology of impact assessment.

Within the domain of consultation, methodological variety is poor. Four in five consultations take place by addressing the consulted parties in writing, thereby presenting the concept legislation in very general terms and refraining from asking specific advice on the matter. A self-assessment of the frequency of use of seven different techniques on a scale from one (never) to five (always) yielded the following results:

---

[27] Jennifer C. Greene; Lehn Benjamin and Leslie Goodyear, 'The Merits of Mixing Methods in Evaluation' (2001) 7:1 *Evaluation*, pp. 25–44.

[28] The results will be published in Manu Dierickx Visschers and Koen Van Aeken, 'Risico-analyse bij en van regelgeving: de rol van het "risicodenken" in de RIA tot verbetering van de wetgevingskwaliteit', *Tijdschrift voor Wetgeving* (due Winter 2008/2009).

[29] The project was funded by WODC (Ministry of Justice, the Netherlands). *Supra* note 21.

[30] For further information, *see* <www.wetsmatiging.be>, 29 August 2008. Also in English.

Table 1. Methods employed by various departments of the Dutch government.[31]

	Internet consult	Public meetings	Opinion polls	Focus groups	Citizen panels	Specialist Panels	Delphi Method	**Row total**
VROM	1,0	3,0	1,0	4,5	1,0	3,0	1,0	**2,1**
FIN	5,0	4,0	1,3	4,0	1,0	3,7	3,2	**3,2**
LNV	1,0	1,0	1,0	1,0	1,0	1,0	1,0	**1,0**
VENW	1,0	2,0	1,0	1,7	1,0	1,3	1,0	**1,3**
SZW	1,3	3,0	1,5	2,3	2,3	3,0	2,0	**2,2**
EZ	3,0	3,0	–	–	1,0	1,0	2,0	**2,0**
BUZA	4,0	1,0	1,0	1,0	1,0	1,0	1,0	**1,4**
JUS	3,3	2,0	2,0	1,3	1,3	2,7	1,0	**1,9**
OCW	3,0	3,0	2,0	2,0	2,0	3,5	3,0	**2,6**
BZK	2,0	2,0	2,0	2,0	2,5	3,0	1,0	**2,1**
VWS	1,0	1,0	1,0	1,0	1,0	1,0	–	**1,0**
Column total	**2,3**	**2,3**	**1,4**	**2,1**	**1,4**	**2,2**	**1,6**	**1,9**

Source: Patricia Popelier, Rob van Gestel, Koen Van Aeken, Vicky Verlinden and Peter Van Humbeeck, *Consulteren over ontwerp-regelgeving: alibi voor vrijblijvendheid of prikkel tot actie? Een zoektocht naar internationale best practices en een toepassing op de Nederlandse consultatiepraktijk als referentiekader voor Belgische beleidsmakers en Vlaamse RIA-ambtenaren* (Politeia, Brussel, forthcoming).

Most techniques are thus never or very rarely applied in the Dutch departments, with a maximum of just 2,3 for internet consultations as well as public meetings. The use of focus groups features regularly in just two departments, whereas this is otherwise a widespread technique with an optimal balance between difficulty and results. In short, civil servants or legislative lawyers stick with the technique that is most familiar to them, i.e. asking for a written, general advice.

[31] Abbreviations: Ministry of VROM (Housing, Spatial Planning and Environment); FIN (Finance); LNV (Agriculture, Nature Conservation and Food); VENW (Traffic, Public Works and Water Management), SZW (Social Affairs), EZ (Economic Affairs), BUZA (Foreign Affairs), JUS (Justice), OCW (Education, Culture and Science), BZK (Internal Affairs) and VWS (Health, Welfare, Sport).

In Belgium as well as in the Netherlands, attempts to introduce or apply new techniques depend on the interest and goodwill of staff and management. Methodological experimentation is nothing but an isolated phenomenon.

These findings to not only concern the actual application of techniques, but also relate to the intended use of methods and techniques. Throughout the interviews conducted, only a small minority of legislative lawyers expressed a motivation to learn new techniques. In some departments, this motivation was entirely absent.

C. *Extended Methodology, Superior Evaluation*

Considering the need for maximum prudence and carefulness when designing rules and regulation, so that the gap between the desired outcomes and the actual effects is maximally reduced, the disproportionate emphasis on the most basic consultation technique and the relative indifference with regard to computational techniques are reasons for concern. Regulation of many of the more complex issues which contemporary government faces, such as environmental problems, welfare distribution, ageing of the population, labour market evolutions and migration, demands careful scrutiny that is not met by just asking for a written general advice. The limits of consultation's potential are well exceeded in this challenging setting. This does not imply that computational techniques are always required or are superior to consultation, but limiting the toolbox to just one family of techniques is certainly not helping to grasp the complexity of the environment in which the future law will operate. Let's study this in more detail.

An on-line governmental document, primary serving educational needs, provides the following instructive observation on predicting: "When we deal with the future, uncertainty is part of any analysis, no matter how sound, but the more precisely we state the degree of uncertainty, the more complete, and the more useful, our prediction will be. Saying "We are 95-percent confident that the number of competitively awarded contracts will increase by between 10,000 and 15,000 for each of the next 4 years" provides more precise information to a decision maker about likelihood than does the statement "More contracts will be awarded competitively in the future."[32]

This example illustrates an importance feature of numerical methods, namely the ability to express levels of uncertainty – and, conversely, confidence – regarding the impact assessment. This is especially relevant since *ex ante* evaluations deal with the future, uncertainty's favourite playground. Yet the use of numbers

[32] United States General Accounting Office, *Prospective Evaluation Methods*, p. 30, <www.gao.gov/special.pubs/10_1_10.PDF>, 1 July 2008.

in se surely does not offer a guarantee for scientifically sound prospective evaluations. Many forms of erratic or even malignous use of figures and statistics thrive. By way of illustration, I point out one typical form of the inappropriate use of numbers, related to the widespread use of mean scores to assess impact.[33] Consider the following real life example: the median household income for the US in 1996 was reported to have increased 1.2 per cent over the previous year. Yet this median percentage conceals the fact that the income of the 20 per cent richest inhabitants improved with 2.2 per cent, while the poorest two deciles were confronted with a *decrease* of 1.8 per cent. Caution should thus be exercised when applying numerical methods – in this case, the use of a frequency distribution would immediately unveil the misleading interpretation resulting from the use of mean scores. The mastering of a somewhat wider array of techniques thus allows for superior insight and understanding and consequently, better-quality evaluations.[34] This is true within the family of quantitative techniques, but also holds with extension to the collection of qualitative techniques, which constitute an integral part of the computational techniques. As discussed earlier, whereas the denominator 'calculation' or 'computation' might suggest the supremacy of numerical methods, the use of techniques based upon the qualitative paradigm, or even the mixed use of quantitative and qualitative methods are now fully accepted.

The ability to choose from a multitude of methods and techniques, whether quantitative or qualitative, whether consultational or computational, allows the evaluator to improve a number of characteristics of *ex ante* evaluation. The prediction becomes more accurate, more complete and less subjective, while at the same time likelihood estimates can be provided. Still, there is more to it. Extending the range of techniques offers possibilities to deepen the 'ontological' meaning of the information at hand. Let me explain. On one occasion, I contributed to a survey on the implementation of risk analysis/risk assessment tools in RIA-operations.[35] Hence, some 30 RIA reports were analyzed starting from the question whether any form of risk analysis was employed. The modest research showed saddening results. In the studied sample of Flemish (mandatory) regulatory impact analyses, just one of the methodologies utilized referred to risk. In other words, an alternative way of looking at information was completely lost, just because the Flemish administration was not familiar with the methodology. Indeed, since regulation is intrinsically linked to risk – risks the rules may cause or, conversely, risks of which the effects might be reversed by the planned regulation – this was a missed opportunity to mine the data

---

33 Burt Perrin, 'How to – and how not to – Evaluate Innovation' (2002) 8:1 *Evaluation*, p. 16.

34 Or allows the reader to protect himself from misleading calculations.

35 *Supra* note 28.

for implicit but probably valid information that could hardly be identified in a traditional consultation process.

With the arguments outlined above, I hope to illustrate that computational methods not only contribute to a higher accuracy, validity and confidence of the data, but in addition grant a much broader research potentiality to the data that are at the evaluator's disposal. Risk assessment is but one of the many computational methods – a quick glimpse at the shortlists above makes clear how large a potential is lost when evaluators stick to techniques they are familiar with since the early days of the rationalization of policy and government. The next challenge is now to explain this situation.

IV. *A Methodologically Challenged Administration*

If the merits of extended methodological knowledge can be easily summarized, why do the administrations involved still stick to the simplest forms of consultation as the legislative evaluation tool *par excellence*? Section IV attempts to provide some answers which will later be helpful in designing a solution.

Numerous explanations compete, many of them related, so that the final answer is far from clear cut. The answers become even more entangled since I make an effort to provide a universal answer, that is, not limited to the Netherlands and Belgium. I will nevertheless try to present the main factors in an orderly fashion, drawing from my own research as well as the international literature addressing this question, typically provided by the international evaluation community.

A. *Political Salience of Evaluation in General*

A first element is undoubtedly the political salience of evaluation in general. Elsewhere, I address this question in more detail.[36] For now, I sketch the main outline of this argument.

Much talk is going on about evaluation *ex ante* and *ex post* these days – commonly referred to as Regulatory Impact Assessment (RIA) and Regulatory Impact Evaluation (RIE), since these assessments are now commonly regarded as excellent or even indispensable means to improve the quality of regulation. The stakes are high: spiraling globalization and the extent of the free market require individual nations to 'clean up' their 'legislative act' in order to stay ahead of the competition. The flux of migrants, the advent of new industrial and financial technologies, the movements of money markets, intercultural exchange and

[36] Forthcoming: Koen Van Aeken, 'Het primaat van de politiek. Een eenvoudige reactie op het preadvies "Impact Assessment als onderdeel van een 'gemeenschappelijke wetgevingscultuur' in Europa" door Anne Meuwese' (Academie voor Wetgeving, Den Haag 2008).

many other phenomena pose serious challenges to the state. This challenge is even more prominent for the Western democracies which have to regulate the gigantic redistribution system that is at the core of the welfare state. Against this background, the quality of legislation – still the favourite instrument to translate policy into reality[37] – is more important than ever. Hence the keen interest in all things evaluative. Yet, strangely enough, much of this political interest is just lip service.[38] While evaluation of legislation has acquired more political salience than ever – and certainly so in Belgium where evaluation was practically unheard of prior to 1998 or so – support, in budgetary and organizational terms, stays at a remarkably low level.

A plausible explanation is that evaluation research does not promise quick and easy landmark victories for politicians. The (positive) results of a well conceived law take about two years to show, since it takes on average two years for the law to obtain 'cruise speed', the level of sufficient implementation that is needed for the law to demonstrate its actual impact. By that time, chances are real that a new government has already been installed as a result of the elections that take place every four years so that the responsible politicians do not enjoy the success they deserve.[39] Conversely, badly designed pieces of legislation might be quickly enforced at the end of the four-yearly legislature, the lawmaker not bothering at all about the real impact, since he will have cleared the political arena by the time cruise speed has been reached by that law.

In short, the system of four-yearly legislatures is not favourable towards careful social engineering and, more specifically, *ex ante* legislative evaluation. With state budgets eternally soaring, it comes as no surprise that individual politicians prefer spending money on short term projects that carry their signature, instead of allocating the scarce resources to a policy domain that is as exotic to the average citizen as it is ungrateful to the politician, namely the evaluation of legislation.

The explanatory power of the following argument is probably much greater than the one of the factor described above. Much of the efforts in the field of better legislation have been 'hijacked' by the movement lobbying for reduction of regulatory burdens and the simplification of administration. I like to illustrate this trend by referring to a simple but meaningful change of names that happened in Belgium: the 'Knowledge Center for Regulatory Management' (*Kenniscel*

---

[37] Koen Van Aeken, 'Legal Instrumentalism Revisited' in L. Wintgens (ed.), *The Theory and Practice of Legislation: Essays in Legisprudence* (Ashgate, Aldershot 2006), pp. 67–92. According to the instrumentalists – which are, still, the majority of law-makers.

[38] Koen Van Aeken, 'Wetsevaluatie tussen droom en daad' (2003) 3 *Tijdschrift voor wetgeving*, pp. 31–37.

[39] *See* also Marleen Brans, Pedro Facon and Dieter Hoet, *Beleidsvoorbereiding in een lerende overheid. Stand van zaken en uitdagingen voor de Belgische federale overheid* (Academia Press, Gent 2003).

Reguleringsmanagent) was rebaptised as the 'Knowledge Center for Legislative Moderation' (*Kenniscel Wetsmatiging*). Much of the resources originally devoted to better regulation have been reallocated to the war against regulatory burdens and the quest for administrative simplification. This shift in attention has multiple causes, the most important being the neoliberal paradigm that inspired a great part of the governing political circles. Neoliberalism prescribes the 'reduction of the state', a process that according to some is best operationalized by reducing the volume of the state's legislation. In fact, one could talk about a new deregulation movement, targeted at the worst legislation. While this is *in se* not a bad thing, it unfortunately correlates with less attention for the question of the *quality* of regulation. Another cause for the shifted attention is the popularity of legislative action which reduces the administrative burdens faced by citizens and companies. By contributing to the reduction of red tape, politicians hope to see themselves rewarded in the ballot box.[40]

A third reason within the political sphere has to do with the background of the political elite. Very often, they are trained lawyers. Parliament counts a disproportionate number of law graduates in its ranks. Since the curriculum[41] of law studies in most civil law countries lacks methodological training, the legislators are not familiar with this kind of reasoning and consequently they feel unsure about funding evaluation initiatives. A side-effect of the dominance of law degrees in political circles in Belgium is that much legislative evaluation is reduced to assessments of juridical aspects of regulation.[42]

All in all, the political class – and thus the legislator – has little interest in evaluation due to a number of causes. This directly affects the position of legislative evaluation in the administration. First, due to the lack of interest and the intense rivalry between policy domains, budgets are severely limited. There is little money available for a variety of things, such as buying or updating software tools, attending courses or seminars, planning interregional or international meetings, and, especially, hiring well-trained personnel or having qualified personnel working on evaluation assignments. Second, structural initiatives with regard to the organizational framework are impossible without support from the political elite. This also includes granting or facilitating access to administrative data, setting up organizations, coordinating activities and more. Thirdly, political

---

[40] Reduction of administrative burdens has short term effects that are often immediately noticeable; as such, the legislator has not to fear that his accomplishments will be annexed by the next government installed.

[41] The situation in Belgium is described in Francis Van Loon and Koen Van Aeken, 'Legal education in Belgium' (2003) 2 *The Takada Law Review*, pp. 1–21.

[42] Koen Van Aeken, 'Wetsevaluatie: intenties en uitdagingen op het niveau van Kamer en Senaat' (2006/2007) 3–648/4 *Handelingen Belgische Senaat*, p. 104.

involvement is essential when contacting certain stakeholders[43] or when trying to avoid inappropriate use of evaluations.[44] The lack of political goodwill is a powerful explanation for the methodological restraints to evaluation research in Belgium and the Netherlands. It is, however, not a justification; not only the political class is to blame. What follows is a concise review of other causes.

B. *The Characteristics of Law-making*

Reliable legislative *ex ante* evaluation demands time. Not only need the data to be collected, the analysis thereof might take up more time than expected and organizing meetings with stakeholders and experts can be a time consuming process. These activities take place under a considerable time pressure, since the coming into being of a law counts many stages of which evaluation is just one – and certainly not the most important one. This time pressure poses serious problems, mostly because it renders it impossible to collect and analyze sufficient and high quality data necessary for a prospective evaluation.[45]

Moreover, the *ex ante* evaluation should take place as early as possible in the policy cycle. If the evaluation comes too late, the possible impact of the evaluation is reduced to zero, since the political-legal machinery has been set in motion and very little can be undertaken to stop it. Likewise, the null-option (jargon for the legislator refraining from taking any action) is only meaningful on the condition that the evaluation takes place in the embryonic stadium of the conceptual legislation. Any subsequent evaluative activity is mere lip service.

The fact that time is a scarce good in the lawmaking process has a number of consequences for *ex ante* evaluations. First, some actors in the political arena resist systematic evaluation since they fear it will only increase time pressure, resulting in even more half-hearted law-making. This off-putting attitude is, of course, not favourable to the development of evaluation *ex ante* in general and, consequently, to the expansion of the in-house knowledge regarding methodology. Second, clever politicians have discovered a strategic function of *ex ante* evaluations. By imposing the obligation to conduct an *ex ante* evaluation on a particular piece of legislation, they are able to postpone the political decision

---

[43] *See e.g.* M. Bamberger, J. Rugh and L. Mabry, *Real world evaluation* (Sage, New York 2006), pp. 373–376.

[44] There are various questionable types of evaluation. Lewis summarizes as follows: eyewash evaluations, focusing on surface appearances; whitewash, covering up legislative or programme failure; submarine evaluations, used to undermine a programme or law of the opposition; posture, the ritual use of evaluation without any policy intentions and postponement, hijacking evaluation to avoid or postpone action. Lewis, J. 'Reflections on evaluation in practice' (2001) 7:3 *Evaluation*, p. 391.

[45] M. Brans, P. Facon, and D. Hoet, *supra* note 39.

making process without this being obvious. Postponement,[46] as it is called in jargon, is a common type of the inappropriate use of evaluations that discredits evaluation as a whole.

C. *Competences of the Civil Servants*

Up to now, the main culprit for methodological one-sidedness pointed at was the political setting of evaluation research. While this setting accounts for a great part of the explanation, it is certainly not the only cause. Arguably more important than the politicians are the people involved in the *ex ante* evaluations proper, i.e. the evaluators and the legislators, responsible for the quality of the legislation produced and consequently, *ex ante* evaluation. Within this pool of people, two categories should be distinguished: internal and external evaluators. External specialists are hired for evaluation projects because of their specific skills and experience in the field. Much of the present day methods and techniques require after all a great portion of software proficiency, social-scientific research competences and extended expertise. This skillfulness comes at a price, however. The scarcity of employees and the generally generous salaries in the IT-sector make consultation expensive, particularly when compared to the more modest pay of civil servants. On the other hand, they secure the administration's access to present days' evaluation's technology. A balance between knowledge and budgets is obtained by limiting outsourcing to the most important or prestigious legislative projects. Still, these expensive outsiders are a thorn in the eye of many, devouring large budgets as they come and go. These costs – in addition to the desire to be self-sufficient – motivate some managers to resort to their own people for solving evaluation problems. Together with the managers, we now have to ask ourselves how much actual skills and how large a learning potential is present among the civil servants of the department. I refer to section V for the answering of the latter part of this question, since it involves a systematic solution.

The question with regard to the skills present, then, is easily answered: complex or difficult evaluation problems are not dealt with in-house, but are outsourced. The reason is simple: most civil servants possess no knowledge of evaluation processes, and those that do, have skills chiefly limited to the basic written consultation. This finding constitutes the third explanation for the methodological narrowness of evaluations in legislative departments. But why are competences limited as they are? To avoid a fundamental misunderstanding, I illuminate again an underlying assumption that is crucial to a good understanding of this contribution. The evaluations I am talking about, are predominantly *impact assessments*. By definition, these evaluations are driven by a research question

[46] M. Bamberger, J. Rugh and L. Mabry, *supra* note 43.

concerning the impact that will be generated by the laws 'in action'. Typical juridical evaluations, on the other hand, are produced within a research frame commanded by criteria such as legal compatibility or clear and precise formulation of the legal articles. These evaluations are not at stake here; after all, I defined the fundamental rationale for (*ex ante*) evaluations as the gap between the 'law in action' and the 'law in the books'. This gap can be tightened by constructing legislation with the utmost prudence and care, which in turn might be obtained by assessing the impact that the law will have in its complex social setting.

This little excursion holds the key to explaining the lack of competence among the civil servants engaged in lawmaking. To start with, the phrasing 'lack of competence' is misleading, since they naturally possess a certain proficiency, but their expertise is predominantly situated in the 'law in the books'-domain. The majority of the civil servants involved are law graduates after all. Their expertise is thus hardly suited for solving predictive time series analyses or building micro-simulation models. Consultation and particularly its forms that do not require methodological or technical skills, such as the written consultation, are, conversely, well served by the education that leads to a law degree. An additional explanation in the field of human resources is worth mentioning. Young people that are able to apply a variety of computational and consultation techniques are often just marginally interested in a governmental career. Many private firms involved in evaluation, audit, consultation etc. promise better career prospectives, better salaries and more fringe benefits than the government is able to offer.

V. *Institutionalization: a Multi-purpose Solution*

In the previous section, I exposed the three main culprits for the one-sidedness of evaluation *ex ante* techniques, namely the lack of political interest in prospective evaluation (or evaluation in general terms), the time constraints to the drafting of legislation and the specific competences of the civil servants involved. Overcoming these obstacles should clear the way for the enlarging of the methodological scope of evaluation, which in turn serves the broader case of the improvement of the quality of legislation.

The solution I put forward should thus be able to deal with the three main causes and the various related problems I sketched in section IV. As such, it should protect against unpredictable, *ad hoc* and strategic interventions by politicians. Budgets should be brought to a decent level and stabilized. Regulatory burdens reduction and administrative simplification should not devour the resources attributed to evaluation. Interdepartmental and multilevel coordination of evaluative activities should be assured. The format of four-yearly legislatures should have less impact on the attitudes of the legislators. The learning capacity of the administration should be expanded and a solid knowledge base should be constructed. Preconditions with regard to data collection and gathering of information should be fulfilled. Sufficient time for scientifically sound evaluations should be foreseen in the lawmaking process. As the body of literature on the topic is huge, I restrict this discussion to a selected number of highlights, pitfalls and unresolved questions.

Despite the considerable number of challenges listed here, there is one solution that addresses most of these challenges: institutionalization. Drawing on national and international literature I will concisely define the concept, sketch its positive features and discuss pitfalls and unresolved questions.

The pragmatic role attributed to institutionalization in this context asks for a down-to-earth definition. As such, I free the term from its embedding in sociological and, more precisely, in neo-institutionalist theory, and follow the Walloon evaluation specialists Varone and Jacobs when they state that institutionalization refers to "a formal organization or a procedural rule that provides actors with a framework guaranteeing a certain predictability of their respective behaviour and, as such, of the outcomes of their collective action... The institutionalization of evaluation is thus understood as a 'systematization' of the expected, if not compulsory, recourse to evaluation, which can also be measured by its level of implementation within administrations, political bodies and policy networks."[47] Central to this process is the steering of the behaviour of the main actors, in this case the administration and politicians. This is in accordance with the problem analysis presented above, in which the lack of interest and involvement of the political elite was identified as a main cause of the problem, implying that it is an equally important starting point for the construction of a solution. Indeed, "L'évaluation des politiques publiques...appelle une forte volonté politique."[48] Not just some friendly politics will do the trick – a *strong* political will is required. The epitethon expresses the need for a powerful political intervention to correct the deplorable state of affairs in France, equally suggesting that the political setting in which the action should take place is a hostile environment.[49] Changing the lamentable attitude of the political elite and chiefs of administration asks for

---

[47] Frederic Varone, Steve Jacob and Lieven De Winter, 'Polity, Politics and Policy Evaluation in Belgium' (2005) 11:3 *Evaluation*, p. 255.

[48] Although referring to France and to 'poliques publiques' rather than legislation, the following heading found in a document on evaluation published by the French Senate could serve our purpose well. *Placer l'évaluation des politiques publiques au coeur de la réforme de l'État*, Chapitre II, Traveaux Parlementaires, Sénat, <www.senat.fr/rap/r03-392/r03-392.html>, 20 September 2008.

[49] This is certainly true in the French context: a great many efforts to introduce a systematic legislative evaluation have yielded minimal results on the working floor, i.e., the number of actual evaluations carried out in the administration is limited to a mere handful. Evaluation has not been able to break free from rhetoric, causing much frustration among politicians that strive for renewal on the domain of administration, policy and legislation.

a drastic remedy that goes way beyond isolated actions and *ad hoc* initiatives. This remedy is thus institutionalization. While it may look and sound like a very abstract concept, it becomes much more manageable and tangible when operationalized. For the sake of conducting comparative research, the Walloon academics Jacob and Varone developed a theoretical index of policy evaluation, containing six chief dimensions which can be measured empirically.[50] These concern the qualified presence of, respectively, an evaluation body within the Executive; an evaluation body within the Parliament; evaluation activities within the supreme audit institutions, a national society of evaluators; a scientific review on evaluation and finally, quality standards.[51] For each dimension, a number of points between 0 and 2 is attributed, along the lines of the level of achievement of the nation within that terrain.

Empirical research indicates that institutionalization is an effective tool to ensure the systematic use of evaluation. As far back in time as in the early nineties, a comparative study pointed out the correlation between the implementation of sound program evaluation and the existence of institutional arrangements.[52] According to the OECD, it is generally acknowledged that a certain level of institutionalization must be accomplished for evaluation to play its full role in public governance. Varone e.a. postulate "that a high degree of institutionalization guarantees... that an evaluation will be carried out. This institutionalization provides the conditions, in turn, for sustained and standardized data collection on policy implementation and its effects. It also makes more likely the presence of highly qualified evaluators within the administration, universities of consultant's offices. As such it contributes to the professionalization of evaluation. It encourages learning processes within policy networks and promotes an efficient implementation of evaluation activities."[53] Especially relevant to our central research question, it can be added that the decision to institutionalize evaluation invokes a minimum set of policy guidelines with regard to purposes

[50] While this index is very manageable, it also simplifies things a bit. Another index includes more dimensions, such as the pluralistic character of some of the evaluation institutions. Such a more encompassing index would even serve better to measure a concept related to institutionalization, *i.e.* evaluation culture.

[51] Frederic Varone, Steve Jacob and Lieven De Winter, 'Polity, Politics and Policy Evaluation in Belgium' (2005) 11:3 *Evaluation*, p. 258.

[52] Frans L. de Leeuw, 'Institutionalisering van evaluatie-onderzoek bij de overheid' in M. Donkers and J. Derks (eds.), *Rekenschap. Evaluatie-onderzoek in Nederland, de stand van zaken* (Nederlands Centrum Geestelijke Volksgezondheid, Utrecht 1993), p 35.

[53] Frederic Varone, Steve Jacob and Lieven De Winter, *supra* note 51, p. 255.

and resources attributed to the evaluation and location and methodological approaches of the tier(s) in the evaluation.[54]

In short, the attribution of a systematic character to evaluation activities is advantageous in many ways. Not only can the reluctance of individual politicians to (prospective)[55] evaluation be overcome; on a more fundamental level, the institutionalization improves the organizational, budgetary, and methodological features of evaluation research. With the advantages of institutionalization being rather self-evident, it is not surprising that the actual academic discussion now focuses on other aspects of the concept. At the heart of the discussion are now the various ways in which evaluation is institutionalized.[56] Besides, an up-and-coming field of research into evaluation concerns its possible negative side-effects. Both themes can be combined in interesting study material that is especially suited for nations with a developing evaluation culture, since they can learn from the mistakes made by their more experienced peers. This is the case for Belgium, a country with an embryonic evaluation culture, yet many of the insights from these studies are of interest to nations with a more advanced level of institutionalization. Since a detailed study of the institutionalization of evaluation *ex ante* would lead us astray with regard to the core research question of this contribution, I conclude this section by concisely highlighting the main challenges involved in the systematic application of evaluation. These challenges are varied and plentiful; as such, the order in which I write them down is of no significance. This final paragraph might be disappointing if one expects to find clear-cut answers to the question how to systematize the implementation of evaluation; rather, it creates more questions than it solves answers.

To start with a classic problem: what is the optimal distance between the evaluator on the one hand and the lawmaker and his administration on the other? If the evaluator is part of the administration, access to information, collaboration and mutual trust are more or less guaranteed, but political impartiality is restrained. The other option is to appoint external evaluators, such as private consultancy firms, research centers and universities. Locating evaluators

---

[54] Zulmira M.A. Hartz, 'Institutionalizing the evaluation of health programs and policies in France: cuisine internationale over fast food and sur mesure over ready-made' (1999) 15:2 *Cadernos de Saúde Pública*, p. 229.

[55] The average politician is not very keen on retrospective evaluation either. Reluctance is even aggravated because of the fear of a personal blame when the *ex post* evaluation yields negative results. *See* Geva-May, I; Thorngate, W., 'Reducing anxiety and resistance in policy and programme evaluations. A socio-psychological analysis' (2003) 9:2 *Evaluation*, pp. 205–227.

[56] *See* the doctorat dissertation on the topic: Steve Jacob, *Institutionnaliser l'évaluation des politiques publiques. Étude comparée des dispositifs en Belgique, en France, en Suisse et aux Pays-Bas*, (PIE-Peter Lang, Bruxelles 2005).

outside the administrative circles hinders data acquisition, yet it might secure the autonomy of the evaluator.[57] In practice – or more precisely, in the practice of countries with a low level of institutionalization – the choice between internal and external evaluation revolves around methodological know-how and budgets. Institutionalization increases or consolidates budgets, but there are limits to the methodological sophistication that can be obtained within the administration. After all, it is not a dedicated research center. With budgets permitting, outsourcing might thus still be necessary for very complicated research contexts or questions. However, depending on the frequency and quality of in-house methodological training and the recruiting policy towards new employees, the need for external specialists will gradually become less stringent.

A second matter is the actual use of the evaluation *ex ante* results. As has become apparent in many an empirical study, once a course is set out by the political machinery, it is very hard to change direction, even if evaluation studies indicate that the planned regulation will have anything but the desired effects.[58] This can be partly avoided by the positioning of evaluation activities at the very beginning of the legislative cycle (*see supra*); furthermore, institutional arrangements should be made to validate its use. One could think of public hearings, more transparency and better communication with the different stakeholders and the general public, all aiming at increasing the pressure on the political actors involved to act upon the results of the evaluation.

Strengthening the relationship between evaluation and democracy is another important challenge.[59] This liaison has many faces. Evaluation may become a tool to counter political alienation, on the condition that the general public or those directly affected by the regulation become informed about the various policy options or are encouraged to actively taking part in the very evaluations. To this end, the government must ask itself whether it makes its reports freely available instead of limiting publication to corporate stakeholders. Evaluation

---

[57] Koen van Aeken, *Proeven van wetsevaluatie. Een empirisch geïllustreerde studie naar het hoe, wat en waarom van wetsevaluatie. Doctoral dissertation* (University of Antwerp, Antwerp 2002), p. 163.

[58] Rob van Gestel and Marc Hertogh, *Wat is regeldruk? Een verkennende internationale literatuurstudie* (WODC, Den Haag 2006). Patricia Popelier, Rob van Gestel, Koen Van Aeken; Vicky Verlinden and Peter Van Humbeeck, *Consulteren over ontwerp-regelgeving: alibi voor vrijblijvendheid of prikkel tot actie? Een zoektocht naar internationale best practices en een toepassing op de Nederlandse consultatiepraktijk als referentiekader voor Belgische beleidsmakers en Vlaamse RIA-ambtenaren* (Politeia, Brussel in print).

[59] Michael Q. Patton, 'A Vision of Evaluation that Strengthens Democracy' (2002) 8:1 *Evaluation*, pp. 125–139. Frans L. Leeuw, 'Evaluation in Europe 2000. Challenges to a Growth Industry' (2002) 8:1 *Evaluation*, pp. 5–6. Koen Van Aeken, *Proeven van wetsevaluatie. Een empirisch geïllustreerde studie naar het hoe, wat en waarom van wetsevaluatie. Doctoral dissertation* (University of Antwerp, Antwerp 2002), p. 93.

might even become a form of empowerment, by involving the public in the evaluations – the methodology allows to, by means of such techniques as internet consulting and citizens panels.

Returning to the government and the administration, a crucial challenge is presented by the proliferation of evaluating bodies and institutions. Even (or just because of) in a country with an underdeveloped evaluation culture, such as Belgium, the number of institutions involved in some form of evaluation is enormous. This calls for robust coordinating efforts, taking into account factors as multi-level government or the pluralistic composition of evaluation bodies. Furthermore, the possibilities of transdepartmental collaboration have to be assessed in order to promote diffusion of information and know-how.

A related question, which can equally be regarded as an opportunity, concerns the (re)positioning of powers. Considering the uneven balance of executive and legislative powers in contemporary politics, the institutionalization of evaluation holds the prospect of reinforcing the role of the parliamentary powers.[60] The ongoing debate about the future role of the Senate and the 'Eerste Kamer' in respectively Belgium and the Netherlands offers a golden opportunity to review the relationship between the two chambers in the light of the controlling function of the First Chamber and Senate.

Currently, a considerable number of varying tests of legislation exist within the administration. Rob Van Gestel states that at least a whopping hundred tests and assessments exist in the Dutch legislative framework.[61] One category consists of the juridical tests, checking principles of good regulation such as consistency with international obligations and the constitution, transparency, legal certainty, proportionality or necessity; next, the law has to pass some accountancy and audit tests; another category includes tests measuring the amount of red tape produced by the future legal disposition, while yet another class of tests reviews the quality of the legal writing. Furthermore, concerns about ecology have introduced new tests, such as environmental impact assessment. In this line of reasoning, one can imagine that the future will hold many more tests, such as checks for the safeguarding of privacy and the protection against discrimination. All these assessments have their own scope, institutions, personnel and procedures. Institutionalization should rationalize these activities by trimming down overlaps, rescheduling time frames, abolishing obsolete tests and so on. After all, this would be an act of administrative simplification, with the added advantage of liberating resources for the sake of the elaboration of the methodology of impact

[60] Koen Van Aeken Koen, Steve Jacobs, Frederic Varone, 'Beleidsevaluatie: een sturingsinstrument voor het overheidshandelen' (2003) 4 *Vlaams tijdschrift voor overheidsmanagement*, p. 32.

[61] Rob van Gestel in Willem Witteveen, Ivo Giesen and Joan Wijkerslooth (eds.), *Alternatieve regelgeving*, Handelingen NJV (Kluwer, Deventer 2008), p. 79.

analysis. The current debate on evaluation in Belgium's legislative forum is still mainly focused upon the juridical aspects of evaluation,[62] neglecting the very rationale for *ex ante* evaluation research: bridging the gap between the desired effects and the actual outcomes.

I have pointed out above the fact that *ex ante* evaluation is just one part of the legislative cycle. Equally important is the retrospective evaluation. As expressed elsewhere in this volume, *ex ante* and *ex post* evaluations cannot function apart from each other. Uneven attention to just one of the types is senseless – nevertheless, Belgian's parliamentary achievement of 2007 to install a systematic legislative evaluation[63] (which has been debated over the course of two legislative terms) exclusively aims at evaluation *ex post*.

Universities and other institutions of higher education must reflect on their societal responsibilities *vis-à-vis* better regulation through the promotion of legislative evaluation. They should undertake and sponsor multidisciplinary research into the domain of the methodology and offer courses in the field to a wide range of students. In addition, these institutions should foreground explanatory and policy theories,[64] which will become valuable tools for policy elaboration as the body of scientific insights grows over time. Assessing the reliability and applicability of theories will gain prominence as one of the basic research questions that steer evaluation projects.

Last but certainly not least, the unintended and undesirable side effects of evaluation should be addressed.[65] As institutionalization progresses, the risks of bureaucratization increase. Institutionalization should not lead to the development of yet another new institution; preferably, existing ones are reconverted. Moreover, the process should not lead to the installment of complicate procedures and time-consuming exercises in redundancy (see also the entry above about the various tests). The performance paradox is well placed here: an organization that wishes to increase its performance by introducing performance testing might be acting ineffectively. Or, "the audit society expends a huge amount of resources in assurance activities whose most immediate consequence is to increase bureaucratization."[66] It would be cynical that all efforts turn contra productive because of 'evaluation fatigue'. That is why the institutionalization

[62] Koen Van Aeken, 'Wetsevaluatie: intenties en uitdagingen op het niveau van Kamer en Senaat' (2006/2007) 3–648/4 *Handelingen Belgische Senaat.*

[63] *Wet van 25 april 2005 tot oprichting van een Parlementair Comité belast met de wetsevaluatie*, B.S., 11 May 2007.

[64] Frans L. Leeuw, 'Evaluation in Europe 2000. Challenges to a Growth Industry' (2002) 8:1 *Evaluation*, pp. 7–9.

[65] *Ibid.*, pp. 9–10.

[66] Robert Schwartz, cited in *ibid.*, p. 9.

of evaluation should ideally start small and grow from the bottom up.[67] In this way, the people involved will have ample time to internalize the necessary ideas and attitudes of an evaluation culture, allowing evaluation to grow as a natural aspect of the legislative cycle.

In short, the challenges that are faced by institutionalization are gargantuan. Books such as this volume are thus badly needed. Yet they cannot replace the 'volonté forte' that must inspire our politicians – political determination holds the key to institutionalization, shaping the conditions for the enlargement of the methodological scope of evaluations in Belgium and the Netherlands.

VI. *In a Nutshell*

My contribution to this volume on legislative *ex ante* evaluation has been inspired by a recurring and somewhat annoying finding. Judging by the steadily increasing number of publications, seminars, public statements by political actors and institutionalization efforts with regard to the topic, evaluation appears to be well on track to become one of the hottest public governance activities in present-day's audit society. But while everybody is talking about impact assessments, the poor souls that are actually able to conduct a methodologically sound evaluation are astonishingly small in numbers.

The statement above is, of course, the victim of some exaggeration. The civil servants or legislative lawyers engaged in evaluation clearly possess the skills to conduct a variety of assessments. But these assessments do rarely touch the question that should be at the very core of an evaluation policy: the issue of impact assessment. Indeed, the ubiquitous use of legislation as an instrument of social engineering – a heritage of the seminal welfare state – disregards the cold fact that the actual outcomes differ from the desired effects due to the complex setting in which the legal dispositions come to life. Prospective evaluation of the impact of legislation might help to bridge this gap.

Unfortunately, empirical research seems to indicate that the methodological spectre of the evaluative activities is severely limited within the administration. The most basic of the consultative methods are common, whereas more advanced consultation techniques and so-called computational techniques are hardly used. Given the complex contexts of current legislative problems, this state of affairs is undesirable. In order to find a solution, I studied the causes of the situation. Lack of true political salience and ill-adapted competences of the civil servants involved turned out to be some of the main culprits. Fortunately, these problems

[67] *See* McDonald, Patricia Rogers and Bruce Kefford, 'Teaching People to Fish? Building the Evaluation Capacity of Public Sector Organizations' (2003) 9:1 *Evaluation*, pp. 9–29.

can be overcome by institutionalization of evaluation. The embedding of evaluation in an organizational framework and other actions related to the process of institutionalization will not only tackle many of the methodological challenges, but offer additional advantages as well. However, a strong political will remains a *conditio sine qua non* to initiate the institutionalization process.

Part II

Ex Ante Evaluation in Practice

Chapter 7

European Impact Assessment and the Choice of Alternative Regulatory Instruments

Anne Meuwese and Linda Senden

I. *Introduction*

One key element of the Better Regulation strategy of the EU is to promote the use of alternative regulatory instruments, including co-regulation, self-regulation, the open method of coordination and soft law more in general. In recent years, an important way or tool for putting the aims of the Better Regulation strategy to practice has been the development and application of impact assessments. In many policy documents of the Commission claims are made that Better Regulation initiatives, including impact assessments, entail enhanced consideration of the use of alternative regulatory mechanisms. Most recently, this was done in the Commission's Second Strategic Review of Better Regulation in the European Union: "Better regulation does not mean deregulation or holding back new rules when they are needed. But policy and regulatory proposals are now systematically assessed, and a wide range of options – regulatory and non-regulatory – are examined for each initiative."[1]

In the Inter-Institutional Agreement 'Better Lawmaking', adopted by the Council, Commission and European Parliament in 2003, we can also find a joint recognition of the need to use alternative regulatory mechanisms by

[1] European Commission, Second strategic review of Better Regulation in the European Union, COM(2008) 32 final, p. 2. At a Public Hearing of the European Economic and Social Committee on 'The Current State of European Self- and Co-Regulation' on 31 March 2008, this basic assumption was explicitly confirmed by Mr. Italianer, Deputy Secretary General of the European Commission, in charge of Better Regulation.

the legislative Institutions.[2] A crucial question, however, is how this aspect of the Better Regulation policy is being put into practice. Do European impact assessments – hereafter 'EU IA', to emphasise that impact assessment is more than a bureaucratic tool used for internal Commission purposes only – show indeed such a built-in preference for alternative regulatory mechanisms? To what extent does the growing practice of EU IA show that 'classical' forms of regulation – i.e. legislative options – are being weighed against alternative regulatory options? More importantly even, how is this assessment made, on the basis of what criteria, and what should these criteria be if the existing ones prove to be non-satisfactory? Given the fact that the use of impact assessments has been 'booming' only in very recent years, little research has been done up to now regarding these questions. We therefore seek to explore these questions in this chapter, with the aim of throwing some new light on the basis on which regulatory choices are made in the EU and the role that impact assessment has to play in this respect.

Dealing with these issues will require first of all an understanding of the way in which the European impact assessment regime has developed and of what the contours of this regime are now (section II). Given that, as will be set out below, one of the shared principles of EU IA is that a range of legislative and alternative regulatory mechanisms should be considered, the initial question that is triggered is what legal and other constraints to regulatory choice have to be taken into account by the framework of EU IA. We will then turn to the issue as to how the tool of IA gives hand and feet in practice to this theoretical starting point of the EU's Better Regulation policy and what conclusions this practice induces as to the actual enhanced consideration and use of alternative regulatory mechanisms (section III). We wind up this chapter with some general conclusions and a short evaluation: what elements of this practice call for improvement and what might this improvement consist of (section IV)?

II. *The Development of a European Impact Assessment Regime*

This section sets out the contours of the EU IA regime as it has developed over the past years, both in terms of procedure and substance.

---

[2] Inter-Institutional Agreement on Better Lawmaking (2003) – European Commission, European Parliament and Council of Ministers, Inter-Institutional Agreement on Better Lawmaking, OJ 2003 C 321/01, point 16. To be further discussed in section III.

A. *What Is Impact Assessment?*

Impact assessment is the common term for *ex ante* analysis conducted in an early stage of policy and/or legislative processes, with a view to making a more informed decision about the content and the type of the intervention. The actual procedure as it is currently in place in the European Commission policy cycle, consists of a series of analytical steps to be carried out at the bureaucratic level: problem identification, definition of the objectives, development of the main policy options, impact analysis, comparison of the options in the light of their impact and an outline for policy monitoring and evaluation.[3] The existing procedures for pre-legislative consultation and collection of expertise have been maintained, but are now encapsulated by the new IA procedure. A 'Roadmap' – a sort of 'mini IA' with a fixed template – is published as part of the Commission's Work Programme so that stakeholders can plan their input into the impact assessment. An IA report,[4] published together with the proposal, contains the findings of the IA *process*, including an explanation of how expertise and consultation have been used. This document reveals the reasoning behind the proposed regulatory intervention as well as the various impacts as estimated by the Commission and the trade-offs between sets of impacts across policy options. To date, several hundreds of impact assessments have been prepared by the European Commission.[5]

B. *Background: Regulatory Reform and Better Regulation*

Meta-level regulatory policies containing principles, tests and procedures generally applicable to regulatory activity have been increasingly enacted all around the world in recent years, partly as a result of intense promotion on the part of the OECD.[6] We can refer to these policies as 'regulatory reforms' or as 'regulatory policies' (if the initiative is meant to have a more structural impact). In the EU this kind of policy has been given the – now commonly used – brand name 'Better Regulation' (BR). As is the case in many regulatory policies of other legal systems, impact assessment is the flagship tool, bringing to the fore some fundamental political choices involved in designing and running such systems.

---

[3] European Commission, Impact Assessment Guidelines, SEC(2005) 791 (update of March 2006). The Guidelines can be downloaded at <ec.europa.eu/governance/impact/docs/key_docs/sec_2005_0791_en.pdf>, 8 September 2008.

[4] Often simply referred to as the 'impact assessment' even if in fact the term 'impact assessment' covers the whole process and not just the report.

[5] For an overview of the EU IAs carried out thus far, *see* <ec.europa.eu/governance/impact/practice_en.htm>, 22 August 2008.

[6] Regulatory Impact Analysis: Best Practices in OECD Countries (OECD Publications, Paris 1997). More recently, Measuring Regulatory Quality, OECD Policy Brief, April 2008.

There are many types and flavours of 'regulatory policies' and in the choices of institutional design that have to be made, administrations face similar dilemmas. For instance, should the rationale behind the regulatory reform be made explicit or left implicit? By way of illustration: in Europe many governments have been struggling with the question of whether to call their reforms 'deregulation' or not. Doing so may please the business world, but also amounts to a fundamental political choice that makes it impossible to present the regulatory reform as a neutral 'win-win' policy.[7] A second dilemma is whether to enact centralised reforms, by means of general requirements for all new policies and/or legislation or to keep it (relatively) sector-specific and work mainly through the departments which carry out their own specialised tests. A third choice to be made is whether to adhere to a 'thick template' (obligatory procedures with a fully fledged enforcement mechanism) or to stick with a minimalist approach (work with best practices and focus on raising awareness with officials rather than imposing procedures upon them). The former runs the risk of enforcing pre-fabricated theories of regulation,[8] which may not suit well every sector or situation, whereas the latter may not have much effect at all.

What can we – at this stage – say on the answers EU IA and the Better Regulation strategy more widely give to these questions? Does the European Better Regulation agenda come with a certain political orientation? Do the Institutions adhere to a common and coherent vision and approach thereof? As we will show below, the EU tries to take the middle road in most of these dilemmas. The result of this compromising is a multitude of conceptions of what EU IA is and should be.

The Better Regulation strategy started out as clearly embedded in debates on constitutional legitimacy, in particular as a tool to make the subsidiarity and proportionality principles operational. In section III we will elaborate on those aspects, but here we would like to point out that a shift towards what could be called 'economic legitimacy' can be witnessed. With the European Commission being forced to put the Lisbon strategy and competitiveness higher on the agenda, Better Regulation and impact assessment also increasingly came to serve these goals. This perception can be coupled with the observation that the EU is moving from a proceduralist type of Better Regulation ('Better Regulation

---

[7] Claudio M. Radaelli and Anne C.M. Meuwese, 'Better Regulation in Europe: Between Public Management and Regulatory Reform' (2009 forthcoming) *Public Adminstration.*

[8] Claudio M. Radaelli and Anne C.M. Meuwese, 'Better Regulation in the European Union. The political economy of impact assessment' in Klaus Jacob *et al.* (eds.), *EVIA handbook* (Springer, 2009 forthcoming).

as an exercise in governance')[9] to a more substantive approach in terms of the outcome to which BR and IA should lead.[10] This is exemplified by the focus on the reduction of administrative burden, pushed by a small group of Member States, most notably the Netherlands and Denmark.[11] The main instrument to achieve an overall relieve in burdens that regulatees experience from EU regulation, is the baseline measurement of existing burdens that is currently ongoing in combination with the overall target of 25% less burdens that has been set for 2012. But the 'Standard Cost Model' (SCM), a methodology for measuring administrative burdens developed by the Dutch government,[12] has also been integrated into the IA methodology of the Commission.[13] The recent political attention for regulating in such a way as to minimise the direct costs that regulatory interventions generate (those costs also being narrowly defined as flowing from information obligations), is a move away from the more balanced approach that assumes that certain costs are outweighed by the benefits of regulation. In the current political climate, it is sometimes forgotten that Better Regulation can also mean regulating in accordance with basic insights from regulation theory: any regulatory action, be it classical or in an alternative form, presupposes that there is a clear necessity for it because of market failure, regulatory failure and/or protection of a public interest.[14]

---

[9] Claudio M. Radaelli, De Nobis Fabula Narratur (The Story Was About Us): Three Better Regulation Tales, Dinner Speech delivered to the meeting on Strategic Policy Making and Regulatory Reform, 4 June 2007; Claudio M. Radaelli, The architecture of regulatory impact assessment, presentation held at the EVIA final conference, 16 January 2008. The presentation is downloadable at <www.centres.ex.ac.uk/ceg/research/riacp/documents/EVIAfinalconference ArchitectureofRIARadaelliwithanimations.pdf>, 8 September 2008.

[10] This also connects to the concepts of input respectively output legitimacy. Fritz Scharpf, *Governing in Europe: Effective and Democratic?* (Oxford University Press, Oxford 1999).

[11] The Member States that have programmes for the reduction of administrative burden in place at the national level, or are interested in initiating one, are united in the informal 'SCM network', *see* <www.administrative-burdens.com/>, 22 August 2008.

[12] The SCM measures administrative costs in terms of time spent by, originally, businesses (but in recent versions the model has been extended to citizens and public authorities) to comply with information obligations imposed by public regulation. The methodology boasts a high degree of precision (bottom-up measurement instead of top-down estimation), but has the drawback of only looking at information obligations. This limitation is often overlooked by proponents on the model and, besides, it is debatable whether burdens flowing from information obligations are a suitable proxy for overall administrative burdens.

[13] IA Guidelines, *supra* note 3, *see* Annex 10 in particular.

[14] *See* Anthony I. Ogus, *Regulation: Legal Form and Economic Theory* (Hart Publishing, Oxford 2004).

C. *From an IA Procedure to an EU IA Regime*

The European Commission experimented with several targeted and often sector-specific regulatory reform initiatives in the 1990s, but none of these seemed to help solve problems regarding the quantity and quality of European legislation, which was perceived to impose heavy burdens on Member States, business and citizens.[15] The new century brought momentum for a more rigorous approach to regulatory reform, including an attempt to put in place a system of impact assessment (IA), apparently modelled on the 'best practice' championed by the OECD[16] and to some extent on the American concept of 'regulatory impact analysis'.[17] Yet, the context in which the European Commission was to use the instrument was very different from its American habitat of delegated 'rule-making' by agencies and adjustments were made accordingly. In 2002, following recommendations from the Mandelkern group on Better Regulation,[18] the European Commission announced its intention to use impact assessment as a 'general purpose impact analysis tool' in the preparation of legislative proposals. Although the European Commission introduced an impressive package of better regulation measures in 2002 and sat around the table with the other lawmaking Institutions of the EU in 2003 to lay down an inter-institutional framework for European impact assessment (*see* below), the issue remained relatively obscure for a few years. A pilot project with some 20 proposals took off in 2003 and continued for a second year in 2004 with a similar number. In 2005 interest in European impact assessment suddenly peaked and awareness was growing that its now routinised use might actually change the way in which the EU makes policy and law. From 2005 onwards impact assessment came to cover all proposals in the Commission's Legislative and Work Programme (CLWP).[19]

The implementation of the IA procedure in the services of the Commission has been sped up by the Commission's adoption of Impact Assessment Guide-

---

[15] Jacques Pelkmans *et al.*, 'Better EU Regulatory Quality: Assessing Current Initiatives and New Proposals' in Giampolo Galli and Jacques Pelkmans (eds.), *Regulatory Reform and Competitiveness in Europe – Volume I, Horizontal Issues* (Edward Elgar, Cheltenham 2000), pp. 461–526.

[16] *Supra* note 6.

[17] Jonathan B. Wiener, 'Better Regulation in Europe' (2006) 59 *Current Legal Problems*, pp. 447–518.

[18] The Mandelkern Group was composed of Member State experts on better regulation and chaired by Dieudonné Mandelkern, a French government official. It was set up by Ministers of Public Administration, in November 2000 to provide recommendations for a strategy to improve the European regulatory environment. The Mandelkern report was presented to the Laeken European Council in November 2001.

[19] European Commission, Better Regulation for Growth and Jobs in the European Union, Communication from the Commission, COM(2005) 97, 16 March 2005 (Brussels 2005).

lines[20] in June 2005.[21] This comprehensive piece of guidance (plus annexes) is meant to provide internal guidance to all Commission officials faced with an impact assessment. Nevertheless, its publication on the Commission's IA website has inevitably made it part of the framework that sets out what the outside world can expect from impact assessment by the Commission. Whereas 2006 was perhaps a year of consolidation, the arrival of 2007 marked a new phase in the development of IA. In 2006 the Commission put out a call for tender for the first external evaluation of its IA system. The Evaluation Partnership, a London based consultancy firm, won the tender and published their findings in 2007, pointing to the 'principle of proportionate analysis' (the idea that the depth of the IA should depend on the magnitude of expected impacts) and the 'blanket coverage' (the requirement to carry out IAs for *all* initiatives in the Commission's Work Programme) as problematic aspects of the current regime.[22] In a simultaneous effort to better enforce the standards for IA, the Commission set up an internal scrutiny body for IAs, the Impact Assessment Board (IAB) at the end of 2006. Recently, the Commission has decided to extend the scope of application of IA beyond the Work Programme; where appropriate this could also include Comitology items.[23] A final development that deserves to be mentioned is the enhanced cooperation with the US – or, to be more precise, the Office of Management and Budget, which is responsible for guarding the quality of the American RIAs – on how to measure impacts on trade.[24]

There is an explicit, basic rationale behind EU IA as it has thus developed, and it can be distilled from various policy documents on the topic and that has been expressed already in the White Paper on Governance: "Proposals must be prepared on the basis of an effective analysis of whether it is appropriate to intervene at EU level and whether regulatory intervention is needed. If so,

---

20 IA Guidelines, *supra* note 3.

21 The Commission already issued internal guidelines in 2002, namely 'Impact Assessment in the Commission – Guidelines' and 'A Handbook for Impact Assessment in the Commission – How to do an Impact Assessment', but the uniform use of these guidance documents was not actively promoted and political endorsement of the content, as happened with the 2005 Guidelines, was lacking.

22 The Evaluation Partnership (TEP), Final Report, p. 90. The report can be downloaded from <ec.europa.eu/governance/impact/key_en.htm>, 8 September 2008.

23 *Cf.* Second strategic review of Better Regulation in the European Union, *supra* note 1, p. 6.

24 EU-US High-Level Regulatory Cooperation Forum, Review of the Application of EU and US Regulatory Impact Assessment Guidelines on the Analysis of Impacts on International Trade and Investment, Final Report and Conclusions, prepared by the Office of Management and Budget and the Secretariat General of the European Commission, Brussels/Washington DC, 13 May 2008, <ec.europa.eu/governance/better_regulation/documents/eu_us_consult/joint_paper_sg_oira_050808.pdf>, 22 August 2008.

the analysis must also assess the potential economic, social and environmental impacts."[25]

So, the primary goal of EU IA is to ground the decision as to whether (subsidiarity) and how (proportionality) to intervene in effective analysis. Thus, the purpose of IA is one of informational value only; IA is merely meant to function as 'an aid to decision-making, not a substitute for political judgment'.[26] This is exemplified in particular by the Commission's choice not to include a particular decision criterion in its IA framework. Whereas 'textbook IA' preaches that the last part of any impact assessment should consist of a choice for either the most cost-effective option, or the option that is expected to generate the highest net-benefits (or to attain any other preordained objective), the Commission Guidelines recommend presenting the options according to a range of various criteria that are chosen on an ad hoc basis (multi-criteria analysis). Yet the reason why EU IA can be characterised as a 'regime'[27] rather than just as a 'procedure' is twofold: a) the fact that IA is used by the European Commission as a policy coordination tool and b) the fact that a common set of standards for EU IA is evolving for all the legislative Institutions, albeit mainly of a procedural nature. The use of EU IA as a policy coordination tool is evident from the Roadmap requirement (*see* above), but mostly from the procedures that are in place to ensure IA helps the internal dialogue between Directorates-General. The Inter-Service Steering Groups, significantly renamed 'Impact Assessment Steering Groups' in the new draft Guidelines of 2008,[28] established in the early phases of the policy or law making procedure, revolve for an important part around the impact assessment.

A complicating factor is that IA is meant to inform both the political decision-makers in the College of Commissioners and those in the European Parliament and the Council of Ministers. With this in mind, the European Parliament has pointed out that EU IA 'only makes sense if the Commission, Council and Parliament operate in accordance with the same system and with the same standards'.[29] However, institutional constraints and power struggles have significantly

---

[25] European Commission, White Paper on Governance, COM(2001) 428 final.

[26] European Commission, Communication on Impact Assessment, COM(2002) 276 final, p. 3.

[27] The following definition of 'regulatory regime' is given by Hood *et al.*: 'the complex institutional geography, rules, practice and animating ideas associated with regulating particular aspects of social and economic life'. Christopher Hood *et al., The government of risk: understanding risk regulation regimes* (Oxford University Press, Oxford 2001), p. 9.

[28] European Commission, Draft Impact Assessment Guidelines, May 2008 (Brussels). The Draft Commission Impact Assessment Guidelines can be downloaded at <ec.europa.eu/governance/impact/consultation/ia_consultation_en.htm>, 22 August 2008.

[29] It is unclear whether this should be interpreted as a common methodology for measuring administrative burdens or for wider categories of costs as the Doorn report seems to equate

watered down the results of attempts to establish a common system with common standards. The umbrella document in this regard is the Inter-Institutional Agreement on Better Lawmaking (2003). On the use of impact assessment it reiterates the obligation imposed on the Commission to carry out IA. It also contains recognition by the three Institutions that IA is a positive contribution to the quality of Community legislation, declares that there is a duty to inform the European Parliament, Council and general public about the results as well as a duty to motivate Commission proposals in the light of the outcome of IA. Furthermore it mentions the possibility for the European Parliament and the Council to carry out their own IAs on substantive amendments and states that the Institutions will consider of a common methodology for IA. The inter-institutional agreement also contains some provisions on the use of alternatives to classical regulation, which will be dealt with below.[30]

The EU Institutions have indeed sought to establish such a common methodology, adopting in November 2005 an Inter-Institutional Common Approach to Impact Assessment, consolidating some 'traffic rules' on the use of impact assessment throughout the legislative cycle. The Common Approach lays down a common framework mainly for the use of impact assessment, but also mentions

---

administrative burdens with regulatory burdens. European Parliament, Report on assessment of the impact of Community legislation and the consultation procedures, Committee on Legal Affairs and the Internal Market (rapporteur Lambert Doorn), Brussels 2004, para 7.

30 Inter-Institutional Agreement on Better Lawmaking (2003), *supra* note 2, p. 4. The full provisions read:

> 27. Pursuant to the Protocol on the application of the principles of subsidiarity and proportionality, the Commission will take due account in its legislative proposals of their financial or administrative implications, for the Union and the Member States in particular. Furthermore, each of the three Institutions will take into account the objective of ensuring that application in the Member States is appropriate and effective.
>
> 28. The three Institutions agree on the positive contribution of impact assessments in improving the quality of Community legislation, with particular regard to the scope and substance thereof.
>
> 29. The Commission will continue to implement the integrated advance impact-assessment process for major items of draft legislation, combining in one single evaluation the impact assessments relating inter alia to social, economic and environmental aspects. The results of the assessments will be made fully and freely available to the European Parliament, the Council and the general public. In the explanatory memorandum to its proposals, the Commission will indicate the manner in which the impact assessments have influenced them.
>
> 30. Where the co-decision procedure applies, the European Parliament and Council may, on the basis of jointly defined criteria and procedures, have impact assessments carried out prior to the adoption of any substantive amendment, either at first reading or at the conciliation stage. As soon as possible after this Agreement is adopted, the three Institutions will carry out an assessment of their respective experiences and will consider the possibility of establishing a common methodology.

the use of co-regulation and self-regulation at the EU level and implementation of the Commission's new simplification programme. The document elaborates the pre-existing commitment of the European Parliament and the Council to not only use Commission IAs, but also produce their own when they propose 'substantive amendments'.[31] The Common Approach contains more concrete norms for EU IA, but they hardly go beyond mere 'traffic rules', regulating the way in which the Institutions are expected to approach the IA work carried out by each, and would not qualify as a true 'common methodology'. The main principle the Common Approach enshrines is that each Institution bears responsibility for assessing its own proposals or modifications as well as for choosing the means to be used for their impact assessment. This principle should be regarded in the light of the reservation made at the beginning of the Common Approach, namely that it is made without prejudice to the decision-making role and autonomy of each Institution and in line with their respective roles and responsibilities. The rules and principles of EU IA set out in the Common Approach aim to balance this consideration with the resolution that '[t]he rigour, objectivity and comprehensive nature of the analysis should mean that the impact assessment is not a simple justification of the initiative or the substantive amendment'.[32]

The Common Approach mentions the integrated and balanced coverage of potential impacts, meaning that social, economic and environmental aspects/impacts ought to be covered. Also, where possible both short and long term costs and benefits should be assessed. Other elements which the Common Approach emphasises are integration of subsidiarity and proportionality tests into IA as well as the obligatory consideration of how the policy would be monitored and evaluated. The Commission's impact assessment (not those by the European Parliament and the Council) should "strive to explore a range of legislative and non-legislative options which could potentially meet the set objectives". On the whole, EU IA must ensure 'rigorous and comprehensive assessment based on accurate, objective and complete information' and take into account the principle of proportionate analysis, meaning concretely that '[t]he impact assessment's depth and scope will be determined by the likely impacts of the proposed action'. Furthermore, the Common Approach prescribes transparency (all IAs are to be published on websites) as well as consultation for IAs ('where reasonably possible and without causing undue delay in the legislative process').[33]

---

[31] Inter-Institutional Agreement on Better Lawmaking (2003), *supra* note 2.

[32] European Commission, European Parliament and Council of Ministers, Common Approach to Impact Assessment (2005), point 5. The Common Approach has not been published in the Official Journal; it can be downloaded at <ec.europa.eu/governance/impact/docs/key_docs/ii_common_approach_to_ia_en.pdf>, 8 September 2008.

[33] *Ibid.*, point 7.

A final principle enshrined in the Common Approach is cooperation, in the sense that the Institutions agree to inform each other of ongoing IA work. The 'Common Approach' is really only that: an agreement on some very basic procedural rules. As far as substantive principles are concerned, the emphasis on institutional autonomy in deciding which methods to use and which impacts to consider (as long as they cover the three pillars 'economic, environmental and social') could be interpreted as an 'agreement to disagree'. However it should not be overlooked that within the Commission, the flexible interpretation of the IA framework was a conscious choice, in line with the commitment to using IA as 'an aid not a substitute for political decision-making'. The very fact that the Institutions have entered into a dialogue on the subject of impact assessment is quite remarkable and an important step in the progressive 'inter-institutionalisation'[34] of the regime.

D. *Quality Control of EU IA*

In 2005, when the implementation of the EU IA system had stepped up a gear, the impression that the current framework was not capable of delivering sufficient quality persisted among stakeholders.[35] Commission President Barroso acknowledged the need to respond to the varying quality of Commission IAs at the European Parliament plenary discussion on Better Regulation on 4 April 2006, after which the Commission committed itself to establishing a quality control body on 14 November 2006: the Impact Assessment Board (IAB).[36] This Board consists of five high-level officials who act independently of their own Directorates-General and other policy making departments. The Board currently consists of the Deputy Secretary General who acts as chair and of Directors from the following DGs: DG Enterprise, DG Employment, Social Affairs and Equal Opportunities, DG Economic and Financial Affairs and DG Environment.[37] The IAB works under the direct authority of the Commission President and reports directly to him. The Board members are supported by a secretariat consisting of officials from the Secretariat-General. Both internal and external expertise may be used on a case-by-case basis. The term of office of the IAB members is two years with the possibility of extension.

---

[34] Anne C.M. Meuwese, 'Inter-institutionalising EU Impact Assessment' in Stephen Weatherill (ed.), *Better Regulation* (Hart Publishing, Oxford 2007), pp. 287–309.

[35] Andrea Renda, *Impact Assessment in the EU. State of the Art and Art of the State* (Centre for European Policy Studies, Brussels 2005).

[36] European Commission, A strategic review of Better Regulation in the European Union, COM(2006) 689.

[37] This composition is entrenched in the current mandate of the IAB, *see* <ec.europa.eu/governance/impact/docs/key_docs/iab_mandate_annex_sec_2006_1457_3.pdf>, 22 August 2008.

The task of the IAB is to scrutinise the quality of individual Commission IAs as part of an internal system of checks and balances. The IAB will 'provide widespread quality advice and control whilst ensuring that the responsibility for preparing assessments and the relevant proposals remains with the relevant departments and Commissioners' and 'contribute to ensure that impact assessments are of high quality, that they examine different policy options and that they can be used throughout the legislative process'.[38] Case-based quality control is the initial focus of the board, but its activities are foreseen to gradually broaden to 'advice on methodology and on the approach at the early stages of impact assessment preparation.'[39] As matters currently stand, the IAB has no veto power but it is entitled to ask for resubmission of draft IAs. Since the IAB gets involved even before initiatives reach the step of Inter-Service Consultation (ISC) – DGs are required to submit their draft IAs one month before the launch of the ISC – there is always a risk that the line between quality control and control over substance will become blurred. The Secretariat General, represented on the Board in the person of the Deputy Secretary General, has a role in ensuring that the Board's advisory powers do not slip into a *de facto* veto power. The IAB also has the competence to send DGs so-called 'prompt letters', asking them to carry out IAs on items falling outside the current obligatory scope of items included in the Commission's Legislative and Work Programme (*see* below). All IAB opinions are published, alongside the impact assessments on the Commission's dedicated website.[40] Anecdotal evidence suggests that the Impact Assessment Board – with now over a 100 IAs scrutinised and a first annual report published[41] – has a real impact on the way Commission officials approach carrying out an impact assessment, especially because it raises awareness of the tool among the higher ranks of the Commission administration.

The Commission has also acknowledged the need to revise and adapt its Impact Assessment Guidelines with a view to improving the quality of its IAs. To this end, it has published new draft IA guidelines for public consultation during the summer of 2008. The main changes are that a) guidance on specific assessments within the IA framework, notably 'risk assessment' and 'administrative cost measurement', have now been included in the main body of the text,

[38] COM(2006) 689, *supra* note 36, p. 8.

[39] European Commission, Better Regulation website, <ec.europa.eu/governance/better_regulation/impact_en.htm#_quality>, 22 August 2008.

[40] European Commission, Better Regulation website, Impact Assessment page, <ec.europa.eu/governance/impact/index_en.htm>, 22 August 2008.

[41] Impact Assessment Board, Annual Report for the year 2007, Brussels 2008, to be downloaded at <ec.europa.eu/governance/impact/key_en.htm>, 22 August 2008.

b) more precise guidance is being offered on how the principle of proportionate analysis should be applied in practice and c) some procedural guidance has been added, such as on the IAB procedure and on the possibility to carry out IAs on comitology items.

E. *In Summary*

To sum up the characteristics of the EU IA regime in particular, as opposed to the generic concept of impact assessment:

- It concerns rigorous comprehensive analysis of potential impacts of several policy options for all major policy and legislative proposals, based on accurate, objective and complete information;
- It takes an integrated approach: environmental, economic and social impacts;
- Subsidiarity and proportionality tests are integrated into the assessment;
- It is a process and a document;
- No decision criterion is imposed on the legislator, instead presenting trade-offs across various options is encouraged;
- It includes consideration of a range of legislative and non-legislative options;
- Cost-benefit analysis is encouraged but only where appropriate; qualitative analysis is better than quantitative analysis that suffers from 'spurious accuracy' bron quote;
- The principle of proportionate analysis means that the depth of the IA depends on the magnitude of expected impacts;
- It aims at being transparent; all IAs are published on websites;
- Consultation of stakeholders is integrated into the IA process and reported on in the IA report;
- There is inter-institutional cooperation on IA (Institutions inform each other of ongoing IA work and build on each other's work), even if this can not be qualified (yet) as a true common approach.

III. *EU IA and Regulatory Choice*

Turning now to one of these shared principles of EU IA in specific, namely the consideration of non-legislative options as a key to successful IA, we can observe that in the policy debates on Better Regulation references to the crucial link between IA and regulatory alternatives are manifold. For instance, the Committee of the Regions 'considers that a preliminary assessment [...] would be particularly important in terms of the application of non-regulatory instruments (co-regulation and self-regulation).'[42] The European Economic and Social Committee has stated that it is "necessary to substantiate the choice of legislative instrument or potential alternative to legislation (co-regulation, contracts, self-regulation) as stipulated in the Inter-Institutional Agreement of December 2003 on Better Lawmaking (hereafter IIA), and from the viewpoint of its contribution to legal or administrative simplification for end-users."[43]

Furthermore, preferential treatment of self-regulation is a recurring request on the part of business stakeholders.[44] At the same time, however, we can also witness a rather ambivalent approach of the legislative Institutions, in particular of the European Parliament and the Commission, towards the use of alternative regulatory instruments. Self-regulation is defined in the IIA as "the possibility for economic operators, the social partners, non-governmental organisations or associations to adopt amongst themselves and for themselves common guidelines at European level (particularly codes of practice or sectoral agreements)".[45] This top down approach to self-regulation (in the sense of 'delegating responsibilities to private or semi-private bodies'[46] which implies that self-regulatory arrangements need a public seal of approval) fits in with the EU's preoccupation with convergence of national (public) regulatory frameworks. In contrast, a more bottom-up definition would be to speak of self-regulation "when an issue of public interest is addressed by standard-setting, monitoring and/or enforcement carried out by private bodies vis-à-vis their members or affiliates who voluntarily subject themselves to this regulation".[47] As others have signalled before, 'co-regulation' has also acquired a rather specific meaning in the EU: the framework of the rules is laid down in legislative acts of the European Union and co-regulation is an implementing mechanism of these general rules. This technique is usually referred to as 'conditioned self-regulation' in national legal systems.[48] Given that regulation at the EU level is geared towards convergence rather than uniformity

[42] Anne C.M. Meuwese, *Impact Assessment in EU Lawmaking* (Kluwer Law International, The Hague 2008), p. 152.

[43] European Economic and Social Committee, Exploratory opinion on the request of the UK Presidency on Better lawmaking (rapporteur Retureau) OJ C 24 (Brussels 2005), para. 8.1.

[44] Meuwese 2008, *supra* note 42, p. 176. *See also* a letter by VNO/NCW and MKB Nederland on the subject.

[45] Inter-Institutional Agreement on Better Lawmaking (2003), *supra* note 2, p. 1.

[46] Giandomenico Majone, *Regulating Europe* (Routledge, London 1996), p. 23.

[47] Zayenne D. Van Heesen-Laclé and Anne C.M. Meuwese, 'The Legal Framework for Self-Regulation in the Netherlands' (2007) 3:2 *Utrecht Law Review*, pp. 116–139.

[48] Philip Eijlander, 'Possibilities and Constraints in the Use of Self-Regulation and Co-Regulation in Legislative Policy, Experiences in the Netherlands – Lessons to be learned from the EU' (2005) 9:1 *Electronic Journal of Comparative Law*, p. 7.

Eijlander sees co-regulation within the European Union not as exceptional and alternative, but as the primary and general starting point.[49]

This state of affairs triggers the question as to when and under what conditions alternative regulatory mechanisms are actually (to be) preferred over legislative instruments; what guidelines and/or criteria have been established with a view to making regulatory choices in the EU and what legal and other constraints are there in fact to regulatory choice? The way in which self-regulation, soft law and other instruments which can be put under the heading of 'alternative regulatory mechanisms' are approached at the policy, legal and practical levels can also tell us a lot about the direction in which the EU is going with its Better Regulation strategy. This will be the focus of this and the next sections of this chapter.

A. *The Policy Framework*

In section II B we have put forward the two basic, but sometimes conflicting, rationales behind EU IA: the constitutional rationale of regulating better in line with the Treaty and the economic rationale of regulating to improve the overall competitiveness of the European economy. We have established that the political and policy orientation has shifted somewhat towards the economic rationale in the past years. Too much attention for administrative burdens risks moving the function that IA has in practice further away from the 'effective analsis' that was meant to give proportionality and subsidiarity 'teeth'. Although there is certainly a place for the consideration of 'burdens' of regulation in the application of the proportionality principle, the particular methodology of the SCM only considers a fraction of the potential regulatory burdens. Similarly, an economic interpretation of the subsidiarity principle amounts to comparative cost-effectiveness, a decision criterion that is only legitimate if a wide range of costs is considered, preferably against the background of regulatory benefits.

Yet, both the constitutional and the economic rationale carry a preference for alternative regulatory mechanisms. Thus, impact assessment and this built-in preference remain an emanation of the obligation contained in Article 9 of the Protocol on the application of the principles of subsidiarity and proportionality (Protocol) to "take duly into account the need for any burden, whether financial or administrative, falling upon the Community, national governments, local authorities, economic operators and citizens, to be minimised and proportionate to the objective to be achieved". The Protocol specifies that proportionality means that "the form of Community action shall be as simple as possible", that the Community "shall legislate only to the extent necessary" and that

---

[49] *Ibid.*, p. 8.

"Community measures should leave as much scope for national decision as possible" (Article 6).

A recurrent theme in the Better Regulation debate is the EU's desire to improve the quality of European legislation by regulating less through hard law and to use alternative, softer regulatory mechanisms whenever these are appropriate and sufficient to achieve the result strived after. In many Community documents, issued over the past 15 years or so, this starting point has been confirmed, leading up to a joint commitment thereto on the part of the three legislative Institutions in the already mentioned IIA 'Better lawmaking', seeking also to operationalise the regulatory guidelines for the application of the proportionality principle. It contains a section dedicated explicitly to the 'choice of legislative instrument and legal basis', followed by a particular heading on the 'use of alternative methods of regulation'. According to these provisions, the Commission has to explain and justify to the European Parliament and to the Council its choice of legislative instrument, in particular in the explanatory memoranda attached to its initiatives. It also has to consider any request in this connection from these two bodies. The Commission will also have to ensure "that the action it proposes is as simple as is compatible with the proper attainment of the objective of the measure and the need for effective implementation." (cons. 12)

In its explanatory memoranda, the Commission must further explain how the measures it proposes are justified in the light of the principles of subsidiarity and proportionality. In doing so, "an account must be given of the scope and the results of the consultations the Commission has conducted and of the impact analyses it has undertaken" (cons. 15). Next, the three Institutions recall the Community's obligation "to legislate only where it is necessary, in accordance with the Protocol [...]" and, most importantly for the purposes of our contribution, it is explicitly stated that "they recognise the need to use, in suitable cases or where the Treaty does not specifically require the use of a legal instrument, alternative regulation mechanisms".

From the considerations that follow, which will be discussed in more detail in the next sections, it becomes clear that by 'alternative regulation mechanisms' the Institutions understand the mechanisms of co-regulation and self-regulation. The Protocol and the IIA thus contain guidelines for the application of the leading principles for lawmaking as contained in Article 5 EC, and thereby for the regulatory choices to be made by the EU. These guidelines are further elaborated in the Impact Assessment Guidelines, which the Commission has drawn up in 2005 and which were under revision at the time of writing (*see* sections III.C.2 and IV).

Even if the legislative Institutions have committed themselves to a common view and approach of the use of certain alternative regulatory mechanisms, there are signs of an ambivalent approach towards such alternative mechanisms. As a 'regulatory power house', with very limited possibilities for steering through spending and built on the principle of conferred powers and defined regulatory mandates in the EC Treaty, the Commission has traditionally favoured regulation through law and legislation. This has also induced a certain suspicion towards alternatives to classical regulation on the part of the legislative Institutions, as we can see reflected in the fact that the IIA takes a rather top-down interpretation of 'self-regulation': self-regulatory agreements or private regulation are not in fact recognised in their pure form and are only labelled as such when they are monitored by the Commission. Apart from this and as touched upon already above, we can see an ambivalent approach in a number of documents issued by the Commission and the European Parliament.

The latter has expressed itself on the use of alternative mechanisms on several occasions. In a reaction to the Molitor report it took a rather favourable stance towards self-regulation, calling for the enactment of several criteria for the assessment of future legislative proposals. The necessity of intervention ("or can self-regulation or other problem management or resolution mechanism be left to solve the problem or the situation")[50] was one of those criteria. About a decade later, however, an own-initiative report by European Parliament on the institutional and legal implications of the use of soft law instruments shows that it has become very critical of the issue, considering that, "in the context of the Community, soft law all too often constitutes an ambiguous and ineffective instrument which is liable to have a detrimental effect on Community legislation and institutional balance and should be used with caution, even where it is provided for in the Treaty". The report and the resolution recall that soft law "cannot be a substitute for legal acts and instruments, which are available to ensure the continuity of the legislative process, especially in the field of culture and education".[51]

The ambivalent attitude towards alternative mechanisms is also reflected in the IA Guidelines of the European Commission of 2005, which provide the following guidance on the consideration of alternative mechanisms in IAs:

> The option of 'no EU action' should always be considered, except in cases where there is an obligation to act laid down by the Treaties. It is also advisable to consider,

---

[50] European Parliament, Resolution on the report of the group of independent experts on simplification of Community legislation and administrative provisions ('Deregulation'), Reaction to the Molitor report, A4-0201/1996, point 1.13.

[51] European Parliament press release, Better regulation in the EU – MEPs adopt four reports, 4 September 2007, <www.europarl.europa.eu/news/expert/infopress_page/008-9997-246-09-36-901-20070823IPR09760-03-09-2007-2007-false/default_sv.htm.ep> (Brussels/Strasbourg 2007); Medina Ortega report on the use of 'soft law' (2007) – European Parliament, 'Report on institutional and legal implications of the use of "soft law" instruments, Committee' on Legal Affairs (rapporteur: Medina Ortega), A6-0259/2007, 4 September 2007 (Brussels/Strasbourg 2007) and the subsequent resolution of the European Parliament on this, P6-TA(2007)0366.

> where relevant, including an alternative approach to 'classical' forms of regulation, *unless a decision by the Commission has already ruled this out.*[52] [our italics]

However, a more recent Commission Communication on the application of Community law shows a preference on the part of the Commission for the use of regulations, in particular with a view to establishing implementing measures:

> Maximum effort should be made to ensure the clarity, simplicity, operability and enforceability of legislation. Increased attention should be paid to aspects of implementation, management and enforcement in the development of proposals, in particular at the impact assessment stage, and throughout the policy cycle. The impact assessment should examine implementation options and their implications, as well as the choice of legal instrument with a view to best facilitating the effectiveness of the measure. *Regulations should be used wherever appropriate and to the greatest extent possible for implementing measures.*[53] [our italics]

Still one can say that, overall, the EU better regulation strategy takes a favourable stance on regulatory alternatives. This is reflected also in the fact that the draft IA Guidelines of 2008 (*see* further section IV) strengthen the call for explicit consideration of self-regulation and other alternative mechanisms, an aspect that was already present in the 2005 Guidelines. Statements like the aforementioned must be read in this broader context and in particular in the light of the duties which the principle of proportionality, established in primary Community law, imposes on the Commission when developing regulatory initiatives. Even if we will see below that this principle does not amount to a strong 'meta-rule' in the sense that self-regulation and other soft regulatory mechanisms should *always* be considered before resorting to hard regulatory solutions and does not award any enforceable rights to stakeholders, it raises expectations among stakeholders and it has a bearing on the political discourse. On a side note, the issue also suffers from a lack of conceptual clarity: we find occasional confusion of 'soft law' and 'self-regulation' in policy documents.[54]

B. *Legal and Other Constraints to Regulatory Choice*

Before digging deeper into the question as to how the Commission takes, and in our view should take, the possibility of alternative regulatory mechanisms into consideration within the IA framework, we must deal with the issue of the legal and other constraints actually restricting the choice of regulatory mechanisms.

---

[52] Impact Assessment Guidelines, *supra* note 3, p. 24.

[53] European Commission, A Europe of results. Applying Community law, COM(2007) 502 final.

[54] European Commission, Better Regulation for Growth and Jobs in the European Union, COM(2005) 97, 16 March 2005 (Brussels 2005). Footnote 5 on p. 4 of this communication mistakenly claims that "'soft law' instruments refers to co-regulation and self-regulation".

The presumption that whoever is allowed to do more – in this case adopt legislation – is also allowed to do less – adopt softer regulatory mechanisms – is wide-spread. It may often hold true in a purely national context, but not within the context of the EU, as the EU has not been given full legislative powers and all its activities are tied to the principle of attributed powers. More in particular, one must note that classical regulation through legislation in this context has another function than in purely national contexts; there is no question of a general EC/EU power to regulate in view of the general public interest, but only in view of certain goals. By far the most important regulatory goal is still the realisation and functioning of the internal market and the regulation of a number of flanking policies.[55] This means that the Treaty drafters have defined the scope and nature of the powers conferred upon the EC and EU, and these may be of a legislative nature or not. We argue here that the above presumption is wrong and that not only the EC Treaty in and of itself imposes limitations on the regulatory choice to be made, but so do certain principles of law. Apart from that, the IIA also formulates some boundaries to the use of alternative regulatory mechanisms, both of a legal and of a more substantive nature. Even if the IIA only covers the mechanisms of co-regulation and self-regulation as alternative regulatory mechanisms, the boundaries identified in it are relevant for the use of other regulatory mechanisms as well, including the open method of coordination and soft law instruments more in general.

1. *Legal basis constraints*

When do the Treaties impose 'an obligation to act' upon the EU, in the sense of the above quotation of the IA Guidelines and what does such an obligation actually entail? Or, to what extent do the Treaties, in particular the EC Treaty, leave or create uncertainty as regards the regulatory method and instrument to be adopted in a certain policy area? The indication in a Treaty provision (or a provision of secondary law for that matter) of a certain instrument would be superfluous, if this would not entail a certain regulation of (the exercise of) power.[56] The drafters of the Treaty have already indicated to a certain extent what level of 'regulatory intensity' of Community action is strived for in a certain area, possibly as an alternative to legislation. The formulation of the Treaty provisions is thus of decisive importance for establishing the actual scope for regulatory choice; the more 'open' a Treaty legal basis has been formulated, the more scope

---

55 *See also* Ernst M.H. Hirsch Ballin and Linda A.J. Senden, *Co-actorship in the Development of European Law-making. The Quality of European Legislation and its Implementation and Application in the National Legal Order* (TMC Asser Press, The Hague 2005), p. 31.

56 *See* Manfred Zuleeg, 'Die Kompetenzen der Europäischen Gemeinschaften gegenüber den Mitgliedstaaten' in Gerhard Leibholz (ed.), *JöR, Band 20, JCB Mohr* (Paul Siebeck, Tübingen 1971), p. 7.

the Institutions have for the use of alternative regulatory mechanisms. At least three types of legal basis can be distinguished in this regard.

At one end of the spectrum we find *obligating* legal foundations, stipulating that the Council or another Institution "shall issue directives or regulations" (e.g. Article 40 EC). Such a provision imposes an unequivocal obligation on the Institution concerned to adopt legally binding measures, in one of the instruments indicated. In such circumstances the legislator cannot suffice with the adoption of other, softer mechanisms and as such there is hardly any scope left for a subsidiarity and/or proportionality assessment. This thought is also implied in point 16 of the IIA, in which the Institutions indicate that alternative regulation mechanisms can only be used "where the Treaty does not specifically require the use of a legal instrument." At the other end of the spectrum we find provisions that we can describe as *prohibiting* legal foundations, because they exclude expressly the harmonisation of legislation, such as Article 151(5) EC. This provision allows the Council to adopt in the area of culture only stimulation measures in the form of recommendations, excluding the harmonisation of legal and administrative provisions of the Member States. So, this kind of legal basis provides already for other instruments than classical Community legislation. In the case of such provisions, the Treaty drafters have considerably limited the scope for any subsidiarity and proportionality assessment beforehand, by defining in a rather strict way the scope and exercise of Community powers in the area at issue.

In between these two extremes we find *enabling* legal bases which are most interesting for our purposes. These vary in degree of openness. Article 13 EC for instance stipulates that the Council "may adopt appropriate measures" to combat forms of discrimination mentioned in that provision. This legal basis leaves the European legislator full discretion to determine, in the light of the subsidiarity and proportionality principles, whether European measures are necessary at all and if so, whether that should be done in the form of classical, hard legislation or in a soft law form. The provision in itself does not compel the adoption of legislation, but it does allow for this.[57] Formulations such as 'the Council shall adopt measures', which are frequent in Title IV of the EC-Treaty regarding visa, asylum and immigration policy, are more complex because they are obligating in the sense that Community measures have to be adopted, but enabling as to their form and legal nature. These provisions thus leave considerable scope for a proportionality assessment.

What the outcome will be of this assessment, whether the choice will be made for legislation or for an alternative regulatory mechanism, will depend mainly

[57] The adoption on this legal basis of Directive 2000/43/EC, OJ 2000, L180/22 and Directive 2000/78/EC, OJ 2000, L303/16 testify of this.

on the goals of such provisions. The European Court of Justice has made clear in this respect that the Institutions are obliged to choose the instrument that is most apt for realising the objectives of the measure in question and of the Treaty provisions it is founded upon.[58] Where for example the Treaty aims at establishing a common transport policy with a view to a good functioning of the internal market, a failure to establish such a policy infringes the free movement of services and forces the legislator to take the necessary measures to remedy this situation.[59] Where a common policy of the EC is envisaged, the mere adoption of soft regulatory mechanisms will not be sufficient to achieve this. So, even where the Treaty leaves open the choice of instrument, this does not bestow a completely free choice upon the legislator.

The obvious difficulty arising in a particular instance, is to define the exact objective or scope of a certain Treaty provision. At the general level, useful indications can be found in the terminology used throughout the Treaty of 'common policy', 'harmonisation' or 'approximation of legislative and administrative provisions of the Member States' and 'coordination (of policy)'. These terms provide important clues as to what competence has been conferred upon the EC in a certain area – exclusive, shared or merely complementary – and as to what regulatory intensity is aimed at. Areas in which the EC is considered to have exclusive competence are characterised by the aim to establish a common policy, as reflected in the predominant use of regulations at the level of instruments. This can be clearly seen in the areas of external trade policy, agriculture, fisheries and transport; achieving a true common policy in these areas generally requires uniform rules that are uniformly applied in the Member States. This in turn can be best ensured by resorting to the instrument of the regulation, as this instrument is directly applicable in the national legal orders without any transposition measures being required, or better, being allowed.[60] We can see a confirmation of this also in the IIA, where it is stipulated that alternative regulatory mechanisms cannot be applicable "where the rules must be applied in a uniform fashion in all Member States".[61] In areas of shared competence, regulatory intervention is often envisaged to be aimed at harmonisation, of which the area of the internal market clearly testifies. The use of directives is predominant here, as this leaves room for both EC and national regulation. Where EC action is only to be complementary to national action, coordination of national policies may be all that is strived for. For instance, the use of non-binding guidelines or

---

[58] For an overview of implementation problems to do with the use of soft instruments by the EU, *see* Gerda Falkner *et al., Complying with Europe: EU Harmonisation and Soft Law in the Member States* (Cambridge University Press, Cambridge 2005).

[59] Case 13/83 Parliament v. Council, ECR [1985], 1513.

[60] Article 249 EC.

[61] *Supra* note 2, point 17.

recommendations reflects this limited power of the EC and the low intensity of Community interference that is correspondingly allowed for.

The existence of these different types of EC (and also EU) competences, contained in and to be distilled from the separate Treaty provisions, reflects a certain division of powers between the EC/EU and its Member States. Every EU/EC exercise of power will thus have to take this division of power into account and justify the result of any balancing of powers that has taken place on the basis of the Treaty provision at play. The catalogue of Union competences as contained in the Treaty of Lisbon sheds more light on the nature and scope of Union competences vis-à-vis national competences, at least at a theoretical level. This innovation, if adopted, may contribute to an easier assessment of the areas which require European legislation and which could possibly be regulated in other ways.[62]

2. *Boundaries imposed by general principles of law*

To summarise our argument above: whether alternative regulatory mechanisms may be resorted to depends on the degree of 'openness' of the Treaty legal basis at issue and its proclaimed goal. Certain enabling Treaty provisions may leave more scope for an assessment in terms of subsidiarity and proportionality, whereas others leave less. These principles serve in particular the vertical division of powers, between the EC/EU and the Member States. However, other principles of law have to be made part of this assessment as well. Where subsidiarity and proportionality pull in the direction of the least intrusive measures and therefore to the use of softer regulatory mechanisms, leaving as much leeway as possible to the Member States, other principles pull into the direction of classical regulation. In points 2 and 8 of the Protocol, the principles of Community loyalty, institutional balance (protecting the horizontal division of powers in-between the European Institutions), and effectiveness (including uniform application and equality) have been formulated as a kind of counterweight. The Protocol even goes as far as to subject the application of the principles of subsidiarity and proportionality to an assessment on the basis of the said principles and thereby seems to imply a certain hierarchy of principles. Apart from this, the principles of transparency and legal certainty impose certain limits to the use of soft regulatory mechanisms too.[63] If such a mechanism for instance creates uncertainty about the rights and duties for enterprises or if the Commission tries to create new legal rules in such a mechanism, this contravenes the principle of

---

[62] *See* articles 2 to 6 of the Treaty on the Functioning of the European Union.

[63] Linda A.J. Senden, *Soft law in European Community Law* (Hart Publishing, Oxford 2004), pp. 331–340. *See also* in this sense the resolution of the European Parliament, *supra* note 51.

legal certainty and the principle of institutional balance, leaving hard legislation as the only option.[64]

Strikingly, the new version of the Protocol, attached to the Treaty of Lisbon, no longer refers to the institutional balance and Community loyalty. Article 296 of the Treaty on the Functioning of the European Union could also give the impression that in the case of enabling legal bases the choice of instrument has to be made predominantly on the basis of the proportionality principle, without any other principles playing a role in this regard. It stipulates that "[w]here the Treaties do not specify the type of act to be adopted, the institutions shall select it on a case-by-case basis, in compliance with the applicable procedures and with the principle of proportionality". However, even if these provisions do not refer explicitly to other general principles of law, the fact remains that all legislative Institutions are obliged to make regulatory choices that can stand the test of all the general – both written and unwritten – principles of law they have to comply with under Community law.

3. *Substantive boundaries*

There are not only formal, legal constraints that impose boundaries to the regulatory choice of the EU Institutions, but also constraints of a more substantive nature which the Institutions have imposed upon themselves in point 17 of the IIA, by agreeing that

> [t]hese [alternative regulatory-AMLS] mechanisms will not be applicable where fundamental rights or important political options are at stake or in situations where the rules must be applied in a uniform fashion in all Member States. They must ensure swift and flexible regulation.

As such, this provision can be said to entail boundaries to the use of alternative mechanisms that are induced by both (democratic) legitimacy and effectiveness concerns. The obvious conclusion to be drawn from this provision is that the use of alternative regulatory mechanisms is deemed effective and should consequently be considered in cases and areas that ask for swift and flexible regulation, for instance because of the high speed of technological developments or because of quickly changing market circumstances. Whenever uniform application is called for in a particular situation, it is made clear that this goal cannot be effectively achieved through the use of alternative regulatory instruments, turning the adoption of classical regulation into a necessity. Elaborating upon what has already been observed above (III.B.1), it should be added here that in the areas which aim at establishing a common policy and for which the EC has been attributed

64 The re-regulation that has taken place in the area of state aid, 'transposing' in fact a number of soft law acts into legislative acts can also be seen in this light. *See* Senden 2004, *supra* note 63, pp. 332–334.

exclusive powers there can be very little discussion about the appropriate choice of instrument. In areas in which the EC and the Member States have shared powers,[65] such as the internal market, there is more legal scope for such a discussion. Yet, one can say that in order for regulation in this area to be effective, a certain degree of uniformity is a *conditio sine qua non*. Hence, a certain degree of classical regulation is an absolute requirement for this area as well.

Whenever there is a need for important political decisions to be taken in a certain area or when issues are concerned that touch upon the protection of fundamental rights, the IIA rules out the use of alternative mechanisms. Without making this explicit, both these limitations will in practice also affect important aspects of social-economic, internal market regulation. In such cases classical regulation according to the Community method, entailing an important role for the European Parliament, is called for. One may argue that this is called for in order to ensure at least a certain degree of democratic decision-making, even if this rationale is not explicated.

Finally, it can also be inferred from the IIA that if the outcome of the IA would point into the direction of using soft law for example, the Commission is not bound by that as it merely imposes a duty upon the Commission "to give an account of the scope and the results of the prior consultation and the impact analyses that it has undertaken" (para. 15). This is also confirmed in other documents ('IA is an aid to decision-making, not a substitute', *see* section IIC).

4. *Conditions Regarding the Use of Alternative Regulatory Mechanisms*

Once it has been established that there is room for choosing alternative regulatory mechanisms and that this will be the appropriate choice in the case at hand, the use of such mechanisms has to comply with a number of conditions. These can be inferred from the IIA, reflecting as such the top-down approach the European Institutions take towards the issue, but some also flow from general principles of law. The IIA stipulates that

[65] According to Articles 2 to 6 of the Treaty on the Functioning of the European Union, these areas are: the internal market, social policy, economic, social and territorial cohesion, environment, consumer protection, trans-European networks, energy, the area of freedom, security and justice, common safety concerns in public health matters and also agriculture, fisheries and transport. The three latter areas are now commonly considered to be areas falling within the Union's exclusive competence, at least in practice. Under the new Treaty, exclusive competences are considered to exist as regards the customs union, the establishment of the competition rules necessary for the functioning of the internal market, monetary policy to some extent, the conservation of marine biological resources under the common fisheries policy, the common commercial policy. Supplementing, coordinating and supplementary powers are considered to concern the areas of the protection and improvement of human health, industry, culture, tourism, education, vocational training, youth and sport, civil protection and administrative cooperation.

> the Commission will ensure that any use of co-regulation or self-regulation is always *consistent with Community law* and that it meets the criteria of *transparency* (in particular the publicising of agreements) and *representativeness* of the parties involved. It must also represent *added value for the general interest.* [...] They must ensure swift and flexible regulation which does not affect *the principles of competition or the unity of the internal market.* [our emphasis]

The IIA further specifies that co-regulation may be used on the basis of criteria that are defined in the legislative act underlying it (point 18). The Commission also has to inform the Council and the European Parliament of those forms of self-regulation that it deems to a) contribute to the realisation of the goals of the EC Treaty whilst in conformity with its provisions and b) considers to be satisfactory as regards the representativeness of the parties involved, the sectoral and geographical coverage and the added value of the commitments given (point 23).

The requirement of representativeness of the parties involved,[66] nor any of the other conditions for the use of alternative regulatory instruments is further explained or elaborated in the IIA. This does not seem to be too problematic for the purely legal assessment of whether the use of such alternative mechanisms is consistent with Community law.[67] That is not to imply that for instance the competition law test which the IIA explicitly foresees, will always be an easy one to perform, but at least the standard by which to assess this use is a fairly established one. It is consistent case law that "Articles 10 EC and 81 EC are infringed where a Member State requires or encourages the adoption of agreements, decisions or concerted practices contrary to Article 81 EC or reinforces their effects, or where it divests its own rules of the character of legislation by delegating to private economic operators responsibility for taking decisions affecting the economic sphere."[68]

Considering the compliance with the other conditions contained in the IIA may be far more complicated, as these actually involve a more political assessment or at least presuppose a certain vision of what socio-economic values underlie the internal market, as a basis for scrutinising the contents of self-regulatory and co-regulatory initiatives. What does the 'unity of the market' actually require and when can one speak of an 'added value for the general interest' of the use of a co-regulatory or self-regulatory mechanism? The IIA does not in any way

---

66 In the framework of Articles 138–139 EC regarding the European social dialogue, representativeness of the social partners even remains a problematic issue until today.

67 For instance, IA should not go against Article 174 TEC which stipulates that lawmaking in the environmental field 'shall be based on the precautionary principle'.

68 Case C-446/05, Ioannis Doulamis, judgment of 13 March 2008, para. 20, building on previous rulings e.g. in Cases: C-250/03, Mauri, [2005] ECR I-1267; C-94/04 and C-202/04 Cipolla, [2006] ECR I-11421 and in particular 267/86 Van Eycke, [1988] ECR 4769.

substantiate these notions nor can these be filled in simply on the basis of the Treaty itself or of the Court's case law. In the next sections, we will consider to what extent the Impact Assessment Guidelines which the Commission has drawn up for its internal use provide more clues as to how to understand these notions and what criteria for their testing it may have elaborated, as demonstrated perhaps also in the IA practice.

Another observation here is that at various instances above, effectiveness has been hinted at as a requirement for the use of alternative regulatory mechanisms. The transparency requirement can be considered to be part of this, but one can add to this that in order to be effective, the use of alternatives must be credible and in line with existing policy as well as clear as far as implementation and enforcement are concerned.[69] The IIA stipulates in this regard that the legislator can provide for measures regarding the follow up of the application of the co-regulation mechanism in the basic legislative act, impose an information duty on the Commission or insert a revision clause in case the legislator is not satisfied with the result of the co-regulation (point 21). In the case of self-regulation, the IIA stipulates that the Commission will examine the possibility of a proposal for legislation upon request of the legislative authority or in the case of failure of the self-regulation practice (point 23).

C. *The Choice of Alternative Regulatory Mechanisms in EU IA Practice*

1. *From Theory to Practice*

How does the tool of IA give hands and feet in practice to the theoretical starting points of the EU's legislative and regulatory policy? Or, what criteria and strategies have been developed in EU IA-practice for the consideration of alternative regulatory mechanisms, in addition to or in clarification of the ones discussed above? A first preliminary observation in response to these questions is that, it is very difficult to assess whether the use of IAs thus far has led to an increased consideration of and choice for alternative mechanisms, including co-regulation, self-regulation, OMC and soft law more in general. Investigating the relationship between the introduction of IA and the use of alternatives to classical regulation in practice poses namely all sorts of methodological problems, one major complicating factor being in this regard, leaving causality issues aside, that there is little data available. Yet, at least three analytical approaches can be taken that can provide us with some answers to the questions posed above.

---

[69] These elements have also been underlined at a recent public hearing about 'The Current State of European Self- and Co-Regulation', organised by the European Economic and Social Committee on 31 March 2008 in Brussels.

A first approach is the scorecard approach which surveys a relatively large number of IAs, as opposed to an in-depth approach building on a few IA case studies and taking into account legal subtleties.[70] An example of the scorecard approach provides Renda's study on the early years of EU IA, who scored the European Commission IAs that were available by late 2005.[71] According to his study, on average 18% of the IAs considered self-regulation, 18% co-regulation and 17.2% soft law. As such this study provides us with a useful first general impression of the extent to which the Commission is putting theory to practice, but one must acknowledge that this concerns still a very rough and still rather imprecise impression. This is the case first of all because only from 2006 onwards the impact assessment system was professionalised to a substantial degree, second, there is simply no data available from before the introduction of IA to compare these numbers to, and third, it tells us very little in itself about what this consideration has actually entailed. Later research by the same author, in collaboration with others, shows that the consideration of alternatives has become a more integrated and structural part of EU IA, which is taken to be an important criterion for measuring the quality of performed EU IAs.[72] While this study stated that between 2005–2007 all IAs considered at least one alternative,[73] it also concluded that this has been "usually the alternative of not regulating".[74] So, these figures do not tell us much as yet about the actual consideration of self-regulation, co-regulation or other alternative regulatory options. Furthermore, this study also shows that the substantive consideration of alternatives still falls short or is at least immature in the sense that these are not sufficiently assessed in terms of their actual costs and benefits and the balancing thereof.[75] So, even if one may conclude on the basis of this scorecard research that in EU IA practice there is some progress in the actual consideration of alternatives to classical legislation, the way in which this is being done still leaves much to be desired.

Apart from that, we are also still largely left in the dark as regards the actual outcome of such consideration: when has it been opted for classical regulation, no regulation or for an alternative solution in-between and on what grounds

[70] An obvious fourth one that could be taken, concerns a case studies approach, but given the scarcity/paucity still of actual research conducted on our research question, we feel this would carry too much an element of 'randomness' in its selection, the findings of which would be very difficult to generalise.

[71] Renda 2005, *supra* note 35.

[72] Caroline Cecot *et al.*, An Evaluation of the Quality of Impact Assessment in the European Union with Lessons for the US and the EU, AEI-Brookings Joint Center Working Paper No. 07–09, December 2007.

[73] *Ibid. See* in particular figure 4 on p. 20.

[74] *Ibid.*, p. 9.

[75] *Ibid.*, p. 9 and Table 1 at p. 16.

exactly? Looking at this from a more general angle and in the light of what the Better Regulation strategy has produced in terms of results up to now, a recent study by the Centre for European Policy Studies (CEPS) interestingly concludes that the number of proposed legislative acts ('hard law') by the Barroso Commission has in fact remained almost stable in comparison to its predecessor (–2.8%) and that the number of 'soft law' initiatives (measured as Green Papers, Communications, etc.) has increased since 2005 (+18.1%).[76] The same study found that the Barroso Commission proposed less new law, and often limited itself to revisions of existing law which could amount to simplification (and thus not necessarily adding to regulatory burdens but actually reducing them), but the data presented do no allow for verification of this assertion. Only in one area, the researchers found a significant decrease of entirely new legislative proposals – a shift they attribute to the Better Regulation agenda – namely in the field of Internal Market regulation.[77] But the temptation to measure success in terms of a reduction of the amount of regulatory output is never far away:

> With the exception of the internal market, neither the 'better regulation'-agenda nor 'saturation' in traditional policy areas appear to have had a major effect on the quantity of Commission output so far.[78]

A second approach consisting of a further analysis of policy documents may contribute to our understanding of what is actually happening in EU IA practice at the level of regulatory choice; what language is used and what strategy or guidelines have been developed at policy level to justify regulatory choices within the framework of EU IA? Are these sufficient for steering those concerned properly in their consideration of alternatives or are we to conclude that these are not fully adequate, which may also help explaining the above outcome of the scorecard research? This will be dealt with in more detail in the next subsection, discussing in particular the 2005 IA Guidelines. In that framework, we will also mention some examples of cases in which the Commission discarded the use of legislation and discussed different options, to see how the Commission goes about in applying its own policy guidelines and determines the different policy options and its regulatory choice in the end.

These two approaches can be supplemented with a valuable third approach, based on the opinions delivered by the Impact Assessment Board. By making use of the growing leverage of this Board and the growing 'case law' that comes with it, we can attempt to find out how Commission services are being both assessed and steered on the issue of considering alternative regulatory mecha-

---

[76] Sebastian Kurpas *et al.*, The European Commission after Enlargement: Does More Add Up to Less? (CEPS Special Report, February 2008), p. i.

[77] *Ibid.*, p. 20.

[78] *Ibid.*

nisms. Of course the opinions do not necessarily represent the core of what went on in the lawmaking debate, but it is the most normative output of an increasingly systematic and well-documented debate on lawmaking. To put it differently: IAB quality control output can be taken as a proxy for the European Commission's interpretation and application of the norms of Better Regulation. Even if the content of IAB reports is removed from what goes on 'on the ground' of the daily reality of lawmaking, we do find in these documents some of the most pressing dilemmas of EU lawmaking and the practical solutions that an authoritative body offers to them. Depending thus on how the IAB deals with the issue of alternatives in carrying out its ex post quality assessment of EU IA, this may contribute to an enhanced and improved *ex ante* assessment of alternative regulatory mechanisms in following IAs and, in the long run, in establishing a clearer vision on this on the part of the Commission.

2. *The 2005 IA Guidelines*

The guidance on when and how to consider alternative mechanisms which flows from the Protocol and the IIA BL can be said to be rather thin. Nonetheless, a few years down the line, the Commission is very confidently pronouncing the link between IA and enhanced consideration of regulatory alternatives. In its first Strategic review of the Better regulation strategy, it thus held already that "[t]he option of no EU action together with alternatives to legally binding legislation (self- and co-regulation) is routinely examined" and that "[a]s a result, some planned measures have been significantly adjusted."[79] Allegedly, impact assessments in the following areas led to the conclusion that binding measures were not necessary: biomass, urban environment and copyright in the online music sector.[80]

The Commission's examination is based on the internal guidelines for impact assessment, which were revised in 2005 and made public. When scrutinising this document on how the Commission is to make its regulatory choice in a given instance, the following elements can be highlighted. First of all, the issue of regulatory choice is to some extent made part of the discussion of the principle of proportionate analysis, which contributes to some terminological and conceptual confusion as regulatory choice is foremost connected to the principle of proportionality. Yet, the guidelines hold that in the case of 'new' regulatory proposals, meaning that when action is under consideration regarding an area that was previously left to the Member States or that concerns an entirely new area, the necessity (subsidiarity) and the proportionality of the proposed action must

[79] Strategic Review of Better Regulation in the European Union, *supra* note 36. This statement was more or less confirmed in its Second Strategic Review, *supra* note 1.

[80] *Supra* note 26, p. 8.

be scrutinised.[81] In the case of revision of existing legislation, the Commission must examine whether the problem has changed and/or whether the original objectives of the legislation are still valid. If not, alternative options will have to be assessed, but the Commission underlines at the same time that "[f]requent change of policy instruments may indeed be costly".[82]

Secondly, the Commission distinguishes six key analytical steps in EU IA: 1) problem-definition, 2) setting of objectives, 3) identification of policy options, 4) analysis of economic, social and environmental impacts, 5) comparison of options and 6) organisation of future monitoring and evaluation. At different stages in the elaboration of these steps, the Commission touches upon the issue of choice of instrument. As part of the first step of problem-definition, the Commission thus recognises the necessity to establish the Union's right to act in regard of a certain problem. Yet, the guidance given in this respect is very superficial and far from representing the full picture. It is merely stated that "it must be possible to link the problem and at least one article of the Treaties", that the Union must act within the limits of the powers conferred upon it and that in the case of shared powers the Commission must demonstrate that the problem cannot be sufficiently solved by the Members States. As seen in section III B, however, there is far more to the issue of legal constraints for the EC/EU to act. It is also stated in this respect that fundamental rights "may pose legal limits to the Union's right to take action on the problem" and that "impact assessment can be a useful tool in identifying possible impacts on fundamental rights and assessing whether those are proportionate." For more detailed information, reference is made to the Commission Communication on Compliance with the Charter of Fundamental Rights in Commission legislative proposals.[83]

As part of the third step, the identification of the policy options, the Guidelines indicate that this may concern different 'basic approaches', including in particular Community legal acts, legal acts of the Member States, self-regulation and economic incentives. It is also observed that different choices can be combined in a package, and possibly coordinated with Member State action. The most appropriate delivery mechanisms must be considered, regulatory versus non-regulatory approaches, also with a view to force those concerned by the guidelines to think 'out of the box'.[84] This is understood to increase transparency and to offer information to policy-makers and stakeholders as to why some options have been discarded at an early stage. This must also be documented

[81] IA Guidelines, *supra* note 3, p. 8.

[82] *Ibid.*

[83] European Commission, Compliance with the Charter of Fundamental Rights in Commission legislative proposals, COM(2005) 172, 27 April 2005 (Brussels 2005). *See also* IA Guidelines, *supra* note 3, p. 18.

[84] IA Guidelines, *supra* note 3, p. 23.

and presented in the resulting 'IA report'. The instruction is further given that policy-makers have to draw up an initial, extensive list of alternative policy options and that the option of no EU action should always be considered, unless when an obligation to act is imposed by the Treaties. In identifying and screening the different options, elements to be taken into account are: can they count on considerable support, do they take account of existing EU policies as well as existing or planned Member State policies or international agreements, how realistic are they and what technical and other constraints are there. What these 'other constraints' may consist of is in no way whatsoever clarified, but one could think here of the legal constraints identified in section III B above. The guidelines put most emphasis, however, on the measurement of the different options against the criteria of effectiveness, efficiency and consistency. This is confirmed by step five, on how the options compare, which considers comparative effectiveness to be an important evaluation criterion, but also mentions proportionality. The results and the alternative options that have been considered need in all cases to be presented "in a transparent and understandable way to provide the basis for a political discussion on the relative advantages and disadvantages of the relevant options", which will allow political decision-makers to examine the trade-offs between affected groups and/or between the economic, social and environmental impacts.[85]

Regarding step four, the analysis of impacts, we can find some of the limits to and conditions for the choice of regulatory instruments that are contained already in the IIA, implied in the tables which the Commission has drawn up and that are to act as an aid for those concerned to think about the wider potential impacts for the different policy options at issue. These include in particular the question as to how the option affects EU competition policy and the functioning of the internal market and the question (in the table on social impacts) as to how the option affects certain fundamental rights, in particular equality of treatment and opportunities and non-discrimination (such as gender equality). Yet, the guidelines nor the Commission Communication on the Charter of Fundamental Rights clarify in what sense human rights actually restrict the choice for an alternative regulatory instrument and when the Commission should opt for a legislative measure because of this. Given this, one wonders for instance how to evaluate the fact that in the area of social law, an area prone to touching upon fundamental rights, quite a lot of soft law is being adopted, often, but not always, linked to the use of the open method of coordination.

A final observation is that, in practice, it appears that what is meant by 'options' varies from one IA to the next: sometimes options are set at the level of broad regulatory techniques that could be used, at other times they consist

---

[85] *Ibid.*, p. 44.

of a detailed set of varying legal solutions. However, it is quite common for IAs to quickly rule out exactly those options that go under the heading of 'self-regulation' or 'co-regulation' by stating that these will not solve the problem, without necessarily providing arguments to support this claim. One example is the IA that was carried out for the Roaming Regulation.[86] A second example can be found in the REACH IA. Here the use of "alternative, more flexible, policy instruments such as co-regulation or selfregulation" was discarded because "[c]hemicals is an area of Community activity that should be governed by full harmonization because of the need to preserve the integrity of the internal market, to avoid trade distortions and conflicts and to guarantee a high level of protection of health and the environment".[87] Circular arguments such as this one (presenting objectives such as 'preserving the integrity of the internal market', 'avoiding trade distortions' and 'guaranteeing a high level of protection of health and the environment' as the solution rather than as the benchmark for assessing impacts of various options) can often be found in impact assessments and form a common pitfall.[88] In other IAs, such as in the IA on data retention, 'do nothing', 'self-regulation'and 'soft law' aproaches are simply brushed aside with a short reference to 'the developments in this area over the past few years'.[89] As the Guidelines do not add much to the Protocol and the IIA in terms of more concrete guidance on how to proceed in the assessment of different regulatory options, this development in EU IA practice is not really surprising.

3. *Analysis of IAB Opinions*

The Impact Assessment Board has asserted that it will take an active role in encouraging the consideration of regulatory alternatives. In its first annual report the Board suggests that its 'early quality support function' could be strengthened, if there are more explicit requirements for Roadmaps. This should ensure that they contain detailed information on up-to-date information on "the need for

---

[86] European Commission, Impact assessment of policy options in relation to a Commission proposal for a regulation of the European Parliament and of the Council on roaming on public mobile networks within the Community, SEC(2006) 925, 12 July 2006 (Brussels 2006); Regulation (EC) No 717/2007 of the European Parliament and the Council of 27 June 2007 on roaming in public mobile telephone networks within the Community amending Directive 2002/21/EC, OJ L 171, 29 June 2007. *See also* Meuwese 2008, *supra* note 42, p. 62.

[87] European Commission, Extended Impact Assessment on Framework Legislation on Chemical Substances (establishing REACH), SEC(2003) 1171, 29 October 2003 (Brussels 2003), p. 5.

[88] Meuwese 2008, *supra* note 42, p. 195.

[89] European Commission, 'Extended Impact Assessment of the Proposal for a Directive of the European Parliament and of the Council on the retention of data processed in connection with the provision of public electronic communication services and amending Directive 2002/58/EC', Commission staff working document, SEC(2005) 1131, 21 September 2005 (Brussels 2005).

EU action, objectives of the initiative, options for action, provisions for appropriate data collection and stakeholder consultation", in order for the IAB to be able to deliver 'reinforced upstream guidance' including suggesting to DGs to consider alternatives.[90] The IAB clearly ties the consideration of alternatives to the perhaps even more pressing issue of how to determine the proportionate level of analysis:

> In general, more thorough analysis should be carried out for options according to the degree that they are a) binding b) have potentially significant economic, social or environmental impacts or administrative burden impacts or c) may be challenged as excessive or as less efficient than alternative approaches.[91]

However, looking at the actual IAB opinions, surprisingly little guidance is given on the topic of consideration of alternatives. The only IAB opinion to explicitly consider the issue states the following:

> The IA report needs to give a more explicit justification for the range of policy options selected for further analysis. The reason why some options, including the options of professional licensing or self-regulation, were discarded at an earlier stage of the analysis needs to be better justified. Also the floor of € 1500 should be better justified.[92]

Of course the IAB's opinion comes at the very end of the policy preparation cycle, making it difficult for services to go back to the moment of choice of instrument. However since the IAB has a clear prevention function, more specific guidance on the issue would seem appropriate. In other words, if the official responsible for carrying out the IA knows he will have to justify his work in front of the Board and one of the main issues the Board will be looking at is the consideration of alternatives, he/she is more likely to make this a core point of the analysis.

The Evaluation Partnership (TEP) which conducted the official evaluation of the Commission IA system, also looked at the issue:

> [T]he question of which types of options are relevant needs to be handled flexibly and take account of the policy context and in particular of the stage and level of definition of the proposal, in order to allow for a meaningful analysis. While it can sometimes be relevant to examine different types of instruments (such as legislation vs. market-based approaches or self-regulation), in other cases the baseline situation means that this results in a purely formalistic exercise. The identification and examination of genuine options has been done very well in certain IAs, but

[90] Impact Assessment Board, Annual Report 2007 (Brussels 2008), pp. 14–15.

[91] *Ibid.*

[92] Impact Assessment Board, Opinion on the impact assessment on the protection of consumers in respect of certain aspects of timeshare, long-term holiday products, resale and exchange, SEC(2007) 745, p. 3.

> less so in others (even on legislative proposals), which have limited themselves to the identification of a few obvious 'non-options' (often including the 'status quo' option, which has already been shown to be untenable in the identification of the problem the proposal is intended to tackle).[93]

One criterion that TEP used for its overall assessment of the EU IA system was 'instrument vs. substance', described as "[d]o the options that are presented focus on the type of instrument (i.e. the form of the intervention, e.g. regulation, self-regulation, market-based approach, etc.), or on the substance of the proposals (e.g. changing the scope or the parameters of the intervention)?"[94] The evaluators report that the number of IAs that interpret 'options' as 'instruments' roughly equals the number of IAs that takes the substantive approach. This figure remains the same over the years 2003–2006, but there is an increase in the number of IAs that considers both 'options as instruments' and 'options as regulatory techniques'.[95]

In the last section of this chapter we evaluate the current guidance and practice and – by means of concluding – offer some suggestions for ways out of the current situation in which there is wide-spread abstract support for alternative regulatory mechanisms, but a lack of concrete direction.

IV. *Evaluation and Conclusion*

There is little evidence of a structured approach towards the consideration of alternative regulatory instruments in the framework of EU IA, in general, nor in the IAB practice thus far. This is exemplified by the fact that, as our analysis in sections II and III has shown, the legal framework for the use of alternative regulatory mechanisms and the framework provided by Better Regulation are not integrated. Although, as seen, there are quite a few legal limitations to and guiding principles for the use of self-regulation, co-regulation and soft law, the policy documents on impact assessment do not deal with these. On top of that, policy and guidance documents on impact assessment tend to treat the use of alternative mechanisms as unproblematic. There may be different reasons for this state of affairs.

Partly, the lack of a structured approach may be due to the absence of a clear vision and consensus on the part of the Commission when alternatives are a) allowed and b) desirable. The mere statement in the IA Guidelines that alternative mechanisms must be considered in IAs reflects a lack of structural thought

[93] *Supra* note 22.

[94] *Supra* note 22, p. 29.

[95] *Supra* note 22, Annexes p. 37.

on how these actually fit into European lawmaking processes. It is plausible that the remaining prominence of legislative instruments plays a role in the difficulties that the Commission is experiencing in routinely and seriously considering alternatives to classical regulation. One small but significant circumstance that inhibits the use of self-regulation is that the successes of actors (DGs, Commissioners or the Commission as a whole) are often still measured in terms of regulatory outputs. And even if Better Regulation has brought about a change in the conception of success in the sense that deciding not to put in place (public) regulation would count as a success, there is no way to measure this. However, on this point the introduction of impact assessment brings a small opening for monitoring the Commission's efforts *not* to regulate, as the Commission has decided to also publish IAs of those instances when the IA process has led to aborting the initiative. So, if the Commission were to decide that self-regulation is really the best solution and there is no legislative proposal, there should still be an IA. But a brief investigation into the few cases in which this has happened, shows that 'no proposal' does not necessarily mean that alternative mechanisms will be at work. A fairly typical example is that of the IA on modernising inland waterway transport in Europe.[96] The Commission decided that, because the comparison of impacts and trade-offs did not show a clear preference for one policy option over the other, that it was best to stick with the cooperation between various public authorities that already existed and perhaps to increase it a bit. So although no new proposal was put forward, arguably in order to comply with the subsidiarity principle (no added value of EU action proven), this was certainly not an instance of self-regulation.

There may be another important reason for this lack of a structured approach towards the consideration of alternative regulatory mechanisms. Giving more specific guidance on the part of the Institutions, in particular the Commission, to policy-makers and legislative actors on when and how to use self-regulation or other alternative mechanisms, would amount to a commitment in sensitive areas such as how the Commission applies subsidiarity and proportionality, thereby reducing its own room of manoeuvre. This is something that the Commission wants to avoid; even if committed to conducting IAs and to considering alternative mechanisms, the Commission wants to remain flexible as to what to do with the outcome of this process. Elaborating on conditions and principles regarding the different policy options and instruments does not tie in with this.

The constant risk of a juridification of Better Regulation may also be a good explanation of the deliberate malleability of the IA framework, even after five years

[96] European Commission, Report on the impact assessment of proposals aiming to modernise and reinforce the organisational framework for inland waterway transport in Europe, SEC(2008) 23, 10 January 2008 (Brussels 2008).

of IA experience.[97] The activities of the Impact Assessment Board may change that because of their explicit normative character, although our preliminary analysis shows that the IAB opinions tend to contain a lot of 'common sense' guidance (e.g. "the IA should justify better why the option of self-regulation was discarded in an early stage") rather than substantive guidance that makes it clearer what the European Commission understands by 'regulatory failure'.

In its new draft Guidelines posted on the Better Regulation website for public consultation,[98] the Commission has aimed to address some of the difficulties signalled by the IAB in its annual report and by TEP in its evaluation report. Two of the main changes proposed may have an effect on the consideration of alternatives: a) more of a 'time sensitive' approach to subsidiarity and b) more guidance on the 'principle of proportionate analysis'. As to the first change, officials are now reminded that

> [i]t is important to bear this in mind when reviewing existing Community activities, for example in the context of the Commission's better regulation and simplification agenda. For this type of initiative, the IA report should demonstrate that EU action is still in conformity with the subsidiarity principle; you should not rely exclusively on a subsidiarity analysis that was made in the past.[99]

The second change implies that the Guidelines state in detail what type of IA effort is expected in case of certain proposals (broad Communications, non-legislative measures, revisions of existing legislation etc.).[100] Thus the application of the principle of proportionate analysis is not 'impact-driven' but 'form-driven'.

The new proposed Guidelines could be the place to elaborate upon and make more concrete the open and vague criteria that are in place at the moment, but in their present form we can say that the Commission has not grasped this opportunity. As such, they still breath very much the wind of flexibility. However, the issue is of particular importance because the very essence of Better Regulation is to temper the predominance of political considerations in the EU legislative process. Whilst keeping in mind the political difficulties involved in providing more explicit guidance on such a sensitive topic as alternative regulatory mechanisms, we present some suggestions on how to make the current policy framework and the draft Guidelines more in line with the state of the law on this point, as set out in the legal analysis presented above.

---

[97] Meuwese 2008, *supra* note 42, p. 157. Christian Joerges, 'Der Philosoph als wahrer Rechtslehrer' (1999) 5 *European Law Journal*, p. 153, citing Majone, *supra* note 46, pp. 291 et seq.

[98] European Commission, Better Regulation website, Impact Assessment page, <ec.europa.eu/governance/impact/consultation/ia_consultation_en.htm>.

[99] Draft IA Guidelines, *supra* note 28, p. 25.

[100] Draft IA Guidelines, *supra* note 28, pp. 14–15.

To start with, the policy framework speaks of 'suitable cases' for the use of alternative mechanisms. Is it possible to define what 'suitable cases' are? Perhaps not in general; after all, we carry out impact assessments in order to determine what kind of regulation is appropriate to solve a certain problem at a certain point in time. However, it is possible to provide some guidance on what are *unsuitable* cases for using alternative mechanisms. For instance when the risk of free-riding behaviour is high or when the cost of monitoring the self-regulatory arrangements are disproportionately high, these may be less appropriate. It would also be appropriate to elucidate in what sense the human rights restriction is to be understood and in what cases it is presumed to apply. More in general, we deem that the Guidelines should spell out in detail what legal constraints there are to choices for policy options and to the use of alternatives. As seen, in a number of areas the wording of the Treaty preempts any consideration of alternative alternative mechanisms and there are good reasons – e.g. with an eye to expectations by stakeholders who may be less familiar with the legal constraints – to reiterate these in the IA Guidelines. Attention should also be paid to competition screening of alternative regulatory solutions, as breaches of competition law and principles are among the most pressing risks relating to self-regulation. A final suggestion for legal precision is to demarcate more clearly the space for balancing subsidiarity and proportionality against other legal principles such as equality and legal certainty. The mere indication in the new Guidelines that there may be legal constraints without clarifying what these actually are, cannot be considered to provide clear and sufficient guidance in this respect.[101]

Secondly, one further problem with IA and the consideration of alternatives may be due to the nature of IA as a policy-making tool: Robert Baldwin has drawn attention to the rigidity of impact assessments, in the sense that a few clear-cut options have to be fixed in an early stage so as to allow for in-depth analysis to be carried out. However, Baldwin argues, 'smart regulation' (the Canadian name for 'Better Regulation') often means a mixture of regulatory techniques, combined in one measure or not.[102] In and of itself, this need not be a problem: the options defined in impact assessments could well amount to 'smart mixtures of regulatory techniques'. However, what we see is that the European Commission's IA framework encourages officials to think about 'options' as *either* self-regulation *or* legislation (to put it crudely). Headings in the 'policy options section' in impact assessments will often read '1. do nothing',

---

[101] Draft IA Guidelines, *supra* note 28, p. 11. It is merely observed that "[w]here such limitations result from the legal context, i.e. limitations/obligation for EU action fixed in primary or secondary EU legislation or international law, the IA should explain why certain policy options are necessary or not feasible."

[102] Robert Baldwin, 'Is Better Regulation Smarter Regulation?' (2005) *Public Law*, pp. 485–511.

'2. self-regulation' and '3. revising the existing Directive'. If such is the choice, it is not surprising that the first two will be dismissed and, perhaps more worrying, the 'smart option' will be missed because there is no opportunity to integrate 'self-regulatory elements' into the 'legislative option'. One improvement here could be to use the Roadmap stage for a first 'vetting' of rough policy options and the actual impact assessment process to develop more sophisticated options. We expect that the 'early quality support function' that the IAB has suggested for itself, could play an important part in developing 'smarter options' that represent real and realistic policy options.

In the same vein, there should be more attention for the fact that putting in place regulation can still be done in such a way as to incorporate 'alternative' elements. This can be done by focussing less on the legal form of the measure (Regulation, Directive etc.) and more on the (combination of) regulatory techniques used. Currently, IAs often do not manage to assess mixes of techniques, because the IA format fosters juxtaposing a few package deals (e.g. 'no action' vs 'self-regulation' vs 'a Directive'). The Guidelines could for instance include a paragraph on the distinction between alternative *forms of* regulation and alternatives *to* regulation. In other words, IAs as well as IAB opinions should speak the 'language of regulation' more often and training in IA should be training in 'regulation' more broadly. A symbolic step towards achieving this goal would be to incorporate the Annex on regulatory techniques into the main text of the Guidelines. A more structural step forward would be to put a legally sensitive consideration of alternatives to classical regulation and of regulatory techniques at the core of IA practice in the EU and to not allow 'hypes' such as administrative burden reduction to steal the show.

Chapter 8

National Experiences with General Forms of *Ex Ante* Evaluation of Legislation: The Cases of Germany and Sweden

Sylvia Veit

I. *Introduction*

'Better regulation' reforms have gained political attention in the whole EU since the mid 1990ies. The growing importance of this area is made particularly apparent by the rapid diffusion of instruments like Regulatory Impact Assessment (RIA) and Standard Cost Model (SCM) in the whole European region.[1] However, *ex ante* evaluation of legislation is not a new topic. Attempts to improve the information base of political decision makers within the legislative process have a long history. Traditionally, political decision makers have relied on formal and informal consultation to fill their knowledge gaps. However, with the blossoming of policy analysis and planning in the 1960ies and 1970ies, people also increasingly thought about the possibility of integrating impact analysis systematically in the legislative process.

This chapter discusses the significance of *ex ante* evaluation of legislation in two European countries: Germany[2] and Sweden. At first, it provides an outline

---

[1] *See* Klaus Jacob *et al., Improving the Practice of Impact Assessment*, February 2008 <web.fu-berlin.de/ffu/evia/EVIA_Policy_Paper.pdf>, 21 August 2008; Kai Wegrich, *The Administrative Burden Reduction Policy Boom. Accelerated policy learning, blind copying or bureaucratic politics?* Paper presented at the Annual ECPA Conference, September 2007, Madrid.

[2] In the following, only reforms on the Federal level will be examined. In Germany the Federal government is primarily responsible for legislation, while the implementation of laws is mostly done by the Federal states ("Länder"). Moreover, the "Länder" have their own legislative competences in certain areas of law, which are determined by the basic law.

of the history of the reform area. Current instruments of reform are presented and legal as well as organizational questions of their implementation are described. Which role *ex ante* evaluation of regulatory impacts plays in present day legislative practice in both countries is afterwards demonstrated by means of the empirical evaluation of numerous draft laws. The insights into present day evaluation practice that were gained in the course of a content analysis of preambles and explanatory memoranda of all German and Swedish government bills of 2006 are furthermore compared to government bills of 1977. By doing this, it can be demonstrated, that *ex ante* evaluation of legislation even then was an important topic and that changes were only achieved in certain areas, despite the reform boom of recent years. When comparing the two countries, it becomes apparent that the integration of *ex ante* assessments in the legislative process is to a great extent dependent on two variables: the cultural and structural characteristics of the national legislative process, as well as matters of organizational institutionalization.

II. *Development and Key Aspects of* Ex Ante *Evaluation of Legislation in Germany*

The question of an amelioration of *ex ante* evaluation of legislation in the FRG first appeared on the political agenda at the end of the 1960ies. This does not mean, however, that preparative analyses of draft laws did not play a role before then. Prospective evaluation as well as ex post evaluation of effectiveness already belonged to the steady repertoire of the legislative process (including: independent commissions, advisory committees, expert advisory boards, hearings of experts and stakeholders, reporting commitments regarding specific laws/political areas, evaluations). However, there was much criticism that these procedures were used mainly ad hoc and not systematically and that scientific-systematic processes of *ex ante* evaluation of legislation in particular were hitherto rarely used. Hence, the overall concept of reform efforts was to design structures and processes of the political-administrative system in a more intelligent way, so that knowledge about the effects of laws is already generated and used systematically in the drafting phase. The 'active state' was to plan political programs rationally and anticipatory with help of science, use synergy effects and learn from experience. Better planning and the use of socio-scientific analyses were to counteract problems like efficiency deficits of political programs, the lack of attention to the long term effects of laws and the absence of an 'overall concept' of political governance.

In the late 1960ies and the early 1970ies, the predominant principles of 'selective perception'[3] of problems and solutions and the 'negative coordination'[4] within the legislative process were identified as main causes for cases of faulty functioning in the political-administrative system. The term 'selective perception' describes the established tendency within specialized departmental divisions of central government administration to concentrate all attention on their own field of responsibility. This leads to the result, that problems outside that field are perceived less clearly and are not considered to be that important.[5] The department in charge of a bill usually looks for optimal solutions for a particular subproblem. Considering all aspects of society, however, the sum of all optimal solutions for a subproblem does not lead to the optimal solution of the problem as a whole because action taken in one area might cause follow-up problems in other areas.[6] The suboptimal solutions to problems caused by the limited problem perception of department officials in charge are additionally facilitated by the principle of 'negative coordination'. This means that other departmental units assisting the department division in charge of a bill with comments on draft regulations within the intra- and inter-departmental consultation process review legal proposals only in respect to possible negative consequences for their own field of responsibility. In this kind of coordination little attention is paid to the question, if the combination of different measures leads to a desired overall effect. The principle of 'negative coordination' results in the tendency to water down drafts and to incrementalist decision-making ('policy of small steps').

During the 1970ies, several test procedures like map exercises, practice tests or model simulations were discussed for the improvement of the prospective evaluation of bills. In the course of pilot projects, first experiences in applying these test procedures were gained.[7] In 1976, the German Ministry of the Interior even published a textbook about the "administrative map exercise as a test method

---

[3] *For selective perception within organizations see* James G. March and Herbert A. Simon, *Organizations* (Wiley, New York 1958), pp. 127 et seq.

[4] Renate Mayntz and Fritz W. Scharpf, *Planungsorganisation* (Piper, München 1973); later on *see* Fritz W. Scharpf, 'Coordination in Hierarchies and Networks' in F. W. Scharpf (ed.), *Games in Hierarchies and Networks. Analytical and Empirical Approaches to the Study of Governance Institutions* (Campus, Frankfurt am Main 1993a), pp. 125–165; Fritz W. Scharpf, 'Games real actors could play. Positive and negative coordination in embedded negotiations' (1994) 6:1 *Journal of Theoretical Politics*, pp. 27–53.

[5] Mayntz and Scharpf, *supra* note 4, p. 81.

[6] Günther Schmidt and Hubert Treiber, *Zur Programmentwicklung der Ministerialorganisation* in G. Schmidt and H. Treiber, *Bürokratie und Politik. Zur Struktur und Funktion der Ministerialbürokratie in der Bundesrepublik Deutschland* (Piper, München 1975b), pp. 122–162, p. 158.

[7] *See for example* Carl Böhret and Werner Hugger, 'Bessere Gesetze durch Test der Entwürfe?' (1979) 10 *Zeitschrift für Parlamentsfragen*, pp. 254–259.

in the decision-making process".[8] In practice, however, the above mentioned test methods were limited to a few isolated cases,[9] due to the expensive nature of these procedures, which are not fit for a standardized integration into the preparatory process of legislation.

While *ex ante* evaluation of legislation in the 1970ies was primarily discussed as a reform approach to improve the overall efficiency of regulations, the focus shifted in the 1980ies to the question of how over-regulation and its negative consequences (limiting freedom of action of state, economy and civil society; high regulatory costs) could be reduced. Important stimuli for reform were given by an 'expert committee hearing about the causes of bureaucratization within the public body', organized in 1980 at the German Federal Ministry of the Interior.[10] Many scientists who were part of the hearing emphasized that over-regulation was inherent to the German political-administrative system. In their opinion, important reasons for the increase in juridification and for the overabundance of legal norms were, for example, party rivalries and the high degree of specialization within the political-administrative system, combined with the already mentioned concentration of attention of department officials on their own areas, as well as a lack of an overall concept or strategy. In order to work against the problem of over-regulation and its negative consequences, it was suggested to

> deliberately design the process of drafting a bill. 'Counterchecks' that neutralize over-regulation tendencies should be integrated into the legislative process. For this purpose, criteria would have to be formulated, which could be considered as a basis for decision in the drafting process. These criteria could be fixed within the process of drafting through corresponding process regulations. Furthermore, methods or institutions could be devised, which work towards the observance of these criteria.[11]

In a scientific analysis of the Ministry of the Interior's expert committee hearing, the German sociologist Renate Mayntz extracted three main criteria from the different reports (1. Is state intervention necessary? 2. Which of the alternative policy instruments is most appropriate? 3. What has to be taken into consider-

---

[8] Bundesministerium des Innern, *Das Verwaltungsplanspiel als Testverfahren im Entscheidungsprozeß* (Bonn 1976).

[9] A departmental survey in the 1980ies showed, that only 11 drafts were complemented by map exercises or practice tests between 1971 and 1987. Bundesministerium des Innern, *Handbuch zur Vorbereitung von Rechts- und Verwaltungsvorschriften* (Köln 1992).

[10] Bundesministerium des Innern, *Sachverständigenanhörung zu Ursachen einer Bürokratisierung in der öffentlichen Verwaltung sowie zu ausgewählten Vorhaben zur Verbesserung des Verhältnisses von Bürger und Verwaltung am 19. und 20. Juni 1980 in Bonn* (Bonn 1980).

[11] Renate Mayntz, *Gesetzgebung und Bürokratisierung. Wissenschaftliche Auswertung der Anhörung zu Ursachen einer Bürokratisierung in der öffentlichen Verwaltung* (Köln 1980), p. 23.

ation, when further developing the program after choosing a policy instrument, e.g. concerning the implementation structures?). These main questions and the basic idea of a 'rationalization' of the preparatory process of legislation within the political-administrative system by posting certain rules of information and decision were formative for the development of the so called *Blaue Prüffragen* ('Blue Test Questions') and RIA in Germany. As early as in 1980, some of the main difficulties with *ex ante* evaluation of legislation were accurately identified, for instance the tendency of politicians and department officials to overestimate benefits and to underestimate costs of 'their' bills. The frequent lack of an (empirical) scientific base and the high level of uncertainty of *ex ante* assessments of societal developments was also already a topic at that time. The idea, that certain test questions and analytical systems could lead to a rational decision-making process was discovered by Renate Mayntz to be an escapist illusion, because political interests and negotiations tend to outweigh factual rationalities in the legislative process (and hence also outweigh them in the program development phase).[12] She admittedly advocated strengthening certain important criteria, like the question of costs, in the decision-making process and thus making them a stronger topic in the political dispute – an argument, that was later reused and enhanced, for example, in the discussion about the measurement of administrative costs with the Standard Cost Model.[13]

The first large scale attempt at systematizing *ex ante* evaluation of legislation in Germany on Federal level[14] consisted in the introduction of the *Blaue Prüffragen* by the Federal government in 1984. They were test standards for drafts, which gave all department officials in charge of developing a draft bill ten basic questions (each with detailed sub-questions) to answer.[15] The idea behind the establishment of the *Blaue Prüffragen* was to ensure a systematic inclusion of questions of effectiveness and efficiency into the legislative process through the procedural institutionalization of a quality check. However, the rationalization that was supposed to set in after the introduction of the *Blaue Prüffragen* did not live up to the expectations, because the test standards were seldom, if ever,

---

12 *Ibid.*, pp. 45, 90.

13 Werner Jann and Kai Wegrich, *Gefangen im ‚Eisernen Dreieck. Über zu viel Bürokratie nur zu jammern bringt nichts. Jedes Gesetz muss auf seine Kosten geprüft werden*, Die Zeit, 17 November 2005.

14 Similar efforts existed on 'Länder'-level, but they will not be discussed in the following. *See e.g.*, Tobias Bräunlein, *Integration der Gesetzesfolgenabschätzung ins politisch-administrative System der Bundesrepublik Deutschland* (Lang, Frankfurt am Main 2004).

15 Prüffragen für Rechtsvorschriften des Bundes. Beschluß der Bundesregierung vom 11. Dezember 1984.

applied.[16] As causes for the extensive ineffectiveness of the *Blaue Prüffragen* mainly structural factors like the absence of control mechanisms and the lack of transparency when answering the test questions were identified.[17] The issue of political and administrative actor's dominant logics of action in the legislative process and the final primacy of political compromise over factual considerations[18] did hardly play any role in the discussion about the non-application of the *Blaue Prüffragen.*

By strengthening the legally binding character and by reducing the substantial list of questions to a few central points one hoped to increase the practical relevance of impact assessments in the legislative process. In the course of the amendment of the 'Joint Rules of Procedure of the Federal Ministries' (*Gemeinsame Geschäftsordnung der Bundesministerien*, in short: GGO) in 2000 the test standards of the *Blaue Prüffragen* were integrated into the GGO in a condensed and revised version, on which an emphasis was put on the responsibility to describe cost aspects (budgetary effects, implementation costs, costs for the economy). In addition to the specific test standards, a comprehensive Regulatory Impact Assessment (RIA) was introduced into the amended GGO. It is established in § 42 (5) GGO, that the "consequences of laws" have to be presented in the explanatory memorandum. § 44 (1) GGO elaborates further: "The consequences of a law are defined as the main impacts of a law. They contain the intended effects, as well as unintended side effects." In addition to the integration of RIA into the "Joint Rules of Procedure of the Federal Ministries", the Federal Ministry of the Interior published a voluminous handbook with a corresponding code of practice about RIA.[19] The handbook and the code of practice were tested in a pilot phase on the basis of eight legislative projects.[20] For a few years now, the Federal Academy of Public Administration has been offering a training module about the process and the instruments of RIA in the course of a basic seminar about legislation to advance the implementation of RIA in the legislative practice.

---

[16] Sachverständigenrat Schlanker Staat, *Abschlußbericht* (Bundesministerium des Innern, Bonn 1998), pp. 18 et seq.; German Federal Court of Auditors (Bundesrechnungshof), *Bemerkungen des Bundesrechnungshofes 1998 zur Haushalts- und Wirtschaftsführung* (BT-Drs. 14/29, 23 November 1998); Brigitte Zypries and Cornelia Peters, 'Eine neue Gemeinsame Geschäftsordnung der Bundesministerien' (2000) 15 *Zeitschrift für Gesetzgebung*, p. 324.

[17] Sachverständigenrat Schlanker Staat, *supra* note 16, p. 18.

[18] Interview with an employee of the Federal Ministry of the Interior in April 2006.

[19] Carl Böhret and Götz Konzendorf, *Handbuch Gesetzesfolgenabschätzung (GFA). Gesetze, Verordnungen, Verwaltungsvorschriften* (Nomos, Baden-Baden 2001); Bundesministerium des Innern, *Moderner Staat-Moderne Verwaltung. Leitfaden zur Gesetzesfolgenabschätzung* (Berlin 2000).

[20] Bundesministerium des Innern, *Moderner Staat – Moderne Verwaltung. Abschlussbericht über den Praxistest zur Erprobung des Handbuches und des Leitfadens zur Gesetzesfolgenabschätzung an ausgewählten Vorhaben des Ressorts* (Berlin 2002).

After the pilot schemes for RIA were completed for some time, it showed, that the new GGO-provisions on RIA were not implemented the way they were intended to. When the German Federal Court of Auditors in 2004 conducted a random examination of 25 bills, with regard to the observation of the GGO-criteria for RIA, a certain need for action became apparent. In its report, the Federal Court of Auditors discovered, that a great part of the legislative material examined, only inadequately considered the criteria of the GGO, that numbers pertaining to the consequences of laws could often not be justified, and that unintended side effects were rarely considered.[21] The German Federal Court of Auditors, in view of the implementation of RIA by department officials, criticized lack of awareness for the usefulness of the instrument, the small amount of resources dedicated to a substantiated impact assessment and the lack of practice oriented guidelines:

> Knowledge about the methods of RIA (...) was not widely spread. Furthermore, the Ministry of Finance has, up to now, not used its authority (§ 44 GGO) to enact general guidelines for the description of budgetary effects of laws. The awareness for the necessity and practical management of a clearly defined RIA was also not generally developed. Insufficient human-resource allocation, deadline constraints and binding political goals very often impaired the realization of a RIA accordant to the guidelines of the GGO. In most cases, the parties hereto felt the criteria of the GGO to be too abstract and theoretical.[22]

The Court of Auditors therefore arrived at a sobering conclusion concerning the implementation of RIA: "A great part of the examined legislative material only inadequately takes into account the criteria of the GGO."[23] An OECD evaluation of Regulatory Reform in Germany in the same year came to similar conclusions and criticized a "significant implementation gap".[24] Implementation deficits were customarily explained with insufficient guidance and support of department officials concerning the realization of RIA in the legislative process. The "RIA Handbook"[25] published by the Federal Ministry of the Interior in 2001 indeed provided a comprehensive overview of the methodology of RIA, but was considered to be much too complicated to gain a realistic chance of

[21] German Federal Court of Auditors (Bundesrechnungshof), *Bemerkungen des Bundesrechnungshofes 2004 zur Haushalts- und Wirtschaftsführung* (BT-Drs. 15/4200, 15 November 2004), pp. 105 et seq.

[22] *Ibid.*, p. 104.

[23] *Ibid.*, p. 106.

[24] OECD, *Government Capacity to Assure High Quality Regulation. OECD Reviews of Regulatory Reform. Regulatory Reform in Germany* (Paris 2004), p. 19.

[25] Böhret and Konzendorf, *supra* note 19.

getting attention within the policy formulation process.[26] Therefore, the Federal Ministry of the Interior in 2005 compiled new RIA-guidelines. The new manual formulates precise test steps which have to be completed during the RIA process. Furthermore, it provides practical examples and phrasing assistance.[27] Because of the growing importance of the EU-level in many policy areas, the Federal Ministry of the Interior additionally published an EU RIA manual, which advises the departments on how to participate early in Regulatory Impact Assessments of EU-institutions.[28]

When the Grand Coalition under Angela Merkel came to power in autumn 2005, the political priorities in 'better regulation' reforms changed. Core instrument of the new strategy became the in the whole European area rapidly spreading Standard Cost Model (SCM). The main focus of political efforts for an improved *ex ante* evaluation of legislation shifted from a comprehensive RIA to the reduction of administrative burdens caused by regulations. Red tape reduction was given top priority. The governing parties CDU (Christian Democratic Union) and SPD (Socialdemocratic Party of Germany) anchored the introduction of the Standard Cost Model, linked with the establishment of an independent National Regulatory Control Council (*Nationaler Normenkontrollrat,* in short: NKR),[29] in their coalition treaty. The government concretized their political plan within the "Programme for the Reduction of Bureaucracy and Better Regulation",[30] which was adopted in April 2006. The eight members of the National Regulatory Control Council started to work in September 2006.[31] The task of the National Regulatory Control Council is to check draft laws and general administrative regulations for their compliance with the principles of a standardized measurement of administrative costs before they are submitted to the Federal cabinet. Because of that, the 'Joint Rules of Procedure of the Federal Ministries' were amended in December of 2006, so that information obligations[32]

---

[26] Werner Jann, Kai Wegrich and Sylvia Veit, 'Verfahren und Instrumente erfolgreicher (De-) Regulierung. Pilotstudie der Universität Potsdam im Auftrag der Bertelsmann-Stiftung' in S. Empter, F. Frick and R. Vehrkamp (eds.), *Auf dem Weg zu moderner Regulierung. Eine kritische Bestandsaufnahme* (Bertelsmann-Stiftung, Gütersloh 2005), pp. 47–77.

[27] Bundesregierung, *Arbeitshilfe Gesetzesfolgenabschätzung* (Berlin 2005).

[28] BMI (Bundesministerium des Innern), *Leitfaden Folgenabschätzung in der Europäischen Union* (Berlin 2006).

[29] Modeled after the independent ACTAL committee in the Netherlands (*see* chapter 5 of this volume).

[30] The Federal government issued a report about the "Programme for the Reduction of Bureaucracy and Better Regulation" in October 2007: Presse- und Informationsamt der Bundesregierung, *Bürokratiekosten: Erkennen – Messen – Abbauen. Bericht der Bundesregierung zur Anwendung des Standardkostenmodells 2007* (Berlin 2007).

[31] BGBl. I 2006: *Gesetz zur Einsetzung eines Nationalen Normenkontrollrates*, p. 1866.

[32] "Information obligations are the obligations arising from regulation to provide information and data to the public sector and / or third parties (e.g. civilians). An information obligation

and administrative costs now have to be described within preambles and explanatory memoranda of draft regulations.

Early in 2007, the Federal Statistical Office started a measurement of administrative costs of the entire German Federal law, parallel to the implementation of SCM-procedures in the *ex ante* process.[33] The reform area was organizationally institutionalized beyond the establishment of the National Regulatory Control Council by anchoring the responsibility within the Office of the Federal Chancellor (Minister of State Hildegard Müller as Federal Government Coordinator for the Reduction of Bureaucracy and Better Regulation; establishment of a central Better Regulation Unit). Moreover, a Committee of State Secretaries for the Reduction of Bureaucracy as inter-departmental guidance and coordination committee was established. Within every department, a contact person with responsibility for reduction of bureaucracy was named. These contact persons regularly meet to prepare Committee of State Secretaries meetings and to coordinate SCM policy.[34]

The Better Regulation Unit within the Federal Chancellor's office and the National Regulatory Control Council developed a "Manual for the *ex ante* evaluation of bureaucracy cost according to the Standard Cost Model"[35] in concordance with the Federal Ministries. The manual was developed to practically realise the *ex ante* evaluation of bureaucracy costs. The implementation of the manual is supplemented by training courses for department officials.[36] The secretariat of the National Regulatory Control Council (NKR) offers support to department officials by helping with methodological questions in the process of *ex ante* assessment of bureaucracy costs. If the responsible officials do not contact staff members of the NKR-secretariat beforehand, then the NKR is informed of the draft through an inter-ministerial consultation and receives the opportunity to give a written comment. The time limit for delivering the NKR-comment according to the 'Joint Rules of Procedure of the Federal Ministries' is at least

---

does not necessarily mean that the information obligation has to be transferred to the public authority or private persons, but may include a duty to have information available for inspection or supply on request." (Definition of the International Standard Cost Model Network: <www.administrative-burdens.com/default.asp?page=14>, 15 April 2008).

33 Including the information obligations based on international and EU-law; for the current state of the measurement see: Report of the Federal Government about the Implementation of the Standard Cost Model. Presse- und Informationsamt der Bundesregierung, *supra* note 30.

34 *For a detailed description of the SCM in Germany see* Werner Jann and Bastian Jantz, 'Bürokratiekostenmessung und Nationaler Normenkontrollrat – erste Bewertung des Programm "Bürokratieabbau und bessere Rechtssetzung"' (2008) 23:1 *Zeitschrift für Gesetzgebung*, pp. 51–68.

35 Bundeskanzleramt, *Leitfaden für die ex ante Abschätzung der Bürokratiekosten nach dem Standardkosten-Modell* (Berlin 2007).

36 Nationaler Normenkontrollrat: *Kostenbewusstsein stärken. Für eine bessere Gesetzgebung* (Jahresbericht des Nationalen Normenkontrollrates, Berlin 19 September 2007), p. 22.

four weeks, in practice however, the time limit is shorter. The comments of NKR about the *ex ante* assessment of bureaucracy costs are attached to draft regulations before they are delivered to Federal Cabinet respectively to Federal Parliament and Federal Council. The NKR statement therefore is publicly available.

The NKR does its work with assistance of a rapporteur system. Every NKR-member and every employee within the NKR-secretariat (which is currently staffed with seven employees) is responsible for one certain department and prepares statements for legal drafts coming from this department. The NKR normally convenes on a weekly basis and during its meetings arrives at decisions formally following the majority rule. In practice however, the council arrives at decisions with consensus of all its members, so far there has not been any case of 'crucial vote'. Because of the large number of legal regulations that have to be reviewed, not all statements are discussed in the plenum. Non-controversial cases are decided upon by the NKR without discussion.[37]

By comparing the introduction of the SCM-assessment of bureaucracy costs in 2006/2007 with the introduction of RIA since 2000 in Germany, differences – especially in the political support of the topic and in the organizational anchoring of the process – become apparent. While the implementation of RIA was scarcely supplied with additional resources, the introduction of SCM was strongly supported by political leaders in a personal and financial manner as well as with words. Apart from the establishment of a central competence for de-bureaucratisation policies in the chancellor's office, the government created an extensive network to coordinate and support the implementation of the SCM-measuring process. Additionally, the NKR has yearly obligations to report to the Federal Chancellor.[38] This report obligation increases the binding character of the implementation of SCM-reforms.[39]

III. *Development and Key Aspects of* Ex Ante *Evaluation of Legislation in Sweden*

In Germany, legislative proposals primarily are worked out within government departments while in Sweden, all important regulatory projects are prepared by Committees of Inquiry (*statens offentliga utredningar*, in the following referred to as 'committees'). In Sweden, committees are appointed by the government for specific topics. They conduct extensive research and inquiries in the forefront of

[37] Telephone interview with an employee of NKR in September 2007.

[38] *Supra* note 31, para. 6.

[39] The first annual report of NKR was published in September 2007. Nationaler Normenkontrollrat, *supra* note 36.

the actual legislative process. Their working time can be anywhere between a few months up to several years, at an average it is approximately two years. Goals, mode of operation, budget and personnel of committees are determined by the government in the framework of committee directives. Size and personnel of committees can be extremely varied. Some committees consist only of one person (one-man committees), others make up a big commission with representatives of public administration, experts, lobbyists and members of Parliament. For their support, the members of a committee have a special committee-secretariat at their disposal. This secretariat attends to the day-to-day committee work, conducts surveys, and documents and prepares the decisions of the committee. The secretariat normally also formulates the written interim and final reports (*betänkande*) of committees.[40] Reports by committees are always published and are subject to an elaborate consultation procedure (*remiss*). Interim and final committee reports together with stakeholder statements from the *remiss*-procedures provide a basis for the compilation of a government bill (*proposition*) within the government offices (*regeringskansliet*).[41] The legislative proposals contained within propositions can be (almost) identical to the recommendations of the committee but sometimes they also differ substantial from the committee's proposals.

It is also common in other nations to prepare certain political decisions outside of the government's own administration by committees, but not to the extent as it is done in Sweden. The importance of committee work is reflected in the financial resources allocated by the government. Nearly one fifth of the annual government offices' resources (except for the Ministry of Foreign Affairs) are allocated to committee work.[42] Another reason why committee's work is an important characteristic of the Swedish political system and political culture is reflected in the fact, that its roots reach back into the 16th century.

Committees are appointed to tackle specific problems and are often dealing intensively with the consequences of national policies, based on empirical studies. They are deep seated institutions within the political-administrative system for the impact assessment of governmental policies (which often take the form of laws or ordinances) even if *ex ante* evaluation is not their only function. Expert knowledge plays an important role in the work of committees. That is why

---

40 Rune Premfors *et al., Demokrati och byråkrati* (Universitetsförlag, Lund 2003), p. 157.

41 About 15 per cent of committee reports are dropped by the government and are not elaborated into a bill. Werner Jann and Jan Tiessen, 'Gesetzgebung im politischen System Schwedens' in W. Ismayr (ed.), *Gesetzgebung in Westeuropa. EU-Staaten und Europäischen Union* (Westdeutscher Verlag, Wiesbaden 2008), pp. 99–131.

42 Viviann Gunnarsson and Marja Lemne, *Kommittéerna och bofinken. Kan en kommitté se ut hur som helst? Rapport till expertgruppen för studier i offentlig ekonomi* (Finansdepartmentet, Ds 1998: 57, Stockholm 1998), p. 13.

scientists have to some extent argued, that the frequent use of committees in the Scandinavian country is an expression of a more 'rational oriented' Swedish style of policy-making.[43] Empirical studies, however, have shown that this judgment is only partly true. Johansson, for example, came to the following conclusion based on several case studies about committees in Sweden:

> It arises, that the different actors in a committee argue about important topics in a very non factual fashion. This is probably because the members know the opposite opinion well from former times. The members have met before in other commissions or in other arenas. Of course it is possible to find the 'technically best' solution for less important parts of the inquiry. (…) But this is not common for the central questions. Instead, committee work is about the different actors' pursuit of influence. Knowledge seems to be an important tool in this conflict.[44]

This quote makes clear, that committees are indeed an arena for the exchange of factual arguments and the evaluation of alternatives for regulation. In practice, however, their work is considerably influenced by political questions of assertion of interests and by the search for a Parliamentary and/or Cabinet majority. Committees further compromises because they include different actors of society into the organization of a reform project. The orientation towards compromise and consensus is structurally fixed: committee members have to arrive at a final report. Every member, however, has the right to write a so called '*reservation*', if the committee could not agree on specific questions. Despite the shortcomings shown in regard to an idealistic belief in rational policy-making in Sweden, the committees are important and internationally unique institutions for a systematic *ex ante* evaluation in the legislative process. They are making an important contribution to the formulation of new legislative proposals and to the disclosure, discussion and adjustment of antagonistic positions.[45]

Apart from the institutionalization of broad *ex ante* evaluations through the work of committees, there were and are numerous efforts to strengthen specific elements of impact assessments in the legislative process in Sweden, not primarily within the framework of committees, but above all on the level of governmental agencies. In this context it is important to know, that Swedish central administration is characterized by a division into a relatively small 'government

[43] Thomas J. Anton, 'Policy-Making and Political Culture in Sweden' (1969) 4 *Scandinavian Political Studies*, pp. 88–102.

[44] Jan Johansson, *Det statliga kommittéväsendet. Kunskap, kontroll, konsensus* (Stockholms universitet, Stockholm 1992), p. 240.

[45] Erlandsson's case study about the development of the proposition for the 'beast of prey' policy graphically shows that many conflicts can be adjusted in the framework of a committee. Magnus Erlandsson, 'Sammanhållen rovdjurspolitik. Om processen bakom regeringens proposition 2000/01: 57' in P. Ehn *et al.*, *Processer i regeringskansliet – sex fallstudier* (2001) 9 *Score Rapportserie* (Stockholm 2001), pp. 34–51.

office' (in 1997, all government departments in Sweden were integrated into one authority, the 'government office') and big central agencies. While draft laws and ordinances are elaborated in committees and by government departments, the implementation of policies as well as the formulation of concrete implementation provisions is done by central agencies.

Since the 1970ies, 'better regulation' policies concerning the regulatory activities of central agencies focused on the improvement of cost assessments. Already in 1970, a regulation[46] came into force, which obligated governmental agencies to submit new or modified regulations, instructions or 'generic suggestions' (*allmänna råd*)[47] to the government for examination if these "influence current standards or rules or if they could lead to a more than immaterial degree of direct of indirect cost increase." In 1977, this regulation was expanded, so that follow-up costs had to be not only qualitatively identified, but also had to be calculated concretely. In the 1980ies, two more regulations[48] were added, which governed the participation duties of stakeholders in the legislative process to prevent unnecessary administrative burdens, e.g. through bad forms.

From the mid-90ies on, the focus of 'better regulation' reforms in Sweden shifted from a hitherto concentration on the prevention of unnecessary regulatory and administrative costs to a more extensive Regulatory Impact Assessment (*konsekvensutredning*). The 'Agency Ordinance' (*verksförordningen*),[49] which entered into force in 1995, obliged central agencies to examine alternatives to lawmaking and to document the "cost consequences and other effects" of new regulations. Furthermore, extensive consultation obligations were laid down. These consultation obligations explicitly comprised the possibility to comment on RIA. The obligation to conduct impact assessments comprised all new or altered regulations and 'generic suggestions', whether they were small adjustments or important changes in the law area. The only exemption were internal regulations and regulations concerning fees levied by the authorities.

In addition to the 'Agency Ordinance', several regulations came into force in the years 1998 and 1999, which committed government departments and public authorities as well as Committees of Inquiry to a specific RIA concerning small enterprises (the so called Simplex Impact Assessment). For public authorities an annual obligation to report to the government about their work with the Simplex Ordinance was introduced. A special unit was installed in the Ministry of Industry (the so called Simplex Unit) to coordinate and control

[46] SFS 1970: 641. Begränsningskungörelsen.

[47] The so called 'generic suggestions' are legally non-binding, general advocacies about how a law or a regulation should be applied.

[48] SFS 1982: 668. Förordning om statliga myndigheters inhämtande av uppgifter från näringsidkare och kommuner; SFS 1987: 1347. Begränsningsförordningen.

[49] SFS 1995: 1322. Verksförordning.

the operative work with Simplex Impact Assessments. This unit was dissolved in the year 2004, due to the disillusioning account of its work. From January 2005 on, the government transferred the responsibility for the support of public authorities at performing Simplex Impact Assessments to a central agency (the Swedish Business Development Agency).

Hence, a dual RIA system existed in Sweden since the end of the 1990ies. This implied that central agencies had to conduct two kinds of Impact Assessment for all regulations pertaining to small enterprises: a general RIA according to the 'Agency Ordinance' and an impact assessment focused on small enterprises according to the Simplex-ordinance. This procedure drew much criticism. The Committee of Inquiry for the reformation of the 'Agency Ordinance', active from December 2001 to February 2004, advocated an integration of the two RIA systems into an independent RIA regulation in its final report.[50] Although the committee's proposal gained broad consensus in the consultation process a new RIA regulation was not issued by the Ministry of Industry until after a long 'meditation period' (and a change of government) in December 2007.[51] The 'Agency Ordinance' and the Simplex regulations were annulled by the new regulation. According to the new RIA ordinance small enterprises are only one item among many in Sweden's new RIA system. In comparison to other follow-up aspects the analysis of economically relevant consequences is emphasized.

Measurement of administrative (or bureaucracy) costs with the SCM was introduced in Sweden in 2004 and was strongly concentrated in the first years on analyzing existing law and identifying methods of simplification.[52] Not until the change of government in autumn 2006, were concrete measures taken to implement an *ex ante* assessment of administrative burdens. In addition to the binding regulation that drafts of new or altered laws, statutory regulations and regulations of administrative agencies have to be subject to a bureaucracy cost assessment, a group of State Secretaries and an inter-departmental task force were established – akin to the procedure in Germany. The group and the task force are responsible for coordinating departmental measures in the reform area of 'better regulation'. In addition to the State Secretary group and the task force, coordinators and contact persons were appointed in each government department. Two central agencies were charged with giving support to agencies

[50] Statens offentliga utredningar (SOU), *Utredningen om översyn av verksförordningen: Från verksförordning till myndighetsförordning* (Finansdepartementet, SOU 2004: 23, Stockholm 2004).

[51] SFS 2007: 1244. Förordning om konsekvensutredning vid regelgivning.

[52] Sylvia Veit, 'Reformen auf die sanfte Art: Bürokratieabbau und Anwendung des Standardkostenmodells in Schweden' (2008) 23:1 *Zeitschrift für Gesetzgebung*, pp. 68–85.

in the RIA process and with organizing further education about RIA.[53] Beyond that, a National Regulatory Control Council (*Regelråd*) was established in May 2008. The Swedish Regulatory Control Council is not only responsible for the assessment of administrative burdens but (other than the German NKR) also for supervising the compliance with all provisions concerning *ex ante* evaluation of legislation (SCM and RIA) in the legislative process.

IV. *Practice of* Ex Ante *Evaluation of Legislation in Germany and Sweden: an Empirical Comparison*

After the development of *ex ante* evaluation of legislation in Germany and Sweden was described in the preceding sections, the following part discusses the empirical reality of *ex ante* evaluation in both countries. A content analysis of all government bills about new or amended draft bills of the year 2006 (Germany: 154, Sweden: 132) carried out by the author serves as a base for this discussion. The basis for the analysis in Germany are preambles and explanatory memoranda of governmental legislative proposals. For the case of Sweden, the empirical basis are the government's so called 'propositions', which consist of one or more draft bills. Swedish 'propositions' usually contain extensive background information about the problem area, the process of policy formulation and about the proposed solution. As a matter of course, the incentives of an 'interest free' depiction of the results of *ex ante* evaluation are rather small, because the focus of the analyzed documents (preambles and explanatory memoranda, propositions) is first of all a justification of the legislative proposal submitted by the government. The author nevertheless argues, that in the case of Germany and Sweden, an analysis of the documents described is reasonable.[54] On the one hand, because the description of certain regulatory impacts and of RIA results in the framework of these documents is legally prescribed and on the other hand, because the explanatory statements constitute an important source of information for Parliamentary decision makers. Suitable alternatives are not available, because in the ministerial process of the composition of draft bills, independent RIA

[53] The Swedish Business Development Agency and the National Financial Management Authority.

[54] It is important to note at this point that the results presented in the following do not constitute a complete implementation analysis of the procedure of *ex ante* evaluation in Germany and Sweden, because neither statutory regulations nor administrative regulation nor the in Sweden particularly widely used committee reports were included in the analysis. Due to the comparative perspective, the analysis' focus solely is on government bills.

documents or papers solely for the documentation of results of *ex ante* assessments are produced neither in Sweden, nor in Germany.

The draft bills and propositions of the year 2006 were compared in respect to five test-criteria. These include not *all* requirements of *ex ante* evaluation, that are fixed in legislative provisions or guidance documents in the respective country, but only those criteria which are compulsory in *both countries*: 'alternatives', 'budgetary effects', 'implementation costs', 'economic impacts' and 'administrative costs for enterprises'. For the Swedish case, the description of the impacts on small enterprises was additionally examined, because this aspect of *ex ante* evaluation constitutes a central point in Swedish 'better regulation' policy. The analyses distinguishes between 'formal compliance' and 'real compliance' to the requirements of *ex ante* evaluation. A 'real compliance' is constituted of an established impact analysis of the individual test criteria in regard to content (detailed statements with a justification). 'Formal compliance' is existent, if one can find a statement about the corresponding variable in the introductory pages of the law and/or in the justification of the law respectively in the proposition, even if the statement is very short and is not justified. 'Real compliance' is defined as a subset of 'formal compliance'.

In respect to 'formal compliance' of the test criteria, Germany performs better than Sweden. Fig. 1 shows, that 'formal compliance' in Germany in 2006 was higher in all test criteria than at the same time in Sweden. The differences between the two countries were especially wide regarding the criteria 'administrative costs for enterprises' (GER: 60%; SWE: 23%) and "economic impacts" (GER: 84%; SWE: 62%). In the other three criteria, the difference between Sweden and Germany amounted to less than ten per cent. The structure of legislative cover pages (preambles) in Germany plays an important role with respect to the very high degree of 'formal compliance' in German proposals. For the specific criteria which have to be on the cover pages as an individual bullet by default there was almost always a statement, even if apparently no impact analysis of the criteria had taken place (or the results of the analysis were not to be published within the cover pages or the justification). This led to numerous cliché-ridden or impact-denying statements in German legislative cover pages, which contained very little substantial information about expected regulatory impacts for Parliamentary decision-makers and the Federal Council.[55]

In Sweden, a purely 'formal adaptation' in the sense of 'ticking off' certain test-criteria was more uncommon than in Germany. The widespread relinquishment of 'ticking off' analysis requirements is pandered by the structure of the propositions. The outline is variable except for some fix subsections and mainly complies with the content of the regulation. On the one hand it is less transpar-

[55] In Germany, the Federal Council participates in many legislative decisions on Federal level.

ent, which points of *ex ante* evaluation are catered to and which are not, on the other hand there is no reason to 'formally investigate' certain aspects because of a given structure. The test criterion "budgetary effects" constitutes an exception. This criterion is often discussed in the bullets "consequences" and "economic impacts", which are present in most of Swedish propositions. There is a higher degree of transparency in regard to this variable and inasmuch a certain 'pressure' to give a statement on this point.

As clarified in Fig. 1, the relation between Germany and Sweden in respect to 'real compliance' compared to 'formal compliance' inverts itself, meaning, that a substantial *ex ante* evaluation had taken place for all five criteria considerably more often in Sweden than in Germany. The difference between Germany and Sweden is especially big in respect to the criterion 'description of alternatives'. There were descriptions of alternatives in only six per cent of German drafts, all other drafts contained only the short and unjustified conclusion, that there were no "alternatives". In Sweden, in most propositions (94 per cent) alternative policy options were described. A characterization of alternatives took place especially often within those chapters of propositions where the necessity for regulation was justified (for instance in terms of a description of the 'zero alternative': What will happen, if nothing happens?). It also occured within the depiction of the committee's report and in line with the presentment of consultation results (transparent description of alternative suggestions from the committee's report and from the consultation process). It becomes apparent at this point, that Swedish propositions are documents, which make many details of the developing process of the final bill transparent and do not completely fade out numerous alternatives in the pre-Parliamentarian phase as it is mostly done in German government bills.

An important cause for the good performance of Sweden in the criterion "alternatives" is the principle of public access to official documents. This principle is anchored within the Swedish constitution and leads to a high degree of transparency in respect to decision making processes. Another relevant factor for the widespread description of alternatives in Sweden consists in the integration of Committees of Inquiry in the legislative process, whose original purpose is the examination of alternatives. The almost exclusively 'formal adaptation' to the obligation to assess alternative regulatory options in Germany shows clearly, that the German explanatory memorandum serves less as a tool to bring about transparency of the legislative process and to argue about the draft in an objective manner. German explanatory memoranda are rather documents, which serve the juristic interpretation and validation of a draft bill. This fact also is reflected in the volume of specifications. While general explanations about the regulation area, alternatives, consequences, benefits and costs of a draft are for the most part very long in Swedish propositions, the corresponding part in German explanatory statements normally is only a few pages long. The average Swedish

Fig. 1: Formal and Real Compliance of Requirements of Ex Ante *Evaluation in Germany and Sweden*

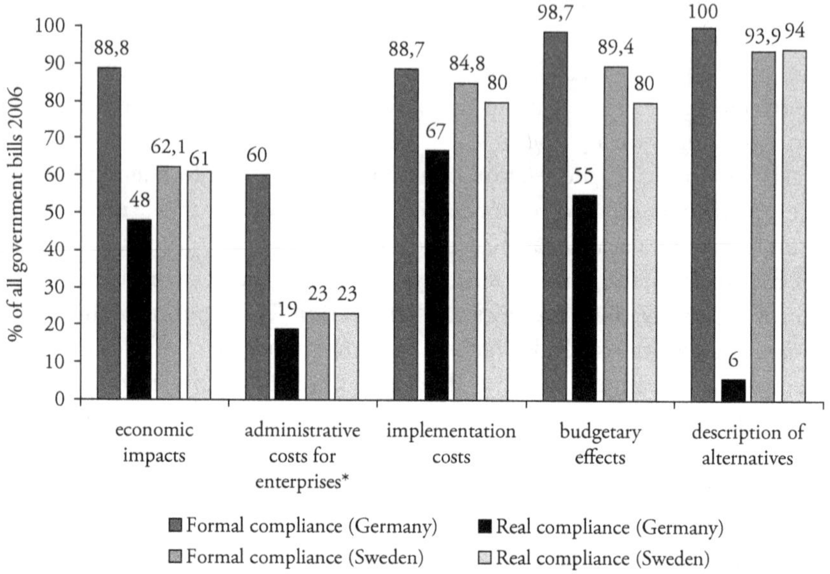

* Deviant period at test-criterion 'administrative costs for enterprises' in Germany, because *ex ante* assessment of bureaucracy cost was only introduced on the 1st of December 2006 via the GGO: Analysis of 75 governmental propositions, which were submitted to Parliament between 1st of December 2006 and 30th of August 2007.

explanatory statement for a proposition in 2006 was 54 pages long. In addition, the propositions contained on average 45 pages of attachments, which provided additional information, in the form of e.g. an index of consultation instances, former regulation drafts, summaries of committee reports, results of studies or the text of an EU Directive. The average German explanatory memorandum in 2006 was only 13 pages long, with 3 pages for the "general part" and 10 pages for the "special part" which concentrates more on juristic questions of detail.

Structural factors of the state's architecture are important reasons for the dominance of judicial and juristic questions in Germany. This particularly pertains to the existence of a Federal Constitutional Court and the Federal setup of the German state. These structural factors involve specific requirements in regard to the constitutionality of laws. The integration of new regulations into the existing legal framework is an important and complicated task which is getting much attention in the pre-Parliamentarian phase of lawmaking. Sweden, however, is a centralist state, with a much lower level of political interweavement and it does not have a central authority responsible for controlling norms in the form of a constitutional court. The requirements for a juristic validation of new legislative norms are lower and not as multifaceted as in Germany. Apart from these structural factors, the respective educational background of the personnel in government departments supports the emphasis on socio-scientific inquiries and explanations in Sweden and the strong emphasis on juristic questions in Germany. The professional socialization has an enormous power of imprint over the prevalent orientation patterns and attitudes in organizations.[56]

Already in 1973, a German group of researchers showed in an empirical study, that the monopoly of jurists in the German departmental administration facilitates specific patterns of communication and unilateral problem perception with a focus on judicial and procedural problems.[57] The study proved that department officials with juristic training put a stronger emphasis on judicial questions than department officials without juristic training. In German Federal departments, compliance with standards and rules was rated higher than the orientation on factual issues.[58] Several empirical studies show, that German department officials in most cases were (and are) fully qualified lawyers. There have been only few changes in the "monopoly of jurists" and the "jurist promotion monopoly"[59] in the last decades. The percentage of jurists in the German administrative elite is constant at about 60 per cent.[60] However, it has to be said, that most of the statistical inquiries looked at positions from the head of a directorate upwards. An inquiry into the educational background of the officials of the lower echelons at the Federal ministries (head of divisions and desk officers) carried out by the author revealed, however, that these positions in most ministries were also primarily occupied by jurists.[61]

---

[56] Walter W. Powell and Paul J. DiMaggio (eds.), *The New Institutionalism in Organizational Analysis* (University of Chicago Press, Chicago/London 1991), pp. 69 et seq., 75.

[57] Gerhard Brinkmann, Wolfgang Pippke and Wolfgang Rippe, *Die Tätigkeitsfelder des höheren Verwaltungsdienstes. Arbeitsansprüche, Ausbildungserfordernisse, Ausbildungserfordernisse, Personalbedarf* (Westdeutscher Verlag, Opladen 1973), pp. 233 et seq.

[58] *Ibid.*, pp. 346 et seq.

[59] The higher the position of employees in the upper echelons of the federal administration the higher the (the already very high) percentage of jurists (*ibid.*, p. 54).

[60] Bärbel Steinkemper, *Klassische und politische Bürokraten in der Ministerialverwaltung der Bundesrepublik Deutschland* (Carl Heymanns, Köln/Berlin/Bonn/München 1974); Hans-Ulrich Derlien and Renate Mayntz, *Einstellungen der politisch-administrativen Elite des Bundes 1987* (Verwaltungswissenschaftliche Beiträge der Universität Bamberg 25, Bamberg 1988); Katja Schwanke and Falk Ebinger, 'Politisierung und Rollenverständnis der deutschen Administrativen Elite 1970 bis 2005 – Wandel trotz Kontinuität' in J. Bogumil *et al.* (eds.), *Politik und Verwaltung* (Verlag für Sozialwissenschaft, Wiesbaden 2006), pp. 228–249.

[61] Exceptions were the Federal Ministry of Food, Agriculture and Consumer Protection (because of the importance of professional expertise in this area) and the Federal Ministry of Research and Education (because of the comparatively small legislative activity and the importance of

Like in Germany, completing law school traditionally provided the usual background for a career in central government administration in Sweden.[62] Formally, a law degree was a necessary condition to enter the civil service in a department until 1964. Jurists also dominated in central agencies. Today, the situation has changed. Until the end of the 1990ies, law school steadily lost importance.[63] This trend was stopped however because a high demand for juristic professional competence resulted from Sweden's EU-membership and the necessary adjustment of national law to EU-specifications. Three subjects dominate the government offices today: jurists, economists and social scientists.[64] The Swedish scientists Rune Premfors and Göran Sundström showed in a questionnaire study that in 2005, only 25 per cent of the desk officers and 34 per cent of the leading officials in the government offices considered themselves to be jurists. Approximately one fourth of the desk officials and one fourth of the heads of division considered themselves to be economists. Another 40 per cent of the desk officers were social scientists. On the executive level, the percentage of social scientists was 27 per cent. On the 'staff level' in the government offices, social scientists are the dominant group by now.[65]

In Sweden, the professional composition of the departmental administration, because of the relatively high percentage of economists and social scientists, provided a particularly 'fertile ground' for the instruments of impact analysis which, because of their methods and focus, were close to these particular disciplines. If the Swedish propositions of 2006 are compared to regulation drafts of the 1970ies[66] significant changes become evident in exactly those areas, on which the reform efforts for a 'better regulation' had focused. This pertains to the presentation of budgetary effects, which in 2006 compared to 1977 took place at a significantly higher percentage of laws and was carried out more detailed. A second area in which significant differences between 1977 and 2006 become evident is the presentation of the impacts of laws on small enterprises. Because of the programmatic setting of priorities by the Swedish government at the end of the 1990ies, linked with the already mentioned introduction of the Simplex-regulation, the Simplex-manual and structural measures, this factor

evaluation of project applications *et al.* from a professional perspective). At these ministries only about a third of the officials in the higher echelons were jurists in 2006.

62 Premfors, *supra* note 40, p. 186; Peter Ehn, *Maktens Administratörer. Ledande svenska statstjänstemäns och politikers syn på tjänstemannarollen i ett förändringsperspektiv* (Stockholm Studies in Politics 59, Stockholm 1998), p. 78.

63 Peter Ehn *et al.*, 'Swedish Bureaucracy in an Era of Change' (2003) 16 *Governance*, pp. 429–458, p. 66.

64 Ehn, *supra* note 62, p. 79; Premfors, *supra* note 40, p. 186.

65 Rune Premfors and Göran Sundström, *Regeringskansliet* (Liber, Stockholm 2007), p. 77.

66 Sample of 27 propositions from 1977.

gained particular importance. Hardly any change was detected between 1977 and 2006 for the other test-criteria like economic impacts, implementation costs and the description of alternatives, which, because of the in (comparison to Germany) relatively high scores of 'real compliance', is seen as an indication, that the grown structures of the Swedish legislative system have pandered *ex ante* evaluation of legislation already in former times.

A comparative analysis of German draft bills of 2006 with draft bills of 1977 does not hint at a substantial change in legislative preparation. There has altogether been no stronger focus on the description of positive or negative impacts of legislation compared to the set goals. The 'formal compliance' to requirements of *ex ante* evaluation has significantly increased during the last three decades, but there is no informative data behind this compliance. There is, however, one exception: the description of implementation costs. 50 per cent of the cases did not indicate a description of implementation costs in 1977, in 2006, it were only 11 per cent of the drafts. This phenomenon can be explained with the fact that 'implementation costs' was not an individual category on the introductory page in 1977, while this was the case in 2006. However, not only the 'formal compliance' with the requirement to describe implementation costs did increase, but also the 'real compliance' with the requirement increased considerably. In so far, it can be assumed that because of a greater political attention to questions of implementation in connection to the shortage of public funds and in the course of modernization attempts under the headword New Public Management an attitude shift took place in the last decades, which diverted the attention of department officials responsible for the composition of explanatory statements in laws to implementation aspects.

Finally, the (in both countries) relatively new assessment of bureaucracy costs for enterprises with the SCM will be discussed shortly. While 'formal compliance' with requirements for the description of administrative costs for enterprises in Germany far exceeded the 'formal compliance' in Sweden, the 'real compliance' was on the same level (GER: 19%; SWE: 23%). It has to be added, that in the German case, the test criterion was based on a different control sample (75 drafts between December 2006 and August 2007) because the *ex ante* assessment of bureaucracy costs was introduced bindingly in Germany only since December 2006. The 'real compliance' was comparatively low, because in the first months of implementation many drafts just referred to the fact, that inter-ministerial consultation started before the December 2006 and that an *ex ante* assessment of administrative costs could not be done because of that. In the course of time the number of drafts with this reference decreased significantly. At least 7 per cent of the German drafts during the transitional period here analyzed contained monetary details of administrative costs. In Sweden however, only one proposition (0.8 per cent) contained quantitative details of administrative costs. This extremely marginal implementation of quantitative administrative cost assessment in the Swedish lawmaking process shows the elementary importance of an organizational institutionalization for the real integration of specific *ex ante* evaluations into the legislative process.

It also shows, that the more convenient structures and cultural legacy in Sweden (especially the committee procedures, the publicity principle and the educational background of department officials) have no impact on the practice of *ex ante* evaluation of legislation, if responsibilities for the implementation of a new aspect of analysis are not clearly defined and established with support of political leaders. A quarter of Swedish propositions indeed contained a qualitative statement about administrative costs for enterprises but this mostly was associated with an extensive description of regulatory impacts, which is customary in Sweden, and did not have anything to do with the introduction of SCM in 2004. This is proven apart from the lack of quantification by the fact that appropriate reform terms like 'information obligation' or 'administrative burden' do not surface in the reports. The Swedish *ex ante* evaluation of administrative costs in 2006 was neither organizational nor legislatively institutionalized, but it was only released as a statement. This deficit has been perceived in Sweden which is why a National Regulatory Control Council has been established to control the implementation. The German SCM strategy is designed differently. An organizational anchoring complemented by the institutionalization of political support for the administration cost topic was conducted right from the start in Germany. The empirical data is hitherto indeed sobering (see Fig. 1) but at least the percentage of quantification is much higher than in Sweden, despite the lack of continuation on a permanent basis because of the short time span between introduction of the legislative obligation and the empirical analysis. In addition, appropriate terms are used and an increase in 'real compliance' of GGO-specifications can be detected in the course of time.

V. *Conclusion*

In summary, it is to be called to mind that efforts to create a systematic *ex ante* evaluation of legislation have a long tradition both in Germany and in Sweden. During the last three decades, a substantial achievement could be reached in respect to an improved assessment of implementation costs in Germany. In Sweden, *ex ante* evaluation of regulatory impacts within many different areas of society has been deeply seated in the lawmaking process through the extensive use of Committees of Inquiry. Defects are existent above all in regard to regulatory preparation within central agencies. That is why 'better regulation' reform efforts in Sweden have to a great extent concentrated on this area. The assessment of regulatory impacts for small enterprises and the improved description of cost impacts for the state were the essentials of Swedish reform policy over the past decades. The empirical analyses shows that in both areas discernible improvement has been reached in respect to *ex ante* evaluation of legislation. The *ex ante* assessment of administrative costs with the help of the SCM was barely implemented in Sweden because in this area, a long term organizational institutionalization and effective political support for the topic is lacking. The establishment of a National Regulatory Control Council could lead to progress in this area, as can be seen on the German example. In Germany, in the first year after the introduction of the *ex ante* assessment of administrative costs with the SCM already verifiable changes in the legislative process were accomplished.

The empirical analysis clearly shows that a purely formal adjustment to provisions of *ex ante* evaluation of legislation plays a larger role in Germany than in Sweden. The inflexible structure of the law introductory pages and the explanatory memoranda, which promote a pure 'ticking off', and in particular the lack of structural and cultural anchoring of impact analysis in the political-administrative system were determined to be the main causes of this. The juristic validation of new legislative norms is of great importance in Germany, while factual issues are negotiated within informal committees of the coalition partners and by departments in accordance with interest organizations, *Länder* and local authorities. Political rationality and questions of interests are in the fore here, because to arrive at a compromise is often that difficult in the complex multi-level system of the FRG, that a once arrived at compromise is not endangered later on, even if factual arguments would speak for it.

The analysis of the Swedish and the German case clearly shows, that the implementation of a comprehensive *ex ante* evaluation of 'all' regulatory impacts is very hard and is to a great extent dependent on structural and cultural factors in the respective country. The establishment of *ex ante* evaluations for specific impact aspects (e.g. assessment of administrative burdens for enterprises, assessment of budgetary effects) however, is more easily. Besides the political support for the topic, what is needed above all is a suitable and enduring legal and organizational institutionalization, which increases the binding character of evaluation requirements and allows an implementation control of impact analysis.

Chapter 9

Assessing the Accuracy of *Ex Ante* Evaluation through Feedback Research: A Case Study

Rob van Gestel and Jan Vranken

I. *The Black Box of* Ex Ante *Assessment of Legislative Drafts*

Most legal publications concerning the quality of legislation are focused on the parliamentary phase of the lawmaking process.[1] What happens during the preparatory phase inside and between ministries and government agencies largely takes place in a 'black box' although this is in fact the place where the action is.[2] This is remarkable because that is where the policy problem underlying a Bill is first defined, where the data/information is gathered through consultations or otherwise, where alternative regulatory options (non-regulation, self-regulation, co-regulation) are explored, and where trade-offs between those options are discussed etcetera. It is during this pre-parliamentary phase that all kinds of *ex ante* assessments of the quality of legislative drafts will take place.

But what do we know about the accuracy and reliability of these assessments and their effect on the quality of legislation after enactment? One way of finding out is by conducting so-called 'feedback research'.[3] This type of research aims

---

[1] *See*, for example, R.W. Bauman and T. Kahana, *The Least Examined Branch: The Role of Legislatures in the Constitutional State* (Cambridge University Press, Cambridge 2006). For the Netherlands, G. Visscher, *Parlementaire invloed op wetgeving* (dissertation Leiden, Den Haag 1994) and more recently: J.Th.J. van den Berg, J.L.W. Broeksteeg and L.F.M. Verhey (eds.), *Het parlement, Staatsrechtconferentie 2006* (Wolf Legal Publishers, Nijmegen 2007).

[2] These words are taken from one of the few Dutch scholars who have done research on the pre-Parliamentary phase of the legislative process, L.J.M. d'Anjou, *Actoren en factoren in het wetgevingsproces* (W.E.J. Tjeenk Willink, Zwolle 1986), p. 274 (dissertation with an English summary).

[3] Not much has been written on the methodology of feedback research. An exception is: E.H. Mory, 'Feedback Research Revisited' in H. Jonassen (eds.), *Handbook of Research on Educational*

to compare the results from *ex ante* evaluations and advisory opinions concerning the quality of legislative drafts with the outcomes of ex post evaluations to find out which judgements and predictions were (not) correct in retrospect and which essential flaws were overlooked.

In this chapter, we will focus on the *ex ante* review of legislative drafts by the Dutch Council of State.[4] The reason for this is that the position of the Council of State in the Netherlands is vital when it comes to *ex ante* evaluation. Other than most of the surrounding countries, the Netherlands does not yet have an integrated system of regulatory impact assessment or an impact assessment board. The Council of State, however, does something reasonably similar to *ex ante* evaluation, namely, assess the policy-analytical aspects[5] of legislative drafts before they are sent to parliament. There is no other institution that has the same authority, the same expertise (the House of Representatives is first of all a political arena), or the same strategic position (the Senate is at the far end of the lawmaking process and has little opportunity to demand amendments to legislative proposals) to be successful in scrutinizing the quality of legislative drafts.

Section II is about the Council of State and its exact role in the review of legislative drafts. In section III, the focus of this study will be specified, leading to the research questions in section IV. Our research involves a pilot study of two cases for which we developed an analytical framework (V–VIII). Finally, in sections IX and following, the research questions will be answered: what observations and conclusions can be drawn from the study?

II. *The Council of State as the Principal Advisor on Legislative Quality*

Together with the House of Representatives, the Senate, the National Chamber of Audit and the National Ombudsman, the Council of State belongs to the High Councils of State. These are government agencies of which the independence is regulated by the Constitution because they fulfil an important role in

---

Communications and Technology (Lawrence Earlbaum Associates, Mahwah 2004), pp. 745–784. *See* especially p. 745, where it is stated that feedback research allows the comparison of actual performance with some set standard of performance. Mory argues that information presented via feedback in instruction might include not only answer correctness, but other information such as precision, timeliness, learning guidance, motivational messages, lesson sequence advisement, critical comparisons, and learning focus. See also Section III.

[4] A detailed overview of the advisory tasks of the Council of State can be found in T. Borman, *Wetgevingsadvisering door de Raad van State in Nederland* (W.E.J. Tjeenk Willink, Deventer 2000).

[5] See Section II.

the constitutional system of checks and balances.[6] Similar to, for instance, the French *Conseil d'État*,[7] the Dutch Council of State (*Raad van State*) has two main functions. First, it is responsible for assisting the executive with legal advice. Secondly, the Council is the highest administrative court with general jurisdiction in administrative law cases. The legal basis for this double mandate can be found in Articles 73, 74, and 75 of the Constitution.[8] In its role as independent legal advisor, the Council of State has to be consulted on legislative drafts before they are sent to Parliament, i.e., the House of Representatives and the Senate.

Our study only concerns the Council's role in scrutinizing the quality of legislative drafts. In that capacity, it provides the government with advice on:

- all bills the government intends to present to Parliament,
- international agreements which the government intends to submit to Parliament for approval,
- orders in council promulgated by the Crown.[9]

The House of Representatives also seeks the Council's advice on bills initiated by members of Parliament before considering them in the House. Both for the government and the House of Representatives, the Council's advice is compulsory, i.e., without the Council's advice Parliament cannot consider bills and the government cannot promulgate orders in council. This privileged position of the Council of State in the legislative process is even strengthened following a significant reduction of the number of advisory bodies on the central government level over the last ten years. Currently, the Council of State is the last and most important advisory body in line before legislative drafts are sent to the House of Representatives. Reports from other government advisory bodies, such as ACTAL (the agency responsible for the assessment of administrative burdens),[10] the Social

[6] For a brief introduction to the Dutch constitutional system we refer to C. Kortmann, J. Fleuren and M. Kindlová, *Constitutional Law of 10 EU Member States: The 2004 Enlargement* (Kluwer Law International, Deventer 2006).

[7] *See* <www.conseil-etat.fr/ce/home/index.shtml>. More information on the competences of different Councils of State in Europe can be found through the European association of Councils of State and Supreme Administrative Jurisdictions of which the secretariat is established at the Belgium Council of State <www.juradmin.eu/en/home_en.html>.

[8] The text of the Dutch Constitution can be found at the website of the Ministry of the Interior and Kingdom Relations: <www.minbzk.nl/contents/pages/6156/grondwet_UK_6-02.pdf>.

[9] *See* <www.raadvanstate.nl> (English).

[10] *See* <www.actal.nl> (English).

and Economic Council, or, for example the National Health Council,[11] have to be sent to the Council of State together with the legislative draft.

In preparing its advisory opinions the Council has traditionally paid particular attention to both the legal and the technical aspects of legislation. Assessing the *legal* aspects means answering such questions as: will the bill fit in the existing legal system? Is the bill in accordance with higher law such as the Constitution, international treatises, e.g., human rights conventions, and European law? Is the bill in accordance with principles of democracy, equality before the law, proportionality, legal certainty, and the rule of law?[12] Assessing the *technical* aspects of legislation concerns, for instance, matters of logical consistency, use of terminology, and transitional provisions.

In the last decade, a third aspect has also become more and more important in the advisory opinions of the Council: assessing legislation from a policy-analytical perspective. In 2003, the Council even developed and published a special 'checklist for policy-analytical scrutiny of draft legislation'.[13] This checklist is quite detailed and covers a wide range of topics. They vary from:

- the definition of the policy problem that is addressed in the draft and the question of whether legislation is really necessary, the availability of alternative modes of regulation (self-regulation, co-regulation, economic incentives) in order to be certain that legislation is the best possible or least troublesome way of solving the problem, to
- the chance that the proposed legislation will prove to be effective, efficient and well-balanced regarding costs and benefits, and
- the possibility of monitoring and enforcing the law, and the side effects, bottlenecks, and problems that may be expected in these respects once the law has entered into force.

At the end of the report that contains the advisory opinion, the Council states its conclusion (*dictum*). This may be negative in that it recommends reconsid-

[11] More information about the Social and Economic Council of the Netherlands can be found in English at <www.ser.nl/en.aspx>. The same goes for the National Health Council at <www.gr.nl/index.php>.

[12] These principles concerning the quality of legislation can be found in such guidelines (Legislation in perspective, *Kamerstukken II* 1990–1991, 22008, nos. 1–2 (available in English)) and in the so-called *Aanwijzingen voor de regelgeving*, which are available in English as "Directives on legislation" at <www.kc-wetgeving.nl/> (the website has restricted access but a guest account can be obtained through the Ministry of Justice). The Directives on legislation are also on archive with the authors (r.a.j.vanGestel@uvt.nl and j.b.m.vranken@uvt.nl).

[13] Published in the Council of State's Annual Report 2003, Annex 4, pp. 151–152, and also available at <www.raadvanstate.nl> (English).

ering the bill and not submitting it to Parliament, or it may recommend that, before submitting the bill to Parliament, some amendments or improvements have to be made, in the text of the bill or in the Explanatory Memorandum. If the Council's *dictum* is negative, the draft has to be re-discussed by the Cabinet. Apart from this, the Minister responsible for the legislative draft always has to present a Report to the Queen (*Nader rapport*) containing a motivated reply to the comments by the Council of State. The Council's advisory opinion and the *Nader rapport* have to be published as soon as the bill is submitted to the House of Representatives.[14] Today the reports are easily accessible both in the national database on legislation and through the Council's website. The *Nader rapport* is supposed to make clear whether the Council's remarks have induced the Minister to amend the bill or to alter or supplement the Explanatory Memorandum.

III. *Focus of the Study*

We will concentrate on the accuracy of the Council's advice in uncovering policy-analytical failures and hidden mistakes in legislative drafts. To determine the accuracy, we will compare the Council's advices with an ex post evaluation of the relevant bill, which usually takes place several years after its enactment. This feedback research involves three aspects. First, it has to be determined whether the Council of State made an accurate assessment of the problems in advance. What bottlenecks and side effects did the Council foresee and were the predictions accurate according to the ex post evaluation? Secondly, it has to be established whether the ex post evaluation indicates that there is reason to reconsider and adapt (a) the procedure in which the Council prepares its advisory opinions, i.e., its working method, and (b) the checklist concerning the policy-analytical review. Thirdly, and most importantly, which lessons can the legislator learn for the quality system of *ex ante* assessment of legislative drafts in general, including the phase before the drafts are sent to the Council of State? More specifically, we will address the possible implications for the methodology of *ex ante* assessment, and the timing and expertise that is required. On that basis we are able to evaluate the potential contribution of feedback research to enhance the Ministries' quality system of *ex ante* assessments of legislative drafts, and therefore the quality of legislation. To answer the third question, we will briefly turn to scholarly literature on *ex ante* evaluation because, on the one hand, we expect that in our evaluation we can probably rely on theories or methods that are used to assess the regulatory impacts of draft legislation, whereas, on the

[14] *See* Article 25a of the Council of State Act 1962 (*Wet op de Raad van State van 9 maart 1962*).

other hand, we will be able to add our findings about the potential contribution of the feedback research we conducted in this project to the current body of knowledge on regulatory evaluation.

By 'the Council's procedure or working method', we mean the approach of the Council in preparing advisory opinions. Does the Council proceed in a transparent and consistent way and with a well-established idea about its own role in the process of preparing legislation? What data were available? Were they sufficient and reliable or should the Council have been more active in gathering information? Considering the preparatory phase of the advice, we will also pay attention to the style of argumentation and the way opinions are underpinned with consultations, empirical research, or other scientific evidence. What we already know from the start is that the Council usually keeps its comments as brief as possible, among other things, by keeping silent about topics in the bill it agrees upon, not giving any comments on possible good practices, and by being hesitant to refer to external sources outside the legislative file as it is presented to the Council. Furthermore, the Council prefers not to enter into debates with other advisors or commentators.[15]

The 'checklist on policy-analytical assessment of legislative drafts' was already mentioned. What role do the criteria in this checklist play in the daily practice of the Council's advisory opinions? Bearing in mind that the list is quite detailed and covers a wide range of topics, it seems almost impossible for the Council to keep a close track of the list and run through it item per item for each and every draft.

IV. *Research Question*

The foregoing leads to the following central research question:

What do ex post evaluations reveal about the accuracy of the policy-analytical review of legislative drafts by the Council of State and what lessons can be learnt for the quality system of ex ante assessment of draft legislation in general?

---

[15] This information is drawn from previous empirical research concerning the way the Council of State uses its advisory competence. In general, all these reports conclude that the Council relies heavily on intuition, experience, and practical wisdom. *See*, for example, Ph. Eijlander and W. Voermans, *Evaluatie regeerakkoord 1998 uit wetgevingsperspectief* (Tilburg 2002) <till.uvt.nl/articles/voermans/internet.pdf>; B.R. Dorbeck-Jung, *Beelden over de wetgevingsadvisering van de Raad van State. Hoe wetgevingskwaliteit gemaakt wordt* (BJU, Den Haag 2003); and J.L.W. Broeksteeg, E.M.J. Hardy, S. Klosse, M.G.W.M. Peeters and L.F.M. Verhey, *Zicht op wetgevingskwaliteit: een onderzoek naar de wetgevingsadvisering van de Raad van State* (WODC, Den Haag 2005) (available at <www.wodc.nl> with a summary in English).

Sub-questions are:

- In retrospect, has the Council of State conducted an accurate assessment of the problems, bottlenecks, effects, and side effects of bills before they entered into force according to the results of ex post evaluation?
- Do the ex post evaluations indicate that there is a reason to reconsider and adapt (a) the procedure in which the Council prepares its advisory opinions and/or (b) the Council's checklist on policy-analytical review?
- What lessons can the legislator learn for the ex ante assessment of legislative drafts in general? More specifically, what are the possible implications for the methodology and criteria of ex ante assessment, and the timing and required expertise?
- Considering the answers on the three sub-questions: what is the potential contribution of feedback research to enhance the system of ex ante assessment of legislative drafts in order to support the quality of legislation?

V. *Pilot Study*

The kind of feedback research we want to conduct ideally requires at least ten to twelve different case studies. We think it impossible to cover all types of files the Council has to deal with in its advisory function, but a certain diversity is needed. Aiming at a realistic variety, our selection criteria are (1) politically controversial or more legal-technical bills, (2) large or small size of the file, (3) establishing national law or implementing European directives, (4) a division of files over the classical areas of law (private law, criminal law, administrative law), and (5) a spread over the various governmental departments (economics, interior, foreign affairs, health, welfare, sport, employment, culture, law, spatial planning, housing, integration, education, science). A precondition is of course that the bill has been properly evaluated ex post.

In order to know already at an early stage whether feedback research will be a useful method, we decided to start with a pilot of two case studies. We have chosen one large, politically controversial statute in the area of private law (the Youth Care Act 2005), and one relatively small and technical statute in the area of administrative law (the Act for the Compensation of Costs in the Administrative Objection Procedure 2002). The *dictum* of the Council's advice in the first case was the most negative one, i.e., not to submit this proposal to Parliament, and in the second case rather moderate, i.e., to make some necessary amendments to the bill before submitting it to Parliament.

VI. *Three Definitions*

A. *Policy-Analytical Review*

The Council itself defines the policy-analytical review as a systematic description, analysis, and review of policy aspects of legislative drafts on the basis of three indicators: problem definition, approach in tackling the problem, and effectiveness and efficiency.[16] For an explanation of these criteria, we refer to section II of this report.

B. Ex Post *Evaluation of Legislation*

Not each collection and evaluation of data concerning the working of a bill can be considered an academic ex post evaluation.[17] The latter requires at least a well-defined research problem and research questions, a methodologically well-founded collection of relevant data, a research strategy including a solid academic analysis and interpretation of relevant data, and a report that shows the results of the evaluation. It is important to realize that an ex post evaluation about the working of a bill can serve different aims, and can therefore stress different questions for which different data are needed. Aims may include, for example, measuring the effectiveness of the bill or its legitimacy; determining bottlenecks and effects of the bill compared with what the legislator intended to achieve; learning about the process of implementing a bill in terms of, e.g., costs and benefits; early warning of possible side effects or administrative burdens; and so forth. The ex post evaluations of both the Youth Care Act and the Act for Compensation of Costs of the Administrative Objection Procedure[18] are early warning studies intended to monitor the working of these statutes in practice as soon as possible in order for the government to be able to adjust them if and where necessary.

---

[16] *See* the article written by the Vice-President of the Council of State on the policy-analytical review: H.D. Tjeenk Willink, 'De beleidsanalytische toetsing door de Raad van State' (2005) 2 *RegelMaat*, pp. 51–59.

[17] About ex post evaluation of legislation: U. Karpen (ed.), *Evaluation of Legislation, Proceedings of the Fourth Congress of the European Association of Legislation*x (Nomos, Den Haag 2002). Also H.B Winter, *Evaluatie van wetgeving: Structurering en institutionalisering van wetsevaluatie in Nederland* (Kluwer, Deventer 2002); K. van Aeken, *Proeven van wetsevaluatie* (dissertation) (Universiteit van Antwerpen, Antwerpen 2002); L. Mader, *L'évaluation législative: pour une analyse empirique des effets de la législation* (Payot, Lausanne 1985).

[18] *See* Chapter 7 of the General Administrative Law Act concerning objections and administrative appeal. The Act can be found in English at <www.justitie.nl/onderwerpen/wetgeving/awb/Wettekst_awb/index.aspx>.

C. *Legislative File*

A file comprises the text of the bill, its Explanatory Memorandum, the reports of advisory bodies which are sometimes compulsory, and, if applicable, (scientific) reports, proceedings of expert meetings and of other consultations which are held by the government before or during the drafting process, data from comparative research, and also all information the Council itself has gathered while preparing its advisory opinion. It is to some extent problematic that the personal knowledge and experience of the members of the Council or its supporting staff about the issue at hand, based on experiences with preceding bills or comparable problems in other policy areas, usually remains hidden for the readers of the advice, unless it is somehow documented in the file. The file also contains the notes of the Council's staff and the proceedings of the deliberations between the members of the Council who prepared the draft advice, including their names, in order to be able to contact them if clarification of certain points is necessary. Not part of the file, but necessary for our feedback research, are the Council's advisory report itself, the report to the Queen (*Nader rapport*), and the text of the ex post evaluations.

VII. *Analytical Framework*

The first sub-question of the study concerns a comparison of the Council's advice with the ex post evaluation as regards its accuracy. To ensure that the comparison in the pilot phase – and afterwards in all the files of the main study – will be conducted in the same way in both cases, we need an analytical framework. This framework provides the lens through which we will look at the object of study. It points out how to go through the legislative file step by step in order to obtain the relevant data. It is purely limited to establishing what happened and what was done, and does not involve any judgements concerning the data collected.

1. First Step

What remarks did the Council make and what was its advice on the definition of the problem, the problem approach, and the effectiveness and efficiency of the bill? How did this influence the Council's final opinion?

These data can easily be extracted from the Council's advice. As to complex and extensive files, it may not be so easy, but if that turns out to be the case, we will distinguish per item.

2. Second Step

On what data did the Council base its findings? Did the Council restrict itself to the data collected by the government? Were they sufficient and reliable? Did it consult other sources of information, and if so, which ones and why?

We should be able to find these answers in the Council's advice, but a problem already mentioned is that the Council usually does not refer to sources of information nor does it enter into debates with other advisors or commentators. This complicates the reconstruction of the information base. The notes of the Council's staff might be more informative in this respect, but if they are not, interviews with the members of the Council and the supporting staff who prepared the advice will perhaps yield more information. The same applies to the knowledge and experience of the Councillors, which we already mentioned in section VI (C).

The background of the queries on data collection is the importance of an adequate, reliable, and solid factual basis of the bill. It belongs to the key responsibilities of the Council as an advisory body to check whether the relevant information has been or will be taken into account as much as possible. This task is difficult for various reasons. The first reason is the broad range of topics the Council has to attend to. The Council cannot be expected to be able to compete on each topic with the special expertise available inside the different Ministries. Secondly, the Council generally has to deliver its advice within three months and in complex files; this time span is too short. Thirdly, a lack of solid factual evidence, needed to check the assumptions underlying the legislative draft, might complicate things. It is a situation legislators, judges, and legal scholars all have to cope with, not only in the Netherlands but in other countries as well. Rarely is it possible to (empirically) test the factual basis of many legislative assumptions or intended societal effects, except with hindsight in ex post evaluations. The same applies to the factual basis of judicial decisions, and of conclusions or recommendations in legal literature. Empirical legal research and inter- or multidisciplinary approaches to law, which could offer testable facts and figures, is still scarce in civil law countries. The Council has neither the time nor the means to do this type of research itself and does not see it as its task.

3. Third Step

How did the Council proceed when preparing its advice on the problem definition, the problem approach, and the effectiveness and efficiency of the bill?

For example, did the Council critically review the problem definition of the government or did it run through the quality of policy analysis checklist item per item? These are crucial questions because the way the Council proceeds indicates to a certain extent what it considers to be its main task in the legislative process in which so many actors are involved. Especially, its attitude towards various forms of *ex ante* evaluation, which the government has to carry out when preparing the bill – see the Directives on Legislation (*Aanwijzingen voor de regelgeving*) – is meaningful.

We already alluded to the Council's policy to keep its advice as concise as possible, among others things by not spending a word on topics in the bill it agrees upon, or by only stressing the most important critical points to make sure that the attention will not be distracted by its remarks on less important issues. In these cases, the Council reviewed the bill on a larger scale than mentioned in its advice. If necessary, interviews with the members of the Council and its staff who prepared the advice can clarify this.

4. Fourth Step

Did the government and/or Parliament adopt the Council's remarks and advice? Did the Council explain its opinions and, if so, how?

As to the government, the answer to both questions can easily be found in the report to the Queen (*Nader rapport*). For Parliament, we intend to carry out a quick scan of the Parliamentary documents that do not belong to the file. With the help of official legislative databases on the Internet, such a quick scan is not too difficult. Regarding the reliability of the quick scan results, it must be borne in mind that Parliament might discuss the Council's advice more extensively due to critical comments that were made, but the various parties in Parliament do not necessarily share the opinions expressed in the remarks. Therefore, it might sometimes be difficult to determine whether a parliamentary amendment has its basis in the Council's advice.

5. Fifth Step

Did the Council conduct an accurate assessment of the problems, bottlenecks, effects, and side effects of the legislative drafts, according to the ex post evaluation?

For the answer to this question, we need to compare the results of the first step of the analytical framework with the findings of the ex post evaluation. One of the problems we might face emerges from the fact that ex post evaluations do not evaluate the Council's advice, but the bill itself as it eventually entered into force. Often this bill was amended or adapted in Parliament. Moreover, evaluation commissions do not necessarily study all aspects of the bill. This impedes a pure comparison between the Council's advice and the ex post evaluation, but with the help of a quick scan of the parliamentary considerations, we are at least able to determine whether amendments and adaptations were made. Another problem is that, in practice, a bad law might be implemented or enforced in such a way that it is hard to distinguish what exactly caused what problems; was it the bill itself or perhaps the way it was implemented that influenced the final outcomes of the evaluation? This problem is more serious because, in our research design, we do not have the tools to even recognize it. Therefore we can only mention it as a warning to be borne in mind, when answering this question.

6. Sixth Step
Provided that the answer to the first sub-question is answered predominantly in the negative, does the ex post evaluation indicate that this is or might (partly) be caused (a) by the procedure in which the Council prepares its advisory opinions and/or (b) by the checklist on policy-analytical issues applied by the Council: What can be learned about (a) and (b) from the scholarly literature on ex ante evaluation of legislation?

The sixth and last step of the analytical framework is the feedback from ex post evaluation to the Council's assessment in advance. What do ex post evaluations reveal about the accuracy of the Council's advice and what do they, and the scholarly literature on evaluation, indicate on whether it could be of help to reconsider and adapt the procedure pursued by the Council and its checklist, at least the way it applies the list?

VIII. *The Litmus Test: Results of Two Case Studies*

In this section, we will summarize the most important findings of the two case studies that formed the pilot phase for a possibly more comprehensive study into the accuracy of the Council of State's policy-analytical assessments of legislative drafts. The two files that we have studied are, as mentioned before, the Youth Care Act 2005 (hereafter abbreviated as YCA) and the Act for the Compensation of Costs in the Administrative Objection Procedure 2002 (hereafter abbreviated as ACCOP). In reporting on the results, we will follow the six analytical steps that we have distinguished in the previous sections.

A. *Analysis of the Youth Care Act*[19]

Preliminary remarks: The YCA entered into force on January 1, 2005. The first draft was sent to twenty different advisory bodies before it was received by the Council of State on July 17, 2001. It took until November 21, 2001, before the Council gave its advisory opinion, while the reply by the government followed on December 14, 2001. For the benefit of our research project, the Council provided us with two ex post evaluations, both finished in 2006. A consulting agency conducted the first evaluation, which was requested by Parliament, while

[19] *Wet van 22 april 2004, houdende regeling van de aanspraak op, de toegang tot en de bekostiging van jeugdzorg* (Wet op de jeugdzorg), *Stb.(Netherlands Bulletin of Acts and Decrees)* 2004, 306 (for a number of corrections, see *Stb.* 2004, 700).

an official working group installed by the Cabinet Office performed the second study, especially concerned with the financial structure of the youth care system in the future.[20] Since the second study is not predominantly an evaluation of the YCA, we will not take it into consideration. The first evaluation study has to be characterized as an early warning evaluation because a huge project such as the YCA will take at least three to five years to get rid of its teething troubles. Moreover the results of the first full-size ex post evaluation are not to be expected before the end of 2009.[21]

The Council's advice identifies twelve general items to comment upon.[22] From these twelve items, only six concern the policy-analytical aspects of the YCA. The other items and the Council's comments on specific articles are not relevant for our study.

Step one: Expectations, comments, and critical remarks concerning the problem definition, approach, effectiveness, and efficiency of the bill

The Council does not systematically assess these aspects of the bill. Problem definition and approach can be considered to be included in the remarks on the aims of the new bill compared with those of its predecessor, the Youth Assistance Act (*Wet op de Jeugdhulpverlening*).[23] Effectiveness and efficiency are not dealt with in a specific section of the advice, but the Council's relevant remarks have to be extracted and combined together from its comments on the various items.

As to the problem definition and approach, the Council was downright sceptical on whether the draft would be capable of providing a remedy for the major problems of the Youth Assistance Act. Its scepticism was fed, among other things, by the fact that there appeared to be much unclarity about what kind of implementation measures would follow from delegated laws and regulations as soon as the bill entered into force. Because of this, the Council had the feeling to be in the blind. Furthermore the Council seriously questions whether the Youth Care Act was capable to overcome the problems that its predecessor had met in practice since an overview of previous shortcomings and their causes was missing in the file. The Council signalled, for instance, that overcoming fragmentation in the youth care system had already been a goal of the Youth Assistance Act. However, the Explanatory Memorandum did not provide any

---

[20] *Het kind en de rekening. Eindrapportage van de werkgroep IBO financiering jeugdbeleid*, 2005–2006, no. 2.

[21] *Kamerstukken II* 28 168, F (Senate).

[22] *Kamerstukken II* 28 168, A (the Council's advice and the 'Nader Rapport'). Items 1–5 and 8 concern the political-analytical aspects.

[23] Item 1 of the Council's advice (*Kamerstukken II* 28 168, A).

information on why that Act had failed in this respect and to what extent the proposed bill would be likely to offer a better remedy here.

The Council also commented on a number of issues related to the expected effectiveness and efficiency of the Youth Care Act. The most serious one had to do with the creation of an individual right to youth care.[24] The Council wondered how such a right could be enforced in court if government budgets proved to be insufficient, or if there were not enough facilities, or in case of a lack of qualified personnel. Another doubt concerned the financial and organizational structure of the youth care system, which was likely to prove to be defective, because of its complexity. Complex structures generally did not invite the actors in the field to cooperate closely and that was disastrous because tailoring youth care – one of the objectives of the YCA – could not become successful without channelling the efforts of all actors involved.

Step two: What data did the Council base its findings upon?
From the file, it follows that the Council exclusively based its findings on the data which the government had provided, including the opinions of the twenty different advisory bodies on an earlier draft of the bill. No indication can be found of whether the Council explicitly tested the adequacy, reliability, and soundness of the information. Preparatory notes from the supporting staff refer to several sources, more specifically to one paper in a legal journal, one judicial decision, one of the twenty advisory opinions included in the file, and one other advisory opinion, which were not contained in the file. The Council's final report only refers to one of the opinions in the file and, without any further specification, to 'existing case law'.

Step three: How did the Council proceed when preparing its advice on the problem definition, the problem approach, and the effectiveness and efficiency of the bill?
Two staff notes can be found in the file. However, the file does not reveal, explicitly or implicitly, any relevant information about the cooperation between the State Councillors and the Council's staff, nor among the State Councillors themselves, nor on any other aspect of the working method. Therefore we cannot say whether the supporting staff was instructed by (one of) the State Councillors – e.g., the State Councillor *Rapporteur* who is responsible for preparation of a draft advice for the Plenary Council meeting –, whether the notes were discussed in (informal) meetings, which items were considered the most important ones, and what was left out in the final version of the advice. Although it does not follow from the Council's advice, it is certain that the draft advice was on the agenda of the Plenary Council, because this is compulsory. Whether the draft

[24] Item 2 of the Council's advice (*Kamerstukken II* 28 168, A).

was accepted without debate cannot be ascertained because there are no records of that plenary meeting in the file.

As to the way the Council handled the checklist, the picture is the same: the advice does not explicitly comprise relevant information about this subject. Nevertheless, from what was said above in step one, it seems safe to conclude that the Council paid much attention to the definition of the problem, the approach, the effectiveness and efficiency, especially regarding the availability of sufficient, qualified personnel, financial means, and a well-structured organisation. It also seems safe to state that, in this file, the Council probably did not systematically go through its checklist, but writing this, it must be recalled that, because of its policy not to waste any words on issues it agrees upon, the bill may have been reviewed on a larger scale or more systematically than mentioned in the advice.

Step four: The attitude of government and Parliament towards the Council's remarks and advice

The government remains silent on the Council's fundamental scepticism and doubt on whether the aim of the bill, to provide a remedy for the major problems of its predecessor, the Youth Assistance Act, will be feasible. Summarizing, it could be said that the government stuck to its views and choices[25] and was only prepared to adapt or supplement the Explanatory Memorandum in order to clarify certain arguments. As to Parliament, a quick scan of the parliamentary documents that did not belong to the file disclosed that especially the House of Representatives supported the Council's fundamental scepticism and doubt, using qualifications like 'severe' or 'crushing', and complaining that the government had given too little weight to the Council's advice. The parliamentary considerations in the House of Representatives led to many amendments, proposed by members of the House, and to three extensive ministerial memoranda of amendment (*Nota's van wijziging*). Whether and to what extent these amendments were prompted by the Council's advice is hard to say.

Step five: The findings of the evaluation report

In the first *ex ante* evaluation report,[26] seven items were studied, three of which were the result of amendments in Parliament supplementing or tightening the bill. They were not part of the Council's advice and therefore cannot play a role in our assessment of the accuracy of the Council's advice. The four items which were reflected in the Council's advice are subsequently: (a) the youth care

[25] *See Kamerstukken II* 28168, A ('Nader Rapport', answers to items 1–5 and 8).

[26] Bestuur & Management Consultants, *Evaluatieonderzoek Wet op de Jeugdzorg. Eindrapport* (Evaluation Youth Assistance Act. Final report), November 2006.

agency (*bureau jeugdzorg*) as the exclusive way of access to youth care; (b) the complex financial structure of the bill; (c) the right to youth care; and (d) the Council's fundamental scepticism and doubt on the necessity and feasibility of the bill. The findings of the evaluation report on each item can be summarised as follows:

(a) The introduction of an exclusive youth care agency caused many problems and bottlenecks. The list in the evaluation report was too long and too detailed to summarize here, but the report's recommendations clearly indicated what was at stake: there was a need for improving the quality of personnel and the process of decision making; improving the cooperation between the agency and the many other actors involved; improving the exchange of policy documents; and improving the openness of the agency for hints from the public about (potential) youth care abuses.
(b) Different financing sources obviously caused problems as to responsibility, accountability, transparency, and applicability, because each of them had, among other things, its own criteria, tariffs, and policies. Nevertheless, the evaluation report did not recommend to integrate the sources immediately, but to start with harmonising their preconditions and policies as much as possible and to wait until the 2009 final evaluation of the bill before definitely deciding upon this issue.
(c) The still existing waiting lists and the relatively long completion time showed that realization of the right to youth care had not been attained, despite the many extra millions of Euros the government had spent since 2005 and continued to spend to cope with the most severe bottlenecks. Partly, this was the consequence of an unexpectedly high increase of the number of clients who sought the help of the youth care agency. Partly, it was the consequence of problems such as a lack of sufficient tailored youth care, not knowing the effects of youth care yet, and, again, a lack of cooperation between the actors involved.
(d) Although the evaluation report showed that the problems and bottlenecks of the Youth Care Act were numerous and severe, and undoubtedly required new policy measures, the evaluation report did not recommend to drastically reform the Youth Care Act system of youth care (and therefore did not recommend to forget about improving the bill, and starting to prepare a new and better one).

The government quite agreed with the analysis and recommendations of the evaluation report and announced to take responsibility for the rapid implementation of the recommendations.[27]

[27] In a letter to the Parliament (DJB/JZ-2721942).

Step six: Comparison of the evaluation report and the Council's advice as to the four items. Was the Council accurate?

On items where the many amendments strongly revised the bill, a pure comparison of the ex post evaluation and the Council's advice is not reliable. This holds true especially for (a) and (d): exclusive access to the youth care agency (*bureau jeugdzorg*) and the Council's fundamental scepticism and doubt on the necessity and feasibility of the bill, respectively. Also relevant is that the essential delegated laws and regulations which the Council had missed while preparing its advice and which was one main reason for its scepticism and doubt, of course, were promulgated (and were often even supplemented and adjusted) once the bill entered into force.

As to the other two items, the financial structure and the right to youth care, a comparison seems justified. The parliamentary debate was extensive and profound, the House of Representatives asked the government to reconsider its view, but the government stuck to its position. The comparison conclusively showed that the Council's critical remarks and advice on the two items were borne out by the ex post evaluation and were, therefore, accurate. Although not with the same details as the ex post evaluation could do, in retrospect, the Council correctly identified the (very nature of the) problems with these two items.

B. *Analysis of the Act for the Compensation of Costs in the Administrative Objection Procedure*

Preliminary remarks: The ACCOP entered into force on March 12, 2002.[28] The Act partly resulted from an evaluation of the General Administrative Law Act (GALA, *de Algemene wet bestuursrecht*). This evaluation made it clear that there was no consensus about the possibilities for compensation of costs in the objection procedure, which is normally an obligatory step for access to an administrative court.[29]

According to the case law of the Netherlands Supreme Court (*Hoge Raad*) compensation was possible. Most administrative courts, however, denied this except for situations in which the disputed administrative order was so blatantly in conflict with existing law that the authorities must have known this. As a consequence, the state Commission for Codification of Administrative Law was asked to find out whether adjustments to the GALA were necessary. In its report, the Commission stated that there were two major reasons to give an affirmative answer in this respect. First, it was considered undesirable if the Supreme Court's case law and that of the Council of State continued to diverge. Secondly, the

[28] Wet kosten bestuurlijke voorprocedures van 24 januari 2002, *Stb.* 2002, 55.

[29] Verslag van de Commissie evaluatie algemene wet bestuursrecht, *Toepassing en effecten van de Algemene wet bestuursrecht 1994–1996*, Den Haag 18 december 1996. *See also Kamerstukken II* 1997–1998, 25 600 VI, no. 46, p. 40.

Commission argued that continuation of the Supreme Court's approach would create a counterproductive formalisation of the objection procedure and increase the threshold for a flexible settlement of legal conflicts.

In relation to this file, we studied two evaluative documents. The first one contained an official evaluation resulting from a request by the Senate to the Minister of the Interior. The Groningen University Faculty of Law conducted this evaluation in the period between June 2004 and January 2005, i.e., within two and a half years after the Act had entered into force.[30] The second study was not a real evaluation but a study by two individual legal scholars three and a half years after enactment, focusing on an inventory of national and European case law.[31] This study was taken into account because it was explicitly meant to be an update of the Groningen study on the aspect of case law.

Step one: Expectations, comments, and critical remarks concerning the problem definition, approach, effectiveness, and efficiency of the draft

The remarks by the Council concentrated on the argument that the Supreme Court should no longer be able to rule on compensation for costs in the objection procedure. By doing so, the Council appeared to agree with the drafters of the law to the effect that excluding this topic from the jurisdiction of civil law courts was the best way to solve the problem. The Explanatory Memorandum, however, also mentioned other elements of the problem definition, such as the risk of formalising the supposedly informal objection procedure and the risk of increasing the costs for the administration due to the fact that plaintiffs would want to safeguard their claim for compensation by resorting to pro forma appeal.

Step two: On what data did the Council base its findings?

Our first impression is that the Council predominantly based its findings on the information available in the legislative file. Studying the internal communication between State Councillors, however, reveals that its experience as the highest administrative court seems to have had a significant influence on the Council's position in the assessment of the legislative draft. In one of the internal notes from the supporting staff addressed to the State Councillor Rapporteur, it is stated that "the bureau notices that there has been a lot of criticism from different sides towards the Council's case law that is now being codified in the

---

[30] H.B. Winter, P.O. de Jong and R. van Dijk, *Evaluatie Wet kosten bestuurlijke voorprocedures* (Groningen 2004). The full report is available at <rechten.eldoc.ub.rug.nl/FILES/departments/Algemeen/Recht1/2005/ evaluatieWkbv/EvaluatieWkbv.pdf>.

[31] R. Ortlep and R.J.G.M. Widdershoven, 'De Wet kosten bestuurlijke voorprocedures in de rechtspraak' (2005) *JB plus*, pp. 147–167.

draft. The same goes for the arguments used to justify the current draft in the Explanatory Memorandum" (our translation).

The bureau also summarized the three most important critical comments in the scholarly literature on the draft.[32] First, some scholars argued that the administrative authority might benefit from a further juridification of the objection procedure because this could increase the pressure to settle disputes without entering into a formal legal discussion. Secondly, some experts felt that it was unfair to expect from an individual citizen to carry the costs of an administrative order that was not only a wrong decision but also an unlawful one. Thirdly, the obligation to pay the costs of the objection procedure in order to retain the right to compensation on appeal might lead to negative side effects, such as an increasing number of pro forma appeals. None of these reservations from the supporting staff were reflected in the final version of the advice.

Step three: How did the Council proceed when preparing its advice?

The file clearly indicates that the draft had led to a lively discussion inside the Council, especially in relation to its own case law. It is rather remarkable that the State Councillor Rapporteur opposed to this case law, which, in practices, boiled down to a standard refusal to grant compensation for costs except in cases where the authorities deliberately disregarded applicable rights or obligations. In this context, the State Councillor wrote: "This is an Alocorp or in other words a reversed Procola matter.[33] If the Council feels its own case law is untenable, it should say so. The 'against better judgement' criterion is unfortunate if it also applies to cases of misinterpretation of current laws and regulations" (our translation).

Other Councillors, however, begged to differ in this respect. One of them concluded that the Council's case law left no room to manoeuvre whatsoever here. Another one claimed that the decisive criterion in the draft, i.e. 'severe carelessness', was far too vague to offer any guidance here. To this he added: "But apparently no criticism on this matter is allowed inside this house". (our translation).

---

[32] They draw attention to publications such as J.J. Simon, 'Kosten van voorprocedures' (1998) *JB*, pp. 68 et seq.; R.J. Tjittes, 'Bestuurlijke proeftuin' (1998) *RM Themis*, pp. 1–2, and N.S.J. Koeman, 'Proceskosten voorprocedures: voorontwerp gepresenteerd' (1998/9) *NTB*, pp. 290–293, and furthermore the case note by Van Ravels (1998) *Bouwrecht*, p. 522.

[33] This remark refers to the case law of the ECtHR, *Procola vs. Luxembourg* judgment of 28 September 1995, Series A, no. 326 (14570/89), concerning the double mandate of the (Luxembourg) Council of State in relation to the requirement of judicial independency as laid down in Article 6 of the ECHR.

These types of remarks indicate that the draft led to fierce internal debate. Nonetheless, the criteria on the checklist for policy-analytical review by the Council apparently did not seem to play a role in these debates. No evidence can be found in the file that such topics as the problem definition, approach, or programme theory behind the draft received systematic attention. First and foremost, the Council seemed to focus on the perceived legal necessity of the draft in order to rule out any further legal uncertainty caused by the fact that both the Supreme Court and the Council of State claimed jurisdiction on this matter.

Step four: The attitude of government and Parliament towards the Council's advice
With respect to the government's position, we can be brief: on almost all points the government stuck to its guns. More interesting, however, was the debate in the House of Representatives. There, the criterion used in the draft, viz., compensation only if the contested administrative decision appeared to be unlawful and severely careless was amended.[34] The rather strict criterion in the draft was toned down in the sense that a revocation of the order because of careless decision-making that could be attributed to the authority is enough to qualify for compensation of costs. According to the Minister of Justice, this came down to a significant broadening of the criterion in the draft. Furthermore he repeated his fear that this might cause an undesirable formalisation and juridification of the objection procedure which ran against the intentions of the legislature as laid down in the GALA. Therefore some members of Parliament asked for a renewed opinion by the Council of State on the amended text but in his formal reply, the Minister advised against this and the House of Representatives ultimately agreed on that point.[35] In response to the fears of some members of Parliament that the amendment was going to lead to a disruption of the informal character of the objection procedure together with increasing costs for the administration, the Minister of Justice did promise an early evaluation of the ACCOP, even ahead of next periodical evaluation of the GALA in 2007.

Step five: Comparison of the Council's advice with the results of the ex post evaluations
The findings in the ex post evaluation conducted by experts from Groningen University show some interesting results. First of all, the empirical part of the evaluation revealed that, in the sample of administrative bodies that had been studied, petitioners requested a compensation of costs in only 5 to 10% of the objection cases. Especially people without legal assistance did not even seem to know about the possibility to get compensation. This did not come as a surprise

[34] *Kamerstukken II* 2000–2001, 27 024, nr. 14.
[35] *Kamerstukken II* 2001–2002, 27 024, nr. 17.

since most authorities do not notify those who file objections of this possibility. For the rest, the law appeared to have been implemented according to the intentions of the legislature, resulting in very few awards for compensation. Only 1 to 2% of the requests were granted.

What is even more important is that the alleged side effect of juridification failed to materialize. Administrative bodies did not put more emphasis on legal aspects than before the Act entered into force in settling disputes with citizens. Besides this, no extra objections seemed to have occurred as a result of pro forma claims. Some authorities did try to bypass the rules for compensation by taking a new decision instead of replying to the objections but this practice already existed before the ACCOP and has in the meantime been blocked by the courts. All in all, there were no signs that the ACCOP had led to a formalisation of the supposedly informal administrative objection procedure. Most authorities still seemed to believe that the fixed compensation rates were not significant enough to fight over in court. As a consequence, the authorities continued to be eager to settle disputes out of court as much as possible.

Step six: Comparison of the evaluation report and the Council's advice as to the four items. Was the Council accurate?

In retrospect, it could be said the Council of State does not appear to have been very accurate in its policy-analytical review. However, it is difficult to draw hard conclusions here for a number of reasons. First of all, we already mentioned that the ACCOP was amended in Parliament. What we do not know, however, is whether the amendment would have stood a chance had the Council been more specific in its criticism towards the decisive criterion in the draft. Secondly, it is not so easy either to conclude what effects the Council overlooked. With hindsight it could be argued, for instance, that it was a good choice that the Council did not warn of possible side effects, such as the juridification of the objection procedure, serious cost increases for the administration, and a growing number of pro forma claims, because they did nor occur. This does not seem to be quite correct, however, since the Council's bureau pointed to scholarly literature criticizing the draft of the ACCOP. Particularly because the Council overstated these risks, it seems more likely that it agreed with the government here and therefore implicitly underlined the same wrong assumptions of the government. Besides, it might be argued that the policy-analytical assessment of legislative drafts is especially intended to uncover unjustified claims about these kinds of risks.

IX. *Feedback: The Council's Working Methods and its Checklist of the Policy-Analytical Review*

Our second sub-question is whether the ex post evaluations indicate that there is a reason to reconsider and adapt the way the Council proceeds in preparing its reports or follows its checklist. Looking back at the two case studies, and keeping in mind the limited scope of our study, we can conclude that the accuracy of the current review by the Council does not seem to depend very heavily on the working methods applied in the assessment or on the checklist. After all, although roughly the same working methods and exactly the same checklist were applied in both cases, the accuracy of the Council's advice differs. As to the YCA, the Council made accurate observations about some weak spots in the draft whereas, with regard to the ACCOP, it overlooked important weaknesses in the draft or was perhaps too easily convinced by the arguments of the government.

The latter might be a consequence of the fact that the Council does not systematically follow its own checklist. From contacts with staff members, we know that there is some sort of implicit proportionality test, meaning that not every legislative draft is put through the same in-depth assessment, but there are no official guidelines for this selection process. Another conclusion is that the working method being used to assess legislative drafts seems to depend to a large extent on the individual staff members and the State Councillors, especially the *Rapporteur*, who happens to prepare the advice. Sometimes other Councillors are consulted, as in the ACCOP file, or even outside experts, but there is no policy on how to proceed in these matters.

On other issues, there are established practices but it may be doubted sometimes whether they be counterproductive. To name just a few: the Council is usually as brief as possible in commenting, no remarks are made about good practices or possible ways to improve the draft, there is almost no reference to sources and no motivation as to the grounds of the Council's criticism. Besides, it is impossible to find out whether and, if so, on what points the Council ignored minor flaws or agreed with choices made in the draft. As a consequence, the assessment process is neither transparent nor systematic. Personal experience, practical wisdom, common sense, and intuition are given free play.

Although our pilot study does not present hard evidence that the accuracy of the Council's review would benefit from a change in the working method or by following the checklist, we believe that a more systematic and transparent approach in both respects will show positive (side) effects. Existing literature on (*ex ante*) evaluation of legislation seems to reveal that relying too heavily on experience, practical wisdom, common sense and intuition is a hazardous approach because legislative flaws, unrealistic assumptions or, as the ACCOP file shows, biased positions,[36] arbitrariness, and subjectivity can easily be overlooked. Moreover, without a systematic assessment with transparency as to the methods, arguments, sources, and evidence which underpin the advisory opinions, an opportunity is missed to challenge those who are responsible for the preparation of the bill to rethink parts of the draft. For them, such an opinion is just an opinion, regardless of the institutional authority of its author.[37] Sometimes they will probably feel taken by surprise because they do not know what to expect from a policy-analytical review which rests so heavily on idiosyncrasies.[38] The same goes for members of Parliament who cannot use the Council's advice as ammunition against legislative mistakes if the advice is unclear or not backed up with facts, arguments, or evidence that uncovers legislative flaws or failures.[39] It is more difficult for the drafters not to take well-articulated, sound arguments seriously, especially when they come from the most important advisor in the legislative process. In the latter case: even if the drafters ultimately do not agree with these arguments, they nevertheless may improve the draft, because they are forced to engage in a serious discussion to explain why they wish to stick to their proposal.

Does all this mean that experience, practical wisdom, common sense, and intuition are no longer useful? Definitely not. Although a systematic approach in the assessment of drafts and more clarity about the Council's own working methods would possibly improve the quality of the advisory opinions, this certainly does not imply that these capacities are no longer to be used. On the contrary, we would say. The fact that most State Councillors know the legislative process from different angles (as former politicians, judges, and ministers, etcetera) certainly has great advantages. However, because most members of

---

[36] In that file, the Council of State missed the openness to critically assess its own case law. For the methodological pitfalls concerning *ex ante* evaluation, *see*, for example, F.L. Leeuw, 'Reconstructing Program Theories: Methods Available and Problems to be Solved' (2003) 24:1 *American Journal of Evaluation*, pp. 5–20.

[37] The idea that *ex ante* assessments of legislative drafts can simply serve as a way of speaking truth to power is refuted by, for instance, A. Meuwese, *Impact Assessment in EU Lawmaking* (dissertation, Leiden 2008).

[38] There is anecdotal evidence that this feeling of being taken by surprise really exists. *See*, for instance, T.C. Borman, 'Zeven stellingen over de (herstructurering van de) Raad van State en de wetgevingskwaliteit' in T. Barkhuysen, T. Borman and R. van Gestel, *De wetgevingsadvisering door de Raad van State* (BJU, Den Haag 2008), p. 7.

[39] This of course does not mean that if the assessment is underpinned by scientific evidence, Parliament will automatically adopt the conclusions that follow from the evaluation report. The interface between evaluation and public policy is far more complicated than that. *See*, for example, C.H. Weiss, 'The Interface between Evaluation and Public Policy' (1999) *Evaluation*, pp. 468–486.

the Council of State have themselves experienced how resistant lawmaking is to unwelcome factual information or institutional changes, the Council could consider it to be a challenge to strengthen the evidence base of its own role as a guardian of the quality of legislation.[40]

X. *Feed Back: The Methodology and Criteria of* Ex Ante *Assessments, the Timing, and the Required Expertise*

Our third sub-question is what lessons the legislator can learn from the *ex ante* assessment of legislative drafts *in general*, and more specifically, what the possible implications are for the methodology and criteria of *ex ante* assessments as such, the timing, and the required expertise. The first lesson – Conclusion I – follows from the foregoing:

> A transparent and systematic methodology is indispensable to be able to prevent arbitrariness and subjectivity, and to avoid overlooking legislative flaws, or unrealistic assumptions or biased positions of the assessment body. Nevertheless, experience, practical wisdom, common sense, and intuition seem to be just as important in order to avoid a tick-box mentality in the assessment of legislative drafts.

The case studies have shown that, while the Council of State does not go about in a systematic way in preparing its advisory opinions and does not possess the methodological expertise to perform state of the art *ex ante* evaluations, its judgments and predictions, especially in the first case study, are often remarkably accurate. This puts the importance of methodological purity in the assessment process into perspective. Apparently there is more to *ex ante* evaluation than 'going by the book'. The 'soft' side of the assessment process should not be underestimated. Methodology, practical experience, intuition, and common sense are inextricably intertwined, as also appears from what the empirical part of our study revealed about the interface between methodology and communication. Those who want to scrutinize the quality of legislative drafts, and cannot explain how they proceed or account for the methods they have used to estimate the impact of a bill before its enactment, will probably have extra trouble in convincing policymakers and politicians to take their advice on board. This does not imply that *ex ante* evaluation is simply a matter of 'speaking truth to power'.

---

[40] The plea for more evidence-based lawmaking in the Netherlands seems to have become stronger lately. *See*, for instance, P. Eijlander, 'Het wetgevingsbeleid na de bruikbare rechtsorde', in: P. Popelier and Ph. Eijlander, *Preadviezen Vereniging voor wetgeving en wetgevingsbeleid 2007* (BJU, Den Haag 2008), p. 52. See also the call from the Senate in its latest annual report to make more use of experiments and sunset clauses in the process of drafting new legislation. See <http://www.eerstekamer.nl/> (search for: jaarbericht).

Ultimately, those with political power will have to make up their own minds in deciding what weight should be given to the outcomes of *ex ante* evaluations. A more evidence-based approach in preparing new legislation cannot and should not replace political judgment.

The second lesson concerns the timing of the *ex ante* assessment. Looking at our pilot study and the international literature on *ex ante* evaluation, it is not surprising that the Dutch Council of State's policy-analytical review of legislative drafts has relatively little effect. The main reason for this is that the Council of State is positioned too late in the legislative process to be able to bring about fundamental changes in legislative drafts. The most likely explanation for this, we think, is what might be called the *path dependency* in the lawmaking process. As soon as there is agreement inside the administration about a proposal for a new law, it will become extremely hard for 'outsiders' such as the Council of State to persuade those who are responsible for the draft to adopt serious changes. Conclusion II is therefore:

> Path dependency of the lawmaking process implies that the later critical remarks from ex ante assessments are brought up in the process, the more difficult it will become to have them taken into account.

This conclusion is not new, but our pilot study empirically confirms what is prevailing in most publications on *ex ante* evaluation, viz., to stress the importance of timely review of alternative policy choices and regulatory options because otherwise they will not stand a chance.[41] However, having said this, the question immediately arises what is meant by "timely". A clear-cut answer will probably be hard to get. On the one hand, a fruitful *ex ante* evaluation requires that a legislative draft should already have a certain level of maturity, especially with regard to collecting the relevant data (which are sometimes not yet available at that time or hard to obtain), the policy choices to be made, the regulatory options to consider, the assessment of the consequences, and the effectiveness and efficiency of the proposed rules. On the other hand, there should still be a genuine openness to other possible policy choices, different regulatory options such as self-regulation or co-regulation, the expected working of the proposed rules, and also, if necessary, sufficient time and willingness to reconsider and adapt the draft in question.

---

[41] *See*, for example, R. Baldwin, 'Is Better Regulation Smarter Regulation?' *Public Law* (Autumn 2005), pp. 485–511. S. Jacobs, *Current Trends in Regulatory Impact Analysis: The Challenges of Mainstreaming RIA in to Policymaking* (Jacob & Associates Inc., Washington DC 2006). For an overview of the international literature on this and other common problems in *ex ante* evaluation *see*, for example, SERV, *Reguleringsimpactanalyse in Vlaanderen, Evaluatie en aanbevelingen* (Brussel, 22 November 2006). *See also*, chapter 3 of this volume.

Does the latter mean that the draft to be sent to the *ex ante* evaluator should explicitly consider and balance the advantages and disadvantages of various policy choices, alternative regulatory options and expectations as to the effectiveness and efficiency of a bill, each of which based on sound factual information? At present, such a way of proceeding is unusual and there are some good reasons for that. First, it would burden the legislator with a very heavy, if not rather unbearable workload. Secondly, it could bring the *ex ante* evaluator in a position that interferes too much with the legislator's responsibilities, which impedes its neutrality, impartiality, and objectivity. However, there is no scientific certainty that these risks will occur. All in all, there is an urgent need for further (empirical) study to determine the most appropriate moment for *ex ante* evaluations, among other things, by comparing and analysing experiences in several countries, and on the EU level. Therefore we would like to add to Conclusion II:

> Determining the most appropriate moment in the legislation process for an ex ante evaluation still needs further (empirical) investigation from a comparative perspective.

The third possible lesson follows naturally from this line of argument. It concerns questions like who is best equipped to carry out *ex ante* evaluations, what sort of expertise is required, and what type of assessment methods are most suited for different types of legislation. Several authors in this volume have already dealt with these questions. We refer to them and, of course, to the authors of relevant, international literature as well.[42] In this contribution we will confine ourselves to what we have learned from the pilot study in this respect and what we would like to add to the existing body of knowledge on this topic. Conclusion III reads as follows:

> It is generally accepted that an ex ante assessment should be carried out as early as possible in the legislative process (see Conclusion II). The subsequent questions to be answered are: who is best equipped to carry out ex ante evaluations, what kind of expertise is needed, and what assessment methods are most appropriate in relation to different types of laws.[43] These questions need further research, also from a comparative perspective, but from our pilot study we have learned four important lessons that may be kept in mind.

---

[42] *See*, for instance, J. Hertin, J. Turnpenny, A. Jordan, M. Nilsson, D. Russel, and B. Nykvist, *Rationalising the Policy Mess? Ex Ante Policy Assessment and the Utilisation of Knowledge in the Policy Process*, FFU report (Freie Universität Berlin, Fachbereich Politik- und Socialwissenschaften, Berlin 2007). *See*, in this volume, chapters 4, 5 and 8.

[43] With different types of laws, we mean temporary versus permanent legislation, politically sensitive laws versus more technical ones, strictly national laws and regulations versus bills that are used to implement European directives at a member state level, etcetera.

First, a professional evaluation board should consist not only of lawyers, economists and social scientists, familiar with the methodology of evaluation research but should also include people with experience in the public administration. The latter are more likely to be blessed with the aforementioned practical wisdom, common sense, and intuition about what works and why. This means that, on the one hand and from an institutional perspective, such a professional board must keep a certain distance towards the political process, while on the other hand, as to the personnel composition of the board, there should be a close commitment.

At the same time, a multidisciplinary setting will probably complicate communications between members of the board, due to their different backgrounds. In our case studies, the Council of State did not have these problems because the majority of its members share the fact that they have a law degree and therefore speak the same type of language.

Secondly, a professional board should be entitled to recommit poor quality legislative drafts to the legislator in order to make sure that the decisions that are being made rest on reliable information and, if necessary, state of the art scientific evidence. Without such power, the board will be toothless and remains the plaything of political institutions in the legislative process. So, only a strong board with real power to enforce adaptation and improvement of draft bills can counterbalance the often preponderant political rationality.

The third observation suggested by our pilot study is that a professional evaluation board should develop a proportionality test to determine which drafts should be evaluated more thoroughly than others. This implies that criteria will have to be developed to distinguish between various types of legislative drafts.

A fourth observation concerns one of the most striking problems, i.e., the fit between the methods to be used – see Van Aeken in this volume – and the kind of legislation at stake. It is often said that methodological flaws are the Achilles heel of *ex ante* evaluation. The importance of ex post evaluation for the *ex ante* evaluation will be discussed in section XI.

XI. *Feed Back: Evaluating the Relevance of Feedback Research for Improving the Quality of* Ex Ante *Assessments of Legislation*

As to the fourth sub research question, we start by stating that evaluation research normally involves assessing the strengths and weaknesses of programmes, policies, personnel, products, or organisations to improve their effectiveness. The idea behind most evaluations is to provide useful feedback to those who designed the rules or to people or organisations otherwise affected by the rules. However, taking feedback into account is not axiomatic.

First of all, *ex ante* evaluation is by nature more future-oriented than most other types of evaluation research and does not automatically include monitoring of predictions that were made earlier in the process or introduce learning loops through feedback by itself.[44] Secondly, the relationship between evaluations and their impact is not a simple one. Scientific studies that seem critical sometimes fail to influence short-term decisions because the policy cycle revolves more quickly than the research cycle,[45] and studies that initially seem to have no influence might have a delayed impact when more favourable conditions arise.[46] As a result, the quest for evidence-based law and policy has turned increasingly to systematic reviews of the results of previous inquiries into a certain policy domain in order to learn more about how legal interventions work instead of just measuring effects, often not knowing what has caused those effects (laws, organisations involved in the implementation and enforcement, social pressure, coincidence, etcetera).[47] Unfortunately, drawing lessons from previous evaluations, either ex post or *ex ante*, through a systematic meta-analysis of a larger sample of studies often suffers from the fact that it is impossible to locate the origin of mistakes or miscalculations in the process of legislative drafting. Hence the lessons to be learned often remain rather abstract ("In what sort of context do certain intervention types have the best chance of succeeding?").

This problem also affects other possible methods that could be used to improve the quality of *ex ante* evaluations, such as learning from previous impact assessments in the same policy domain in other jurisdictions (comparative legal research);[48] trying to generalize the effects of the same type of interventions in different policy areas (horizontal learning); reconstructing the programme theory that lies behind laws or regulations in order to be able to translate underlying assumptions into hypotheses that can be tested by using existing empirical research or factual information (programme evaluation).[49] None of these methods can serve as a real-life litmus test of the prospective value of *ex ante* evaluations. It does not follow that they are worthless, on the contrary. These methods are useful to ensure that the causal assumptions underlying legislative action are

[44] *See also*, in this volume, chapters 2, 3, 4 and 5.

[45] R. Pawson, *Evidence-Based Policy: A Realist Perspective* (SAGE, London 2006), p. 8.

[46] C.H. Weiss, *supra* note 39, p. 472.

[47] R.A.J. van Gestel, Evidence-based Lawmaking and the Quality of Legislation: Regulatory Impact Assessments in the European Union and the Netherlands, in: H. Schäffer and J. Iliopoulos-Strangas (eds.), *State Modernization in Europe* (Ant. N. Sakkoulas-Berliner Wissenschafts-Verlag-Bruylant 2007), pp. 139–165.

[48] See C. Kirkpatrick and D. Parker (eds.), *Regulatory Impact Assessment. Towards Better Regulation?* (Edward Elgar, Cheltenham 2007).

[49] F. Leeuw, 'Trends and Developments in Program Evaluation in General and Criminal Justice Programs in Particular' (2005) 11 *European Journal on Criminal Policy and Research*, pp. 18–35.

as explicit and precisely formulated as possible and based on the most reliable scientific information that is reasonably available.[50]

Nonetheless, monitoring and evaluation of *ex ante* assessments is essential to measure the accuracy of methods for the scrutiny of legislative drafts. This is an important *conditio sine qua non* for creating a 'learning legislator', especially now that many problems with legislation are not only a matter of analytical failures or legal technicalities but also of institutional difficulties.[51] As long as those who are responsible for *ex ante* evaluation or policy-analytical scrutiny of legislative drafts do not match their research findings with the outcomes of ex post evaluations, they will continue to be in the dark about the accuracy of their own criticism. For this reason, our fourth and final conclusion is:

> Feedback research which links the results of ex post evaluation with the outcomes of ex ante evaluation can be a fruitful method, in the preparatory phase, to test the prospective value and consequences of legislative drafts, and therefore deserves more systematic attention.

That it might be worthwhile to monitor the results of *ex ante* evaluations is of course not a new observation. Many guidelines on how to conduct regulatory impact assessments stress the importance of monitoring the outcomes of *ex ante* evaluations after a bill has entered into force. Very little has been written, however, on the methodology that is needed to perform this feedback research and the benefits that it might or might not have. Further research is necessary here but our study has proven that feedback research might serve at least three goals.

First, a regular and more systematic comparison of ex post and *ex ante* evaluations could help to develop more sophisticated methods of regulatory impact assessment and make predictions about future effects and side effects of legislative drafts more accurate. It shows in retrospect which observations that were made somewhere in the assessment process (data collection, interpretations of findings from consultations, alternatives modes of regulation and so forth) were right or wrong, and sometimes even what caused a certain mistake. Secondly, more regular feedback research can stimulate learning from evaluation results in adjacent policy domains (horizontal learning). Currently this does not happen very often, at least not in the Netherlands, because it calls for a more systematic approach towards evaluation research, which is less concentrated on measuring the (direct) effects of legislation and more on the underlying mechanisms and pathways determining the impact of legal rules. Reconstructing the programme theory behind laws through *ex ante* evaluation and afterwards comparing the

---

[50] L. Mader, 'Evaluating the Effects: A Contribution to the Quality of Legislation' (2001) 22:2 *Statute Law Review*, pp. 119–131 (p. 124).

[51] J.B. Wiener, 'Better Regulation in Europe' (2006) 59 *Current Legal Problems*, pp. 447–518 (p. 476).

results with the outcomes of ex post evaluations increases the chance of discovering the rationale behind different types of regulatory interventions such as permit systems, taxation schemes, or subsidies. It also encourages reflecting on why certain identical legislative interventions might work in one policy context and not in another.

Thirdly, feedback research is an excellent means to uncover a biased position of those responsible for drafting a bill or for conducting an *ex ante* evaluation.[52] Questions such as what possible (side) effects have been overlooked or overstated during the pre-parliamentary phase can only be answered with hindsight.

Nevertheless, our pilot study has also shown that an essential condition for proper feedback research is that the questions that are raised ex post and *ex ante* match. That is why we follow Mader where he states that ex post and *ex ante* evaluations should be seen as complementary because the more explicit and differentiated prospective evaluation is, the easier it will become to perform a solid ex post evaluation that will provide relevant and reliable feedback.[53]

[52] The case of the compensation of costs in the administrative objection procedure can serve as an example here. In retrospect both the commission who prepared the working draft as the Council of State itself focused to much on the case law and overlooked signs indicting that juridification of the objection procedure might not be a realistic threat.

[53] L. Mader, *supra* note 50, pp. 124–125.

Chapter 10

Assessing Corporate Tax Reform: Incomplete Information and Conflicting Interests

Henk Vording and Hans Gribnau

I. *Introduction*

Legislation in the area of corporation income taxation is highly complicated and typically an experts' area of law. The interests at stake can be high, with large corporate taxpayers owing amounts of € 100 mn and more per annum. Large taxpayers therefore have a clear incentive to develop political pressure for tax reform, both in terms of tax rate reduction and special tax incentives. At the same time, they also engage in international tax planning – relocation of taxable profits to lower-tax jurisdictions. Governments try to limit this behaviour by anti-avoidance rules, in themselves an important source of complexity of the law. Rigid enforcement of rules, however, creates risks in terms of regulatory competitiveness – a dominant issue in corporation tax policy throughout Europe. In fact, governments tend to pursue asymmetric policies – they try to discourage outward tax planning, but they also try to encourage inward tax planning and flows of real investment. This latter element of their policy is usually called tax competition. But national options to engage in tax competition are limited by an EU legal framework. This framework, consisting of heterogeneous elements, in effect provides a bias in national tax legislation – away from special tax incentives, towards general tax rate reductions.

It is against this background that national corporate tax policies develop their shape. With minor local variations, Member States are now all walking along the same road:

1. lower corporate tax rates
2. broader statutory definition of taxable profits
3. stricter anti-avoidance rules to regulate outward tax planning

4. fine-tuned special tax incentives to promote inward tax planning and foreign direct investment (FDI).

The first two measures can be seen as complements: rate reduction is paid for by using a more inclusive concept of profits for tax purposes. Measures 3 and 4 are both aimed at protecting and increasing the national tax base (the total amount of taxable profits), potentially at the expense of other countries' tax revenues.

This chapter reflects on the most recent pieces of corporate tax legislation in the Netherlands. It introduced as per 2007 a sizeable reduction of the corporate tax rate (to 25.5%) and corresponding measures in the personal income tax, tighter rules for deduction of costs and losses, changes in existing anti-avoidance rules, and two special tax incentives: one for profits from research and development (R&D, effective tax rate 10%), and one for profits from intragroup financial services (effective tax rate 5%).

This package raises two types of questions, which will both be addressed. One is the balancing of interests in the legislative process: is this typically large firms' policy? The second, more basic, question is how the aims of this legislation were chosen, or rather, how the process of choosing these aims was affected by the different interests at stake. Both questions, we will argue, touch upon the same problem: the strategic use of information in the process of choosing the purposes and instruments of corporate tax reform. Both the legislator and large firms have private information about the effects of alternative policy options, which they may use to affect the outcomes of the legislative process. The legislator – or at least the Ministry of Finance – has unique information about the tax base, and is able to monopolise budgetary estimates of alternative policy options.[1] Corporations know better than the legislator how they will actually respond to lower rates, new tax incentives, tax planning opportunities etc. Jointly, they have some information about the overall impact of reform which they may not wish to discuss publicly. As we will argue, the economic literature suggests that measures as those undertaken in 2007 tend to create an inflow of 'paper profits' rather than real foreign direct investment. Lower rates *and* special incentives provide large multinational enterprises (MNE's) with an incentive to report more of their worldwide taxable profits in the Netherlands.

[1] In the Netherlands, as in many European countries, government is the main driver of (tax) legislation. Although the power to enact Acts of Parliament rests with the government and the States General jointly, in practice, most Acts of Parliament are the result of government initiatives. This also holds for tax legislation. Here, the State Secretary of Finance plays a pivotal role. In his capacity of co-legislator, he is responsible for initiating government tax policies. In practice, the State Secretary and his Ministry of Finance dominate the tax legislative process due to their lead on Parliament in terms of knowledge and technical skill.

The rhetoric of reform, however, stressed something different: real investment, additional jobs and economic growth.

This brings us to our final issue: that of an *ex ante* evaluation. No such evaluation was in fact undertaken. Would a full *ex ante* evaluation of aims, options, and effects of corporation tax reform have been a useful tool in the legislative process? Would it have helped to make information about plausible aims and effects more publicly available?

II. *The Dutch Corporation Tax Reform 2007: an Outline*

In the running-up to the reform process, the organisation of large businesses had been pressing for two initiatives. One was a special scheme for intragroup interest flows, to compensate for the loss of a comparable scheme that had been found incompatible with the State Aid rules in 2002. The idea behind it was that group financial activities can only be performed in the Netherlands when a low effective tax rate is offered for such activities. The other request was a special regime for R&D, in addition to existing tax arrangements for the labour input in this sector. The idea here was that Dutch-based multinationals were on the verge of relocating their R&D activities to locations with a more competitive tax environment.

The start of the process leading to the corporate tax reform of 2007 was explicitly innovative, because it tried to mobilise debate before a White Paper was actually conceived. The Dutch Secretary of State for Taxation formulated his goals for corporate tax reform in early 2004 as follows:

- to increase the competitiveness of the Netherlands for international investors through a substantial reduction of the tax rate;
- to make corporate taxpayers pay for the rate reduction by broadening the corporate tax base;
- to make the corporate income tax fully compliant with EU rules.[2]

The Secretary of State added that he wanted no time-consuming overhaul of the tax, but a set of practical proposals to be introduced by 2007.

[2] In the discussion with parliament, additional goals and restrictions were added, including:
- to develop new tax incentives for intragroup financial activities and for R&D;
- SMEs should also enjoy the rate reduction;
- and (more implicitly) sectoral effects on tax burdens should be limited.

Soon afterwards, the Ministry of Finance undertook an open and informal consultation. One element was a website offering a discussion platform; a second element was the organisation of an academic conference on priorities in corporate tax reform. This consultation process was, however, not well-structured – it did not end in something like conclusions nor in a review of ideas provided and arguments exchanged. Looking back at the input in this early stage of the process, one can only say that it was very heterogeneous. One possible explanation was that academics were not sure how fundamental the discussions were meant to be. On the one hand, the idea of a major tax rate reduction to be funded by broadening of the corporate tax base seemed to require a basic rethinking of that tax base. On the other hand, the political intention was clearly to have quick results rather than fundamental discussions.

It seems that what the Ministry was trying to do, was to invite 'good ideas' in a non-lobbyist setting. As such, it achieved a limited success at best. From the start, some experts voiced their suspicion that nothing useful would be done with the outcomes of the process. A more structured form of consultation would perhaps have produced more useful output, or at least would have made it easier for the Ministry to account for the use of this output. On the other hand, if the main aim of this informal consultation was to generate attention for the subject, and a sense of urgency, the success was more obvious.

The actual development of proposals in the form of a White Paper was a much more covert process. It took about six months from late 2004 up to May 2005. The White Paper contained a set of specific proposals:

- a reduction of the corporation income tax rate to 25.5%
- comparable tax rate reductions for SMEs in the personal income tax
- special tax regimes for intragroup interest flows and for R&D costs
- a streamlining of anti-avoidance rules
- tighter depreciation rules for buildings used in business
- reduced deductibility of losses.

In the optional sphere, two special tax incentives were suggested for R&D activities and for intragroup international treasury functions, respectively.

The White Paper also provided and idea of 'distributional effects' in terms of economic sectors and size of business. As most of the tax rate reductions were to be funded by tax base increases, the business sector as a whole enjoyed only a slight reduction of tax burden. In such a context where business pays for its own tax rate reduction, every gain for one taxpayer will be mirrored by a loss for another taxpayer.

The Netherlands Bureau for Economic Policy Analysis (NBEPA, a state advisory body) reported on the expected economic consequences of the government's corporate tax proposals in November 2004 – at the end of the consultation stage.[3] At the time, the government plans were still unspecific; a wide array of potential funding measures had been mentioned. Therefore, the NBEPA estimated the economic effects of (1) a 5% point corporate tax reduction and a comparable tax measure for unincorporated small businesses, combined with (2) a range of funding measures which in effect meant that less than half of the costs was borne by business. The distributional effect was that the tax burden on business would be reduced by an amount of 0.3% GDP, while the tax burden on family households would be increased by 0.2% GDP. On this basis, the NBEPA predicted +0.6% growth in GDP and employment. This considerable effect was explained by the reduction of the effective tax burden on business – implying that a revenue-neutral approach would not have significant economic effects.

In its report of 10 May 2006 the State Council addressed the government's proposal as a (largely) revenue neutral tax rate reduction. Its main criticism concerned the proposed tax base broadening to fund the tax rate reductions. The Council argued that a tax base broadening of this size should have been based on a systematic approach, and that the proposal should have made the tradeoffs between alternatives transparent. The Council saw no evidence that the measures actually proposed to broaden the tax base were the least burdensome among available options. The Council advised the government to reconsider its proposal from this perspective.

It saw two other problems with the strong emphasis on tax rate reduction. First, the original aim of making the corporation income tax more 'EU proof' had in fact been overshadowed, leading only to some minor proposed adjustments. Secondly, the government had no clear idea how its tax rate reduction would affect the policy choices of other countries. The Council advised the government to discuss these issues in more depth in its explanatory memorandum.

On 24 May 2006, the government published its draft law and explanatory memorandum on corporate tax reform. The draft followed the broad lines set out in the White Paper. The proposed broadening of the tax base funded three quarters of the rate reductions: revenue neutrality had been achieved to a large extent. Responses from business organisations were predictably lukewarm; they had hoped for a sizeable tax burden reduction. The organisation of large businesses published its own list of preferred tax measures, with practically no funding out of tax base broadening.[4] The package would cost close to 1% of GDP.

---

3 CPB, Economische effecten Vpb-pakket, 30 November 2004.

4 J.A.M. Klaver, 'Verbetering fiscale concurrentiepositie Nederland' (2004) 1379 *Weekblad Fiscaal Recht*, pp. 1379 et seq.

This position perhaps reflected the organisation's problem in finding a common stance acceptable to a variety of sectoral interests.

III. *Corporate Income Taxation: the Actors and their Interests*

One of the aims of impact assessment is to show how consultations, costs and benefits, and trade-offs between policy choices have been taken into account by the legislator. Proper consultation of interested parties (stakeholders) results in information on the expected effects and side-effects of potential new legislation and of the possible effects and side-effects of alternatives, including the alternative of not regulating at all. Parties consulted in the impact assessment process will try to bend the policy aims to their objectives and interests. After all, policy does not start with an aim and proceed to action: people seek to make sense of the action, and frame and refine statements of aims.[5]

Knowledge provides an essential basis for policy-making; data influence the whole policy-making and regulatory process. Knowledge depends on information – readily available, or specifically "tailored to the micro-impacts of the proposal in terms of benefits, costs or risks."[6] Information should meet quality standards such as transparency, objectivity, utility and integrity (security). Objectivity means that the information is accurate, reliable and unbiased; utility focuses on the usefulness to the intended users. Other quality standards are reproducibility, and acceptance by independent experts. Information is often costly. Thus, information can be considered a scarce and usually unevenly distributed commodity. At the same time, equal levels of information among all actors is a sine qua non condition for effective policies.[7] Interested parties will behave strategically with regard to the information on the potential effects of new policies, especially the disclosure of information at their disposal and not known by others.[8] The control of information may be an important means to achieve one's goals. Therefore, it is important that information meeting the general quality standards is produced by independent research institutes or statistical services who make their findings available to the public at large. The result is a kind of equality of arms among stakeholders.

---

[5] H.K. Colebatch, *Policy* (2nd edition, Open University Press, Maidenhead 2005), p. 65.

[6] S.H. Jacobs, 'Current Trends in the Process and Methods of Regulatory Impact Assessment: Mainstreaming RIA into Policy Processes' in C. Kirkpatrick (ed.), *Regulatory Impact Assessment: Towards Better Regulation?* (Edward Elgar Publishers, Cheltenham 2007), p. 26.

[7] P. Knoepfel et al., *Public Policy Analysis* (Policy Press, Bristol 2007), pp. 71–73.

[8] The withholding of information may not only be motivated by strategic intentions, but also by financial ones ('our organisation paid for the production of the data'); Knoepfel, *supra* note 7, p. 72.

Lawmakers may use impact assessments to remedy their information deficiencies. Bohne divides information deficiencies into asymmetries and deficits. He refines this analytical distinction by using the principal-agent theory which distinguishes four types of information asymmetries: relevant information available to interested parties but 'hidden' from the legislator may regard characteristics, action, knowledge and intentions.[9]

Strategic informational behaviour is determined by the actors' aims and interests. We start, therefore, with a discussion of different actors (stakeholders) and their interests involved. Thus, in this section, we discuss the interests of five types of players in the field of corporate income taxation and legislation:

- the state (government)
- small and medium sized business
- large (multinational) corporations
- tax advisers
- European institutions.

A. *The State*

The evident interest of the state in the field of tax law is to generate revenue. The optimal tax rate is, however, not necessarily the one that maximises tax revenues. The tax system is also being used for providing implicit subsidies, e.g., to promote specific types of investment and employment. These tax incentives may be hidden in complicated pieces of regulation. For any given level of tax revenue, tax incentives imply higher tax rates, because tax incentives make the tax base smaller. Corporation tax policy therefore requires a balancing of interests: state revenues, entrepreneurial incentives, employment, investment climate etc.

The optimal tax rate is reduced by international mobility of corporate profits. This has two separate reasons. On the one hand, a low tax rate attracts 'paper profits' from countries with higher tax rates.[10] This is because (multinational) firms have some freedom to reallocate their revenues and costs between locations (text box 1). On the other hand, a low tax rate also attracts real investments. This means that (multinational) firms do not just reallocate their profits, but their real business activities in response to differences in national tax rates. Conversely, if a state's corporate tax rate exceeds the rates in alternative tax jurisdictions, it has to combat reallocation of 'paper profits' to those jurisdictions by anti-avoidance

[9] Chapter 4 of this volume.

[10] E.J. Bartelsman and R.M.W.J. Beetsma, 'Why Pay More? Corporate Tax Avoidance Through Transfer Pricing in OECD Countries' (2003) 87:9–10 *Journal of Public Economics*, pp. 2225–2252.

rules, while its attractiveness for real investments can be bolstered by providing good public services to businesses.

Corporation tax policy typically requires different types of information. The kind of information that allows the legislator to set his priorities include information on neighbouring states' priorities, on the performance of domestic capital and labour markets, on trends in international investment flows etc. Much of this information can be collected and processed by independent research institutes or statistical services. But the information required to make 'good' tax policy also includes knowledge on taxpayer responses to taxation. This is the kind of information that is partially being produced by economic research, but also provided on a more anecdotal basis by large taxpayers themselves. Choices concerning alternative tax instruments require both technical skills and budgetary information. In information on the budgetary aspects of tax rules, the Ministry of Finance has a virtual monopoly. However, in matters of legal technique, it may have difficulty in keeping up with highly specialised tax advisers.

Part of the government's lack of information will have to do with deficits, e.g. economic research cannot answer all relevant questions on international investors' behaviour. But there may also be asymmetries. E.g., the tax planning options open to large corporate taxpayers may be fairly clear to those taxpayers but more obscure to the legislator. And on the other hand, taxpayers have no independent (i.e., non-governmental) information on the budgetary costs and revenues of alternative policy options.

Text box 1. The concept of 'paper profits'

The concept of 'paper profits' stems from the economic literature. It refers to the disentanglement of (a) business profits and (b) the tax jurisdiction where these profits have been 'earned'. A simple example is a Dutch firm, conducting its business mainly on the continent, which has a subsidiary in Ireland. This Irish subsidiary is the firm's financial centre. It provides loans to the Dutch firm. As a result, the Dutch firm will have to pay interest to its Irish subsidiary. This interest is deductible in the Netherlands and taxable in Ireland. As the Dutch tax rate is considerably higher than the Irish, there is a net (and risk-free) gain to the firm. What actually happened here is that profits earned in the Netherlands have been relabelled as 'interest payments' and turn up as profits again in Ireland. This explains the term 'paper profits', and the process of relocating 'paper profits' is called 'profit shifting'. An economist would argue that, from the perspective of the firm's shareholders, the firm owes the loan and the interest to itself – in reality, no profits have been earned in Ireland. A tax lawyer's analysis would be more subtle. He would accept the economic reality of intragroup financial activities, even if located in low-tax jurisdictions. His idea of 'paper profits' would be limited to typical 'avoidance' cases where nothing really happens. E.g., a Dutch firm distributes profits to its Irish holding company, but instead of actually paying the money, it acknowledges a debt. The combination of these legal acts has no apparent economic substance, and anti-avoidance rules may deny deduction of interest in such (and comparable) cases.

Recent research on the financial structure of large German firms provides evidence that profitable firms use intracompany loans to siphon profits to lower-tax jurisdictions. However, there was also clear evidence that intracompany loans are used as an alternative to equity investments in case of low or negative profitability of a German affiliate. This makes economic sense, as debts are easier to recover in case of bankruptcy than equity capital. The overall implication is that 'intracompany borrowing' *per se* does not equate 'tax avoidance'. F. Ramb and A.J. Weichenrieder, Taxes and the Financial Structure of German Inward FDI (2005) 141:4 *Review of World Economics* pp. 670–692.

Additional ways to relocate profits include the allocation of R&D and headquarters costs. R&D costs in particular seem to account for a sizeable part of total profit shifting; this indicates that much of the 'paper profits' problem is connected to specific industries such as pharmaceuticals. H. Grubert, Intangible Income, Intercompany Transactions, Income Shifting, and the Choice of Location (2003) 56:1 *National Tax Journal* pp. 221–242.

The overall effect of tax rates on paper profit flows is sizeable. Huizinga and Laeven estimate a semi-elasticity of 1.31 for European countries on average. This means that a reduction of the tax rate by 1% point increases the tax base by 1.31%. Assume that the corporate tax rate is 25%, then a reduction to 24% takes 4% of the tax revenue, but inward profit shifting will generate 1.31% additional revenue. On balance, the cost of the tax reduction is reduced by one third because of the mobility of the tax base. Smaller countries, such as the Netherlands, tend to have much higher semi-elasticities, making tax rate reductions even more profitable. H. Huizinga and L. Laeven, International profit shifting within multinationals: A multi-country perspective, *Journal of Public Economics* (2008) 92:5–6, pp. 1164–1182.

B. *Small- and Medium Sized Enterprises*

For SMEs, the main interest in corporate tax legislation is its effect on their tax burdens, and therefore, their net profits. This effect operates through two channels.

Corporation tax rates matter for SMEs' choices to adopt legal personality (i.e. incorporation). SMEs can 'opt in' and 'opt out' of the corporation income tax by way of their incorporation decisions.[11] Unincorporated business is taxable under the personal income tax; corporations are taxable under the corporation income tax, while dividends may be taxable in the hands of their shareholders (either as personal or corporate income). While both taxes have basically the same concept of taxable income, they differ in rate structure and special incentives.

[11] J.K. Mackie-Mason and R.H. Gordon, 'How Much Do Taxes Discourage Incorporation?' (1997) 52:2 *The Journal of Finance*, pp. 477–505; A. Goolsbee, 'The Impact of the Corporate Income Tax: Evidence from State Organizational Form Data' (2004) 88:11 *Journal of Public Economics*, pp. 2283–2299; R.A. de Mooij and G. Nicodème, 'Corporate Tax Policy and Incorporation in the EU' (2008) 15:4 *International Tax and Public Finance*, pp. 478–498.

The choice whether or not to incorporate may have important consequences in terms of tax burdens and, therefore, net profits.[12]

Corporate tax legislation may affect SME interests in a more indirect way as well. Whenever a specific corporate tax policy entails changes in the definition of taxable profits, unincorporated businesses are usually affected. This is because the corporation income tax has no separate concept of taxable profits; it refers to the personal income tax (with some modifications, esp. for large international corporations).

C. *Large Corporations*

For large corporations, corporate tax legislation also affects their tax burdens and net profits. However, disincorporation is not usually an option open to large (multinational) firms. Therefore, the comparative treatment of profits under personal and corporate income tax is not a relevant consideration to these firms.

What does matter are the cross border options, both in terms of reallocating profits to foreign branches and subsidiaries ('paper profits') and in terms of reallocating real business activities. To put it differently, large corporations have an opportunity to 'vote with their feet' against unfavourable tax policies, and perhaps more importantly, they can make credible threats to this effect. They may, therefore, strategically disclose some possible future action, but they will mostly not fully do so. The same goes for information with regard to their relevant characteristics, available knowledge and intentions.

Furthermore, large corporations make use of highly specialised international tax advisers, which may result in information asymmetry with regard to recent tax law changes in other countries.

D. *Tax Advisers*

The role of tax advisers in the field of tax legislation is considerable, because of the highly technical nature of the corporation income tax. Their impact operates in several ways. One is the development of new tax planning techniques[13], in response to regulatory developments both domestic and abroad. The national legislator will often respond with new anti-avoidance rules which may themselves create new tax planning opportunities. Tax advisers also have an (indirect) influence on the legislative process in their role of informal 'gatekeepers' – whatever

---

[12] Other factors affecting the choice whether or not to incorporate are social insurance legislation, personal liability and the statutory obligation to publish an annual statement of accounts for corporations.

[13] Tax planning is just one part of the tax adviser's work. Due to the extreme complexity of the corporation income tax, taxpayers simply cannot fulfil their statutory obligations without the aid of a specialised tax adviser.

(other) stakeholders want to achieve through corporate tax legislation needs to be phrased in the technical language of the law and to fit into the basic 'ideas' behind the law. Furthermore, advisers in the field of international tax are often better informed on recent tax changes in other countries than national governments. This results in information asymmetry between their clients, usually MNE's, and the tax legislator (government).

E. *The Average Taxpayer*

Taxpayers in general are affected by corporation tax measures in several ways. One is that any net tax reduction in the corporate sphere must be paid for by others in some way. The criterion of revenue neutrality – in the corporate sphere – therefore represents the interest of the general taxpayer. The idea that some tax reform should be revenue neutral reflects the concept of internalisation of costs: the group of taxpayers that gains from tax reform should also bear the costs of that reform instead of making others pay for it. On the other hand, like other changes in the tax regime, a reduction of corporate tax rates and burdens may have a broader economic impact. Tax reductions may be of benefit to more (and even, to other) people than the ones who get the lower tax bill. This is where economic analysis comes in.

The results of economic analysis belong to the category of generally available information, which does not (directly) depend on disclosure by interested parties. But the use of information may require skilled interpretation. The economic analysis of changes in tax legislation tends to be confusing to non-economists. The case of corporation income taxation is no exception. To mention the most important issues:

- *the incidence of the tax.* An important question in tax policy debate is 'who really pays the tax'. This is not necessarily the person who makes the payment. In the case of corporate taxation, the taxpayer is in fact a legal person, unable to suffer a loss in welfare. The traditional assumption is that the tax is borne by the shareholders. This assumption has long been challenged. There is now a basic agreement among economists that a tax on mobile capital is in fact borne by immobile labour.[14] That is to say, an increase of the corporation income tax will deter foreign investment, will reduce local demand for labour, and will ultimately result in lower wages. As a consequence, changes in the

[14] The assumption that capital is perfectly mobile is not warranted, however. R.H. Gordon and A.L. Bovenberg, 'Why is Capital so Immobile Internationally? Possible Explanations and Implications for Capital Income Taxation' (1996) 86:5 *American Economic Review*, pp. 1057–1075. Also A.J. Auerbach, 'The Future of Capital Income Taxation' (2006) 27:4 *Fiscal Studies*, pp. 399–420.

corporate tax burden may look as something affecting investors only but have in fact more subtle effects.

- *the benefit character of the tax insofar as capital is immobile.* There are different reasons why real business investments are not perfectly mobile, or indeed rather immobile. One is the existence of agglomeration effects and location-specific rents. Specific industries may cluster near a specific labour market (Silicon Valley), large consumer market (Germany), or natural resources (oil).[15] Corporation income tax then operates as a kind of 'entrance fee', reflecting the benefits connected to those specific locations. More generally, governments can use their corporate tax rate to find a balance with locally provided benefits.[16]
- *the impact of the tax on location choices for real investments and for corporate financial activities.*[17] There is ample economic evidence that changes in corporate taxation have a substantial impact on MNEs' financial decisions: how to organise their subsidiaries, where to locate their financial and holding centres, how and when to distribute income between group affiliates.[18] Much of the rhetoric of corporate tax reform is, however, about attracting real investments in plants and employment. Economic research shows that corporation tax has an effect there, as well. This effect is, however, probably smaller in size than the 'paper profits' effect.[19] If the rate reduction is funded by broadening the legal concept of taxable profits, the tax planning effect may indeed be much

---

[15] For a broader discussion L. Weiss, *The Myth of the Powerless State* (Cornell University Press, Ithaca 1998), pp. 186–187.

[16] T.J. Goodspeed, 'Tax Competition, Benefit Taxes, and Fiscal Federalism' (1998) 51:3 *National Tax Journal*, pp. 579–586.

[17] J.R. Hines, 'Lessons from Behavioral Responses to International Taxation' (1999) 52:2 *National Tax Journal*, pp. 305–322; R.A. de Mooij and S. Ederveen, *Taxation and Foreign Direct Investment* (CPB Memorandum, 27 September 2001); M.P. Devereux, *The Impact of Taxation on the Location of Capital, Firms and Profit: A Survey of Empirical Evidence*, mimeo (University of Warwick, April 2006).

[18] R. Altshuler and H. Grubert, 'Taxes, Repatriation Strategies and Multinational Financial Policy' (2003) 87:1 *Journal of Public Economics*, pp. 73–107.

[19] R.A. de Mooij and S. Ederveen, 'Taxation and Foreign Direct Investment: A Synthesis of Empirical Research' (2003) 10:6 *International Tax and Public Finance*, pp. 673–693 summarise the existing economic literature on the impact of corporate tax rates on foreign direct investment (FDI). A 1% point decrease in a country's effective tax rate increases the stock of FDI by 3.3%. This does not mean that tax revenue will increase by a comparable figure. First, the total stock of investment in a country (and the corporate tax base) is typically dominated by domestic investment. Secondly, much of FDI inflow is typically not "greenfields investment" but mergers & acquisitions. Such a change in ownership of taxpaying corporations will not affect national tax revenues. The positive revenue impact of a 1% point decrease in tax rate through increased FDI will typically be in the range of 0–1%, i.e. smaller than the effect of profit shifting reported by Huizinga and Laeven, supra textbox 1.

larger than the effect on real investments (see text box 3). MNE financial activities are, by their nature, more mobile than real investments. The economic effects of corporate tax rate reductions in Europe should therefore be distinguished between a short-term, large but temporary impact on flows of 'paper profits' and long-term, probably smaller and less volatile effects on the location of real investments.

- *the impact of tax rates on SMEs.* While it is intuitively plausible that lower tax rates (or burdens) encourage entrepreneurial activity, the outcomes of economic research are mixed. Income taxes affect entrepreneurial decisions in several ways, not just as a cost, but also as a form of risk-sharing – because the money value of loss deduction increases with the tax rate.[20] Perhaps the conclusion should be that the effect of tax policy on entrepreneurial activity is modest.[21]

These (and other) economic intricacies of corporate tax reforms cannot easily be communicated to the general public discussion. This probably means that the average voter considers corporate tax reductions as something that has no clear connection to his own interests. Discussions on corporate tax legislation and policy are typically dominated by 'insiders'.[22]

F. *The EU Institutions*

The main notion that the EU institutions, esp. the European Commission (EC) and the European Court of Justice (ECJ), bring into the national legislative process is 'non-discrimination'. Both the EC (in the State Aid framework) and the ECJ (in its application of the Treaty Freedoms on national tax rules) may use information on national policy intentions as evidence in their proceedings. On the policy level, the EC presses for corporate tax co-ordination between the Member States to reduce tax barriers.[23] The EC has frequently warned the Member States that increasing corporate tax competition may lead to a 'tax race

---

20 H.J. Schuetze and D. Bruce, 'Tax Policy and Entrepreneurship' (2004) 11:2 *Swedish Economic Policy Review*, pp. 223–265.

21 D. Bruce and M. Mohsin, 'Tax Policy and Entrepreneurship: New Time Series Evidence' (2006) 26:5 *Small Business Economics*, pp. 409–425.

22 J. Snape, 'Corporation Tax Reform – Politics and Public Law' (2007) 103:4 *British Tax Review*, p. 382.

23 European Commission (2001), Company taxation in the internal market, COM(2001)582 and annexes. The size of these tax barriers has been thoroughly documented in Commission Staff Working Paper, *Company Taxation in the Internal Market*, Brussels, 23.10.2001, SEC(2001) 1681.

to the bottom',[24] potentially resulting in a shift of the tax burden to workers and consumers. It should be noted that there is neither political nor academic consensus on the definition of harmful tax competition and that even "empirical evidence is somewhat disputed by both economists and political scientists."[25]

Even if the evidence for such a race to the bottom is unclear, the concept suggests a collective decision-making problem. For a single Member State it may be sound policy to reduce its tax rate, as much of the cost is probably covered by inflowing 'paper profits'and FDI. But what if neighbouring countries follow (text box 2)?

Text box 2. Pro's and con's of tax co-ordination
The underlying theme in national corporate tax policy is tax competition. Two views can be distinguished:

1. Tax competition is the outcome of a prisoner's dilemma. While it is optimal for every Member State *not* to compete with tax rates and special incentives, there is no credible way that all states can commit themselves to a co-operative policy. In this analysis, it is up to the European institutions to provide mechanisms for co-ordination of national policies. And indeed, the EC is now working with a number of Member States on a future Common Corporate Tax Base, though the EC has never ventured to propose minimum corporate tax rates.
2. Tax competition is a form of beneficial regulatory competition. National corporate tax policies have thus far made for more efficient tax rules. Lower tax rates are less distorting to the economy; broadening of tax bases means that politicians have less opportunities to meddle with private investors' decisions. To the extent that corporate tax burdens are effectively being reduced, economic effects will be positive. More investment means more employment and economic growth; the EU as a whole becomes more competitive.

Both views are not fully incompatible, to the extent that the struggle against 'harmful tax competition' is effectively limited to profit shifting. Profit shifting is a problem also under the second view, because it undermines states' ability to make investors pay a reasonable price for locally provided benefits.

---

[24] Fiscal degradation is "the loss of tax revenue borne by countries engaged in the lowering of taxes on income derived from inbound investment or, in other words, the excessive erosion of their taxable bases on such income" C. Pinto, *Tax Competition and EU Law* (Kluwer Law International, The Hague/London/New York 2003), p. 11; R.S. Avi-Yonah, 'Globalization, Tax Competition, and the Fiscal Crisis of the Welfare State' (2000) 113:7 *Harvard Law Review*, pp. 1573–1676 refers to empirical studies which suggest that countries seek to compensate the decline in (corporation) income tax revenues by increasing "relatively regressive taxes, such as consumption and pay roll taxes." A.J. Menéndez, 'The Purse of the Polity' in E.O. Eriksen (ed.), *Making the European Polity: Reflexive Integration in the EU* (Routledge, London 2005), p. 208 points to "the connection between corporate taxation and distributive justice (tax dumping leads to social dumping)."

[25] C.M. Radaelli, 'The Code of Conduct against Harmful Tax Competition: Open Method of Coordination in Disguise?' (2003) 81:3 *Public Administration*, pp. 513–531, at p. 522.

According to settled case law, although direct taxation, such as corporate taxation, falls within their competence, Member States must nonetheless exercise that competence consistently with Community law.[26] Thus, the Member States may not enact or maintain direct tax laws or administrative practices which discriminate against or restrict enterprises, employees or capital of other Member States. The case law of the ECJ has consequently struck down many national tax regulations on the ground of violation of the free movement rules.[27]

The EU competition rules, in particular, in the field of taxation, the ban on State aid to enterprises (Arts. 87–89) are another constraint on domestic corporate tax policy. According to the Court, the effects rather than the objectives of a state measure count.[28] Tax measures, therefore, in principle constitute State aid if their effects favour certain enterprises or productions.[29] Note that, like taxation, State aid is at the heart of state sovereignty, and therefore an extremely politicised EU policy area.[30] The case law of the ECJ constitutes essential information readily available to all. However, because the ECJ like all courts proceeds case by case, it is often hard to predict its course. Consequently, future rulings of the ECJ on national tax measures constitute an information deficit shared by all.

One part of the proposed Dutch scheme for intragroup financial activities has led to an in-depth State aid investigation by the Commission. The opening of this investigation also enables interested third parties to submit their comments on the proposed measures.[31] The proposed R&D facility was approved.

Tax measures may also constitute harmful tax competition. In this respect the Code of Conduct for Business Taxation, a soft law instrument, is also part of the framework. Its adoption by the ECOFIN Council in 1997[32] marked an

[26] *See* already ECJ 14 February 1995, Case C–279/93 *Schumacker*, para 21.

[27] The ECJ has adopted a "much more robust concept of discrimination than that found in international tax and trade law"; M. Graetz and A.C. Warren, 'Income Tax Discrimination and the Political and Economic Integration of Europe' in R.S. Avi-Jonah *et al.* (eds.), *Comparative Fiscal Federalism: Comparing the European Court of Justice and the US Supreme Court's Tax Jurisprudence* (Kluwer Law International, Alphen aan den Rijn 2007), pp. 279 and 300. *See also* F. Vanistendael (ed.), *EU Freedoms and Taxation* (IBFD, Amsterdam 2006).

[28] ECJ 2 July 1974, Case 173/73, *Italy v Commission.*

[29] An example is the recent approval by the Commission of a French tax credit aimed at encouraging video game creation. This measure qualified for the exemption provided by the EC Treaty for state aid to promote culture; IP/07/1908, 12.12.2007.

[30] The State aid policy area "pits the Commission directly against the member states, with governmental authorities rather than firms, targets of Commission regulation"; M. Cini, 'The Soft Law Approach: Commission Rule-Making in the EU's State Aid Regime' (2001) 8:2 *Journal of European Public Policy*, pp. 192–207, at p. 198.

[31] IP/07/154, 07.02.2007; another part of the group interest box scheme was approved by the Commission.

[32] This package (OJ No. C 2, 6.1.1998), was based on a proposal put forward by the Commission: *see* Paper *Towards Tax Co-ordination in the European Union – A Package to Tackle Harmful Tax*

important step towards further tax coordination. "By proceeding softly where hard approaches have failed, the Code has garnered agreement in principle to coordination, broadly phrased."[33] The non-binding nature of the Code may be considered a strength rather than a weakness. The managing of the Code by high-level tax-policy makers (the Primarolo group) can be seen as a means to overcome the information deficit with regard to harmful tax competition. The Primarolo group had to cope with information asymmetries among the Member States' governments. They were not eager to disclose much information on their tax measures, necessary for their assessment, and on their intended behaviour with regard to future corporate tax law. By engaging in an interpretative community the ground for a of convergence in 'talk' was prepared.[34] The subsequent discursive practice allowed for the shaping and reshaping of attitudes, the establishment of a common vocabulary, and the coordination of action. Member States have taken the Code seriously and amended most of their tax measures to comply with it.[35] The Code of Conduct is generally regarded to be a fairly effective political instrument.[36]

For corporation tax measures such as the Dutch corporation tax reform, the most important part of the Code is Member States' commitment to refrain from introducing new potentially harmful tax measures. EU Member States, therefore, have to test their intended tax measures *ex ante* against the Primarolo-criteria. They also have to present their intended potentially harmful tax measures to the Primarolo-group for assessment. The Dutch government did this with the group interest box scheme. According to a communication of the Dutch State Secretary of Finance to the Dutch parliament, the Primarolo group will decide upon investigating the group interest box scheme after the State aid procedure will be finished.[37]

Competition, COM(97) 495, 1.10.1997, and *A Package to Tackle Harmful Tax Competition in the European Union*, COM(97) 564 final, 5.11.1997.

33 W.W. Bratton and J.A. McCahery, 'Tax Coordination and Tax Competition in the European Union: Evaluating the Code of Conduct on Business Taxation' (2001) 38:3 *Common Market Law Review*, pp. 677–718 at p. 685.

34 Radaelli, *supra* note 25; H. Gribnau, 'Soft Law and Taxation: EU and International Aspects' (2008) II:2 *Legisprudence*, pp. 67–117.

35 Pinto, *supra* note 24, pp. 205–206. B.J. Kiekebeld, *Harmful Tax Competition in the European Union: Code of Conduct, Countermeasures and EU Law* (Kluwer, Deventer 2004), at p. 51.

36 *See* Menéndez, *supra* note 24, p. 201: The Code of Conduct (also) had a limited but not irrelevant impact on the definition of national corporate income tax bases.

37 Letter State Secretary of Finance, 1.10.2007, no AFP2007–703, *Vakstudie-Nieuws* 2007/48.9.

G. *Summing up: Some Conflicts and Congruencies in Interests*

In this section, we analyse some structural features of the (perhaps of any) debate on corporation tax reform: where do actors' interests usually conflict, where do they meet?

There are several conflicts of interest to be noted. One is basic to the field of taxation: while the state has an interest in raising revenue, taxpayers have an interest in minimising their own contributions. The nature of tax law is to enforce duties against private interests. The idea that taxpayers also have an interest in the public services funded by taxation may be thought of as a relevant moral consideration, but does not preclude that 'free riding' pays to the individual taxpayer.

Taxpayers' strategies at minimising tax burdens can use two channels. One is their private tax planning strategies. A firm which is successful in its tax planning choices may gain a competitive advantage in the market. The second channel is the one relevant here: organised taxpayers can try to change the tax code to their advantage.

Such attempts will obviously conflict with the state's interest in raising tax revenue. The key concept here is 'revenue neutrality' of tax reform. A tax reform can be said to be 'revenue neutral' when the overall tax burden on the group of taxpayers affected by the reform does not change. This will, for example, be the case whenever a tax rate reduction is paid for by a reduction of tax incentives for the same group of taxpayers. A tax reform is non-neutral if it changes the overall tax burden on the relevant group. If the tax burden is reduced (as stakeholders will obviously try to achieve) the burden of the tax is shifted to other social groups.

Text box 3. Tax rate, tax burden and revenue neutrality

Assume that the corporate tax base is p, then the average corporate tax burden is pt, when t is the statutory tax rate. If a reduction of the tax rate t is funded by increasing the statutory tax base p, the average tax burden will not be affected. That is to say, despite the tax rate reduction, the average firm will not pay less tax, because its tax base has increased. In fact, corporate tax rate reductions throughout the EU have frequently been funded out of tax base broadening (e.g. reduction of investment incentives and depreciation allowances). See A. Haufler, Prospects for Co-ordination of Corporate Taxation and the Taxation of Interest Income in the EU (1999) 20:2 *Fiscal Studies*, pp. 133-153; Griffith, R. and A. Klemm (2004), What has been the tax competition experience for the last 20 years?, *IFS Working Paper* 04/05. In these cases, the combined effect of corporate tax measures is said to be revenue neutral.

In principle, such a revenue neutral change will have limited economic impact. Its most important effect will be to enhance inward tax planning. This is because a firm's tax planning ('paper profits') decision to reallocate one additional Euro of profits from e.g., Germany to the Netherlands typically depends on differences in statutory tax rates. The effect of rate reduction, if revenue neutral, on real investment decisions is much more modest. This is because, on average, the effective tax rate is not affected – corporate taxpayers still pay the same amount of tax on their overall profits. However the operation may not be neutral to individual corporations. Effects may depend on sector and size of firms. There is also a systematic effect related to profitability. Highly profitable firms will suffer comparatively little by the loss of deductions and incentives (which usually depend on the size of the investment, not on its profitability), and gain a lot by the rate reduction. Generally speaking, corporate tax rate reductions funded by base broadening favour successful investments. The overall economic impact is, however, more difficult to judge. Rate reductions also imply that risk taking is discouraged, as the value of loss deductions decreases. This may have a negative impact esp. on small entrepreneurship; Schuetze, H.J., and D. Bruce (2004) 11:2, Tax Policy and Entrepreneurship, *Swedish Economic Policy Review*, pp. 223–265.

It is important to see, however, that the concept of revenue neutrality reflects the perspective of the state (and behind him, one could say, the general taxpayer). In the relevant group of taxpayers, important shifts in the tax burden may occur, even when they add up to zero. In corporation tax legislation, one may think of two types of divide within the total group of taxpayers: the diverging interests of SMEs and large multinational firms, and the role of sectoral interests (e.g., services, pharmaceuticals, infrastructure industry). Corporate taxpayers will therefore have to divert their efforts in two directions: trying to reduce their overall tax burden, and trying to shift the tax burden to other groups of corporate taxpayers.

There are also congruencies of interest between actors. To mention a few examples:

- *corporate tax rate reduction.* To the state, reducing the corporate tax rate is a way to signal a 'good investment climate' to international investors. To large firms already present in the Netherlands, a lower tax rate increases their net (shareholder) value. This may strengthen their position on the international M&A market. Another effect of lower corporate tax rates concerns tax planning. Outward tax planning is discouraged (because foreign jurisdictions become comparatively less attractive); inward tax planning is encouraged (for the same reason). In effect, a lower tax means that more firms will locate their group financial and holding services in the Netherlands. This may be of advantage to domestic multinationals; it will also allow the state to recapture part of the costs of tax rate reduction.
- *special tax incentives.* To the state, providing special tax incentives, e.g., to group financial and holding activities, is a much cheaper form of tax compe-

tition than general reduction of tax rates.[38] In fact, such special schemes can even generate net tax revenues because of inflowing 'paper profits'. To large firms, special incentives are attractive because they can be fine-tuned to their needs during the legislative process. The state and large firms have a common interest: how to introduce new special incentives without openly confronting the EU regulatory environment?

IV. *Conclusion: the Process in Retrospect*

A. *Problems: Balancing of Interests and Access to Information*

Looking back on the Dutch corporate tax reform process of 2004–2007, we see two separate problems that could have been addressed in a full-scale *ex ante* evaluation of priorities and instruments.

1. The different stakeholders did not have equal effective access to the process of choosing purposes and instruments of legislative reform; more specifically, the process seems to be biased towards the interests of a relatively small group of large firms. It is intuitively plausible that large corporate taxpayers have a stronger lobbying position than SMEs. Their group is smaller and easier to organise. In addition, they have an 'exit threat' which is not credibly available to SMEs. More in particular, a handful of the largest Netherlands-based multinational firms is able to play on public sentiments if needed. But for precisely this reason, it is also plausible that many features of the corporate tax code, and many characteristics of its administration, have been modelled with an eye on those biggest firms' interests (such as explicit or implicit acceptance of a certain level of outward tax planning). And indeed, it seems that the largest corporations pay relatively little corporate tax in the Netherlands. As a result, this select group of Dutch multinationals may not have much to gain by taking a publicly visible stand on issues of corporate tax legislation. Arguably, their position in the legislative process was a bit too conspicous – recently, the low and declining corporate tax burden of MNEs in the Netherlands has developed into an issue of public debate and concern.

[38] This is because special incentives can be focused on the most mobile types of investment. A. Haufler and S. Stöwhase, *Taxes as a Determinant for Foreign Direct Investment in Europe*, CESifo DICE Report 2/2003, pp. 45–51.

2. Information on the costs and benefits of alternative options was used strategically by stakeholders during the process. As revenue neutral tax reforms will always have an impact on the distribution of tax burdens and on the size/direction of incentives, this impact matters to the design of the reform. Actors use their private information on the possible effects of alternative options strategically, to promote their most favoured options and to block alternatives. Detailed revenue information on corporate taxation is collected and processed at the Ministry of Finance, but not made available to the public. This offers the state, in its role as draft legislator, an opportunity to use revenue estimates strategically – e.g., pushing its preferred alternatives by over- or underestimating the revenue impact. At the same time, business representatives may be better informed on business responses to alternative tax rules (including international tax planning opportunities) than the state. This offers them some scope to over- or underestimate economic effects of alternative options. In the process, both the Ministry of Finance and business representatives have been able to make claims about costs and benefits, about effectiveness and side-effects, without providing sufficient empirical evidence.

A problem which is not explored here, is the uncertainty that all national actors face with respect to the policy responses of other states. One aspect of this uncertainty is whether a Dutch tax rate cut (and special tax incentives) will induce countries like Belgium or Germany to follow. In that case, any Dutch gains may be very temporary in nature. Another aspect is the European response, which may be nurtured by national concerns in other Member States. In both cases, perceptions matter: if a few large taxpayers visibly respond to new Dutch tax rules, neighbouring countries will not be slow to notice.

B. *Revenue Neutrality as a Second-Best Solution?*

Evidently, an *ex ante* evaluation of priorities and available instruments could have done much to improve the quality and the outcome of the legislative process as described here.

We described the process of corporation tax law-making as a typical insiders' debate. The language of the law is not accessible to the public though the issues at stake are clearly relevant to it. But even among insiders, there are differences in how 'inside' they really are. On the one hand, there is no independent information to test the revenue neutrality of the tax reform. The only source of information is the Ministry of Finance, which has considerable freedom to push its favourite reform ideas with the help of budgetary arguments.

On the other hand, business representatives, both of SMEs and of large corporations, had to operate in a context of sectoral interests. These sectoral interests were triggered, and strongly accentuated, by some of the tax base broadening proposals. There were evident losers of the tax reform. Especially the tighter depreciation rules for buildings (by far the most important element of the tax base broadening) implied a shift of the tax burden from sectors like business services to sectors like domestic industry and retail trade. At the winners' end, there were changes like the R&D facility and a certain relaxation of anti-avoidance rules, which were of benefit to a limited group of large firms.

An explicit *ex ante* evaluation would have helped to develop a realistic idea of feasible goals. What can be achieved with a corporate tax rate reduction? And what, if this reduction is largely paid for by the taxpayers themselves? Is it more foreign investors, more jobs? Or rather, a temporary advantage in tying 'paper profits' to the Netherlands? And what about special incentives for R&D and intragroup interest flows? Though the economic literature in this field is still developing, it seems that both fields are at the heart of the tax planning industry. The financial centers of MNEs are mobile enough to relocate quickly in response to changes in the international tax environment. Competition is fierce in this area: while the original (2005) proposal was to introduce an effective 10% tax rate, the final version (end 2006) has 5% (still awaiting EC approval, and possibly a review under the Code of Conduct criteria). An *ex ante* evaluation of international developments to be expected in this area, might have focused political (and stakeholders') attention to more radical approaches of intragroup interest flows.

As to the R&D facility, the economic literature suggests that R&D-intensive industries engage more heavily in profit shifting. This might imply that the actual physical location of R&D is not very sensitive to local tax rates, as profits can be shifted away easily. In that case, the rationale behind a low effective Dutch tax rate is not to tie high-skilled employment to the Netherlands, but to turn the tide of outward tax planning.

A formal consideration of feasible goals, in an early stage of the process, would probably have been dominated by economists. Their message would probably have been something like: a revenue-neutral tax rate reduction is not without economic merit, but much of the merit is to improve the Dutch position in international tax planning flows; don't expect too much of new jobs and FDI.

It is very doubtful whether this kind of input would have been welcomed in the political process. It seems that politicians actually avoided to mention any positive revenue effect of profit shifting at all, e.g., in the budgetary calculations underpinning the legislative proposals. One can think of several explanations for this hesitance. One is that it may be unwise to attract neighbouring countries' attention to what is basically *their* loss of tax revenue, and the attention of the Primarolo group for what looks like harmful tax competition. With respect to special facilities aimed at large firms, such as the R&D incentive and the scheme for intragroup financial flows, politicians and large taxpayers had to some extent a joint interest in keeping silent about purposes, and about expected costs and benefits.

Another role of *ex ante* evaluation could have been to improve the level of information available in the legislative process. When taxpayers claim that a special tax incentive for intragroup interest flows is needed, or that stricter depreciation rules have a negative impact on investment decisions, how can they be made to substantiate those claims? Comparable questions have been raised in areas such as environmental regulation. There, private parties may have knowledge on environmental risks of specific products, about the most efficient ways to reduce those risks, etc. which the regulator has not. It has been argued[39] that under such circumstances, the regulator should look for differences in firms' interests for (non-)disclosure. E.g., the firm that is best equipped to reduce environmental risks, may gain a competitive advantage when it helps the regulator to develop costly risk-reducing rules.

To some extent, such divergent interests can also be used in acquiring information for tax policy choices. Firms do have different interests with respect to a package of rate reductions and base-broadening measures. From this point of view, the requirement of revenue-neutrality is not just a way of protecting the average taxpayer's interest. It is also a way to promote disclosure of information and to facilitate negotiations. Though firms do not have to disclose their own data, they have to disclose the policies they prefer on the basis of their data. Speaking out one's policy preference makes negotiations possible. In other words, all taxpayers favour rate reductions; they all reject base broadening. A package deal requires them to make up their minds: is it worth it? Are the negative consequences of tax base broadening outweighed by the rate reductions? We may assume that these questions have indeed been raised – and answered – within the organisations representing business interests. In this sense, applying a criterion of revenue neutrality to discussions about changes in the tax system, may offer a second-best alternative to a proper *ex ante* evaluation of priorities and options.

However, not all elements of the tax package have been subjected to the 'revenue neutrality' approach. The notable exceptions were the special tax schemes for R&D and for intragroup interest flows. And indeed, the consequence is that there is no reliable information about the cost and the (expected or intended) impact of these tax incentives. Large corporations have claimed that these incen-

[39] C. Coglianese, R. Zeckhauser and E. Parson, 'Seeking Truth for Power: Informational Strategy and Regulatory Policy Making' (2004) 89:2 *Minnesota Law Review*, pp. 277–340.

tives were needed to keep the Netherlands competitive, to prevent an outflow of economic activities, etc. But they were not asked how much they would be prepared to offer in return; there was no mechanism to make them reveal their true preferences. But in this field of tax law, national actors are very much aware of the European dimension, which may make them disinclined to open debate.

Conclusions

Chapter 11

Conclusions. A Conditional Yes to *Ex Ante* Evaluation of Legislation

Jonathan Verschuuren and Rob van Gestel

I. *Introduction*

In the first chapter of this book we set out to develop a critical analysis of various forms of *ex ante* evaluation of legislation. We defined *ex ante* evaluation of legislation as:

> Future oriented research into the expected effects and side-effects of potential new legislation following a structured and formalised procedure, leading to a written report. Such research includes a study of the possible effects and side-effects of alternatives, including the alternative of not regulating at all.

In various ways, legislatures around the globe try to assess what can be expected when a new piece of legislation is going to take effect. Will the targets be met, will there be any side-effects? If so, what will they be, and how can they be redressed? The aim of this book is to assess the prospects of *ex ante* evaluation of legislation. What are the benefits of *ex ante* evaluation and what not? Under which conditions should which form of *ex ante* evaluation be applied? What should be their role in the legislative process? In order to answer these questions, two paths have been followed: a more or less theoretical path focusing on the context of *ex ante* evaluation, and an empirical path, focusing on past and present experiences of various forms of *ex ante* evaluation. This chapter summarizes the results of our venture and tries to stir up the debate on the role that *ex ante* evaluations or impact assessments should (not) have in improving the quality of legislation and the reduction of regulatory burdens. Special attention is paid to the methodology, or perhaps better the methodologies, of *ex ante* evaluation and the rationale behind the current popularity of this type of evaluation research in the lawmaking process throughout Europe.

Gaining more insight in the methodological possibilities and constraints of prospective evaluation seems crucial because to a large extent the methodology that is followed, such as cost-benefit analysis, stakeholder consultation or micro simulation, determines what kind of 'beast' *ex ante* evaluation will be in practice.

The importance of raising a debate about the expectations behind the use of regulatory impact assessments in the European Union and its member states lies in the intrinsic tension there will always be between a wish for more evidence-based lawmaking on the one hand and the fact that political judgment can always be used to overrule the outcomes of any kind of evaluation research on the other hand.

II. *The Context of* Ex Ante *Evaluation: Opportunities and Constraints*

Starting with the issue of the rationale behind *ex ante* evaluation one may conclude that over the last decades of the twentieth century, the legislative process has become more and more rationalised. Until fairly recent, there was no such thing as a 'legislative policy' in most EU-countries. As far as the scientific study of legislation is concerned, the legislature was, at least from a legal perspective, for a long time the least examined branch of government.[1] With the rise of the interventionist state, legislation became an important tool for policymakers engaged in what Roscoe Pound once coined as 'social engineering'.[2] The problems that arose from this instrumentalist use of legislation, including implementation deficits, non-compliance and increasing administrative burdens for business, led to a growing awareness among legislators that behaviour modification is a lot more complicated than the codification of unwritten rules or principles that represent shared values and beliefs in a certain society.

Because of the aforementioned difficulties, the public, politicians, and legal commentators, increasingly require the legislature to underpin proposals for new laws with solid empirical evidence as to the need for legislative intervention, the choice between different types of regulation (self-regulation, co-regulation, economic incentives etcetera), the possible trade-offs between alternative regulatory options, and the expected effects and side-effects in terms of social, economic and environmental effects. Government decisions, including those of the legislature, have to be justifiable on the basis of present information and

---

1 R.W. Bauman and Tsvi Kahana, *The Least Examined Branch: The Role of Legislatures in the Constitutional State* (Cambridge University Press, Cambridge 2006).

2 Roscoe Pound, *Social Control Through Law* (Transaction, New Brunswick 1997), p. 65.

should be adaptable to changes in insights and in the socio-economic environment. In this situation, *ex ante* evaluation takes up a prominent position in several influential theories on legislation, governance and public management, as was shown in chapter 2 by Popelier and Verlinden. *Ex ante* evaluation of legislation can provide transparency about the decision-making process that is needed to inform citizens and to create democratic legitimacy, as is required by the New Public Management theory. Stakeholder involvement, as required by the Corporate Governance theory, only works when the citizens involved can assess the impact of decisions, thus providing an important reason of existence to *ex ante* evaluation. Internal and external controls that can be found in business corporations found their way into government organisations, leading to the rise of various forms of *ex ante* and ex post evaluations.

Against this background, the 1995 OECD Recommendation on Improving the Quality of Government Regulation became very influential. The OECD considers *ex ante* evaluation to be an essential element of the lawmaking process, as it can improve the quality of legislation, and contribute to getting simple, efficient, consistent legislation that is necessary to achieve a certain public policy goal. In addition, Popelier and Verlinden show that there also exists a legal obligation to carry out an assessment of the effects of new legislation. Courts may annul legislation when they find that these laws were not created in a transparent and well-informed way. In other words: underpinning new laws with clear data, obtained from *ex ante* and ex post evaluations, can be seen as a necessity in order to make a new law legally justified and at the same time reliable in terms of effectiveness and efficiency. Populier and Verlinden, however, rightfully warn that *ex ante* evaluation is not simply a matter of 'speaking truth to power' and depoliticising legislative decision-making. Rationality, they claim, is context-bound and therefore the scientific, legal, and socio-economic dimension of lawmaking can come into a conflict that can only be 'solved' by way of making political choices. In that sense there really is no contradiction between a political rationality and, for example, an economic or legal rationality. Democratically elected legislators are supposed to serve the public interest. In order to do that political decision-making presupposes the balancing of different types of interests and as a consequence taking an overarching perspective.

The latter does not suggest that, besides the legal rationale for *ex ante* evaluation of legislation, the economic rationale has not been a powerful motivator for the rise of *ex ante* evaluation as well. On the contrary, especially in the United States, but since the launch of the Lisbon strategy also on the level of the European Union, more focus has been put on economic growth and the creation of jobs accompanied by regulatory reform to lift the burdens for business and simplify the existing body of legislation. The 'better regulation movement' has certainly emphasized the relationship there is between economic development and regulatory policy. In this context of regulatory reform *ex ante* evaluation is often considered to be a tool to block unnecessary new legislation and give preference to 'lighter' regulatory alternatives in comparison with legislation.

In chapter 3, Larouche describes the rise of *ex ante* evaluation in the context of the public interest theory of regulation, whereby public authorities intervene to remedy market failures. Impact assessments are meant to study the options to correct undesirable effects of a free market system, such as a communising of costs through a privatisation of profits, which in game-theory is called a 'double P, double C, game'. Well-known is of course the idea of a 'tragedy of the commons' that was developed by Garret Hardin.[3] In that story the metaphor of a society of herders sharing a common parcel of land on which they were entitled to let their cows graze was used to show the possible damaging effects of a totally free market encouraging the herders to act in their own self-interest, neglecting the interests of the community as a whole.

Unfortunately, however, public intervention may in practice also be driven by private interests rather than by the public good, leading to an even more harmful intervention in the market. According to Larouche, impact assessments can only prevent this from happening, if they are set up and carried out properly. According to him, this means that the assessment should begin without any *a priori* bias in favour or against regulatory intervention, that it is conducted with an open mind (for instance with regard to the choice of regulatory options to be evaluated, including the option of non-regulation, and that it is carried out at an early stage so that it can still fully influence the decision-making process.

The latter process is essential for the success of *ex ante* evaluation: the results of the evaluation have to be taken seriously in the subsequent decision-making process, but we would like to add that there are no guarantees that politicians are willing to let themselves be surprised by the outcomes of either ex post or *ex ante* evaluations. Furthermore, in the complex globalised society of the 21st century, information of the effects of new legislation is, at least in part, often likely to be unavailable because national laws and regulations are increasingly influenced by supranational decisions. Particularly in the multi-level governance structure of the European Union it is becoming more and more difficult to study national laws as 'stand-alone projects'. It is needless to say that this complicates the question of how to conduct a proper regulatory impact assessment. While some relevant information concerning for example administrative costs for small and medium sized business may be generated in the process of the assessment, other information, such as the benefits from EU-directives for companies that operate on a transnational level may very well remain unavailable or extremely

[3] G. Hardin, 'The Tragedy of the Commons' (1968) *Science*, pp. 1243–1248.

difficulty to grasp. Larouche argues that in such cases, the assessment process becomes a discovery process among the various actors involved. Game theory then offers a theoretic environment for such a process. In this view, the *ex ante* evaluation is only one step in a multi-period game involving the decision-maker and private actors.

As Larouche shows, *ex ante* evaluation helps the private actors because the decision-making process gets more open and transparent. However, such a vision on the process also explains why *ex ante* evaluation can and will be politicised and misused every now and then, as both the private actors and public policymakers may consider regulatory impact assessments or stakeholder consultation as a means to an end. The way they perceive the ends does not necessarily correspond with the scientific ideal behind *ex ante* evaluation (providing objective information to support regulatory decisions) and contribute to the public good.

First of all, policymakers who dislike interference from outsiders, such as an impact assessment board, may argue against regulatory impact assessments by pointing at the fact that they are costly and will slow down the decision-making process. Second, decision-makers and regulators may use the *ex ante* evaluation to convince potential partners to produce legislation, because they have an *a priori* bias in favour of public intervention through legislation. If that is the case, the impact assessment only studies a pre-determined set of policy options, in a linear fashion (leaving no room to redefine the problem or add new options), without evaluating all possible implications, and it runs in parallel to the drafting of a legislative proposal. Although empirical data are lacking, those that follow specific *ex ante* assessments will recognise these characteristics. Third, and closely related to the previous argument, is the influence that those who conduct *ex ante* evaluations may have on the outcomes. As for example Robert Baldwin has argued,[4] it is all but unlikely that evaluators will prefer traditional command and control types of regulation because of the fact that the impact of these 'single shot interventions' can be estimated more easily than the effects of more responsive types of regulation that consist of mixtures of both hard and soft law, such as co-regulation and legally conditioned self-regulation (see hereafter where we summarize the findings of Meuwese and Senden).

In chapter 4, Bohne indeed shows that *ex ante* evaluation of legislation runs the risk of becoming discredited as merely a political instrument. First of all, there are often important information deficiencies that make it hard for the legislature to draft effective and efficient legislation. Regulatory information asymmetries do exist. Often, the necessary behavioural and technical information rests with those that are to be regulated. Large corporations, for example, will usually have more accurate information about what are the best available techniques to

[4] R. Baldwin, 'Is better regulation smarter regulation?' (2005) *Public Law*, pp. 485–511.

achieve a high level of environmental protection, taking into account the costs and benefits. The question is, however, to what extent they will see it as being in their best interest to share (all) this information with regulatory agencies. Experience has shown that in the field of environmental law it is not unusual that companies only provide strategic information that benefits their short-term interests thereby disregarding legitimate interests that others might have. Bohne gives striking examples of this mechanism, and reaches the conclusion that *ex ante* evaluation of legislation should not involve information asymmetries, but is only suited to repair information deficits. These exist when the lawmaker lacks the necessary information, simply because it does not yet exist. Bohne, however, warns that while technical information may be gathered in an *ex ante* evaluation process, reliable information about human or corporate behaviour is normally much harder to obtain. Regulators usually share all kinds of assumptions about the way the addressees of the rules are going to react to intervention(s) that are aimed at a change of behaviour. Very often, however, they have little or no empirical evidence to underpin these assumptions. Even more important is that those who are primarily responsible for the drafting of legislation are often trained as lawyers and not as social scientists. As a consequence they will often have very little feeling with the use of empirical evidence as input for making regulatory decisions about, for example, the necessity of legislation, the costs and benefits that will accompany the implementation and enforcement, or the consequences for the judiciary in terms of possible conflicts that will arise about the interpretation of a new law.

Because of these reasons, Bohne concludes that the legislature should emphasise ex post evaluations, rather than *ex ante* evaluations. He feels that ex post evaluations provide harder evidence about real-life effects of legislation than *ex ante* evaluations. To a certain extent this is probably true. Nevertheless, one has to bear in mind that most ex post evaluations are also meant to provide more insight in the effects and side-effects that have occurred after the enactment of a law or regulation. In other words: did the intended effects the legislature was aiming for indeed occur? That, however, does not yet prove that there is necessarily a causal connection between the societal effects and the regulatory intervention! To be able to establish such as connection one at least needs an experimental research design with a group of addressees that is exposed to a certain regulatory intervention and a control group on which the intervention does not apply. In practice these kinds of randomized trials are pretty rare in the field of legal research. Moreover, one might question if ex post evaluations and *ex ante* evaluations should be seen as opposites. Would it not be more fruitful to consider them to be complementary? The more explicit and differentiated, for example an *ex ante* evaluation is, the easier it will probably become to perform a solid ex post evaluation that will provide relevant and reliable feedback afterwards.[5] The other way around, ex post evaluations of previous legislation often provide important input for the drafting of new laws and regulations.

The preference that Bohne seems to give to ex post evaluations has to do with the danger that *ex ante* evaluations are more likely to be politicised. He argues that, while *ex ante* evaluation may improve the quality of legislation when used sincerely, it should not be seen as a handy tool to reduce the number of laws that exist, since information deficiencies about the need for regulatory intervention and the availability of alternative policy options contribute to overregulation only to a small extent. Political and institutional factors, such as the wish of politicians to show strength and decisiveness by pushing a bill through Parliament or the influence that lobby organisations have on legislators, seem to be far greater motivators for an over production of laws and regulations, both at a national and at the EU level. According to Bohne, overregulation is the real reason why there is an increasing gap between legislative promises and their actual fulfilment.

In chapter 5, Hoppe puts *ex ante* evaluation of legislation in the public policy context. When looked at from a policy studies perspective, it is clear that there can be no such thing as an independent, completely objective, *ex ante* evaluation in the legislative process. Hoppe convincingly shows that knowledge is a joint construction of policymakers, experts, public opinion, and the media, each of which strategically uses information to influence and bias the eventual authoritative definition of the problem and its underlying realities. Moreover, *ex ante* evaluations, such as a cost benefit analysis, usually are far from comprehensive as they do not (fully) cover non-economic costs and benefits. An interesting underlying question is: why is this the case? Is it because of methodological difficulties in estimating and quantifying the indirect benefits of legislation or determining what is the price of immaterial things, like the value of a human life (risk regulation)? Or does it have to do with the fact that policymakers and politicians are perhaps more interested in cutting back on government spending through deregulation than in showing the 'softer' benefits of regulatory intervention, such as the value that rules and regulations might have for the stability of financial markets or the trust that people will put in governmental decisions that have a legal basis.

Another reason for Hoppe to be sceptical about *ex ante* evaluation has to do with the fact that the forecasting of policy effects is still in its infancy, and may, because of severe methodological problems that surround prospective evaluation and, to which we will come back later, never grow old. We just remind

[5] L. Mader, 'Evaluating the Effects: A Contribution to the Quality of Legislation' (2002) 22:2 *Statute Law Review*, pp. 124–125.

the reader of the famous quote of Nobel Prize winner Niels Böhr: "predicting is very difficult, especially about the future". Still, like Bohne, Hoppe argues that *ex ante* evaluation of legislation can be a sensible choice in the process of preparing new legislation as long as we accept that the evaluation itself is part of the political process. He proposes two strategies that can be considered. The first strategy is to cut the ties with the political process as much as possible by creating independent professional interdisciplinary bodies in which economists, lawyers and social scientists, all of whom are specially trained to do this kind of research, together carry out the assessments, under a system of independent peer review. One could think of an evaluation committee consisting of experts with different scientific backgrounds, appointed by parliament on the basis of their specific expertise and professional status. The second, and more or less opposite, strategy is to improve the quality of *ex ante* evaluation as it is carried out within the (political) process of legislative drafting. This can be done by paying more attention to the checks and balances in the process of lawmaking, for instance by trying to circumvent information asymmetries. An interesting method that is sometimes used is to try to detect and correct overestimation by self-interested stakeholders through the invitation of parties that are not well organized (the 'silent mass') to the consultation process and lowering the threshold for their participation. Also, those that conduct regulatory impact assessments should think of themselves more as professionals who know how to bridge the gap between science and political practice by demarcating and coordinating these different institutional spheres in a creative division of labour. An example of this we find in the compilation of the Impact Assessment Board that has been established by the European Commission in 2006. The members of that board are high-ranking officials from the Commission's departments that have been appointed in the personal capacity and on the basis of their expert knowledge.

Methodological constraints appeared in both chapters 4 and 5. They are the main topic of chapter 6. Van Aeken shows that in practice only a very limited number of methods and techniques are applied to the bulk of *ex ante* evaluations or impact assessments. Most lawmakers stick to the consultation methods that they are familiar with. They are reluctant to try new and perhaps more promising techniques. An interesting question here is, of course, what could be the reasons for this reluctance. Van Aeken sums up three main culprits for the one-sidedness in the use of methods to perform *ex ante* evaluations, namely: a lack of political interest in prospective evaluation and/or evaluation research more in general, the time constraints to the drafting of legislation, and the specific competences of the civil servants involved (those are often people with a legal education not trained in doing sophisticated evaluation research). Another, rather trivial, reason might be that stakeholder consultations are a much cheaper method of *ex ante* evaluation than, for example, experiments with draft legislation in pilot projects or setting up large-scale computer simulations.

Van Aeken sharply criticises this approach: the method should fit the data, not the evaluator. Today's legislation requires in-depth evaluation rather than a quick, superficial or intuitive assessment of the consequences. A simple assessment, for instance by doing some interviews or bringing together a group of experts in a workshop, often misses the effects caused by psychological, societal, cultural, economic, and other non-legal factors, and their interactions. Van Aeken: "It is, to start with, very hard or even sometimes impossible to determine which events will take place in the future. Next, calculating the effect of these events on the legislative project requires much effort and skills. This is furthermore complicated by the rise of multiple interaction effects between all of the events involved." The lawmaker can think of a logical causality chain behind his desk, but research has shown that, in practice, this chain is broken by numerous societal, psychological, socio-psychological and other factors. Bill Bogart has compared the claims of this causal model with throwing a bowling ball down an alley.[6] The impact of the law is in that case measured by how many pins succumb to the force of the ball. When many fall, the impact is considered to be great, but when all or most pins remain standing, the throw was causally insignificant and the bowling agent ineffective.

In reality, the street-level effects of legislation cannot be measured in such a way. Hence, the need for far more sophisticated methods of *ex ante* evaluation that are able to better take the context in which laws have to function in society into account. For some part the methods and techniques of *ex ante* evaluation that put less emphasis on causal connections can be listed under the heading of 'computation', as they can be employed from behind a desk and a computer. They are such methods as goal attainment scaling, prospective evaluation synthesis, multi criteria analysis, scenario analysis, game theory, risk assessment, micro simulation, modelling, experiments and quasi experiments, etc. etc.

Interestingly, Van Aeken claims that institutionalisation (among other things the presence of an independent evaluation body and a forum for evaluation research) is an effective tool to ensure the systematic use of evaluation research. He seems rather optimistic about the possibilities to overcome the 'lamentable attitude' of the political elite and chiefs of administration by this process of institutionalisation. Without denying the importance of institutional factors, we wonder if there is not more to it than just a lack of political interest in the outcomes of *ex ante* evaluations. Is it not more likely that those in power are sometimes unwilling to take the evaluation results into account? The fact that explanatory memoranda ('travaux preparatoires') that accompany legislative drafts sometimes show signs of great dedication by leaving unwelcome facts or critical

[6] W.A. Bogart, *Consequences: the Impact of Law and its Complexities* (University of Toronto Press, Toronto 2002), p. 88.

comments that are made during the consultation process aside, should at least cast some doubts in this respect.[7]

III. *Practical Experiences with* Ex Ante *Evaluation of Legislation*

There has been ample experience with various forms of *ex ante* evaluation of legislation in various countries, and at the EU level. At the EU level, however, the experiences are rather recent. Only since 2005, all proposals in the European Commission's Legislative and Work Programme are subjected to an impact assessment. The EU impact assessment is usually characterised as a comprehensive analysis of potential impacts of several policy options, based on accurate, objective and complete information, without prescribing a specific or common methodology. It takes an integrated approach towards environmental, economic and social impacts, and also a subsidiarity and proportionality test have been integrated into the instrument, as well as stakeholder consultation. The aim of an impact assessment is not only to make the legislative process more transparent and enhance the public support for new legislation but also to present to the legislature which trade-offs there are between various regulatory options without the pretensions of providing legislators with a decision criterion.

In chapter 7, Meuwese and Senden critically assess the first experiences of the EU impact assessment system. There definitely are some interesting results. The institution of the Impact Assessment Board in 2006, for instance, has been an impetus for quality control and for a more systematic development of a common methodology. The introduction of impact assessments also lead to opening up the lawmaking process to at least one alternative option. On the whole, however, we must conclude that the experiences are still somewhat disappointing, particularly from the point of view that the impact assessment is supposed to contribute to the better regulation strategy laid down in the inter-institutional agreement on 'Better lawmaking', which demands more attention for alternatives to direct regulation. The alternative that usually is considered but very often rejected, is not to regulate a certain topic at all. Alternative regulatory solutions that take the form of self-regulation or co-regulation are often not evaluated, and a mix of regulatory instruments ('smart regulation') is not at all considered. The impact assessment builds upon a few clear-cut options that have been fixed in an early

[7] In the Netherlands there is until today no legal duty to submit consultation documents to parliament together with the legislative draft. This is different, however, in for example Austria where Members of Parliament do receive a copy and where an electronic parliamentary database exists that includes consultation documents. *See* H. Schäffer, 'Evaluation and Assessment of Legal Effects Procedures: Towards a More Rational and Responsible Lawmaking Process' (2001) 22:2 *Statute Law Review*, p. 135.

stage of the process, such as direct regulation, no regulation or self-regulation. A study of mixtures of direct regulation and self-regulation usually stay outside the scope of an assessment and guidance documents on impact assessment tend to treat the use of alternative modes of regulation as fully unproblematic.

Meuwese and Senden partly explain the lack of a systematic approach by pointing to the fact that the Commission does not seem to have a clear vision on when alternatives are allowed and desirable. On the other hand they argue that the 'success' of, for instance DGs and Commissioners or the Commission as a whole is very often still measured in terms of regulatory output. Furthermore, Meuwese and Senden show that even if an impact assessment leads to the conclusion that it is best not to come up with a proposal for new regulation that does not mean that self-regulatory alternatives are actually considered. Sometimes negotiated agreements between public authorities are preferred. Another interesting thought that they come up with to explain the lack of a structured approach towards the consideration of alternative regulatory mechanisms is that specific guidance on when and how, for instance, to use self-regulation would amount to a commitment in sensitive areas such as how the European Commission applies the subsidiarity principle, thereby reducing its own room for manoeuvre.

Last but not least Meuwese and Senden are holding a plea for more guidance on the legal possibilities and constraints regarding self-regulation and co-regulation. The mere indication in the new impact assessment guidelines that there may be legal constraints without clarifying what these actually are, cannot be considered to provide clear and sufficient guidance. The same goes for the way the guidelines encourage to think about regulatory options as either doing nothing, opting for self-regulation *or* relying on legislation. Just like the aforementioned Robert Baldwin, Meuwese and Senden argue that very often it might be wiser to integrate self-regulatory elements into a proposal for new legislation thus making a distinction between alternatives *for* and *in* legislation. According to them, the Commission should invest more in knowledge about the legal and practical conditions under which such a mix of soft and hard law elements is appropriate and pay less attention to regulatory 'hypes' as the reduction of administrative burdens. This last remark clearly indicates that Meuwese and Senden are convinced that the use of self-regulation and co-regulation in the process of EU-lawmaking should not be regarded as a temporary hype but is there to stay.

The case studies to *ex ante* evaluation of legislation in Germany and Sweden, presented in chapter 8 by Veit, show that these countries have a history of *ex ante* evaluation of legislation dating back to the 1970s. In Germany, evaluation of various forms of assessments showed that these were not very successful. The comprehensive regulatory impact assessment, for instance, was not carried out the way it should. Standard questions about, for instance, the necessity of legislation and the availability of alternatives were all too often treated as formalities (tick-box mentality). The availability of an extensive regulatory impact assessment handbook, which provided a comprehensive overview of the methodology of *ex ante* evaluation did not provide much help since it was considered to be far too complicated to gain attention for impact assessments in the drafting process.

A new phase in the history of *ex ante* evaluation in Germany was introduced in 2005 when a new Coalition government came to power and made reduction of administrative burdens a top priority. As a consequence, in 2006, an assessment of administrative burdens following the Standard Cost Model was introduced. Although the scope of the assessment was reduced, the resources made available for it, and the political backing of the assessment are much larger than that of the previous forms of *ex ante* evaluation of legislation. An independent National Regulatory Control Unit, directly reporting to Federal Chancellor, checks all draft laws and general administrative regulations for their compliance with the principles of the standardised measurement of administrative costs before they are submitted to the Federal cabinet. All this explains why the assessment of administrative burdens has been more successful than the introduction of previous forms of *ex ante* evaluation.

In Sweden, all new or altered regulations, big or small, are subject to a broad regulatory impact assessment. An assessment of the effects of new legislation on small enterprises was integrated in the normal assessment in 2007. In 2008, Sweden followed the German example and established a National Regulatory Control Unit to not only assess the administrative burdens (like in Germany), but also to supervise compliance with the statutory provisions on *ex ante* evaluation.

A comparison of a large number of *ex ante* evaluations in Germany and Sweden shows remarkable differences, particularly with regard to the 'real' compliance with the assessment criteria. In Germany, there is a high formal compliance of up to 100%; each legislative proposal has a cover page on which all criteria are 'ticked off'. The real compliance, however, in some categories, is as low as 6%, as is the case in the category 'description of alternatives'. In Sweden, this important criterion has a real compliance rate of 94%: in almost every proposition, alternative policy options are seriously considered.

The reasons for these difference are remarkable. In Sweden, legislation is often prepared by Committees of Inquiry. These committees are organisationally located outside the government and conduct extensive research during a period of, on average, two years, in preparation of new legislation. They always have seen a study into alternative options as one of their tasks. Other factors that contribute to a good performance of *ex ante* evaluation in Sweden are the high degree of transparency of the legislative process (everybody is watching!), and the fact that in Sweden, other than in Germany, there is no dominance of judicial and juristic expertise in the preparatory phase of the lawmaking process. The latter is caused by both structural factors (the federal set up of the German state and the role of the German federal constitutional court) and social factors (the educational background of staff, which in Germany predominantly is a legal background). Veit concludes that professional socialisation has an enormous power of imprint over the prevalent orientation patterns and attitude in organisations, and thus on the way *ex ante* evaluation is carried out. However, there is more to it than that. Also the state's architecture is an important reason for differences in the evaluation culture. The fact that Germany is a federal state with a constitutional court explains why the integration of new regulations into the existing legal framework gets more attention during the drafting of new legislation. Sweden, on the other hand is a centralist state, without a central authority responsible for controlling norms in the form of a constitutional court, which explains why there is less focus on the way legislative drafts fit in the overall legal system. Constitution changes can alter these conditions as the membership of the EU by Sweden has shown. This has caused a high demand for professionals with specific legal expertise to supervise the necessary adjustments of national law to EU-specifications.

An interesting empirical study about the prospective value of *ex ante* evaluation is presented in chapter 9 in which Van Gestel and Vranken have compared *ex ante* evaluations of the effect of new legislation by the Council of State in the Netherlands with ex post evaluations of the same pieces of legislation in order to find out how accurate the predictions by the Council have been. They call this evaluation method 'feedback research'. It is a combination of methods of prospective and retrospective evaluation.

An important reason why Van Gestel and Vranken have selected the advisory opinions of the Dutch Council of State as their object of study is that the Netherlands are one of the few countries in Europe that has not yet introduced a system of integrated regulatory impact assessments. The assessment of legislative drafts by the Council of State is what comes closest to an impact assessment, especially now that the Council does not limit itself to an assessment of legal technicalities but also considers the policy-analytical aspects of draft legislation on aspects such as: necessity, efficiency and enforceability. Another thing that makes the Council's policy-analytical scrutiny of legislative drafts interesting is the fact that State Councillors are combining judicial tasks with providing advice on the quality of legislation. Moreover, most of them have a background in politics or have worked as high-ranking governmental officials, which might encourage a politicisation of the evaluation process.[8] Finally, compared to most

[8] Especially the case of the Compensation of costs in the administrative objection procedure seems to reveal some signs of politisation of the assessment process. In that case the double mandate of State Councillors as judges and advisors on the quality of legislation appears to be a relevant factor in the outcomes of the assessment.

ex ante evaluations in other countries, the Council plays its role at a relatively late moment in the process of legislation, after the Council of Ministers has taken position. This might weaken the role that *ex ante* evaluation can play. One of the strengths of the Council of State's assessment, on the other hand, is that it is entitled to receive an explicit reaction on its advisory opinions, which makes it more difficult to quickly and smoothly put aside the advice and impossible to keep silent about it.

Rather exceptional is that Van Gestel and Vranken got access to all relevant confidential internal documents belonging to the Council of State and had the opportunity to discuss their findings with State Councillors, which sometimes gave them more insight in the way the Council proceeds and how, for instance, the guidelines for policy-analytical review are being used. One of the most striking results of their case study is that the accuracy of the current review by the Council does not seem to depend very heavily on the methods or checklist applied in the assessment. Roughly the same working methods and exactly the same checklist were applied in the two cases that were studied. However, whereas the Council often did hit the nail on the head in the draft for a new Youth Care Act, it overlooked important weaknesses in the second draft concerning compensation of costs in the administrative objection procedure. Perhaps the Council was in that case convinced by the arguments of the government too easily. In both cases, however, the advisory opinions of the Council had relatively little effect on the final draft that was sent to Parliament. According to Van Gestel and Vranken, the most likely explanation for this is the 'path dependency' in the lawmaking process. This makes that, as soon as there is agreement inside the administration about a proposal for a new law, it will normally become extremely hard for 'outsiders' such as impact assessment boards or other *ex ante* evaluators to persuade those who are responsible for the draft to adopt serious changes.

Notwithstanding these outcomes, Van Gestel and Vranken do believe that improvements in the *ex ante* evaluation by the Council of State are possible. Currently, the Council is usually as brief as possible in commenting. No remarks are made about good practices or possible ways to improve the draft, there is almost no reference to sources and no motivation as to the grounds of the Council's criticism. It is impossible to find out whether the Council perhaps ignored minor flaws or agreed with choices made in the draft. As a consequence, the assessment process is neither transparent nor systematic. Existing literature on *ex ante* evaluation of legislation shows that relying heavily on experience, practical wisdom, and intuition, as the Council has been doing until today, is a hazardous approach because legislative flaws, unrealistic assumptions or biased positions can be overlooked quite easily. Moreover, without a systematic assessment with transparency as to the methods, arguments, sources, and evidence which underpin the advisory opinions, an opportunity is missed to challenge those who are responsible for the preparation of the bill to rethink parts of the draft. For them, such an opinion is just an opinion, regardless of the institutional authority of the author.

Van Gestel and Vranken suggest further empirical-legal research as to the possibilities and constraints of feedback research, especially since little has been written about this method of evaluation research, at least not by experts in the field of legislative studies. For the time being they suggest that probably the biggest potential for feedback research lies in the fact that it might serve to make methods of *ex ante* evaluations more accurate because it can show in retrospect which observations that were made at various moments in the assessment process (data collection, interpretations of findings from consultations, alternatives modes of regulation and so forth) were right or wrong, and sometimes perhaps even what in particular caused a certain mistake.

In chapter 10, another highly interesting case study is presented in the field of corporate tax reform. Vording and Gribnau show that the reform of corporate tax law in the Netherlands was carried out by a small group of 'insiders', more or less behind closed doors, using a type of language that is not understandable for those outside this group. Independent information is not available. In the end, the decision-making process seems to have been biased towards the interests of large corporations, or/and by the government's wish to avoid any reference to the revenue effects of inward tax planning. The authors convincingly argue that an *ex ante* evaluation could have helped to overcome these biases. *Ex ante* evaluation might have helped to develop a realistic idea of feasible goals, given the international developments in the area of multinational enterprises (What can be achieved with a corporate tax rate reduction?). Economists probably would have dominated a formal consideration of feasible goals. As already stated before, the decision-makers were probably not interested in an economic perspective on the tax reform, as they apparently wanted to keep the decision-making process 'under control'. Legislators are perhaps not always willing to let themselves be surprised by reality.

A second role of *ex ante* evaluation would have been to improve the level of information available in the legislative process. Information that rests with private parties, and that they are not willing to disclose for tactical reasons, could have come to light when the diverging interests among the various stakeholders involved were used to acquire this information by those carrying out the assessment. Nevertheless, Vording and Gribnau rightfully argue that *ex ante* evaluation is not necessarily a policy-neutral activity. Those who are the information owners in the field of tax law are not always interested in sharing it with others, especially not if they feel the information might used against them later on in the lawmaking process. The same thing we saw in the field of environmental law where Bohne claimed that corporations are often unwilling to share information about the possibilities for emission reductions with public authorities because they feel that is not in their best interest. In such circumstances *ex ante* evaluation is a highly complex undertaking, which starts with problems of data collection. Average consultation procedures are probably insufficient to provide reliable information about the impact of legislation in these circumstances and *ex ante* evaluators will have to pursue a more active and investigative role, not only in retrieving the relevant data but also in assessing the validity of the information that stakeholders have provided. It goes without saying that this calls for high quality expert knowledge, and for safeguards concerning the confidentiality of information and an independent position. Finally Vording and Gribnau also show that the use of expert committees to prepare legislative drafts, as Veit has described for the Swedish situation, will not always be the answer in tackling information asymmetries, especially not if most of the experts (tax advisers) have there own interest in the outcomes of the process.

IV. *Prospects for* Ex Ante *Evaluation of Legislation*

The chapters of this book provide a wealth of new information on *ex ante* evaluation of legislation. The general conclusion that arises from all of the chapters is that *ex ante* evaluation of new legislation certainly is a valuable tool to improve the quality of legislation, but that its value must not be overrated because of tremendous methodological and political constraints. Let us go into both aspects of this central conclusion.

It is beyond doubt, that *ex ante* evaluation of new legislative projects, when carried out properly, has a positive influence on the quality of the decision-making process. It prevents tunnel vision and biases towards a certain option that may not be the optimal option. More in general, it leads to a better-informed and more transparent decision-making process. Having carried out some form of *ex ante* evaluation can be seen as an indication of the quality of legislation. In fact, courts already begin to refer to (the absence of) regulatory impact assessments as a quality indication of the piece of legislation that they have to judge in a specific case.

The parenthetic clause 'when carried out properly' is, however, essential. *Ex ante* evaluations can easily be misused to push a certain option forward or to push into the direction of using direct regulation as an instrument to deal with a given societal problem. 'Misuse' of the process of *ex ante* evaluations cannot be entirely prevented, as we must understand that any evaluation that is carried out in the process of decision-making or lawmaking is part of the political process within which the lawmaking takes place. There is nothing wrong with that. It is simply a fact of life in a democratic society. The various actors within the lawmaking process will all try to play their role in the process, including in the *ex ante* evaluation part of the process. What constitutes 'use' or 'misuse' probably is hard to say: what is 'use' for one actor, can be regarded as 'misuse' by the other.

It is essential, though, that all relevant information on relevant policy options reaches the table of the decision-makers, so that political decision-makers at least are well-informed. The main contributing factors to that are:

- *Ex ante* evaluations should start early in the decision-making process, when all relevant policy options are still open, and they should be transparent.
- There should be room for an in between redefinition of the problem or the introduction of a new policy option.
- They should cover 'smart regulation' options, i.e., options in which various instruments of direct and indirect regulation are applied simultaneously.
- They should be carried out, preferably, by an independent institution with staff that is well trained to take a multidisciplinary approach, and that is able to use the wide variety of evaluating methods and techniques that is available. Therefore, staff should not mainly consist of lawyers, but should also consist of social scientist and economists. Attention for methodological issues should be centre stage within this organization, as well as attention for the issue of the relationship between science and political practice.
- All evaluations should be peer reviewed, be it by an Impact assessment board or another independent organisation.
- Ex post evaluations should be used as a basic source of information in an *ex ante* assessment, and to improve the quality of *ex ante* evaluations by providing feedback on the accuracy of predictions and comments that were made (introduction of 'learning loops').

The above contributing factors are strongly interrelated. Therefore, they should not be aimed for in isolation. Organizing the assessment away from the government, i.e., in an independent institution, for example, is good for the quality of the assessments in the sense that they will be less politically biased. At the same time, however, the assessment's influence on the decision-making process is likely to be less because of the gap between the evaluation process and the political process. An early start of the assessment process enables a full assessment of all possible options. At the same time, however, the temporal distance between the assessment and the political process may be so big and so many political or practical changes may, meanwhile, have occurred, that the results of the assessment can hardly be used and a whole new assessment has to be carried out. While the factors mentioned above all strongly influence the quality of *ex ante* evaluations, for *ex ante* evaluations to be used in the decision-making process, concessions will have to be made. It all boils down to finding the right balance between scientific soundness and practical usefulness, given the specific situation. What is the right balance is different for each country and for each legislative institution.

More research needs to be done in order to further improve *ex ante* assessments. In several of the chapters of this book, new research questions pop up. For the instrument of *ex ante* evaluation to be further improved, the following research projects should be carried out:

- First and foremost, research into improving the methodology (or rather: methodologies) of *ex ante* evaluations is vital. As was shown in this book, there are many methodological pitfalls, all of which have to be further mapped so that they can be avoided. Research has to show the relevance of the various new methods (such as goal attainment scaling, prospective evaluation synthesis, multi criteria analysis, scenario analysis, game theory, risk assessment, micro simulation, modelling, experiments and quasi experiments) for the various types of problems to be evaluated. Which method is best suited for which case? And what conditions have to be met at the side of the evaluators and at the side of the decision-makers/regulators to fully deploy the specific method?
- Further empirical information as to the quality of existing *ex ante* evaluation instruments needs to become available to show the intensity of the problem of the a priori biases that are presumed to be present, biases towards a specific policy option, and biases towards using direct regulation.
- *Ex ante* assessments should be monitored and their quality should be assessed when new ex post assessments become available, so that we can learn from these ex post assessments and are able to constantly improve the mechanism of *ex ante* evaluation and try to overcome the many difficulties *ex ante* assessments by nature have. More research is necessary in order to establish the potential link between ex post and *ex ante* assessments. Under what conditions should ex post evaluations be carried out in order to be of maximum benefit to *ex ante* evaluations? Can, for instance, the results of ex post evaluations be corrected for changed legal, political, or socio-economic circumstances at the time of the *ex ante* assessment?

Let us hope that the conditional yes to *ex ante* evaluation of legislation that is presented in this book, is a stimulus for the further improvement of what may become a valuable instrument in the lawmaking process on all levels of regulation, national and international.

Index

www.ingramcontent.com/pod-product-compliance
Lightning Source LLC
LaVergne TN
LVHW080847300926
849162LV00003B/357